OSAMA BIN LADEN

ALSO BY MICHAEL SCHEUER

Imperial Hubris: Why the West Is Losing the War on Terror

Through Our Enemies' Eyes: Osama bin Laden, Radical Islam, and the Future of America

Marching toward Hell: America and Islam after Iraq

MICHAEL SCHEUER

OSAMA BIN LADEN

OXFORD
UNIVERSITY PRESS

Oxford University Press, Inc., publishes works that further
Oxford University's objective of excellence
in research, scholarship, and education.

Oxford New York
Auckland Cape Town Dar es Salaam Hong Kong Karachi
Kuala Lumpur Madrid Melbourne Mexico City Nairobi
New Delhi Shanghai Taipei Toronto

With offices in
Argentina Austria Brazil Chile Czech Republic France Greece
Guatemala Hungary Italy Japan Poland Portugal Singapore
South Korea Switzerland Thailand Turkey Ukraine Vietnam

Published by Oxford University Press, Inc.
198 Madison Avenue, New York, New York 10016

www.oup.com

First published as an Oxford University Press paperback, 2012

Oxford is a registered trademark of Oxford University Press

Library of Congress Cataloging-in-Publication Data
Scheuer, Michael.
Osama bin Laden / Michael Scheuer.
p. cm.
Includes bibliographical references and index.
ISBN 978-0-19-973866-3; 978-0-19-989839-8 (pbk.)
1. Bin Laden, Osama, 1957– 2. Bin Laden, Osama, 1957– —Political and social views.
3. Bin Laden, Osama, 1957– —Psychology. 4. Terrorists—Saudi Arabia—Biography.
5. Terrorism—Religious aspects—Islam. 6. Islamic fundamentalism—Political aspects.
7. Islamic countries—Relations—Western countries. 8. Western countries—Relations—
Islamic countries.
I. Title.
HV6430.B55S33 2011
363.325092—dc22
[B] 2010021715

1 3 5 7 9 8 6 4 2

Printed in the United States of America
on acid-free paper

All statements of fact, opinion, or analysis are those of the author and do not reflect the official positions of the CIA or any other U.S. Government agency. Nothing in the contents should be construed as asserting or implying U.S. Government authentication of information or Agency endorsement of the author's views. The material has been reviewed by the CIA to prevent the disclosure of classified information.

CONTENTS

For Alec, Emily, Jessica, and Sarah, first, last, and always

For Betty, Walt, Dave, Hank, and Frank, who make a difference

For A.W. and J.M., thank you, may you rest in God's care

For the U.S. Marine Corps and the CIA, the Republic's first and best defenders

NEW PREFACE
Another Victory on the Road to Defeat

The killing of Osama bin Laden on May 2, 2011 may well have represented the last chance for the United States and its Western allies to avoid becoming embroiled in the "clash of civilizations" Samuel Huntington warned of two decades ago. The tragic irony is that Huntington would probably never have thought that those responsible for this clash would hail not from the Islamic universities of Mecca and Medina but—as he did—from the Ivy League.

American national security always required that bin Laden be killed. As the materials taken from his residence demonstrate, bin Laden was not isolated from his al-Qaeda organization and running for his life from rock to rock, and cave to cave. Rather, bin Laden led a relatively sedentary life at the time of his death, and continued to play a substantial role in managing al-Qaeda's activities and media operations. He also was participating in talks meant to quell squabbles between competing Islamist groups in Pakistan's tribal region. In May, 2011, then, bin Laden was what he had long been: America's foremost, and most lethal, enemy. His death was an enormous tactical victory for the West.

But all coins have two sides. The obverse of this triumph has been a full-scale retreat—by both U.S. political parties, much of the media, and the academy—from a serious effort to understand what bin Laden had thought, stood for, and, most importantly, accomplished. Admittedly, understanding these issues was never their priority to begin with, but his death does not merit the end-of-an-era rhetoric now commonplace in discourse about U.S. foreign policy in particular. Much of the governing elite's rhetoric and analysis clearly betrays their dismissal of bin Laden as a mere "celebrity," rather than what he truly was, and what this book hopes to prove: a seminal figure in history whose legacy will continue to pose a serious danger to the West. Post-bin-Laden rhetoric has also manifested the most self-defeating components of Western policy in the Islamic world—ignorance and arrogance.

Bin Laden's death has further shrunk the American governing elite's already short attention span. The threat that al-Qaeda and its allies still pose to America has been lost to the noise of the of some tabloid celebrity's latest misadventure. President Obama, Secretary of State Hillary Clinton, and Republican leaders, such as Senators John McCain and Lindsey Graham portrayed bin Laden's demise as something akin to final victory and, more than that, as a signal for the reinvigoration of bipartisan U.S. military and cultural interventionism in the Islamic world—the very thing that most effectively motivates America's Islamist enemies.

Seventeen days after bin Laden's death, President Obama announced his intention to reform the Islamic world in the West's image. In a speech on May 19, 2011, Obama pledged to bring secular democracy to Muslims from Mauritania to Pakistan; called for regime change in five Arab states; pledged to resolve Sunni-Shia and Muslim-Christian animosities; and signed up as a full partner in the Secretary Clinton-Ambassador Susan Rice crusade to impose Western-style feminism on Muslim civilization. Not to be outdone in this combination of Wilsonian interventionism and Kipling-esque white-man's-burden-ism, most if not all Republicans—aside from Ron Paul— complemented the Obama-Clinton cultural offensive with calls for war on Iran and, as the Arab Spring unfolded, Libya, Syria, and Yemen. With Islamists motivated by the impact of U.S. intervention in the Muslim world, America's political leaders acted as if one dead Saudi exile had been the only thing standing between them and a Western-orchestrated salvation—via secularization and Westernization—of the Muslim world.

In the wake of bin Laden's death, what was called for was not less but more intervention, the parameters of which now looked very much like a war on the tenets of Muslim culture, faith, and civilization. The more things change....

Ignorance of Islam is endemic to Washington. The morning after bin Laden's death, Obama's Terrorism Czar, John O. Brennan, told the media bin Laden had been buried at sea. Asked why, Brennan replied that had bin Laden been buried on land his followers would have built a shrine to him, and this would have drawn large numbers of pilgrims. Brennan once defined "jihad" as primarily a non-martial concept, akin to self-improvement efforts and campaigns for community betterment, such as those conducted by Moose and Kiwanis clubs. Bin Laden was a Sunni Salafist, an Islamic sect which hews to the traditions of the Prophet Muhammad and his immediate successors. One of these traditions is strict opposition to such things as saints, shrines, and other means of glorifying man in ways that should be reserved for God. In other words, had anyone built a shrine to him bin Laden's own followers would have been the first to tear it down. Brennan's comment reveals too clearly the standard level of expertise Washington brings to bear on the Muslim world.

With bin Laden dead and Washington, as always, groping in the dark, it is worth estimating what he left behind.

The first thing to note is that bin Laden died a complete success in terms of the goals he set for himself and for al-Qaeda. Beginning with his first public utterances in the 1990s, bin Laden stressed that because he was but one Muslim, and because al-Qaeda so small, they could not expect to defeat the United States. Al-Qaeda's main goal would therefore be to expand its international presence, to be better able to inspire other Muslims to fight Western interference in the Muslim world. Bin Laden, in short, meant to light a fuse. At his death it was not only burning brightly but headed for the powder house.

Despite Western claims of victory after bin Laden's death, the threat of jihad against the United States and its allies remains clear and—al-Qaeda remains at its core. Since September 2001, al-Qaeda has not only kept a major part of its pre-9/11 base in Afghanistan, but has built substantial operational bases in Pakistan, Yemen, Somalia,

Lebanon, Palestine, the North Africa and Sahel regions, and in Iraq, where a regrouped al-Qaeda is a key part of emerging Sunni resistance toward the Shia tyranny that Washington helped install in Baghdad. In addition, the continuing appeal of bin Laden's words and example, as well as widespread Muslim hatred for Western intervention is motivating growing numbers of young Muslim males in Europe, North America, and Australia to join jihadist organizations in Somalia and Iraq; to seek paramilitary training in Yemen and Pakistan; and to plan and attempt violent attacks in their own countries. For more than a decade, polling has shown consistently that a large majority of Muslims think U.S. and Western policy in the Islamic world is meant to destroy Islam and its followers—a finding more pertinent to predicting the duration of the Islamists' war on America and their potential manpower than answers to such silly, *People* Magazine-like questions as: "Do you support Osama bin Laden and al-Qaeda?"

But what of the future? Despite the fact that al-Qaeda's geographical reach has dramatically expanded since 2001, Washington, its allies, and many in the media and the academy now argue that the secular-democratic orientation of the so-called "Arab Spring" sealed al-Qaeda's fate and consigned it to history's dustbin. Actually, the Arab Spring offers a tremendous opportunity for al-Qaeda—now led by Ayman al-Zawahiri—and other Islamist groups, whether politically or militarily oriented, an opportunity that has been either grossly misinterpreted or studiously ignored by the West.

The media's jejune assessment of the revolt in Egypt provides the finest example of the West's naiveté when dealing with the Islamic world. For eighteen days Americans and Europeans watched the activities of 200,000 Egyptians in Tahrir Square. Over that period, CNN, BBC, and FOX reporters interviewed a few score young, educated, well-groomed, English-speaking, middle-class Egyptians. The journalists then read the pro-democracy emanations of these young people on Facebook and Twitter and decided that this small sample proved that 100 million devout and mostly unilingual and illiterate Muslim Egyptians—living by a faith that brooks no church-state separation—were thirsting for secular democracy. The reporters, in essence, exchanged their journalistic credentials for those of cheerleaders. They then did the same in Libya, where they portrayed the birth of secular democracy via the actions of a resistance movement whose military power depended on the combat skills of former mujahedin and U.S. and NATO air forces, directed by their political leaders to intervene and bomb another Muslim country with impressive oil reserves.

No one can ever lose money by betting on the superficial and wishing-makes-it-so reporting of Western journalists; their vapid performance in Egypt and Libya was more or less par for the course. The shock came, however, when leaders in the United States and Europe jumped on the journalists' band wagon and predicted in certain and glowing terms the advent of secular democratic states across the Arab world, embracing the ludicrous idea that the Egyptians in Tahrir Square had somehow accomplished in less than three weeks what America, Britain, Canada, and Australia have been working on since the signing of Magna Charta, nearly 800 years ago.

If facts are faced in the Arab Spring's wake, al-Qaeda, its allies, and unassociated Islamist groups face a more favorable operational environment than they ever have before, so favorable, in fact, that victory is theirs to lose. Four factors arising from the Arab Spring are behind this:

First, as noted, the West has completely misinterpreted what the Arab Spring will yield. While the Western view of the Arab Spring envisions the growth of secular democracy in the region, the Islamists have won every election held since the Tunisian uprising. In reality, the Arab Spring has destroyed the West's strategic position in the Arab world and left it aligned with tiny, minimally influential, and largely irrelevant pro-democratic groupings that will sink—or be sunk—into oblivion as the Islamists solidify their hold on power.

Second, the Arab Spring has created a situation throughout much of the Arab world that favors al-Qaeda and other Islamists militant groups. Through their pro-democracy crusade, Washington and its allies have alienated the military and security services of Tunisia, Libya, Egypt, Syria, and Yemen, services that, to varying degrees, were assisting the counterterrorism work of Western intelligence communities. The result is a large blind spot, one to which Western services must now devote even more manpower and financial resources to cover; the cultural and linguistic expertise lost to the West is, in the near-to-medium term, irreplaceable. In addition, the Arab services have been purged of many of their best officers and thus less capable and interested in detecting and stopping militant activity on their own turf.

Third, the Arab Spring has given the Islamists greater means to attack Israel, whose security has long depended on the maintenance of tyrannies in Egypt, Syria, and Jordan. These regimes were intimidated by Israel's WMD and bribed by U.S. dollars to control their borders and prevent al-Qaeda and other non-Palestinian Islamist groups from launching anti-Israeli attacks from their soil. The Egyptian revolt already has yielded a more porous Egypt-Gaza border, encouraged attacks on the Egypt-to-Israel natural-gas pipeline, and left the Sinai Desert largely under the sway of militants. The West also is actively working to destroy the Syrian regime, thereby weakening security on the Syria-Israel border. When the Arab Spring envelops Jordan—which hosts large Palestinian, Sunni Iraqi expatriate, and Islamist militant populations—the elimination of Israel's longstanding partners in border control will be complete.

Fourth, because the Arab Spring produced serious deterioration in domestic security across North Africa, Islamist military forces in that region, the Sahel, and, increasingly, in eastern and southern Africa have been reinforced with experienced fighters and large quantities of modern weaponry. In Egypt, Tunisia, and Libya the forces that overthrew incumbent regimes opened prisons, freeing thousands of incarcerated Islamist militants, and emptied police and military armories. These militants and weapons are likely to continue bleed into other areas of Africa and, as they do, the threat to Western interests—especially energy, strategic materials (including uranium), and the freedom of the seas—will substantially increase.

Again, all these factors must be deemed potential opportunities for al-Qaeda and other Islamists groups; whether they will be fully exploited is an open question. Still, thanks to Osama bin Laden's example and efforts the Islamist movement is larger, better organized, and more geographically dispersed—all, in large measure, the product of al-Qaeda's incitement activities—than ever before. And, perhaps most important, even after more than fifteen years of war, Western leaders have no true conception of what motivates the Islamist militants, nor that their interventionist policies are the Islamists' center of gravity. Out in the Great Beyond, bin Laden has good reason to praise Allah and to smile.

What follows is a portrait of Osama bin Laden without the preconceptions about him that formed the core of most Western analyses during his lifetime? The terms "nihilist," "mass murderer," "Nazi," "atrocity," "messianic," "Islamo-facscist," "madman," and "criminal"—all part of the traditional Western-centric definition of a "terrorist"—are inapplicable. While such words salve the wounds, buttress the egos, and satisfy the emotions of those who have written or talked about the man who traumatized and humiliated America and its allies, they also move us no closer to understanding him or his legacy. Instead, I will focus on what bin Laden said and did; on what those who knew him best said about him; and on how his words and actions were and continue to be perceived in a part of the world that is desperate for credible, pious leaders and is intimately familiar with centuries of Islamic history. Along the way, I will discuss earlier assessments, weigh the quality of the evidence they present, and at the end—I trust—provide a more balanced portrait of Osama bin Laden.

To be clear, my intention is not to praise Osama bin Laden but to show why, though dead, he remains a presence. To do that, we need a fair-minded, clear-eyed assessment of whom and what he was. And while it is true enough that bin Laden did not wear a uniform, he posed every bit as much as a threat to America's security—and perhaps even its survival—as any enemy general ever did. Washington did not chalk off Lord Howe as a fool and a womanizer; Grant did not dismiss Robert E. Lee as a fanatic (nor did Lee dismiss Grant as a drunk); and Eisenhower did not think he could defeat Rommel in North Africa by calling him a criminal. Each took his opponent's measure and then went about the job of countering his strengths. Understanding Osama bin Laden as he was and what his legacy remains means facing facts. "Live in the world you inhabit," Lee wrote his son George Washington Curtis Lee, then attending West Point, in 1852. "Look upon things as they are. Take them as you find them. Make the best of them … Do not imagine things are going to happen as you wish. Wish them to happen right. Then strive to make them so." We would do well to treat the world bin Laden helped to create in the same manner. Let us first take it as we find it, and show the part he played in making it so.

OSAMA BIN LADEN

1

OSAMA BIN LADEN AS SUBJECT

The flood of words written about Osama bin Laden has overwhelmed a much smaller pool of reliable assessments available to the biographer. Foremost among the latter are the statements, speeches, interviews, and poems bin Laden himself produced from the time he began speaking in public in 1993. In addition, the past decade has seen a growing number of memoirs, reminiscences, and commentaries about him written by men who knew him as a youth, a father, a husband, a construction engineer, a nascent warrior in the anti-Soviet Afghan jihad, or as the leader of al-Qaeda. Many of these works are valuable, even essential, to understanding and assessing his life, but all need to be examined carefully for agendas other than providing the truth about bin Laden.

We often come across the notion of "narrative" in contemporary biography, historical writing, and political analysis. The term suggests the notion that in war situations there is no reality; rather, there are a host of competing narratives, and if one side does not understand its foe's narrative it will lose. To win, it must first understand it and then adjust its own in ways to reflect that comprehension. Getting the narrative right is the key to prevailing.

Now, if "narrative" takes into account that perception dictates reality, then I would agree and, moreover, would argue that it forms the basis of wisdom. Americans ought to understand that bin Laden and the Islamists have attacked the United States and its allies precisely because of the negative impact their governments' actions have had in the Muslim world. But that does not seem to be what the proponents of "narrative" intend. Instead, for them, it means something like producing and sticking to a script essentially written by rather than about a particular actor for his own purposes. Such a script is thus constructed to appeal to the target audience's preconceptions. Reality enters into it only so far as needed to give it certain plausibility. It is, at day's end, a vehicle for obscurantism.

This preconceived-script kind of "narrative"—one substituting plausibility for reality—has been an engine of distortion for works about bin Laden and al-Qaeda. Three versions, in my view, can be dismissed out of hand: one that asserts that bin Laden and al-Qaeda have been tools of Iran; a second that argues that they have been tools of the CIA; and a third that posits that they have been tools of Pakistan's Inter-Services Intelligence Directorate (ISI). Believers in one or another of these versions manifest an almost fanatic fervor, ignoring an abundance of discrediting evidence. Five other versions, however, influence the study of bin Laden because they present a mix of valid and false information. These narratives have been generated by, respectively, traditional terrorism analysts, former mujahedin who fell out with bin Laden, Saudi regime spokesmen, pro-Israeli writers and their colleagues in the United States, and Western experts who have not relied on the primary sources pertaining to al-Qaeda's chief.

The "Old Hands" Narrative

There remain a significant number of veteran journalists and terrorism experts—in the universities, think tanks, and governments—who have argued that bin Laden and his allies have been merely new iterations of the same old terrorism. They fill books, blogs, learned journals, and the airwaves with analogies between al-Qaeda and other Islamist groups and, for example, the Irish Republican Army, Lebanese Hezbollah, Colombia's FARC, Abu Nidal and other Palestinian secular groups, Peru's Sendero Luminoso, Russia's nineteenth-century socialist revolutionaries, Robespierre and the Directory, and the Assassins of Saladin's era. The old hands are keen to protect their status and reassure their readers: "We experts have seen this all before." They are arguing that it's simply political theater and it will go as it came. Their advice is to be patient and to use the police to control and contain the bad guys. Military action is counterproductive.

Their narratives are well argued, thoroughly documented, and, sadly, locked in a time warp. None of the groups mentioned above posed even remotely the threat to the nation-state they fought that al-Qaeda has posed to the United States and its allies. Neither did any of the groups have the Islamists' geographical presence, reach, funding, manpower pool, media capabilities, or immunity to war-weariness. None of them, moreover, had a leader armed with the mental and rhetorical skills to appeal to an entire culture, an appeal that will endure for decades via the record of his spoken and written words. Although I disagree with him on one key issue—that bin Laden was a figurehead in the years before his death—*Al-Quds al-Arabi*'s editor in chief Abdel Bari Atwan, in his book *The Secret History of al-Qaeda*, succinctly undercuts the old hands' narrative.

> Al-Qaeda is unique in the history of radical organizations. It is the first to have a significant global constituency, due to two factors—the diasporas of Muslims throughout the world and, even more critically, the Internet. Any Muslim anywhere in the world can immediately be part of the electronic ummah whose jihadi wing is fronted by al-Qaeda first and foremost.
>
> Al-Qaeda is unique in organizational terms: with a central leadership functioning as figurehead and inspiration, the day-to-day logistics have become the domain of the field commanders in more than forty countries around the world. Again, this is possible because of the Internet; which provides, maintains and updates the ideological and strategic framework within which these commanders—and indeed, any group or individual—can operate.
>
> Finally, al-Qaeda is uniquely dangerous because it has the potential to mobilize thousands, perhaps millions of the world's 1.3 billion Muslims by applying an interpretation of Islam which, alone among world religions, encompasses the obligation to fight among its tenets.[1]

Al-Qaeda and its allies have presented an altogether different kettle of fish from traditional terrorist groups, and the old hands experts have poignantly and dangerously ignored this. Their recommendation when it comes to handling al-Qaeda is a combination of law enforcement and far greater intervention in the Muslim world—to build nation-states, reconstruct economies, promote women's rights, and generally to make 1.5 billion Muslims more Western. Thus they have recommended (a) imposing democratization in the Muslim world; (b) starting worldwide anti-defamation leagues to stop hate speech by Muslims; (c) relying on "smarter policies and better police cooperation"; (d) increasing U.S. intervention in the Arab-Israeli war, the Afghan war, and the Kashmiri insurgency, and massively increasing U.S. funding for those efforts; (e) developing a strategy to send assistance from all pertinent U.S. government agencies "to the whole of an at risk society"; and (f) encouraging Western states to adopt tolerant policies.[2] Perhaps the surest sign that the old hands' time has passed is their nearly unanimous call for more U.S. intervention to stop a war caused by U.S. interventionism.

The "Former Comrades" Narrative

There has been a growing body of writings by retired, jailed, or sidelined jihadis who have been critical of bin Laden. Many were legitimate mujahedin who voluntarily fought alongside the Afghans during the war against the Soviet Union (1972–1992), and so their views are firsthand, are well informed, and need to be included in any research on bin Laden and al-Qaeda. The three men whose works I have chosen to review briefly are intelligent and heroic, and they have often condemned bin Laden. Whatever the differences between them, their criticism has been based on three common factors: (a) their views did not prevail in jihadi councils; (b) they failed to achieve a personal goal, and/or their preferred jihad leader lost out; and (c) they reject bin Laden's tactical modus operandi. Again, each of these men is an authentic mujahedin and has much to contribute to our understanding of the Islamists' movement; but each also has an axe to grind.

The Algerian mujahedin Boudejema Bounoua—aka Abdullah Anas—fought bravely as an insurgent in Afghanistan, although his record hardly merits Lawrence Wright's calling him the "greatest exemplar of Arab Afghan warriors."[3] He was Shaykh Abdullah Azzam's organizational partner and son-in-law; and he expected to win control of Azzam's NGO and funding and recruiting networks after the shaykh's assassination in November 1989. Anas's views on the handling of non-Afghan Muslim volunteers mirrored Azzam's, and, like Azzam, he believed Tajik commander Ahmed Shah Massoud was the only Afghan who could lead the country after the Soviets withdrew. Massoud, Anas said, was "a first rate military planner who was by nature a simple person who had the knack for creating a spirit of camaraderie among his Arab and Afghan soldiers."[4] None of these things came to pass for Anas. As Steve Coll correctly points out, bin Laden thwarted Anas's plans "to take control of Azzam's jihad and recruiting and supporting network."[5] Anas now has political asylum in Britain and from there sniped at bin Laden until the latter's death in 2011.[6]

Anas's criticism has followed predictable lines. Osama bin Laden had broken with Azzam over the handling of foreign Muslim volunteers to fight in Afghanistan. Azzam and Anas favored dispersing them among the Afghans, and bin Laden wanted them concentrated. Bin Laden had sidelined Anas after Azzam was killed, and bin Laden had ultimately aligned with the Taleban in the post-Soviet civil war, thereby opposing Massoud—whom Anas and Azzam had championed—and arranging his assassination. Anas believes bin Laden was successful not because of the Saudi's organizational and political skills, but because the Egyptian Islamists who had won his heart and mind had come between him and Abdullah Azzam, and Anas claims that Azzam had warned that al-Zawahiri was a "troublemaker."[7] Bin Laden, Anas also infers, was one of the Arab volunteers who "had chosen to remain in Peshawar over going into Afghanistan."[8] Bin Laden not only lacked bravery but also organizational skills ("as an organizer—completely a catastrophe")[9] and had "no private circle or an infrastructure of camps depots, and supplies." Indeed, bin Laden had had nothing until he met the Egyptians.[10]

Hashim al-Makki—aka Abu Walid al-Masri and Mustafa Hamid—fought in the anti-Soviet jihad and is regarded as an important theorist by the mujahedin. While he stoutly denies ever having been an al-Qaeda member,[11] al-Makki is fervently anti-American and shares

Shaykh Azzam's and bin Laden's belief in the need for military activity against the West. "I had agreed with Shaykh Abdullah Azzam," he wrote, "that jihad was the only means left for the Islamic nation to defend its religion and interests in facing the forces that are working against it, that the main battle of the Muslims is their battle with the Jews and their Crusader allies."[12]

Al-Makki's criticism of bin Laden has pivoted almost entirely on his respect and affection for Taleban leader Mullah Omar and his Islamic Afghan state, and the negative impact bin Laden had on both. Al-Makki worked as Al-Jazirah Television's Kandahar bureau chief from 1998 to 2001, and there he became close to Mullah Muhammad Omar.[13] Although al-Makki claims that Omar believed the media was "immoral" and depended "mainly on lies," the Taleban chief hired al-Makki to publish the Arabic-language version of the Taleban's monthly journal, the *Emirate*. Al-Makki grew to respect Omar, a man of "quiet but firm character," and is said to have been the first foreign Muslim to swear allegiance to him, and to devote himself to aiding the Taleban's Islamic state.[14]

Al-Makki seems to have made no public criticism of bin Laden before 9/11, but after that event and the Taleban's fall he became open about his "reservations" about bin Laden's approach and its "overall consequences," as well as what he saw as the "extreme weaknesses" of bin Laden's political and military capabilities.[15] In retrospect, he wrote, bin Laden "was not qualified to lead [al-Qaeda]."[16] In addition, he complained of bin Laden's "crazy attraction" to the media, and the international media in particular, which had caused Omar endless problems with the United States and other powers right at the moment that the Taleban was still consolidating power.[17] He accused bin Laden of wanting "absolute individual leadership"; damned him for making "jihad synonymous with the explosive belt and the car bomb"; and condemned his rashness—bin Laden was, he wrote, "fond of jumping in the air" without caring whether "his feet will hit the ground after that or not."[18] Because of bin Laden's faults, al-Makki concludes, the Taleban was defeated and Afghanistan, the Islamic state that "historically holds the strongest fortresses in Islam," was lost.[19] Oddly, al-Makki does not condemn the 9/11 attacks; he focuses on the trouble bin Laden caused Mullah Omar, "this pious man, . . . [who]

became a fugitive in the mountains of Afghanistan after he gave up everything . . . so he may not sacrifice any of the Muslims who sought his protection."[20]

Veteran Arab Afghan Abu Musab al-Suri's stock is currently very high among Western analysts of al-Qaeda and Islamist militancy.[21] Al-Suri—aka Umar Abd al-Hakim; true name: Mustafa bin Abd al-Qadir Setmariam Nasar—is often termed the "successor" to bin Laden, the Islamist leader with the right approach to keeping the movement going. That approach features autonomous individuals and cells staging small, independent, and dispersed attacks around the world rather than large 9/11-like attacks. This, al-Suri has argued, would prevent the West from destroying the attackers because the latter would lack "fixed bases or traceable organizational ties."[22]

Such a plan is, of course, old hat. Terrorist groups have used this tactic for decades both in a national context—the IRA and ETA in Europe, for example—and internationally in the activities of Abu Nidal and Carlos the Jackal. None has amounted to more than a pin prick nuisance. Success would require some sort of systematic and coordinated approach, which is anathema to al-Suri and others who have championed the dispersed strategy. And, in any event, this is a secondary tack used by al-Qaeda since the 1998 formation of the "World Front against the Crusaders and Jews," and was recommended in al-Zawahiri's 2001 book *Knights under the Banner of the Prophet*. Bin Laden encouraged this type of attack, but believed—unlike al-Suri—that although such attacks could produce casualties, as well as consternation among law enforcement agencies, they could never produce victory.

Al-Suri was close to bin Laden for a number of years, working with him on strategy and media operations; he was an al-Qaeda member from 1988 until 1992.[23] He tended to be aggravated by bin Laden's refusal to accept all his ideas, and proceed "irrespective of my opinion," as al-Suri complained.[24] Al-Suri also seems to have regarded himself as smarter and more capable than bin Laden, although al-Suri's excellent biographer Brynjar Lia points out that his fierce criticism of bin Laden has stemmed in part from a deep, abiding dislike and distrust of Saudis.[25] Like others of bin Laden's Islamist rivals—including, at one point, Ayman al-Zawahiri—al-Suri attacked bin Laden for playing to the international media to publicize his war plans and to incite Muslims.

This, al-Suri claimed, focused Western anger on Mullah Omar's regime—of which he was an ardent supporter—and thereby undercut the non-Afghan mujahedin's reliance on Taleban hospitality.[26] Bin Laden's frequent media interviews angered Mullah Omar, al-Suri wrote in July 1999: "I think our brother has caught the disease of screens, flashes, fans, and applause."[27] Al-Suri claimed the solution to the problem was to compile the advice of "knowledgeable and experienced people" (including himself, of course) and send a delegation to force bin Laden to apologize to Mullah Omar.[28] This did not occur, and al-Suri's criticism of bin Laden largely disappeared after 9/11. Al-Suri was captured in 2005, reportedly by Syrian authorities, and remains incarcerated.[29]

Notwithstanding the opposition to bin Laden of former comrades like al-Suri, they were never possible Western allies. Their quarrels with bin Laden have involved timing and tactics; they did not believe bin Laden was a bad Muslim or had an unworkable strategic aim. "Is there anyone who does not know the value of this man, bin Laden," al-Makki has asked, "his valor, generosity, piousness and heroism, his devout worship and jihad?"[30] Al-Makki also echoed bin Laden in condemning U.S. intervention in the Muslim world. "We will continue this fight . . . [until] they . . . leave us free to decide what is in the interest of our people."[31] For his part, al-Suri shared al-Makki's anger over bin Laden's role in the Taleban's downfall, but he regarded bin Laden's creation of the World Front against Crusaders and Jews as "a great step forward," and is reported to have praised the 9/11 attacks, believing they had a positive "mobilizing affect" and "immensely improved" prospects for mujahedin unity.[32] He was seeking to mend ties with al-Qaeda when he was captured.

The Riyadh Narrative

The 9/11 attacks undermined the Saudi regime's ability to keep Americans and their government believing the Kingdom was a true, dependable ally. With fifteen Saudi nationals among the nineteen mujahedin who committed the attacks, suspicions naturally and quickly formed in American minds and, to some extent, across the Western world. That idea that our Saudi friends might be duplicitous was reinforced when the Bush administration authorized the evacuation of bin Laden family members from the United States before they could be questioned, probably because they were carrying Saudi diplomatic passports that afforded immunity. The Saudis, then, had to keep their image of being a U.S. ally alive in the wake of seemingly definitive proof to the contrary.

Fortunately for Riyadh, its damage-control effort was focused on an audience—the Bush administration—that wanted to believe the Kingdom was a friend. While constructing the "good-Saudi-boy-led-astray-by-evil-Egyptians" narrative, the Saudis could rely on the bipartisan goodwill of most of official Washington; on U.S. media willingness to sell as much media air time as Saudis wanted to spread their Madison-Avenue-slick, pro-American propaganda commercials; on the willingness of journalists to lap up what high-ranking Saudis—especially Prince Turki al-Faisal—said about bin Laden; and on the pro-Saudi lobbying of Congress by U.S. arms makers who profit from Riyadh's outsized military spending.

Despite the willingness of its audience to be manipulated, the Saudis had to take care not to offend their domestic religious establishment and its rough-hewn Afghan offspring, the Taleban. (It should be noted that the official breaking of ties between two Middle East entities—such as the post-9/11 Saudi-Taleban break—often means little or nothing substantively.) Were Osama bin Laden perceived as evil as opposed to misled by outsiders, the Saudi clerics and the educational system they ran would be seen as blameworthy, deliberately producing evil Muslims at home as well as abroad, in the form of the 9/11 hijackers, Mullah Omar's regime, and other Sunni Islamist groups. Such a portrait would offend Saudi religious leaders, increase domestic dissent and instability, and handicap the Saudi royals' ability to ultimately restore a Taleban like government in Kabul, their consistent foreign-policy goal for Afghanistan.

Looked at in this context, the Saudis' first propaganda initiative was a misstep. They identified Osama bin Laden's mother as a Syrian-born outsider and the least favored of Muhammad bin Laden's wives, and her son as a teenage wastrel renowned for brawling, drunkenness, and whoring in the bars of Beirut.[33] Neither portrayal would wash, because neither was true. Osama's mother, Allia, was well liked by the large bin Laden family, and Osama's reputation for piety and asceticism was untarnished. Only naïve or pro-Saudi Americans bought the story, and, more troubling for the regime, it reflected poorly on Saudi society, picturing it not as a pious society but as one characterized by bad marriages and roistering youth.

Having failed in this first effort, the Saudi regime next crafted what has proven to be remarkably effective propaganda. It worked by dividing bin Laden's life into two parts. In the first part—from childhood until the 1990–1991 Gulf War and its aftermath—Osama was portrayed as a well-mannered, family-oriented, hard working, and thoroughly pious son of one of the country's most important, accomplished, and loyal families. The pre-1991 Osama loved his family, worked hard in school, and labored in his father's company. (I have used "Osama" in parts of chapters 1–3 not for the sake of familiarity, but to avoid confusing him with other bin Ladens.) Like all good Saudi boys, he was educated in a faith that was nonviolent unless called to defend itself, as in Afghanistan. Then, again like all good Saudi boys, he shouldered his musket and went off to fight the Red Army. In the Riyadh scenario, no Sunni Muslim is an extremist or terrorist unless and until he becomes anti-al-Saud. This remains the case today.

As a coda to bin Laden's pre-1991 life, a number of significant Saudi figures—close boyhood friends, mujahedin, relatives, and regime princes, officials, and clerics—were wheeled out after 9/11 to express shock at what bin Laden stood accused of. Each explained that bin Laden was not at all worldly, and that as a young man he had shown neither leadership skills nor any desire for a leadership position. "What caused such a good Saudi boy to go bad?" The Saudi thespians who asked and answered the question were eagerly listened to and believed by credulous Westerners, and especially American journalists. The key Saudi cast members follow.

PRINCIPAL PLAYERS

Prince Turki al-Faisal—Former chief of the Saudi Intelligence Service and Saudi ambassador to the United States

Ahmed Badeeb—Turki's former chief of staff and a biology teacher who taught bin Laden at the al-Thagher Model School in Jeddah

Jamal Khashoggi—Friend of bin Laden's youth, once an adviser to Prince Turki, and until recently a senior Saudi journalist

Muhammad Jamal Khalifa—Friend of bin Laden's youth, fellow mujahedin, and brother-in-law (now deceased)

Khalid al-Batarfi—Friend of bin Laden's youth, medical doctor, and a now-and-then Saudi journalist

Shaykh Musa al-Qarni—A respected Saudi religious academic who in the 1980s was closely involved with bin Laden and the Afghan mujahedin. He was then bin Laden's adviser for interpreting the rules of Shariah. He now supports the Saudi regime against bin Laden. He later helped the Saudi regime craft anti-bin Laden propaganda.

Shaykh Salman al-Awdah—Once bin Laden's favorite Saudi cleric and a fellow anti-al-Saud reformer. Imprisoned by the Saudis in 1994 and persuaded to recant after several years in jail. He now is a prominent opponent of bin Laden's ideas and his legacy. Pro-Saudi religious scholar, with high academic standing, his own television program, and a popular Web site.

SUPPORTING CAST

Prince Bandar bin Sultan—Former Saudi ambassador to the United States, now Saudi national security adviser.

Prince Nayef bin Abdul-Aziz—Saudi interior minister.

After establishing Osama as a good boy gone bad, Riyadh needed a plausible evil influence over young Osama. Enter Ayman al-Zawahiri, leader of the Egyptian Islamic Jihad (EIJ). The Saudi story predicated Osama's fall as starting with his association with al-Zawahiri in Peshawar in the 1980s. Al-Zawahiri turned this nice (if none-too-smart) Saudi lad into what President Bush called an "evildoer" and the Obama administration called a "murderous thug." Bin Laden's son Omar reinforced this portrait, saying, "The Egyptian doctor had an evil influence over my father."[34]

In phase one of the spin, al-Zawahiri befriends a young and inexperienced Osama; poisons his mind against both Shaykh Azzam—claiming that the shaykh was a U.S. and Saudi agent[35]—and the sainted Afghan commander Ahmad Shah Massoud; slowly inserts his senior lieutenants into bin Laden's circle and thus into al-Qaeda when it is being formed in 1988; and transforms bin Laden into a man who lives only to kill. In phase two—set in the Sudan—al-Zawahiri extends nearly total control over Osama. After the 1996 return to Afghanistan, al-Zawahiri is the puppeteer who makes bin Laden dance. Speaking publicly in 2006, for example, Shaykh Musa al-Qarni, a former bin Laden friend and adviser, said that Osama had fallen into Egyptian hands. "He [Osama] is now part and parcel of the fabric of [the Egyptian] al-Jihad Organization's ideology. He operates in line with its plans."[36]

As absurd as this narrative was—bin Laden, as we shall see, altered al-Zawahiri much more than vice versa—it was bought by many in the West, although nowhere so completely as in *The Looming Tower: Al-Qaeda and the Road to 9/11*. Riyadh's successful Osama spin served its interests well. It convinced American politicians, always eager to believe the al-Sauds to be fine, loyal fellows, and allowed them to in turn reassure a skeptical public that all was well on the Arabian Peninsula. The spin also suited the Saudi religious establishment—which played a major role in peddling the story to the media. And it did not offend the Taleban leaders who would lead the Islamist Afghan regime that the Kingdom intended to reinstall later. Parenthetically, because the scenario played so well in official Washington, Riyadh cooked up an even more outlandish version, one that heralded the creation of reeducation camps to transform mujahedin into peaceful, productive private citizens. Officials in Washington and in the NATO capitals found it convincing.

As noted, the core of the Saudi narrative is the unwarranted influence on Osama by al-Zawahiri.* Having bought the Saudi narrative, Western writers duly produced a bin Laden literature in which Osama is portrayed as an effete Saudi ne'er-do-well who enjoyed "a tea-pouring, meeting-oriented life," as one put it. "Days would drift by in loose debates, fatwa drafting, and humanitarian project development—a shifting mix of engineering, philanthropy, and theology."[37] But then Satan appeared in the form of al-Zawahiri and put bin Laden under a spell. Before the Saudi version made the rounds, the Egyptian journalist Isam Darraz—who is also a former Egyptian military intelligence officer—ascribed no undue influence on bin Laden to al-Zawahiri or

Egyptian Islamic Jihad in his book chronicling the anti-Soviet jihad, but in later interviews he suddenly recalled that "the Egyptians formed a barrier around the curiously passive Saudi."[38] The British journalist Mark Huband has written that al-Zawahiri provided "the political vision that is the foundation of al-Qaeda today."[39] The French scholar Stéphane Lacroix has claimed that al-Zawahiri was "the chief ideologue and brain of this organization [al-Qaeda] . . . [and] is considered the true thinker behind the September 11 attacks on the United States."[40] Lawrence Wright—a true believer in the Saudi scenario, as I have said—has presented the idea that al-Zawahiri orchestrated al-Qaeda's international aspirations by giving bin Laden "a class in how to become a leader in an international organization."[41] Wright never tells the reader that at the time al-Zawahiri had no experience whatsoever, nothing to prepare him to be the tutor of a would-be international leader. The person who would disagree with the Saudi narrative most heartily (aside from me) is al-Zawahiri himself.

It would take a good deal of ink to refute all the assertions, but here is a shorthand catalog of points establishing that, rather than al-Zawahiri influencing bin Laden, the opposite was the case.

1. Al-Zawahiri was single-mindedly intent on overthrowing the Egyptian government and believed the "road to Jerusalem must pass through Cairo"—*until he met bin Laden.*
2. Al-Zawahiri believed Islamist groups should focus on the "near" rather than the "far" enemy—*until he met bin Laden.*
3. Al-Zawahiri believed in small, highly secretive clandestine organizations, like his EIJ—*until he met bin Laden.*
4. Al-Zawahiri believed that the way to topple Arab tyrannies was through military coups, not insurgent warfare—*until he met bin Laden.*
5. Al-Zawahiri strongly tended toward takfirism (deciding who is not a good Muslim and then killing them)—*until he met bin Laden.*
6. Al-Zawahiri was obsessed with secrecy and avoiding publicity, except in the realm of theological debate—*until he met bin Laden, who excelled at media operations.*

7. Al-Zawahiri often praised and quoted the work of Sayyed Qutb and the EIJ's theologian Abd al-Salam al-Faraj—*bin Laden never quoted either, or al-Zawahiri, for that matter.*
8. Al-Zawahiri was inept at running the EIJ's international cells, and his mistakes allowed U.S. and Egyptian intelligence to wreck the network—*forcing al-Zawahiri to seek out bin Laden's aid and accept his direction.*
9. Al-Zawahiri and his lieutenants completely failed to damage the Egyptian government—*and so accepted bin Laden's plan to knock the U.S. props from under Mubarak's regime.*
10. Al-Zawahiri was an arrogant Egyptian nationalist who believed Egyptians superior to other Arabs—*until he met bin Laden, who thrives in multinational working environments.*
11. Al-Zawahiri was unable to raise any significant amount of money and was all but broke—*and so was forced to begin working with bin Laden.*
12. Al-Zawahiri's avuncular personality and reputation as a thinker, not a fighter, gave him no international stature and no potential for such—*until he joined bin Laden's organization.*

Separating out true from false assertions in the Saudi version of events poses a challenge of the first order for any biographer of bin Laden, for what becomes clear is how thoroughly Western politicians, pundits, journalists, and scholars have been hoodwinked by it. Nonetheless, the Saudis' spin mixed a good measure of truth in with its lies. Much of the Saudis' pre-1991 story is accurate, though many of the Saudi claims are simply too good to be true, much like Parson Weems's tales of George Washington. The pre-1991 material can also be vetted against what has become available in the last several years, especially the books by Carmen bin Laden and Omar and Najwa bin Laden.

The post-1991 portion of the Riyadh story is a bit easier to sort out because there is an ample record of what bin Laden said and did, what role al-Zawahiri played in al-Qaeda, and how al-Zawahiri's views changed over time. The data pertaining to the 1957–1994 years are most helpful to our understanding of bin Laden. Indeed, one comes away from the materials believing men like Ahmed Badeeb, Muhammad Jamal Khalifa, and shaykhs al-Qarni and al-Awdah were once so close to bin Laden that they cannot entirely hide either their affection for him or their respect for his bravery and personal sacrifices. Such sentiment seeps out at times as they recite from their anti-bin Laden script.[42]

The Imperialist Narrative

It must be accepted, the historian Victor Hanson Davis wrote, "that bin Laden and Zawahiri—like all fascists who seek state power to implement an all-encompassing reactionary ideology—have not so much an identifiable and specific gripe, but rather total and general hatred of the influence of liberal Western civilization."[43] If Davis meant that Islamists do not want "the influence of liberal Western civilization"—as well as its militaries—occupying the Muslim world, he would be correct. But that is not what Davis meant. He meant that the two Islamists were "mass murderers" who were not "in any sense systematic thinkers who outline a logical belief system."[44] He wanted his readers, in short, to ignore anything the Islamists have had to say. Like many neoconservatives, he has offered a mixture of Wilsonian imperialism and blind faith in the moral superiority of Israel in general and Likudites in particular.

Although the time is long past when it could be credibly argued that al-Qaeda and its allies are motivated by something other than the impact of U.S. policy in the Muslim world, there is still a legion of pro-Israel writers—commentators, academics, and journalists—who endorse this notion. "Contrary to widespread assumptions," Efraim Karsh wrote in his 2007 book, which portrayed al-Qaeda and all Muslims as relentless, land-grabbing imperialists on a level with the Nazis, "these attacks [of 9/11], and for that matter Arab and Muslim anti-Americanism, have little to do with U.S. international behavior or its Middle Eastern policy. If today, America is reviled in the Muslim world, it is not because of its specific policies but because, as the preeminent world power, it blocks the final realization of this same age-old dream of regaining the lost glory of the caliphate. As such, it is a natural target for aggression. Osama bin Laden and other Islamists' war is not against America per se, but is rather the most recent manifestation of the millenarian jihad for a universal Islamic empire (or umma)."[45] Karsh goes on to say that for many Muslims, bin Laden has represented nothing less than a reincarnation of Saladin—vanquisher of the Crusaders—and, like Saladin, has signified the "House of Islam's *war for world mastery*," a phrase Karsh deftly uses to evoke comparisons to Hitler.[46] Karsh neglects to mention that the wars Saladin fought were in his era perceived as defensive, waged to retake Egypt from heretical Shia and to reclaim Jerusalem and the Levant from Christians. How "world mastery" figures into this Karsh does not explain, but he does claim that Saladin's "elaborate holy-war propaganda was a fig-leaf for an unabashed quest for self-aggrandizement . . . [and] his lifelong effort at empire building."[47]

Sadly, examples of this ideological analysis are everywhere at hand, in the works of Douglas Feith, Bernard Lewis, Charles Krauthammer, George Weigel, John Bolton, William Kristol, and Norman Podhoretz; in articles in such journals as the *Weekly Standard*, *National Review*, *Wall Street Journal*, and *Commentary*, and on Web sites like FrontPageMagazine.com and Powerline.com. The hold their views have on much of the media and most leaders in both parties is stunning. Why do they have such influence? Because they offer politicians an easy way out. They reassure them that their failed foreign policies are entirely beneficent, indeed ought to be pushed diplomatically and militarily, as in the current Iraq war. In turn, the politicians react with a mixture of pride and relief—proud to be offered certification of their visionary brilliance and relieved they do not have to publicly admit that the U.S.-Israel relationship dominates and distorts America's domestic politics and endangers its national security.

The result of the neoconservatives' efforts is that since bin Laden declared war on America in 1996, our leaders and media have been duped (often willingly so) into fighting a nonexistent enemy—that is, a gang of would-be world dominators. While Western leaders engage in efforts to slay this phantom dragon, the foe we do face, the one that wages jihad against U.S. intervention in the Muslim world, is growing in numbers and geographical reach. Ironically, the great medieval Arab intellectual Ibn Khaldun (1332–1406) discusses the process by which those he calls "opportunists"—a fair name for the neoconservatives—have come to manipulate troubled urbanized societies and dominate their policies. "To the opportunist," Lenn Evan Goodman has written of Khaldun's analysis, "whether political or intellectual . . . society appears to be no more than a bloated and moribund body whose resources (and last vigor) exist only to be sapped—often under the guise of response to its own desperate recognition of its needs for help. Thus an infusion of a new spirit of resolution may forestall the inevitable decline, but cannot prevent it, for highly organized, urbanized societies *by their very nature* seek remedies to their problems in professionalism and expertise, and thus offer themselves as bait to charlatans and political (and ultimately military) opportunists. But militarism, demagoguery and the intellectual authority of the pseudo-prophets whom the situation calls forth are as destructive of the fabric of society as decadence itself."[48]

There is no better description of what Lewis and others offer than the "militarism, demagoguery, and the intellectual authority of the pseudo-prophets," and their substitution of what they say Islamists say for what the Islamists actually do say has delayed America from taking the Islamists' measure and devising the best means to defeat them. At a minimum, their hubristic militarism and democracy-mongering "has lost not simply hearts and minds [in the Muslim world], but the possibility even of reaching those hearts and minds ever again," as Michael Vlahos has put it.[49] When speaking to Americans in September 2009, bin Laden himself urged them to break away "from the fear and intellectual terrorism being practiced against you by the neoconservatives," and noted that, whether under George W. Bush or Barack Obama, "the bitter truth is that the neoconservatives are still a heavy burden to you."[50]

The "bin Laden Experts'" Narratives

The "bin Laden experts'" narratives are the most obscurantist because they all but ignore what bin Laden has said. Indeed, the bulk of the most heralded works on bin Laden is based on everything except his actual words. On the other hand, the authors extensively quote bin

Laden's enemies—his Saudi rivals; various U.S. government officials, behavioral scientists, and so-called terrorism experts. It is as if a historian were to set out to write a biography of George Washington and decided both to ignore the collected works of Washington and to rely exclusively on the testimony of those most opposed to him—political rivals, American Tories, King George III, British army officers, and today's presentist caste of history professors who see Washington purely as a slave-owning dead white male. The resulting assessment might well win a Pulitzer but would shed little light on Washington's life and career. So it has been with works on bin Laden.

Since 9/11 several books have been written by Western and non-Muslim authors about bin Laden that focus on his character, intelligence, leadership style, international influence, and organizational skills. The best works are by Peter Bergen, Abdel Bari Atwan, Steve Coll, and Brynjar Lia.[51] Among the rest, about a dozen fit the characterization of "essential works" on bin Laden and al-Qaeda. I have listed them below. In each case, the author and title are followed by the number of citations of bin Laden's works—speeches, interviews, statements, and so on—contained in their endnotes.[52] I have also noted where a large number of citations pertain to relatively few primary documents. The books are listed by date of publication. I make no judgment regarding the quality of each—some are fine works, others are noted only because so little serious work is available on bin Laden.

Rohan Gunaratna, *Inside Al-Qaeda: Global Network of Terror* (2002)—20 citations to 8 documents

Jason Burke, *Al-Qaeda: Casting a Shadow of Terror* (2003)—5 citations

Jonathan Randall, *Osama: The Making of a Terrorist* (2004)—2 citations

Marc Sageman, *Understanding Terror Networks* (2004)—2 citations

Steve Coll, *Ghost Wars: The Secret History of the CIA, Afghanistan, and Bin Laden, from the Soviet Invasion to September 10, 2001* (2005)—2 citations

Fawaz A. Gerges, *The Far Enemy: Why Jihad Went Global* (2005)—15 citations to 5 documents

Mary R. Habeck, *Knowing the Enemy: Jihadist Ideology and the War on Terror* (2006)—52 citations to 14 documents
Lawrence Wright, *The Looming Tower: Al-Qaeda and the Road to 9/11* (2006)—28 citations, 22 of which refer to 4 documents
Steve Coll, *The Bin Ladens: An Arabian Family in the American Century* (2008)—17 citations to 10 documents
Bruce Riedel, *The Search for Al Qaeda: Its Leadership, Ideology, and Future* (2008)—12 citations
Roy Gutman, *How We Missed the Story: Osama bin Laden, the Taliban, and the Hijacking of Afghanistan* (2008)—11 citations[53]

One does not expect a reputed "terrorist leader" to produce a corpus of primary sources for historical investigation, in the manner of an eminent politician or statesman. Bin Laden, however, is an odd duck in this regard. My own archive of primary documentation for bin Laden contains 159 documents that total 791 pages. Of course, I have no way of knowing how complete my archive is, and yet its size suggests that the information in the list of books referred to is not exhaustive, and ignores much of what there is to be learned from bin Laden's own works.

A good rule of thumb is that if you are going to analyze someone's thoughts and actions by using the words of his rivals and enemies, you will need to balance them with what he himself said about them. This is particularly the case when the subject is someone most authors—and readers—deem among history's monsters. I would imagine Ian Kershaw disliked the task of reading Adolf Hitler's papers and musings, but he did it. Yet bin Laden's story has thus far been told almost exclusively from the perspective of others. Thus, Lawrence Wright's work puts great stock in what bin Laden enemies, Abdullah Anas, Prince Turki, and Ahmed Badeeb, had to say. Their books suggest that Roy Gutman and Steve Coll worship at the feet of Ahmad Shah Massoud; and Fawaz Gerges' *The Far Enemy* revels in a slew of unnamed anti–bin Laden sources.[54] Most offer quasi-psychological explanations for Osama's behavior, most of which amount to no more than "if only Osama (and implicitly all Muslims) were more like us Westerners."[55]

At times, these one-sided efforts spill into a bit of blindness. In *The Bin Ladens: An Arabian Family in the American Century*, for example, the cast of characters is large and largely contemptible. If the book has a hero, it is Muhammad bin Laden's son and successor, the late Salem bin Laden. In my view, Salem effectively and insincerely played both sides of the street—Islamic and Western—and was hedonistic, hypocritical, and self-centered. In other words, he fits an archetype familiar to many in the West (Bill Clinton, for one, comes to mind). He is also one of the least representative bin Ladens, Saudis or Muslims. Indeed, in the book only three Saudis come off as decent, pious, hard-working, and persevering men—Muhammad bin Laden, King Faisal, and Osama bin Laden himself.[56] That alone is enough to suggest that the primary sources pertinent to Osama merit fuller exploitation.

2

EDUCATION, 1957–1979

Osama bin-Muhammad bin-Awad bin Laden was born in the al-Maz district of Riyadh, Saudi Arabia, on March 10, 1957. The name Osama means lion, and bin Laden explained that he was named after one of the "venerable companions of the prophet," Osama bin Zaid. "He was someone whom the prophet, God's peace and blessings be upon him, has loved and has loved his father before him."[1] Bin Laden's family moved to Medina six months after his birth, and until his departure from Saudi Arabia in 1991, he lived primarily in Mecca, Medina, and Jeddah.[2] Osama was born into a large, wealthy, and prominent family of Yemeni origin whose males rose to positions of business and family leadership via unrelenting hard work, perseverance, stubbornness, genuine religious faith, self-reliance, and risk-taking. This shaped the man bin Laden would become, and to this day influences the way al-Qaeda is run.

Osama's father, Muhammad bin-Awad bin Laden, was born into Yemen's Kenda tribe around 1908. He lived in the village of al-Rubat Ba'eshn in the inland valley of Wadi Doan in the country's Hadramut region. As a young man he emigrated to Ethiopia—where he permanently lost the use of his right eye in an accident—and then to Jeddah, Saudi Arabia. He worked as a porter and a bricklayer, and in 1931 he founded a construction company he called simply the

Bin Laden Company.[3] Muhammad bin Laden, Steve Coll has written, was "a hands-on foreman who sang with his men at jobsites and did not hesitate to work alongside them. . . . [He also had] a gift for sensing the qualities of people around him, and for retaining their loyalty."[4] And while barely literate, Muhammad was a talented engineer and a brilliant businessman whose risk-taking was based on the calculations of a "mind [that] was like a computer for figures."[5] The rags-to-riches story of Muhammad bin Laden and his company has been documented by several writers, and was publicly discussed by Osama.[6] Muhammad was a much-married man—his grandson has said his two passions were work and women—and Osama was his seventeenth son, born of a Syrian wife named Allia Ghanem.[7]

The major themes of Osama's youth seem to be the immediate and long-term impact of his father's example; his relationship with his mother; his ties to the large bin Laden clan; his schooling; his early development of an appetite for hard work; and his love for Islamic history and for the Muslim ummah. All shaped his character and actions.

Osama and His Father

What kind of man was Osama's father? "Shaykh Muhammad bin Laden," his former daughter-in-law Carmen bin Laden wrote in 2005, "was a giant among men." "He was honest, pious, and beloved by everyone who met him. . . . In [his children's] eyes he was a hero, a distant figure, legendary, austere, and profoundly religious."[8] Although he died in an airplane crash on September 3, 1967, Muhammad was remembered by a Pakistani newspaper as recently as January 2010 as a sincere, keen, and loyal man of "very strong will power." The article went on to point out that despite being illiterate, he had a mind "like a computer," and out of his own pocket had rebuilt the al-Aqsa mosque, the Dome of the Rock, in Jerusalem. "He laid a golden sheet weighing several hundred maunds [an Indian measure of weight equal officially to about 82 pounds] of gold on its dome."[9] This certainly is the way Osama viewed his father. Osama's first wife, Najwa, has written that "he had greatly loved and respected his father," and that while he was always "unusually restrained in his manner and his speech," he became more so after his father's death.[10] Bin Laden's own words confirm Najwa's assessment.

> When he learned that the Jordanian government had offered a tender for the renovation of the Dome of the Rock, he gathered his engineers and asked them to determine how much it would cost to do the job without profit. They told him we would include the profit with the cost price. He—may God bless his soul—lowered the cost price to win the tender. By the grace of God, he occasionally prayed in the three mosques on the same day. It is no secret that he was one of the infrastructure builders in Saudi Arabia.[11]

> My father . . . was a minister during the reign of King Faisal. . . . King Faisal was still alive when my father died. King Faisal cried at the death of only two persons, one was Muhammad Ibrahim and the other was my father. . . . King Faisal said upon the death of my father that today I have lost my right arm.[12]

There is, however, a wide divergence between the writings by and those about Osama regarding how much time he spent with his father, and in what circumstances. Osama himself suggested a close relationship, and others that their contact amounted to Osama "sitting quietly in his company."[13] Osama once told his sons that he only saw his father five times, and the bulk of the scholarship on this issue supports this. Steve Coll's work, for example, argues that Osama hardly knew his father, and bin Laden's late brother-in-law Muhammad Jamal Khalifah recalled that he "was not with his father very much."[14] Not only did Muhammad spend little time with Osama, he appears to have spent no more than a minimal amount of time with any of his children, save the eldest sons who would inherit his business and family responsibilities. Osama was no more deprived of his father's company than most of his other fifty-two siblings: twenty-eight brothers and twenty-four sisters.[15]

What made the greatest impression on Osama was his father's piety. Muhammad bin Laden was a conservative Muslim who raised his children in the Wahhabite tradition, which advocated piety and austerity.[16] To his children, he stressed frugality, hard work, piety, and self-reliance. "He impressed upon them, too," as Coll has reported, "the rituals and glory of Islam. Muhammad prayed faithfully and expected the boys [his sons] to do the same."[17] Though a very rich man and much married, as we have seen, Muhammad led an ascetic religious life and valued the company of scholars and jurists. In his youth, Osama regularly met prominent Islamists in social and religious settings arranged by his father and—after Muhammad's death—his older brothers. These events, one observer noted, "started forming an Islamic responsibility in him at an early age." Osama's father, for example, underwrote *halaqat*, which were evening meetings with scholars and clerics to discuss particular theological topics.[18] In addition, the bin Laden family hosted in its many residences "hundreds of pilgrims"—prominent scholars, jurists, and leaders—from overseas who came to the Kingdom for hajj, umra (the minor pilgrimage), or other business, and developed a range of good contacts that later benefited Osama.[19] Apt examples of these contacts were those he made with future Afghan insurgent leaders Burhanuddin Rabbani and Abdul Rasul Sayyaf, as well as with Qazi Hussain Ahmed, the leader of the Jamaat-e-Islami, Pakistan's largest religious party. These men were "common faces" to him before the 1979 Soviet invasion.[20]

Beyond establishing personal ties with leading Islamic scholars from the Kingdom and overseas, Osama came away from these experiences with deep admiration and respect for the role scholars play in Muslim society. Both the Koran and the Prophet assigned a special leadership role to "men of knowledge," making them responsible for keeping Islamic rulers on the religious straight-and-narrow. Scholars were willing to speak truth to power—as we say today—no matter the consequences. Until well into the 1990s, a central aspect of Osama's faith was his belief that all Islamic scholars merited respect and that the best of them were the natural leaders in reforming Muslim regimes and defending Islam. He long held this view, but when he changed his mind he did so with a vengeance.

Muhammad bin Laden also left Osama with the conviction that a man's words must match his deeds, both in earthly endeavors and in his dedication to Allah and defense of Islam. It was his father's attitude toward jihad that Osama followed most closely. "My father used to say that he had fathered 25 sons for jihad," Osama said in the late 1990s, "[and] for 40 years my father waited for the Hazrat Mahdi [the Prophet sent by Allah just prior to the end of the world] to arrive." To match that expectation, his father set aside $12 million.[21]

Muhammad bin Laden had a deep-rooted hatred for the state of Israel. Having interviewed Osama several times, the Pakistani journalist Hamid Mir said that he told him that after the 1967 Arab-Israeli war his father asked his engineers if the firm's bulldozers could be converted into tanks. Based on Osama's words, Mir concluded that Muhammad bin Laden "was very, very, very anti-Israeli, and anti-Jewish."[22] If Mir is recollecting accurately, Osama's youthful pro-Palestine views were inspired by his father.

As will be discussed later in greater detail, young Osama developed an admiration for the work of the thirteenth-century Syrian Islamic scholar Taqi al-Din Ahmad Ibn Taymiyyah (1263–1328), who fought as a jihadi and served prison time for questioning the theological basis of the caliph's decisions. "Do you reckon," Ibn Taymiyyah wrote in words sounding much like those of Muhammad bin Laden, that "the giving of water to pilgrims and the inhabiting [of] the Holy Mosque [are] the same as one who believes in God and the Last Day and struggles in the way of God? Not equal are they in God's sight. . . . Those who believe, and have emigrated, and have struggled in the way of God with their possessions and their selves are mightier in rank with God; and . . . they are the triumphant; their Lord gives them good tidings of mercy from Him and good pleasure; for them await gardens wherein is lasting bliss, therein to dwell forever and ever."[23]

Perhaps the most distinctive trait Osama inherited from his father was a determination to be decisive—to set a course of action and hold resolutely to it. Few dared question Muhammad bin Laden once he made up his mind. "Despite his serene demeanor," Najwa bin Laden has written, "no one ever thought of Osama as being weak-willed."[24] Her estimate of her husband's will has held up. In recent years, a prominent Yemeni Salafi scholar, Shaykh Abd al-Majid al-Zindani, has described bin Laden as "a Sunni teacher" who was "courageous" and "consistent." In al-Zindani's view, bin Laden's "language in support of Islam hasn't changed much" over the years.[25]

Osama and His Mother

Anyone writing about Osama notes the close relationship between him and his mother, Allia, as well as Allia's stout defense of her eldest son. His half-brother Ahmad Muhammad al-Attas has said that Osama adored his mother. "First comes God and then his mother."[26] Allia had a profound impact on his religious faith. "I tried to instill in him [Osama] the fear and love of God, respect and love for his family, neighbors and teachers. I didn't need [to do] much work on that."[27]

While impossible to quantify, Allia Ghanem's influence included broadening her son's knowledge of the Muslim world. She came from a largely secular middle-class Syrian family of Yemeni origin. The Ghanem family is based in Latakia, a seaside city of 300,000 that is heavily Alawite, an Islamic sect that is disliked by Sunnis but that controls Syria's government.[28] The Ghanems deny being Alawite, and it does seem unlikely that Muhammad bin Laden would have brought an Alawite into his family and the Kingdom. Still, there is some speculation that Allia is not Sunni. Some Saudi critics of Osama have insisted that his mother was an Alawite, and for that reason Muhammad bin Laden never married her; she was simply a concubine or a "slave wife" with no social standing.[29] These comments obviously have been designed to denigrate Osama's lineage. There is no evidence that Allia was ever an outcast among the bin Ladens, and, as Steve Coll has argued, rightly I believe, the bin Laden family never treated Osama as a lesser member.[30]

Allia was different from Muhammad's many other wives, not least in taking the initiative to ask her husband for a divorce.[31] While in Saudi Arabia, she dressed appropriately and behaved as women are expected to. When abroad, however, Allia is said to have donned Western clothes and moved about easily and comfortably in countries less strict than the Kingdom, such as Syria and Lebanon. Osama's first wife, Najwa, recalled her "Auntie Allia" was "lovely in every way, inspiring awe in everyone who met her . . . she dressed so fashionably when visiting us [in Syria]."[32] For Osama this meant that he saw his mother in two distinct modes—Saudi and at least semi-Western—and learned that it made no difference in her piety. He also accompanied Allia and his step siblings on summer holidays in Syria for his first seventeen years, experiencing a more cosmopolitan atmosphere than that in the Kingdom.[33] Thus in watching his mother and traveling with her during the summers, Osama was further acquainted—as he had been at his father's *halaqat*—with the diversity of the Muslim world, learning how to get along with devout Muslims who did not embrace the Kingdom's puritanism.

In terms of his personal habits, manners, and social behavior, Allia appears to have had greater impact on Osama than his father. Osama's son Omar has written that "my father laid down the guidelines but left the upbringing to my mother,"[34] and that seems a fair assessment of how Osama himself was raised: Muhammad set guidelines but Allia enforced them on a daily basis. Allia was known for her generosity. Najwa bin Laden claims, "Whenever she heard of a struggling family, she would secretly provide for their upkeep."[35] As a young man, Osama also devoted much time to charity work—a friend noted "everything he spends is spent on poor people"—and as he grew he steadily developed a reputation for quiet generosity.[36]

Osama and the bin Ladens

As recently as 2008, Steve Coll noted that Osama "has never denounced or openly repudiated his own family." Coll argues that their occasional statements of condemnation were "merely the product of heavy pressure brought to bear by the Saudi government."[37] In fact, bin Laden went out of his way to praise his family even after it disowned him. He told a Pakistani magazine in August 2000, "My family members are pray[ing] for me and no doubt have gone through a lot of difficulties. But God gave them the courage to face all that."[38] Until his death, bin Laden refused to criticize either his family or his former Saudi friends who turned on him: Prince Turki al-Faisal, Shaykh Salman al-Awdah, Khalid al-Batarfi, Jamal Khashoggi, Ahmed Badeeb, his late brother-in-law Muhammad Jamal Khalifah, and his fourth-eldest son, Omar. Had bin Laden lived, his family would have remained immune, but ultimately he would have attacked his former friends as he believed the al-Sauds were—to stand trial before an Islamist judiciary after the corrupt Saudi monarchy is toppled.

There is no solid evidence to suggest that bin Laden ever found anything but warmth and acceptance from the family (which today is estimated to include six hundred descendants of Muhammad bin Laden).[39] His half-brother Ahmed has said Osama greatly enjoyed his family and that he eagerly played big brother to the four children his mother had with her second husband, Muhammad al-Attas.[40] Carmen bin Laden wrote "Usama was perfectly integrated into the family." "Never once did I hear anyone murmur that his fervor might be a little excessive, or perhaps a passing phase."[41] Carmen's view was validated by Osama's wife Najwa, who remembered that at the start of the Afghan jihad in 1979 no one in the family "took umbrage at his new political awareness and religiosity."[42] Even the most westernized of the bin Laden clan, Osama's half-brother Yeslam, pledged in 2006 to pay for the cost of Osama's legal defense if he was ever captured.[43]

A contentious point involving Osama and his family was whether or not he continued to receive his share of the profits from his father's company. In February 1994, family chief Bakr bin Laden—in tandem with Riyadh's termination of Osama's citizenship—issued a statement cutting the family's ties to Osama and expressing its "regret, denunciation, and condemnation" of his activities.[44] Several years later, however, Osama responded to a question about the state of his relationship with his family by stating, "blood is thicker than water," but he later balanced that response—which might have cast doubt on his family's loyalty to the Saudi regime—by telling Pakistani journalist Rahimullah Yusufzai that he was not receiving "his share of proceeds from the family business."[45] On this point, Carmen bin Laden's words are worth citing, even while keeping in mind that she was engaged in a prolonged and nasty divorce battle with Osama's half-brother Yeslam. "A Saudi—a bin Laden—cannot confront and split from his brothers, in business or any other way," she wrote in 2004. "I cannot believe that the bin Ladens have cut Osama off completely." "No matter what a brother does, he remains a brother."[46] Suggesting that Carmen's words were not merely meant to spite the bin Ladens, the London-based Sa'd al-Faqih, Osama's former colleague in Saudi Arabia's Islamic awakening, has said, "There is a very interesting thing in the structure of [the Islamic] family. You are obligated to support your family members. . . . Well, [the bin Ladens] have to say that [that they disowned

Osama]. They have to pretend to be cutting off bin Laden. But in all actuality they admire him, they respect him. . . . I do not claim that all . . . the bin Laden brothers do. But quite a significant number of them work hard to get [rid of] what they see as sinful money—which has to reach the rightful owner."[47]

School Years

Of Muhammad bin Laden's sons, Osama was the only one to have received his entire education in the Kingdom and without being exposed to either Western schooling or the broadening experience of frequent or prolonged international travel. This suggests that his mind was formed by Islamic instruction alone. Well, yes and no. Osama did not attend schools outside of Saudi Arabia—with the possible exception of a Lebanese grade school—but he did not attend schools teaching the Islamic religion exclusively.

That said, somewhere along his educational trail Osama developed a love for and a deep knowledge of the Koran, Islamic history, and the sunnah (the Prophet Muhammad's sayings and traditions), and these went far beyond what he learned in school. One close observer of bin Laden's writings and statements would later note that he used "a dizzying array of scriptural and historical sources," a conclusion with which anyone with cursory knowledge of his works would agree.[48] Bin Laden did not see himself or his movement as unique in Islam's history, but rather as part of a continuum; citing applicable precedent, after all, is the key to making valid decisions in the Islamic world. His references to the Prophet's battles, strictures, and deeds, for example, were not meant to compare himself to the Prophet—an egotistical slant often attributed to him by Western writers—but instead to stress the historic context to what he was trying to achieve. And, in any event, Muslims would regard any effort to model one's behavior on the Prophet's as praiseworthy. No believer would deny that Allah made the Prophet "the best of men" and intended him to be the model for all believers. Finally, bin Laden's use of scripture, history, and the sunnah insulated him to a large degree from criticism by Islamic scholars employed by the nation-states he denounces. "Religious condemnations issued by state-appointed ulama," the scholar

Malise Ruthven has said, "carry much less weight than the appeal of the Muhammadan paradigm, the model of the Muslim Prophet as the archetypical religious-political reformer against incumbent regimes deemed to have departed from the 'straight path' of Islamic rectitude."[49]

Documentation of the courses bin Laden took in high school and college is thin. Nonetheless, at some point in his youth he became interested in Islamic history, and would over time master it and its applications. The history of the Prophet's life, that of the Muslim nation (the ummah), and that of Islam's most celebrated figures—the Prophet's companions, several scholars and jurists, and military figures like Khalid bin Walid, Nur al-Din, and especially Salah-al-Din al-Ayubbi, better known in the West as Saladin—loomed large in bin Laden's rhetoric. Mark Long has noted that especially in terms of war-making, bin Laden "consciously adopted the traditions of the Prophet with respect to defending Islam."[50] As already noted, Osama was focused on historical precedents and unfailingly tied his own behavior and that of al-Qaeda to leaders and events in Islam's past. When inciting young men to join the jihad, for example, he invariably invoked Saladin's spirit. Just before the 9/11 attacks, for example, bin Laden did this in verse.

> All Muslims await another Salahuddin Ayoubi, who shall come and liberate this sacred country from their [Christians' and Jews'] subjugation.
>
> I envision you all as Salalhuddin Ayubi himself, wielding his all conquering sword dripping with the blood of infidels.
>
> I envision Salahuddin Ayubi coming out of the clouds, and in our hearts and minds is recreated the remembrance of the battles [of the Prophet Muhammad].[51]

As for the formalities of schooling, bin Laden attended the prestigious al-Thagher Model School near downtown Jeddah, a boys-only, K–12 institution that educated the sons of the Kingdom's elite, including the royal family. The school had been sponsored by Crown Prince Faisal—who became King Faisal in 1964. Al-Thagher, Steve Coll has written, reflected Faisal's interest in science and Western educational methodology and was meant to "prepare young Saudis for roles in the kingdom's modernizing economy."[52] Osama first enrolled in al-Thagher in 1968, at age eleven, and graduated in 1976—two years after he married his first wife—in a class of about sixty students.[53] He took "demanding" courses in mathematics, as well as history, English, religion, biology, Arabic, and other subjects.[54] He enjoyed the school, was proud of its ties to King Faisal—one of the few Saudi rulers he has publicly praised—and did not mind being required to wear an English-style schoolboy uniform, consisting of "a freshly ironed shirt and grey trousers." Indeed, his wife Najwa has recalled that he prepared carefully for school each morning and was "very particular about his appearance."[55]

Two aspects of bin Laden's experience at al-Thagher merit attention. The first is the quality of the education he received and the second is the manner in which he performed as a student. The portrayal of bin Laden as limited intellectually has been key to the Saudi narrative discussed above. Most of what is known about Osama's education and performance at al-Thagher comes from Peter L. Bergen's indispensable book *The Osama bin Laden I Know*. Bergen interviewed Brian Fyfiled-Shayler, who taught English to Osama bin Laden at al-Thagher. "The school didn't owe much to the old Koranic madrassas of Arabia," said Fyfield-Shayler; "the school prided itself on its sciences."[56] He goes on to provide a sketch of Osama as a student whom it would be a mistake to write off as dim-witted. Like most Saudi students, Fyfield-Shayler recalled, Osama was

> extraordinarily courteous . . . I think he was, in fact, more courteous than the average student, probably because he was a bit shyer than the other students. For example, when the teacher asked questions, a forest of hands [would go up]. "Ask me! Ask me!" And Osama would not do that. . . . [He] would sit quietly with a very confident smile on his face, but he would not push forward to display his knowledge. And of course, if you actually asked him, then he was usually right, but he didn't push himself forward.
>
> [Osama's] English was not outstanding. He was not one of the great brains of the class. On the other hand, he was not in the bottom. But this does not necessarily mean he is middling

> because [al-Thagher] was one of the two top schools in the country. So to be in the middle of the top class in the top school really puts you in the top fifty students in the country. So although he did not shine at that particular school, he would be one of the top fifty students of his age education-wise [in Saudi Arabia].[57]

The second aspect of Osama's al-Thagher years that seems significant—reflecting on him personally as well as the way the West has perceived the movement he led—is his participation in an after-school religious study group. Most who have written of bin Laden's life have described a Syrian gym teacher—probably an exiled Muslim Brotherhood member—who led the group, first instructing his students in the Koran and then shifting to a concentration on the hadith, the record of the Prophet Muhammad's sayings and practices.[58] Steve Coll portrays the study group as a semi-clandestine organization in which "bin Laden received his first formal education in some of the precepts of violent jihad."[59] Two points need to be made. First, al-Thagher offered religious courses as part of its curriculum, and so Osama needed no introduction to the Koran, the hadith, or the concept of violent jihad from an after-school organization. In addition, bin Laden attended mosque frequently, and he regularly was in the company of Islamic scholars and jurists from across the Muslim world at events hosted or sponsored by his family.[60]

It would therefore be inaccurate to contend that it was only through the after-school group that Osama learned "some of the precepts of violent jihad." In each of the four venues mentioned above, Osama would have learned that jihad is a primarily military enterprise, because that is the way it is presented in the Koran and the sunnah. Some U.S. and Western government officials, journalists, and historians—abetted by the clerics of Arab regimes assigned to mislead them—have labored hard to portray jihad as a vigorous but peaceful endeavor through which the individual Muslim struggles first to control himself and then to master his baser tastes and inclinations. These writers often cite a hadith claiming the Prophet spoke of a "greater jihad" and a "lesser jihad," considering the "greater" to be the individual struggle just described, and the "lesser" to involve specific military activity. This is an indefensible position. When mentioned in the Koran—which is God's word spoken to Gabriel, who repeats it to Muhammad—jihad is almost invariably used in a martial sense.[61] Moreover, the hadith prized by the jihad-is-personal-struggle advocates is so poorly sourced—hadiths' reliability depends on a validated chain of transmitters who passed the data from the person who heard the Prophet speak or saw his deeds—that it is not included in the two canonical hadith collections, those by al-Bukhari and Muslim.[62]

All this is to say that there is nothing secretive or selective about the way Osama learned about jihad. He simply learned that in almost all cases in the Koran and the hadith the term is understood as martial; he would later explain—correctly—that if people did not understand that using "spearheads" is a "justified right" when Islam is threatened, it was because they were confused. "The jihad is part of our Shariah and the nation [ummah] cannot dispense with it [in fighting] against its enemies."[63] It is the West's failure to accept this simple, irrefutable fact, I believe, that keeps it from understanding that bin Laden and most Muslims—not just his followers—have defined jihad as a military activity; where there is disagreement among Muslims, it involves how, when, and against what jihad is to be launched. Although in my view he understates the prominence of war in Islamic theology, Georgetown University professor John Esposito provides a useful distinction between jihad as a Koran-based martial concept and jihad as a name for individual or civil improvement efforts, much as Americans use the word "war" for public or private campaigns against cancer, drugs, and poverty. In addition to its martial aspect, Esposito writes, "today jihad . . . is used to describe the personal struggle to lead a good or virtuous life, to fulfill family responsibilities, to clean up a neighborhood, to fight drugs, or to work for social justice."[64] Esposito also notes that whether the term is used in its Koranic martial or civil society sense the "word jihad has only positive connotations [for Muslims]."[65]

In 1978, Osama entered King Abdul Aziz University in Jeddah to study economics, business administration, and management; he is said to have developed an enthusiasm for the latter.[66] He did not finish his studies or earn a degree, and I have found no transcript of the courses he took or grades he achieved. Because of this paucity of evidence, the default position is to assume he was most influenced by the

Islamist professors—including members of the Muslim Brotherhood who had fled Jordan, Egypt, and Syria—who were teaching religion there at the time. Several authors claim bin Laden took formal courses from the Jordanian Abdullah Azzam and the Egyptian Muhammad Qutb; Steve Coll writes that under such scholars Osama "studied the imperatives and nuances of contemporary Islamic jihad."[67] While this may be so, and Osama is likely to have heard both men in public lectures, there is no way to prove it. Even his wife Najwa could only say that her husband "took a particular interest in his [university] religion classes."[68]

It is worth noting, however, that bin Laden never directly quoted Azzam or Muhammad Qutb in his public words, and Osama's late brother-in-law Muhammad Jamal Khalifah said only that he and Osama read Sayyed Qutb's most influential books, *Sign Posts* and *In the Shade of the Koran*, and mainly learned "how to educate our children" from Muhammad Qutb.[69] Steve Coll claims that in the late 1970s Osama read Muhammad Qutb's book *Concepts That Should Be Corrected*—which argued that impious Muslim rulers must be opposed—and bin Laden publicly recommended that book and another by Muhammad Qutb titled *Are We Muslims?*[70] Bin Laden also may have been influenced by Muhammad Qutb through his friendship with Saudi Shaykh Safar al-Hawali, whose master's thesis was mentored by Qutb.[71] Thus, between reading the works of the Qutb brothers and that of Ibn Taymiyyah, bin Laden was well versed in what these men described as a Muslim's duty—to fight impious rulers—before meeting Ayman al-Zawahiri in 1986, although it has frequently been argued that al-Zawahiri first taught bin Laden this.[72]

The Millionaire Laborer

Osama claims that from his childhood he was involved in his father's company, helping to construct roadways, tunnels, and urban buildings in or around Mecca, Medina, and Jeddah. "I started working for my father at an early age," Osama said in 1997, "[and] for construction purposes, I received training in explosives in blasting mountains [for tunnels and roads]. . . . I [also] supervised the work of the extension of the Masjid-i-Nabawi [in Medina]."[73] Several of Osama's boyhood friends have verified this claim, one noting that he worked "as a trainee for his father's construction company, he operated tractors in the heat of the summer from early morning to late afternoon, sitting on the ground with the laborers for breakfast and lunch."[74] This image was also attested to by a Palestinian who supervised the teenaged bin Laden's work in Mecca. Osama showed "interest in the smallest details," Walid al-Khatib told Steve Coll. "His technical ability [with construction machinery] was impressive. . . . He liked to solve technical problems for himself."[75] Al-Khatib added that bin Laden worked on complex problems involving engineering and demolition and studied the structural weaknesses of buildings targeted for destruction, a talent presumably useful in planning the 2001 attacks.[76] Later, when Osama was given his first supervisory jobs, he faced and successfully executed the task of managing a workforce that included many non-Saudis, including Egyptians, Palestinians, Kuwaitis, Jordanians, Bangladeshis, Yemenis, Pakistanis, and others.

Over time, bin Laden developed a reputation as a "workaholic" by juggling his studies and a position with his father's firm.[77] He also had married his cousin Najwa Ghanem—the daughter of his mother's brother—in 1974, and by 1978 the couple had two sons.[78] "Despite his position as a bin Laden son," Najwa has written, "Osama would do the most difficult and dangerous work alongside his men. He knew how to drive the biggest equipment, including huge machinery with giant shovels that scraped out mountain roads. He actually worked on paving roads, although he said that he most enjoyed digging safe tunnels through the hard rock of the mountains in the Saudi desert."[79] While hard work is a trait for which the bin Laden family is known, Osama took the family's ethos far beyond most of his relations. "That is the way the bin Ladens are," Khalid al-Batarfi has said. "They study and work all of them, all the people I know, but he [Osama] was different because he used to work with his own hands, go drive tractors and like his father eat with his workers, work from dawn to sundown, tirelessly in the field. . . . He was responsible for some project in Mecca for the bin Ladens and he used to go from dawn to sundown; he works hard, really hard. . . . [He tended to family and social activities in the evening] and at night he would be doing prayer. He would sleep and then wake up a few hours later and do more prayers. This is optional [for a Muslim].

It's just [Osama] following the example of the Prophet. And then he would sleep a couple of hours and then start his day."[80]

Even Osama's recreational activities had a hard, often dangerous edge to them. From his youngest days, he preferred volleyball, soccer, swimming, hunting, and other strenuous outdoor activities. His wife recalled that when they met he "always enjoyed long walks more than most," and his son Omar said that from his own experience no one "could keep pace with my father. He had physically trained himself from his youth. Although he was not a man of muscles, no one could hike with the relentless persistence of Osama bin Laden."[81] A boyhood friend also said that during summer vacations Osama greatly enjoyed mountain climbing in a range on the Syria-Turkey border, where, according to his sister, he could be found "climbing mountains too rugged for any human being."[82] He also spent as much time as possible at al-Bahra, the family's farm about fifteen miles from Jeddah. There he enjoyed hunting, growing crops, raising horses—one was named after the steed of a companion of the Prophet—and driving cars in the desert, to see how fast they could go.[83]

As he grew older, bin Laden's love for nature and the rural life also grew. Early in their marriage, for example, Najwa bin Laden has written, Osama told her Jeddah was "growing too fast, that the city was beginning to feel overcrowded," and Abdullah Azzam's son Hudhayfah recalled that in the early 1980s bin Laden "liked to be away from the hustle and bustle of cities.[84]As the family spent more time on the farm, Najwa said "my husband treasured nature more than anyone I have ever known. . . . He was highly interested in everything made by God, down to the smallest plant and the smallest animal put on our earth."[85] Later his son Omar would write, "My father loved the outdoors. He very carefully laid out an orchard [on the bin Laden farm], planting the area with hundreds of trees, including palms and other varieties. He also created a costly man-made oasis, cultivating reeds and other water plants. My father's eyes would sparkle with such happiness at the sight of a beautiful plant or flower, or pride at the spectacle of one of his prancing stallions."[86]

Bin Laden's belief in the superiority of rural over urban life would come to dominate his thinking. Part of this preference was survival-based; the mountains were easier to hide in than the city. But he also came to believe a Spartan rural life made society stronger, better able to resist threats; that it preserved man's martial spirit; and that it equipped him to renew decaying urban societies. This suggests that at some point in his schooling or reading bin Laden studied the writings of the aforementioned Ibn Khaldun, whose work theorized that societies that are rural, pastoral, and organized tribally have a stronger sense of solidarity than others, as well as a greater will to fight. On the latter point, Ibn Khaldun adhered to the Prophet's position that without a martial spirit Muslims would lose the ability to "help the truth become victorious." Urbanized societies encourage effeminacy, tyrannical government, and societal decline.[87]

So far as I have found, bin Laden never quoted Ibn Khaldun, but his thinking and lifestyle have left the impression that he followed the medieval historian's contention that the forces for renewing Islamic civilization would come from rural tribal societies. Bin Laden's admiration and respect for Shaykh Abdullah Azzam, for example, stemmed not only from Azzam's piety and scholarship but also from his decision to leave the urban milieu. "The Shaykh left the atmosphere that was familiar to Muslims," bin Laden explained, "the atmosphere of the mosque and the narrow confines of the city and launched a struggle to liberate the Islamic world [from South Asia's mountains]."[88] As for himself and al-Qaeda, bin Laden said, "the mountains are our natural place . . . [our only] choice is between Afghanistan and Yemen. Yemen's topography is mountainous, and its people are tribal, armed, and allow one to breathe the clear air unblemished by humiliation."[89]

Bin Laden was also at one with Ibn Khaldun on the necessity of inculcating a martial spirit in men. "Fighting is part of our religion and Shariah," bin Laden argued, "[and] getting military training is the duty of every Muslim. . . . The people should be given easy access to arms."[90] Bin Laden's extreme wariness of any form of luxury, even things that have long stopped being luxuries and become essentials, like air-conditioning, ice cubes, running water, and television, also followed Ibn Khaldun's teachings. Bin Laden's stridency on this issue, and the lifestyle he lived, which reflected it, have been described by those who knew him best.[91] He did not see luxuries as inherently evil, but rather as leading to physical weakness, material and monetary obsessions, and a refusal to sacrifice comfort and well-being to surmount the tests God inevitably puts before all Muslims.[92] For bin Laden, the American lifestyle could be expected to yield benefits for the mujahedin in Afghanistan. "The Western mentality in general and [the] American one in particular," bin Laden told the journalist Ahmad Zaydan, "was materialistic [and] accustomed to luxury and peace and not willing to make sacrifices in a country [Afghanistan] about which a Congressman or U.S. official would take hours to explain to the ordinary taxpayer, including its location on a map."[93] Bin Laden concluded it was better for him, his family, and al-Qaeda "to live under a tree here in these mountains" than risk being "immersed in luxury" such as that that once had made a companion of Muhammad—Ka'ab ibn Malik—decide not to accompany the Prophet on a military expedition against the city of Tabuk.[94]

Regarding Ibn Khaldun's possible influence, the scholar Malise Ruthven wrote that bin Laden and al-Qaeda might be seen as less "nihilistic" than was supposed. "Despite its modernist elements, the structure of al-Qaeda and its purposes broadly fit the historical pattern of cyclical revolt and renewal observed by Ibn Khaldun more than six hundred years ago."[95]

Allah, the Prophet, and the Companions

Perhaps the hardest aspect of Osama's youth to pin down with precision is the development of his religious beliefs. His father was a devout Muslim, of course, and raised his children accordingly; he appears to have been the fundamental source of Osama's fervor. Muhammad bin Laden, according to Steve Coll, was a man who "bequeathed to his children . . . a religious faith in a borderless world."[96] This surely rings true; after all, part of every Muslim's belief is that God plans for Islam to become over time the whole earth's faith, and Osama repeatedly emphasized that "borders mean nothing. . . . The entire earth belongs to God."[97] But Muhammad bin Laden's role in Osama's religious development did not merely lie in inculcating theological tenets—though it did that—but in convincing him that every Muslim's duty was to act on the words of God and His Prophet to defend his faith. And Muhammad bin Laden was as good an example of a Muslim who matched beliefs with actions as it would be possible to find. Not only was he the king's main contractor for building palaces for the royal family, he was central to the construction campaign to modernize Saudi Arabia's roadways, airports, port facilities, military bases, and other infrastructure. Osama would know his theology but, thanks to his father, also believe it insufficient unless acted upon.[98]

Osama received regular religious instruction throughout his youth—in school, at home, and in the mosque—as does every youngster in the Kingdom. Osama was raised by his parents to be a devout follower of the puritanical Wahhabi creed dominant in Saudi Arabia, although neither parent could be described as a particularly fierce Wahhabi. The key texts Osama studied were the hadith (also known as the sunnah), which are considered the second most important source of Islamic thought and law after the Koran. In his public pronouncements, in fact, bin Laden gave slightly more prominence to quotations from the hadith than to Koranic quotations. He clearly loved the Prophet Muhammad and the example he set. And in his words, demeanor, activities, and reasoning—which often amounted to asking "What did the Prophet do in a similar situation?"—Osama fully justified Steve Coll's conclusion that he was "particularly drawn to teachings that a righteous Muslims should imitate the dress and customs that pervaded in the Prophet's time."[99] All Muslims must act as the Prophet acted. "The hadith is taught to Muslims," he said, "but young Muslims need to be taught—along with learning—they need to be taught to act on that knowledge. . . . If you are taught [religious] learning but do not act on it, it is evidence against you. . . . The fruit of knowledge is that we should act in the way that Muhammad, may God bless him and grant him peace, made clear, so that we obtain the approval of God, Who is praised and exalted. As we read in the Sahih of al-Bukhari [one of two canonical hadith collections], when the Prophet was asked about actions, which is the best of them, he said, on him be blessings and peace, 'a man who goes out to risk his life and wealth [in jihad] in the way of God.'"[100]

Bin Laden began interacting with Islamist groups and scholars outside of school and home in the early 1970s.[101] One writer claims that by then "he preferred the company of the ulemas" to that of anyone else.[102] This is supported by his mother's memory of when her son started focusing on Islamic issues. "Osama became politically aware in his early teens," she said after 9/11. "He was frustrated about the situation in Palestine in particular, and the Arab and Muslim world in general. He thought Muslim youths were too busy having fun to care about what they should do to propagate Islam and bring back the old glories of the Muslim nation. He wanted Muslims to unite and fight to liberate Palestine. He had been a devoted Muslim all his life but he was a moderate one. He played football. Went to picnics, rode horses and socialized. He never caused me to worry about him in his teenage years."[103]

Khalid al-Batarfi also has cited Osama's early concerns with the broader Islamic world and especially his focus on Palestine. "Unless we, the new generation, change and become stronger and more educated and more dedicated," bin Laden told al-Batarfi, "we will never reclaim Palestine."[104] Najwa also has written that this continued after their marriage. "As my husband became older and more educated," she has written, "I noticed that a new and broader awareness of the outside world began to occupy his mind."[105]

Allia and Najwa bin Laden hit upon three preoccupations that stayed with bin Laden until his death. First, he was focused from his youth on inspiring young Muslims to join an effort to defend Islam from the Western powers and to take back from them the Muslim land they had occupied. Even before he became involved in the Afghan jihad, bin Laden—as his mother said—believed it was the responsibility of youth to "propagate Islam and bring back the old glories of the Muslim nation." Inciting jihad was, indeed, one of the major roles played by the Prophet Muhammad in the founding days of Islam. "The most important function of the doctrine of jihad," according to scholar Rudolph Peters, "is that it mobilizes and motivates Muslims to take part in wars against unbelievers."[106] The role of inciter in chief is one bin Laden began moving toward early in life.

Second, Osama's mother's reference to the "Muslim nation" suggests that at an early age he was quite conscious of and concerned about the larger world. He also had obviously made his own what Steve Coll has described as his father's faith in an eventually borderless Muslim world.

Third, bin Laden always argued that if Islam was to be defended there must be unity among Muslims. As will be seen below, bin Laden consistently avoided attacking those who betrayed, disappointed, or abandoned him (with the exception of Saudi Prince Turki al-Faisal). Likewise, he rarely faulted others because their beliefs differed from his; indeed, he consistently argued that Muslims must work together regardless of specific religious beliefs and practices. While regrettable and needing eventual remedy, such differences were natural, and must not be allowed to hamstring Muslims from uniting against a common enemy. When the U.S.-led invasion of Iraq was launched in 2003, for example, bin Laden declared that there was no harm in Islamists fighting alongside Iraqi socialists against the U.S.-led coalition. Al-Qaeda is a unique organization in the Muslim world due to its multiple nationalities, languages, religious practices, and ethnicities. Khalid al-Batarfi perceptively underscored his friend's tolerance for religious diversity, a fact that ought to be kept in mind by those arguing that bin Laden espoused takfirism—the least tolerant brand of Islam, as we will see. "He did not try to force his [religious] views on the rest of us, who were not as strict Muslims as he was," al-Batarfi told the journalist Jonathan Randall. "He had a very nice way of winning over young people who did not pray, often leading them by example to become good Muslims. He would encourage us to go to mosque, especially to *fajr*, or dawn prayer. . . . He sort of hoped you would follow his example and if you did, so much the better, but if not, you were still good friends. He had a very strong, quiet, confident, and effective charisma."[107]

Although he received substantial religious instruction during his school years, bin Laden did not become in any formal sense a trained religious scholar, and his discourse lacked the dogmatism often associated with the professional theologian. His knowledge of Islam was based on the Koran and the sunnah, as well as on his education, his family life, talks with scholars he met in his youth, his independent study of theology and Islamic history, and working and fighting alongside men who were trained scholars, most especially the Palestinian scholar Shaykh Abdullah Azzam. In an earlier book, *Through Our Enemies' Eyes*, I wrote with rather too much certainty that bin Laden was heavily influenced by Sayyed Qutb (who to my everlasting embarrassment I mistakenly identified as Muhammad Qutb, Sayyed's brother). In the decade since writing that book it has become clear that Sayyed Qutb—to whom common wisdom assigns the role of "father of modern Islamic fundamentalism"—did not have much, if any, impact on bin Laden's thought. Indeed, although it has been argued that Osama studied Sayyed Qutb and that it was "Qutb's ideas that provoked bin Laden to inflict them on the world," I have found no evidence that fully supports this assertion.[108] Khaled Abou El Fadl, a law professor, has noticed—alone among bin Laden analysts in the West—that bin Laden "rarely mentions Qutb."[109] I would go further and say that I have found not a single mention of Sayyed Qutb in any of bin Laden's writings or statements, and that I would agree with the Salafi scholar Husayn bin Mahmud, who has written "that ignorant people affiliate al-Qaeda with Shaykh Sayyed Qutb," and claim that al-Qaeda is an extension of the Egyptian al-Zawahiri's jihadist group. "These are incorrect assumptions," asserts bin Mahmud.[110]

In any event, many of the ideas attributed to Qutb are really of much older vintage. Qutb is most often cited as having been the first to call for a vanguard to incite and lead other Muslims to return to pure Islam. He also advocated and justified the use of violence against Muslim rulers who do not rule according to the Shariah. Neither idea is original with Qutb. The Prophet Muhammad and his companions, for example, clearly saw themselves as armed with God's revelation and so duty-bound to incite all the Arabian Peninsula's peoples to accept God's call and live by His design. "Our Prophet Muhammad, God's peace and prayers be upon him," bin Laden wrote in describing the Prophet's creation of this vanguard, "spent thirteen years preaching in Mecca and the result was a few hundred Muhajirin [immigrants], may God be pleased with them," and this group later established "the small Medina state . . . [and] good was established."[111] The duty to attack rulers who refuse to govern according to Islamic law was set down in the early fourteenth century by the Syrian Islamic jurist Ibn Taymiyyah. Often referred to as Shaykh al-Islam—an honorific understood as a designation for Islam's most important scholar—Ibn Taymiyyah was a key formulator of Salafism, a puritanical form of Islam centered on the Koran, the hadith, and the practices of the first three Muslim generations, known as the *salaf* or the "pious ancestors." Ibn Taymiyyah articulated the doctrine to deal with what he identified as the un-Islamic governance of the recently converted

Mongols, who mixed their own customs and laws with the Shariah. In Ibn Taymiyyah's view, Rudolph Peters has written, "this is sufficient cause to regard them as unbelievers, even if they pronounce the profession of faith."[112] The mixing of Islamic with pagan tenets, Ibn Taymiyyah argued, proved the "Mongols were apostates and therefore legitimate targets of jihad."[113] On both topics—a vanguard and fighting un-Islamic rulers—Qutb offered nothing that was not already long available in the Koran, sunnah, and Islamic jurisprudence—and Osama was thoroughly indoctrinated with all of these sources during his school years.

More important to assessing Qutb's influence on Osama accurately is asking why he did not accept all of Qutb's major ideas. The Egyptian Islamist argued that the world had reverted to the paganism of the period before the emergence of the Prophet Muhammad. And by "world" he meant the entire world. Anyone—Muslim and non-Muslim—who did not lead a pure life was in danger. Qutb was a leading proponent of takfirism, the belief that one Muslim can take it upon himself to decide whether or not another is a good Muslim, and, if not, kill him. Osama consistently rejected the takfiris' philosophy—although Muslim and Western critics alike consistently tried to hang that tag on him. Current U.S. Afghan policy is still based on the assumption that al-Qaeda is a takfiri organization. Yet Osama was himself the target of at least three assassination attempts by takfiris.

A close reading of bin Laden's work makes clear that he never embraced Qutb's Hobbes-like doctrine of a religious war of everyone against everyone else. Bin Laden did not even call for the deaths of the members of the Saudi royal family—the target of his most scathing rhetoric—but rather their delivery to the Islamist judiciary for trial once they were toppled from power. Indeed, bin Laden even held out an alternative to the idea of punishing the al-Sauds, saying that the path to peace in the Kingdom would be easy were the Saudi royals simply to repent and change their ways. "Correcting the mistakes [you have made] is not hard at all," bin Laden told them in December 2004, "if the ruler is willing and capable of doing what it takes to bring about the needed change. Furthermore, to make corrections, the ruler need not invent any solutions, but all he needs is going back to Allah's religion: Islam that is. As to us [al-Qaeda], Allah knows that we want nothing but changing course so that internal and external policies are crafted according to what Allah and His messenger mandated. . . . To make the story short, let me say that the only way to a safe and happy ending is to embark on the straight path of Allah and His messenger."[114]

Bin Laden also rejected outright Qutb's argument that it was no longer sufficient for Muslims to wage a defensive war against Western influences and corrupt Muslim regimes, but their duty was to wage an offensive war against all opponents until the entire world lived under the banner of "There is no God but God, and Muhammad is His messenger." Since first declaring war in August 1996, Osama left no doubt that he knew that God's plan was for a world that would eventually be entirely Islamic. Nonetheless, he also made it clear that he would have no truck with Qutb's call for an offensive jihad. In statement after statement, and interview after interview, over the past sixteen years, bin Laden called for a defensive jihad: to rid the Muslim world of the U.S. presence; destroy Israel; overthrow rulers who did not govern by Shariah law; and recover the lands taken from Muslims by conquest, including Palestine, Spain, southern Thailand, and Mindanao. Whether or not Western scholars and commentators define these goals as "offensive" war was irrelevant because they were fully covered by the theological guidelines of a defensive jihad. In waging defensive jihad, in other words, Osama was in keeping with the tenets of the Koran, the sunnah, and the mainstream of Islamic jurisprudence; this was the case especially after the 2003 U.S.-led invasion of Iraq.

Why did Qutb have such little impact on bin Laden's thinking? There are several answers to the question. First, Osama was the product of the Saudi educational system; indeed, notwithstanding denials by the al-Saud family, he was the poster boy for that system. Bin Laden was nursed on a pure diet of the Koran, the Prophet's sayings and deeds, and the teachings of a limited number of revered Islamic scholars and jurists. To the end of his life he carried the certainty that God's truth was to be found in these sources alone. Sayyed Qutb, moreover, was a follower of the teachings of the Sunni scholar Abu al-Hasan al-Ash'ari, who championed a nonliteralist approach to the Koran and who argued that the sunnah "differed radically" from the literalist Hanbali school of Sunni Islam that dominates Saudi religious thought and education.[115]

Overall, bin Laden probably would have agreed with the official Saudi position that Qutb was a takfiri who "was out of touch with reality and rejected even widely accepted interpretations of the Koran."[116]

Second, bin Laden almost certainly was wary of Qutb because the Egyptian was not an Islamic scholar. As noted above, he recommended the work of Muhmmad Qutb—a trained scholar—but never mentioned Muhammad's brother Sayyed Qutb. The more famous Qutb's university training was in literature. He was therefore a questionable figure for bin Laden. Untrained in Islam, an on-again, off-again ally of the infidel Gamal Abd-al-Nasser, disrespectful of Islamic scholars he did not agree with, and fundamentally wrong about advocating an offensive jihad—only a caliph can order an offensive jihad, and there has been no caliph since 1924—Qutb simply did not represent someone bin Laden would turn to for guidance or inspiration.[117] This became crystal clear when Osama returned to Saudi Arabia from Afghanistan in 1989 and became a member of what was, at that time, a peaceful reform movement in the Kingdom. Led by prominent Salafi scholars, the movement intended to reform, not dismantle, Saudi society, and bin Laden's writings—as will be seen—in support of the movement clearly show that he was far more comfortable with the movement than with a Qutb-style revolution.

The Emerging Osama

The twenty-two-year-old Osama who went to Afghanistan, while still immature—trusting others too easily and too quickly, for example—took with him a fully developed set of traits and skills. He was a young man of good manners, and was, according to his mother, "kind, respectful and good to all those around him."[118] He was also a man who sought to avoid confrontation and recrimination, and did not regard conflict as the first option for resolving a problem. Both in school and in his father's company, Osama sought to settle disputes between people peacefully. Khalid al-Batarfi relates a story of how he came to Osama's rescue when the latter was being roughed up by an opposing player in a soccer game. Instead of thanking al-Batarfi for pushing the offender away, Osama told him, "You know, if you gave me time, I would have solved the issue peacefully."[119] "He was a quiet and conscientious boy," Najwa writes. "He was a mystery to his cousins, yet we all liked him because he was very quiet and gentle in his manners."[120] Osama has always held his cards close to the vest, and would later demonstrate an almost preternatural ability to use the power of silence to avoid creating new enemies while also driving his existing foes—especially nonstop-talking Westerners—to distraction, as well as encouraging them to draw absurd conclusions.

By 1979, bin Laden was displaying a quality that would shape his career: the desire to be in charge. "He was a natural leader," Khalid al-Batarfi explained; "he leads by example and by hints more than direct orders. He just sets an example and then expects you to follow, and somehow you follow even if you are not 100 percent convinced."[121] This represented more than noblesse oblige; he did not consider leadership his due simply because he was a bin Laden. Indeed, he consistently proved that he was prepared to play the role of loyal subordinate until he felt he had acquired the skills needed to take command of a particular endeavor. His desire to lead, then, seems to have been born in a growing self-confidence that he could master any situation in which he found himself and then rightfully claim a leadership position. Until the first Iraq war (1990–1991), bin Laden's deference to credentialed religious scholars and jurists was nearly complete. However, after Saudi Arabia's grand mufti—Shaykh Abdul Aziz bin Baz—permitted Western/Christian troops into the Kingdom, that deference began to be reversed dramatically.

Osama was aware early of the Muslim world's pervasive sense of defeatism, not only about its chances of retaking Palestine but also regarding confrontation with the West generally. This is shown in his mother's reference to her son's dissatisfaction with Muslim youths, who seemed to him more interested in fun than in Palestine, and in his own eagerness to renew Islam's glory. His generation of Muslim youth has often been referred to as the "generation of defeat," one that witnessed Israel defeat Arab armies three times, and Hindu India defeat the Islamic Republic of Pakistan three times. The Egyptian journalist Isam Darraz—who covered Osama's fight against the Soviets—has written that after the 1967 Arab-Israeli war, bin Laden's generation was in a state of shock. "It wasn't a military defeat," Darraz told Peter Bergen. "It became a civilization defeat. We didn't know we were so backward, we were so retarded, so behind the rest of modern civilization."[122] Bin Laden and others recognized this failure because as "we grew up, American weapons were on our heads and the heads of our children and mothers."[123] Unlike Darraz, however, bin Laden did not think defeat came because Muslim society was "retarded" in terms of the Western definition of "progress"; rather, it had simply failed to live by God's law. He believed that victory depended on returning to the faith as it came from the Koran and the sunnah, as well as on Muslims learning to trust in God. As his life progressed, bin Laden would find that Islam's long road back to glory was made incalculably harder by the ingrained fatalism of Muslims, a defeatism that endured even after the Red Army was beaten in Afghanistan.

Finally, Osama's education was an egalitarian one, giving him exactly what he would need in the years ahead. As noted, many who have written about Osama have argued that because he did not have the benefit of a Western education he grew up unaware of the world's diversity. This is clearly partly true. The education he did receive, however, put him in direct contact with Muslims from across the Islamic world, including Muslim Brotherhood members exiled from Egypt and Syria; his mother's semi-secular Muslim family and their neighbors in Syria and Lebanon; prominent graduates of Egypt's al-Azhar University from Afghanistan, the Arab world, and Indonesia; and working-class Muslims with whom he labored in his father's construction projects. Based on these experiences, his friend Khalid al-Batarfi recalled that the young Osama "believed that all Muslims were equal, and he did not just hang around with rich kids. He had some very poor friends and in fact married poor women."[124] Given the career Osama chose, he could not have had a better education. And, in late 1979, he was about to matriculate in an intense postgraduate course of action: fighting the Soviets in Afghanistan.

3

APPRENTICESHIP, 1979–1989

Decades hence, even historians may begin to recognize the size and significance of the transformation in the Muslim world that began with the Afghan jihad's victory over the Soviet Union. In the West in recent years, many have used the Afghan war to blame the United States—and the CIA in particular—for "creating" bin Laden and the Islamist movement and therefore for the "blowback" they are generating. As a result, the war has been a tool for many in the academy to discredit Ronald Reagan's foreign policy (having failed to do so by praising Gorbachev as the true hero who ended the cold war, which did not wash with very many Americans) as—most pertinent to a study of bin Laden—having played no substantial part in the USSR's demise.

Those who have written about him often seem unable to comprehend how essential the Red Army's defeat in Afghanistan was to bin Laden, as well as to the Islamist movement and Muslims generally. That Afghans and non-Afghan Muslims have embellished their victory, arguing that the Red Army's defeat alone caused the Soviet Union's collapse, is true. That non-Afghan Muslim fighters—Shaykh Azzam's volunteers, al-Qaeda, and so forth—contributed little to the Soviets' defeat is also true. The investigative journalist Camille Tawil has written—correctly, in my view—that the contribution to the victory by non-Afghan Muslims equaled a "drop in the ocean compared to the Afghan mujahedin."[1] But the Red Army's defeat was—for all Muslims, save the most secular and Westernized—a military victory for Islam, the first in several hundred years, and it undermined the pervasive defeatism that had haunted the Muslim world for more than a century. The Afghans' victory did not eradicate this defeatism, which is to this day a major problem for all Islamist leaders. But it did give strong support to those arguing that Muslims could arm themselves and beat God's enemies. Moscow's withdrawal from Afghanistan—which was due overwhelmingly to Afghan, not non-Afghan, mujahedin—gave instant plausibility to the idea that non-Muslim interference in the Muslim world justified a defensive jihad, and that such a jihad could succeed. Bin Laden would build on the example of the Afghan jihad until the need to do so was rendered moot by the 2003 U.S.-led invasion of Iraq, which provided the irrefutable Koranic predicate for defensive jihad.

Arrival

Osama bin Laden dashed to Pakistan soon after the December 1979 Soviet invasion without a clear idea of what he wanted to accomplish, at least beyond using his money to "help" Afghan Muslims repel the Red Army. A question always asked about bin Laden's participation in the Afghan jihad involves when he arrived in Pakistan. Bin Laden said that he learned of the invasion while at prayer, and was in Pakistan before the end of 1979—that is, within five days of the Soviet invasion.[2] (His former sister-in-law says Osama "left quickly—there were no farewell parties.")[3] If true, he made pretty good time. The invasion occurred on December 26, and so to absorb its meaning, decide on a course of action, secure his family's blessing, get the approval of Saudi clerics and officials, and make the arrangements to go from the Kingdom to Karachi speaks to sheer determination. While bin Laden's exact arrival date in Pakistan is of little consequence, the claim by the journalist Ahmad Muwaffaq Zaydan—who had ample pre-9/11 access to al-Qaeda and its leaders—that Osama arrived "only two weeks after the invasion" probably is close to the mark.[4] Bin Laden first went to

Lahore and met with Qazi Hussain Ahmed, chief of Pakistan's Jamaat-e-Islami party, telling him that he intended "to support the mujahedin against the communist invasion."[5] There is no reason to doubt that he had easy access to such important leaders as Ahmed, as well as to the Afghans Gulbuddin Hekmatyar and Abdul Rasul Sayyaf, who would have been well aware of bin Laden's family's fortune and political influence from their attendance at the Hajj-related Islamic discussions hosted by Muhammad bin Laden and his successors. Not surprisingly, Osama's first role in the Afghan jihad was to collect and then distribute funds to the mujahedin from Saudi Arabia and the other Gulf countries.

Benefactor and Point Man

Bin Laden's energies in Pakistan between his arrival and late 1984 were focused upon getting to know the key Pakistani and Afghan players; finding his way around the cities of Peshawar and Islamabad; dispensing money and other forms of aid; and working in cooperation with Saudi Prince Turki, then chief of the Saudi intelligence service, the General Intelligence Directorate (GID). Steve Coll and Mary Anne Weaver's assessment that bin Laden spent much of 1980–1983 "as a commuter who did little more than carry cash and hold meetings" and became known as "the Good Samaritan or the Saudi Prince" seems justified, though incomplete.[6] His shuttling of funds between the Gulf and Pakistan contributed to the Afghans' ultimate success, and was also a useful exercise for him. That he moved easily among the Gulf's royal and business elite is not a surprise; he had grown up among them and studied and played with their sons. That he displayed empathy and generosity toward the wounded and toward refugee Afghans—visiting hospitals for wounded mujahedin and distributing cashews, chocolates, and checks for the families—squares with his father's precept to combine actions and beliefs.[7] His dealings with Pakistani clerics, businessmen, politicians, and generals, not to mention Afghan insurgent commanders, Pashtun tribal chiefs, and men of importance from other Muslim countries, however, required far more of him than had bossing multinational work gangs on construction sites in the Kingdom. It made him acutely aware of the diversity of the

Muslim world. Not all Muslims thought and behaved like Saudis. This awareness—and the tolerance it induced—would be key to bin Laden's success in the years ahead.

The role bin Laden played with the Saudis in this period is more difficult to assess. Prince Turki claims to have met bin Laden only a few times during the Afghan-war years and—true to the Saudi narrative—described him as a "nice guy" who was "shy, friendly, and almost gentle. He always spoke in a low voice; he was man of pithy statements."[8] In public statements after 9/11, Turki always made sure to emphasize that bin Laden "never enjoyed any official status [with the Saudi government]."[9]

Another and, I suspect, more accurate story reflecting bin Laden's role with Turki's GID is told by Ahmed Badeeb, Turki's chief of staff at GID and a former biology teacher at bin Laden's Jeddah school. Badeeb's description of the relationship clearly suggests there were many more Turki–bin Laden meetings than the "one or two" the prince recalls,[10] and that bin Laden also worked with the Saudi embassy in Islamabad and met with the Saudi interior minister Prince Nayef. Badeeb notes that Nayef "liked" Osama and "appreciated" his efforts to aid the Afghans.[11] Bin Laden also took directions from the GID, using his family's construction equipment to cut roads to ease arms delivery to the mujahedin, as well as to build hospitals and other facilities for NGOs in Pakistan.[12] "We [GID] were happy with him." Badeeb remembers, "He was our man. He was doing all that we asked of him." Bin Laden made a deep impression on Badeeb, who said, "I loved Osama and considered him a good citizen of Saudi Arabia."[13]

Badeeb is correct: at this point Osama was not yet alienated from his native country, its religious authorities, or its ruling family despite his unease with the al-Sauds' blatant corruption, their use of French military personnel to design and manage the recapture of the Grand Mosque in Mecca from Islamists in late 1979, and a ruling that permitted fighting in the mosque's sacred precincts.[14] Osama went to Afghanistan a loyal Saudi citizen, did not waver from that stand during the conflict, and apparently did not tolerate open disparagement of the al-Sauds. The Lebanese journalist Jamal Ismail, for example, said that in 1986, after King Fahd had accepted and worn a British decoration resembling a cross, bin Laden stopped his comrades from saying the medal symbolized Christianity and therefore that Fahd was not a Muslim. "For God's sake," Ismail quoted bin Laden as saying, "don't discuss this subject. Concentrate on your mission. I don't permit anyone to discuss this issue here."[15] This reaction offers, I think, some basis for accepting much of the pre-1990–1991 Saudi narrative: bin Laden as a poster boy for the Saudi religious education system. "Osama bin Laden and many of the Saudi youths who arrived in Afghanistan," wrote Abu Musab al-Suri in his book *The Global Islamic Resistance Call*, "were deeply influenced by the Saudi Sahwa [Islamist Awakening], or revivalist current. . . . Against this background, it was natural for bin Laden and his Saudi contingent to accept the Saudi regime, by and large, as legitimate rulers, and to possess a deep respect for Saudi official clerics."[16]

The Influence of Abdullah Azzam

Shaykh Abdullah Azzam (1941–1989) was born in Palestine, trained as a teacher, joined the Jordanian Muslim Brotherhood and fought the Israelis, earned a doctorate from Cairo's al-Azhar University, and, in 1980, moved his family to Saudi Arabia and joined the faculty of King Abdul Aziz University in Jeddah. In 1981, Azzam took a post at the International Islamic University in Islamabad and taught there until resigning in the summer of 1986 to devote himself full time to serving the Afghan jihad. Azzam was the foremost Islamist scholar to champion the Afghans' war against the Red Army, and produced a body of writings that gave theological grounding to the contemporary international jihadist movement.[17] And, as one analyst has written, Azzam was one of the few Islamist scholars who "put his principles into action."[18]

Shaykh Azzam would be one of six men who had the greatest impact on bin Laden's life, the others being the Prophet Muhammad, Ibn Taymiyyah, Saladin, Muhammad bin Laden, and the Taleban chief Mullah Omar. Their influence had a common cause: each matched faith with deeds. "Hardly any key Islamic figures responded to fulfill this obligation [to join the mujahedin]," bin Laden wrote, adding that the "only notable personality from among the scholars of the ummah, who bothered to make a move, was Shaykh Abdullah Azzam, may Allah accept him and his two sons from among the martyrs."[19] Bin

Laden later would be acerbically critical of the failure of Saudi scholars to share the risks the young men they encouraged to go to the Afghan fighting front were facing. He said the scholars were frightened and maintained that "the Russians cannot be resisted."[20] "Almost twenty years ago," bin Laden wrote in 2006, "I used to visit our scholars and shaykhs [in Saudi Arabia], asking them to go out and take part in the jihad, when the jihad first began against the Russians [in Afghanistan]. Many of them came out with many excuses. . . . I still remember what some of them said. They said: 'Usama, go forth all of you with God's blessing. What you believe is the truth and the way, but we are not accustomed or used to it and we are afraid of it.' People are the enemy of what they do not know. They [the scholars] were not accustomed to [going to jihad] because, as I have said, this is a religious duty over which many decades have passed without those responsible for it [i.e., the scholars] going among the people."[21]

Bin Laden may have met Shaykh Azzam before the Afghan war and while attending King Abdul Aziz University, but there is no conclusive proof of such a meeting.[22] Indeed, Azzam's son Hutaifa has claimed that Osama and his father first met in Jeddah during the Hajj season of 1984 and became fast friends.[23] Their relationship was close, but it would be a stretch to describe it as a father-son relationship. A master-apprentice relationship is more apt. That bin Laden respected and initially deferred to Azzam is unquestionable, but he never was Azzam's lackey. Throughout his life, bin Laden was willing—for a time—to play a subordinate role to those with more experience with or knowledge of specific fields, whether construction work, military activity, or organization building. But such subordination was never an admission of inferiority; rather it was his way of preparing to take a leadership role. And he was never involved in an activity that he did not aspire to lead. "Usama is the kind of man who can influence others, not be influenced by others," Shaykh Musa al-Qarni, bin Laden's former anti-Soviet colleague, said in 2006. "Before he went to Afghanistan to carry out jihad, many people advised him not to go, to remain in his country, and confine his role to financial support, that is, to collect donations and send them to the mujahedin. They believed that this was a more important task than going there himself. He did not find this a satisfactory state of affairs. He wanted to be a leader not a follower. . . . He does not have a hesitant or timid character. Usama is a man who loves death, seeks it, and would like to be martyred."[24]

Creating the Mahktab al-Khadamat

Later in 1984, Azzam, bin Laden, and Azzam's son-in-law, the Algerian mujahid Boudjema Bounoua (aka Abdullah Anas), formed an organization called the Makhtab al-Khadamat (MK), or the "Services Bureau." Azzam was recognized as its chief, but bin Laden financed MK's operating costs, which were about $300,000 per year.[25] He also agreed to provide Azzam with funds to settle and maintain in Peshawar the families of fifty or sixty Arabs who would be involved in MK's activities.[26] Its leaders established several committees—military training, logistics, transportation, and so forth—to manage its affairs, but even with them, several writers have argued, organizationally the MK ranged from messy to chaotic. The Egyptian journalist Isam Darraz has said that bin Laden eventually established permanent residence in Peshawar to try and improve the MK's operations, as well as to be nearer the fighting in Afghanistan.[27]

The MK was an all-purpose, NGO-type organization. It initially operated in Afghanistan and Pakistan and then expanded its activities throughout the Muslim world and into Europe and the United States. Its offices outside South Asia appear to have been mainly intended for acquiring and then funneling funds, and channeling recruits to the Afghan warfronts. The MK's Pakistani offices would welcome Muslim volunteers and then shelter, feed, and clothe them until they were given a task. Some volunteers were assigned combat roles and sent to various Afghan field commanders for training and eventual deployment; joining the forces led by Gulbuddin Hekmatyar and Abdul Rasul Sayyaf was most common. Others would be designated to support the MK's manifold humanitarian activities, such as staffing clinics for wounded mujahedin, building shelters in refugee camps, caring for refugees, and establishing schools for the refugee children. The MK's activities allowed its founders to get a better handle on how many non-Afghan Muslims were coming to Pakistan, and to track their whereabouts and conditions. Azzam, bin Laden, and Anas also intended the MK to protect non-Afghan Muslims "from the political games of the Afghans."[28]

Azzam and bin Laden also used MK assets to produce and distribute propaganda for the Afghan jihad across the Islamic world, as well as to keep the Afghans' cause in the forefront of Muslim consciousness. Azzam himself was a major MK propaganda asset, and he spent a good deal of time informing audiences about the Afghan struggle against Soviet barbarity, appealing for donations, and recruiting young men to join the jihad. Azzam also used the talks to spread his theological position that it was an individual's religious duty to participate in the Afghans' defensive jihad. He traveled everywhere, including the United States, where between late 1984 and 1989 he established fifty-two MK offices.[29] Azzam, bin Laden later told his sons, "was the best coordinator, organizing rallies and meetings all over the world, gathering charity, recruiting Muslims to go to Afghanistan to fight the Russians." He also told his sons that Azzam was the embodiment of words matching deeds. "After recruiting [trips] Abdullah would travel to the war zone and fight on the frontlines himself."[30]

Bin Laden also engaged in such proselytizing, but his efforts seem to have been limited to Pakistan and the Gulf countries, where he raised funds and talked to small groups. He also played a major role in helping to fund and produce Azzam's popular monthly magazine, *Al-Jihad*, which first appeared in the fall of 1984 and was the successor to an earlier magazine called *Al-Mujahid*. The MK would eventually print seventy thousand copies per month.[31] This probably was the time bin Laden began to think seriously about the potential power of modern media to promote the mujahedin's cause. His familiarity with Islamic history gave him a keen awareness of propaganda's critical role in furthering the jihad's goal.

For years bin Laden received a good deal of criticism, from both friends and enemies, about his love of the media and for his apparent zeal for the limelight. This criticism betrayed ignorance of Islamic history and tradition. Even before Islam's inception, for example, poetry had been a prized propaganda vehicle, because it is the most respected art form in the Arab world. The power of poetry grew after the founding of Islam because it was then based on a common and shared culture-wide resource—the Koran and sunnah—and so resonated with and motivates both religious and nonreligious Arabs.[32] As avid students of Islamic history, Azzam and bin Laden viewed the media through the eyes of the Prophet Muhammad and Saladin. "Muhammad understood the role of propaganda in the struggle for hearts and minds of the uncommitted," Richard Gabriel has written, "and went to great lengths to make his message public and widely known. In an Arab society that was largely illiterate, the poet served as the chief conveyor of political propaganda. Muhammad hired the best poets that money could buy to sing his praises and denigrate his opponents. He publicly issued proclamations regarding the revelations he received as the Messenger of God, and remained always in public view to keep the vision of the new [Islamic] order and promise of heavenly paradise constantly before his followers and those he hoped to convert. He sent 'missionaries' to other clans and tribes to instruct the pagans in the new faith, sometimes teaching the pagans to read and write in the process."[33]

During the era of the Crusades, Nur al-Din and his successor Saladin built on the Prophet's example, and developed well-oiled information machines. In conducting his campaigns, Amin Maalouf has written, Nur al-Din "understood the invaluable role of psychological mobilization." Al-Din recruited scholars and religious leaders to win hearts and minds, and to force Arab leaders to join his cause. "Nur al-Din supervised his corps of propagandists personally," notes Maalouf. "He would commission poems, letters, books, and always took care that they were released at the time when they would produce the desired effect."[34]

Saladin continued the jihad against the Crusaders both militarily and through propaganda.[35] On October 2, 1187, the day Saladin captured Jerusalem, for example, notes Professor Geoffrey Hindley, "the scribes and clerks of the sultan's chancellery had worked into the small hours writing dispatches to every part of the Muslim world."[36]

Finally, Azzam and bin Laden also faced a propaganda hurdle not faced by the Prophet, Nur al-Din, or Saladin. Were they to succeed in the effort to "instigate the [Islamic] nation to liberate its land and carry out jihad for the Almighty God,"[37] they would have to battle and overcome government-controlled media in the Muslim countries opposed to the mujahedin. From Riyadh to Cairo to Algiers, state-run media, censorship offices, and, increasingly, scholars beholden to the regimes shaped only the message the rulers wanted heard. "These media," bin Laden said, "strive to beatify the persons of the leaders, to drowse [lull?] the community, and to fulfill the plans of the enemies of [Islam]."[38] In addition, bin Laden considered the Western media even more powerful. "The United States has monopolized the media and succeeded by its huge media power to maintain a double standard when it is suitable for it."[39] Thus, Azzam and bin Laden knew their message to the Muslim masses would never be heard unless they devised the means to spread it. The Internet—which came after Azzam, who was killed by a bomb late in November 1989—helped bin Laden and other Islamist leaders to circumvent regime censorship, but many regimes—especially in Cairo and Riyadh—developed means to reduce access, and prosecute those who post antiregime content.

The massive domestic security and bureaucratic disruptions caused in several Arab states by the the Arab Spring surely have enabled the Islamists to use the Internet with less concern about interdiction by the now-neutered regimes' counter-Internet capabilities.

Bin Laden most despised noted Islamic scholars who preached sermons that praised tyrannical Arab rulers, argued that jihad was not justified, and denigrated the mujahedin. Such scholars had always been present, but earlier in Islamic history the harm done by the "imperfection" of their message had been limited by the difficulty of communicating it to the masses. "Today, however," bin Laden explained, "the imperfection touches the entire public because of the communications revolution and because the media enter every house. . . . None will be spared."[40] Bin Laden made it clear, in fact, that the priority he put on media operations came in large measure from his own late recognition of the degree to which the Saudi regime had controlled the media. In a mid-1990s letter he wrote from Sudan to an Islamist scholar in the Kingdom, bin Laden admitted that he had not fully understood the degree of the Saudi regime's distortions until he moved abroad. He had not openly attacked the al-Sauds while living in Jeddah because he had not realized the extent of their "deception." While the Saudis seemed to be administering some of the Shariah laws, maintaining the holy sites, and spreading the D'awa—the call to Islam—the regime had "largely succeeded in deceiving and misleading the nation as to its secular reality. . . . His [the king's] deception over the nation became stronger as he began utilizing governmental media sources and scholarly agencies, which spared no effort in establishing in the minds of the people the picture of the Saudi rulers as leaders of the Muslims and defenders of the religion. In the shadow of this confusion, we didn't have a chance of knowing the real regime. Whoever lived in al-Jazeera [the Arab Peninsula] under the influence of this reality knows the truthfulness of what we say."[41]

Bin Laden played an essential role in the MK—especially financially—and the lessons he took from the experience involved the importance of effective management and control of media operations. The MK's humanitarian activities—clinics, refugee care, education, and so forth—were not ones he would later bring into al-Qaeda. He did not oppose such activities, of course, and maintained an enviable reputation for personal generosity and compassion in Saudi Arabia, Sudan, and Afghanistan, but they were secondary to the cause.

There are two main reasons. First, he and his co-founding colleagues designed al-Qaeda to be an insurgent organization, so that it would focus on military activities. Their goal was to keep the organization compact and secretive. Humanitarian activities are manpower-intensive, expensive, and very public; they would contribute little in the near term to the jihad's military capacity. Second, other entities already performing humanitarian work were better at it than al-Qaeda, which would benefit from that work without having to devote resources to it. Saudi Arabia, Kuwait, and the United Arab Emirates were all involved—via official charities and nonofficial NGOs—in providing humanitarian relief. Central to their operations was and is education, and all taught a Wahhabi or Salafi form of Sunni Islam in programs operating from Baltimore to Bosnia to Bangladesh. The Islamist NGOs' approach was identical to the Jesuits': "Give us your young for schooling and they will be God's forever." Although these nations and bin Laden would grow estranged and eventually violently opposed, they were then—and remain to this day—aligned in their belief that charity should inculcate the belief that jihad represents the sixth pillar of Islam. As Michael Vlahos has written, the Islamic NGOs, especially those backed by the Saudi regime, "have seeded the world with new local [Islamist] movements . . . and helped radicalize others."[42]

Life after Azzam

Bin Laden began moving away from Azzam in 1986—although his funding for the MK continued through 1988. At issue were what role the Tajik commander Ahmed Shah Massoud should play in the jihad and how Arab and other non-Afghan volunteers should be handled.[43] Azzam was a great champion of Massoud, believing he was the best commander in Afghanistan and "the hero of Islam . . . [and] the hope of the whole [Islamic] nation."[44] Bin Laden at the time felt no personal animosity toward Massoud—his friend and al-Qaeda's future military commander, Abu Ubaydah, had fought with him—but bin Laden's closest Afghan colleagues were Pashtun leaders such as Khalis, Sayyaf, Haqqani, Hekmatyar, and others. He did not concur with Azzam's position that a greater percentage of incoming Arab aid should go to Massoud.

Second, and as noted, Shaykh Azzam preferred to parcel out the non-Afghan volunteers designated for combat to the Islamist Afghan groups, primarily those commanded by Hekmatyar, Sayyaf, and Khalis. Shaykh al-Qarni recalled that "ninety-five percent of the Arabs who joined the jihad divided themselves between Hekmatyar and Sayyaf. A small percentage joined Yunis Khalis and [his senior commander] Jalaluddin Haqqani."[45] Bin Laden, however, saw this as a missed opportunity. He formulated a plan that would keep the Arab volunteers together in a group to train and fight, a process he believed would prepare these fighters to join Islamic resistance movements in other areas of the world after the Afghan jihad ended. He took this idea to Azzam but could not convince him of its value. The two men remained friends but, according to Abdullah Anas, each started to go his own way.[46] Anas also said that bin Laden's separation from Azzam was gradual, and not done in "a rude way, or unacceptable way. Both men agreed to keep their differences private." Bin Laden continued to consider Azzam "a great Imam of the Imams of Islam" and "a Mujahid champion."[47] Indeed, bin Laden had said publicly that before Arab-only units were ready to fight and were still training in 1986–1987 in the mountains of Afghanistan's Paktia Province, Azzam was "sending the young men to us."[48] Despite constant rumors, no evidence proves that bin Laden was in any way involved in the 1989 assassination of Azzam and his two sons.[49]

Combat Engineer

When bin Laden decided to become active inside Afghanistan, he began, naturally enough, with construction work. He would later say that after he had witnessed the "brutality" of the Soviets' bombing, he decided to transport heavy equipment from Saudi Arabia, including bulldozers, loaders, dump trucks, and trench diggers. In 1997, bin Laden told CNN's Peter Arnett that "by the grace of God we dug a good number of huge tunnels and built in them some storage places and in some others we built a hospital. We also dug some roads, by the grace of God, and glory be to Him, one of which you came by to us tonight."[50] The impact of bin Laden's efforts was noted by Hashim al-Makki, a mujahedin who later became a strong critic of the al-Qaeda chief. "Perhaps everyone [now] realizes," he wrote in 1994, "what it means to neutralize a sophisticated air force by a cheap and primitive weapon like digging some caves in the mountains, and what it means to control heights and important passages with a number of good trenches. The weaker side militarily is always in need of digging. The Chinese wise man Sun Tzu said 2,000 years ago: 'If you are weak, dig deeper in the ground and when you become strong attack from above like an eagle.'"[51]

Bin Laden described the difficulty of using construction equipment under Soviet fire, but refused to let it stop the work.[52] This made an impression. The journalist John Miller wrote that when he was in Afghanistan to interview bin Laden in May 1998 he found that "grizzled mujahedin fighters still tell of the young man [Osama] who rode the bulldozers himself, digging trenches on the frontline."[53]

Bin Laden also again showed his willingness to act under men with better skills then his. While he arranged and paid for transferring equipment from the Kingdom to Pakistan, he borrowed an expert engineer named Abdullah Saadi from his father's company to plan and direct the jobs.[54] Bin Laden and his engineers helped build Islamic Union for the Liberation of Afghanistan (IULA) leader Sayyaf's major training and educational facility—called "Sada"—in the Parichinar area; caves, trenches, tunnels, and artillery positions in Khowst for Jalaluddin Haqqani's forces; and at least four other mujahedin camps in eastern Afghanistan.[55] Ahmed Badeeb also suggested that bin Laden's builders worked under contract for the Saudi intelligence service to construct health facilities for Islamic NGOs in Peshawar, and to level roads in eastern Afghanistan to allow truck deliveries of ordnance to the mujahedin.[56] Through these projects, bin Laden became a familiar face to the Pashtun tribes on both sides of the Pakistan-Afghanistan border, which would later aid his 2001 escape from Pakistan, and help with his recruiting them to join him and the Taleban in fighting the U.S.-NATO occupation of Afghanistan.

Foot Soldier, Then Leader

Bin Laden's decision to train an Arab-only unit reflected not just his aspiration to prepare well-trained fighters for future struggles, but a level of naiveté and cultural obtuseness. Bin Laden had come to oppose the distribution of Arab volunteers to Afghan commanders in part because he claimed the latter treated the volunteers as guests and kept them from going into battle with their mujahedin. As a result, Arab volunteers were not getting the combat experience they would need in the future. The reality is that Afghan field commanders were not eager to have Arabs in their units because they were undisciplined, unwilling to take commands from Afghans they thought religiously inferior, and, more than anything, were seeking martyrdom at the earliest possible opportunity. They were, in effect, "racing to die." Thus, the Arabs were a disruptive element in Afghan units, and endangered both the safety of their comrades and the success of operations. "They were not organized," Commander Saznur of the IULA said, "and only wanted to become martyrs."[57] While Afghans certainly are willing to die for God's cause if necessary, they much prefer to die in bed as very old men. During the anti-Soviet jihad, suicide attacks by Afghans were unknown, a situation that has changed dramatically.

Before he could start an Arab-only unit, bin Laden needed a place inside Afghanistan to use as a base for training, for caching ordnance and other supplies, and for launching operations. He turned to Abdul Rasul Sayyaf, chief of the IULA and the Afghan leader closest to the Saudi regime and its intelligence service. Isam Darraz has written that bin Laden approached Sayyaf at some point in 1984 and requested his permission to set up an Arab-only camp in the IULA's area of operations in the mountains near Jaji in Paktia Province.[58] Sayyaf concurred, but for reasons not fully understood, bin Laden's engineers did not begin building the camp—called "Al-Masadah al-Ansar" (Lion's Den of the Companions) after a verse written by a companion of the Prophet—until late in the last quarter of 1985.[59] Bin Laden displayed something of his taste for risk-taking by picking a mountaintop site for the camp. The camp was ideally situated to observe Soviet and Afghan communist military movements on the plain below, but for that reason would be a magnet for Soviet artillery and airpower once the Arabs' presence there was discovered.[60]

Bin Laden brought construction equipment to Jaji, and he and his men cut a road up to the campsite—to make it accessible during the winter—and then another from the base of the mountain toward Jalalabad.[61] They next dug trenches, caves, tunnels, and fighting and anti-aircraft positions; they also built living quarters and storage facilities. The first tent was pitched at the Lion's Den on October 24, 1986, by bin Laden and eleven others—including two Egyptians with significant military or paramilitary experience, Abu Ubaydah al-Panshiri and Abu Hafs al-Masri—and by mid-April 1987, the camp featured seven or eight buildings and was manned by about seventy fighters.[62] As construction proceeded, volunteers were detached for military training under Abu Ubaydah and Abu Hafs, or sent across the Pakistani border to Sayyaf's military camp at Sada. The men also received religious training because, as one veteran of the Lion's Den said, the goal was to produce "a coordinated and principled [military] group."[63]

The process of building and training proved a difficult task for bin Laden and his lieutenants, due in part to the personnel they worked with. Although often well educated, the Arab volunteers presented the same problem to bin Laden and those working with him as they did to the Afghan commanders: they were eager to die and stubbornly averse to anything that would delay reaching that goal. For bin Laden this was the toughest management challenge he had yet encountered, far harder than supervising construction gangs working for his father's company. By all accounts, he handled this problem well, persuading the volunteers that they first needed to construct a campsite and complete fortifications before attacking the enemy. As Isam Darraz, an Egyptian journalist, notes in "Impressions of an Arab Journalist in Afghanistan," bin Laden "preached patience to his brothers and trained them to be patient because there were no battles."[64]

Besides channeling this religious zeal, bin Laden, Abu Ubaydah, and Abu Hafs also had to learn how to manage young men of various nationalities and ethnic groups. While Saudis and Yemenis dominated the group, there also were North Africans, Kurds, Egyptians, and

Sudanese. The men also differed in educational levels—some had attended college, others high school, and some were semi-literate—and work experience. The volunteers included businessmen, soldiers, policemen, laborers, and dilettante sons of the wealthy. Their degree of commitment and dedication to jihad also varied. There were those who joined for the duration—and are with al-Qaeda or other Islamist groups today—those who came on a lark, and those who wanted to go home as soon as winter started. On top of such variables, each volunteer reacted in a different way to living in a foreign country, many for the first time. Unable to speak the local language, they were working and fighting without almost any creature comforts and in arduous terrain. Many were exerting more physical effort on a daily basis than they ever had before. Bin Laden and his lieutenants were constantly engaged in negotiating with or mollifying local Afghan commanders, some of whom who did not like Arabs, seeing them as reckless would-be martyrs with whom they could not communicate. Bin Laden is reported to have said he always considered these days as the "happiest days of our lives," but added, perhaps a bit ruefully, that "when one is with his brothers, one becomes more patient."[65]

Bin Laden's Arab-only unit staged its first operation on August 17, 1987, under the command of Abu Ubaydah al-Panshiri, and under the observation of Abdullah Azzam; his assistant, Shaykh Tamim al-Adnani; and Sayyaf, the leader of IULA. The operation was unsuccessful because the Arabs had failed to do sufficient reconnaissance and planning. They encountered the enemy in unexpected positions on the battlefield and consumed their ammunition at a far faster pace than anticipated.[66] The mujahedin left to guard the camp and cover the unit's rear were hit heavily by Soviet planes and artillery.[67]

Interestingly, when the Arab-only unit was at last ready to fight, bin Laden did not put himself in command of it. He deferred to Abu Ubaydah and Abu Hafs. Since childhood, Khalid al-Batarfi has said, Osama had been "a good soldier; send him anywhere and he will follow orders," and Isam Darraz—an eyewitness—said that at Jaji bin Laden "fought in this battle like a private."[68] Steve Coll has said that bin Laden acquitted himself "honorably" in the Jaji engagements.[69] The recollections of bin Laden's associates bore this judgment out. "I saw Osama in the midst of severe fighting," Shaykh Musa al-Qarni said in

2006, by which point he had become one of the Saudis' anti-Osama spokesmen. "He was not the type of man to flee and withdraw. There were battles when Osama was left alone with only two or three mujahedin. They used to stand and fight to cover the entire mujahedin force's withdrawal. He would withdraw only when this was accomplished."[70] Darraz concluded that at the end of the battle, bin Laden had grown significantly in stature. "It was clear now that he'd be the leader. I was near him in the battle, many months, and he was really brave. That's why he got respect from Afghans and Arabs."[71]

The August 17 engagement started off about three weeks of intense fighting around Jaji. The Arabs did not defeat the Soviets, but they held their own until the enemy withdrew. Overall, bin Laden and his men benefited from the battle not only in terms of morale but also with gains in experience. Bin Laden later said Muslims would come to see the Jaji engagement, while small in scale, as an important battle in Islamic history, because a superpower had confronted a lightly armed force that stood its ground. Bin Laden said Allah had protected and guided the mujahedin in a battle that "pitted Muslims against the leading idol-power of the time."[72] Allah's grace had facilitated Muhammad's military victories over stronger enemies at Badr and the Trench, and now it had returned.

After the Jaji fight, information about bin Laden's unit grows sparse, to say the least. The unit must have engaged in other fighting in the two years that followed, but reports citing dozens or hundreds of engagements are surely exaggerations. The last documented fighting of bin Laden's unit occurred around Jalalabad in the spring of 1989, a few weeks after completion of the Soviet withdrawal. This engagement has been much discussed in the Afghan jihad literature, most of which focuses on whether or not the Pakistani military pushed the mujahedin into a semi-conventional battle before they were adequately prepared. A thorough analysis of the fight is beyond the scope of this book, so I will focus instead on the performance of bin Laden and his men, and assess the lessons bin Laden and lieutenants took from their combat experiences.[73]

The Afghan mujahedin and their Arab allies—most of whom had at best a rudimentary grasp of conventional military operations and tactics—began their Pakistan-backed assault on Jalalabad in early

March 1989. Savage fighting raged around the city for three months. When the mujahedin's initial attacks failed, the Afghan communist ground forces—alone for the first time since the Soviet withdrawal—attacked from the positions to which they had fallen back, but the insurgents held their ground. They then went back on the offensive. This proved a fatal mistake. From the city's strong defensive positions, the Afghan army employed their conventional firepower with devastating effect on insurgent forces advancing across flat and open terrain.[74]

When the battle began, Bin Laden had just returned to Peshawar from Saudi Arabia. He quickly went to the battlefield. Initially, he focused upon logistical support for the Arab force, purchasing with his own money thirty truckloads of arms and ammunition in Pakistan and arranging for them to be convoyed by truck to the front. He also established a makeshift hospital near Jalalabad, and bought cars and small pick-up trucks, which he sent to the mujahedin to give them increased mobility on the battlefield. One insurgent later recalled the great value of the vehicles, concluding that "Toyota is good for jihad."[75] Bin Laden thereafter joined the fighting, at one point leading his men onto the tarmac of Jalalabad airport before being driven back.[76]

Bin Laden was wounded at Jalalabad, and the physical bravery and leadership skill he displayed there, and earlier at Jaji, earned him the respect and affection of many Afghan commanders in Nangarhar Province. His actions also became well known in Saudi Arabia where, according to his friend Wael Julaidan, "everyone started to know about Osama."[77]

The Afghans were badly beaten at Jalalabad, due in almost equal parts to the artillery and airpower of the Jalalabad garrison and the failure of mujahedin commanders to coordinate with each other. Both Afghan Arabs and Afghans incurred heavy casualties in the drawn-out, back-and-forth struggle. Bin Laden took note of the Afghan insurgent groups' lack of cooperation—indeed, he strove to overcome it while the battle was in progress. He later claimed that over 170 Afghan Arabs were killed in the Jalalabad fighting, and that this number exceeded all Arab fatalities in the war until then.[78] By admitting this, he was also admitting that fewer than 500 Afghan Arabs were killed in the thirteen years of the jihad, a minuscule total compared to the several hundred thousand Afghan mujahedin killed in the same period. He was conceding that the war had been won by "poor, barefooted Afghans."[79]

Bin Laden's frankness about the comparatively small role played by Arabs in the Afghans' jihad did not change 1989, when he appeared in a video prodding young Muslims to act, noting that "the number of volunteers who joined jihad is still small considering the size of the Islamic world."[80] By not inflating the numbers, or using the rhetoric of an "Arab victory" in Afghanistan, he revealed a realistic assessment of the war. Nonetheless, the Afghans' victory was further proof that faithful Muslims could prevail even against a superpower, despite the latter's far superior military forces. From 1989 onward, bin Laden no longer wasted any time worrying *whether* the infidels could be beaten; he moved on to devising *how* they would be beaten. And *how* Muslims could win emerged from a combination of the lessons bin Laden and his lieutenants learned during the Afghan jihad.

Faith

As noted, bin Laden came out of Afghanistan convinced that God's promised victory over Islam's enemies was certain if Muslims persevered. "Do not be pessimistic, brothers," bin Laden told his impatient, often discouraged, men. "It is a sin to be pessimistic."[81] In Afghanistan, he said, it was "God alone who protected us from the Russians. . . . Reliance upon God is the main source of our strength and these trenches and tunnels are merely the military facilities God asked us to make."[82] No combatant force wins every battle and mujahedin losses were simply God testing their resolve. "Whatever God has ordained," he explained in 1999, "He has always in the past given us the ability to be patient and accept whatever he has ordained for us. A true Muslim should thank God in prosperity and be patient in adversity."[83]

Training

That many of the casualties Afghan and Arab fighters suffered in Afghanistan resulted from their impatience with training became a fixed belief for bin Laden. After the losses at Jaji and Jalalabad, bin

Laden decided operations should be launched only after training had been completed; eagerness for martyrdom would henceforth be subordinated to a professionalism inculcated at the military training camps.[84] That he achieved this goal is evident in al-Qaeda's operations after 1998, both in terms of terror attacks and insurgency combat.[85] "[You must] excel in your actions," bin Laden told the Afghan and Iraqi mujahedin in 2007, "for among the things that sadden Muslims and delight the unbelievers is the hindering of some combat operations against the enemy because of negligence in any of the stages of preparation for the operation, whether it be reconnaissance of the target, training, integrity and suitability of weapons, ammunition, quality of the explosive device or other such arrangements. And when you lay a mine, do it right, and don't leave so much as one wounded American soldier or spy."[86]

Experience

Bin Laden learned in Afghanistan that no one wins every battle. "One day we win and one day we lose."[87] Mistakes were God's means of teaching them. After the Jalalabad battle, Isam Darraz recalls bin Laden "stood between the youth and lectured them saying 'it is possible that the enemy's success in attacking the mujahedin is due to our mistakes, we must learn from our mistakes.'" And despite defeat, "The brethren's experience in using rockets, mortars, and artillery has been broadened."[88] In later years, bin Laden's bodyguard Abu Jandal, himself a senior al-Qaeda trainer, would explain how bin Laden insisted that al-Qaeda training camps be as rigorous as possible. In the case of al-Qaeda's al-Faruq Camp in Afghanistan, Abu Jandal said, "it was established on the basis of a clear military methodology, a military college where cadets passed through a number of stages and levels until they finally graduated at the command level, as military commanders capable of leading any jihadist action anywhere. The idea of establishing that military college was a global issue. Thus, if the jihad in Afghanistan ends, graduates of the college can go anywhere in the world and capably command battles there. Those objectives have been actually achieved by the young men who have moved to many fronts outside Afghanistan, in Bosnia-Herzegovina, Chechnya, the

Philippines, Eritrea, Somalia, Burma, and elsewhere. The fronts do not arise from a vacuum, but were the outcome of the action of well-trained cadres who had received methodical military training."[89]

Security

After Afghanistan, security considerations dominated bin Laden's planning. He often invoked the Prophet's admonition to "seek help in fulfilling needs by keeping them secret," and saw attempts to infiltrate the mujahedin by Arab governments—especially the Saudis—as the most dangerous threat. While advising that "you must protect your secrets," bin Laden also warned his men that they must "beware of . . . the hypocrites who infiltrate your ranks to stir up strife in the mujahid ranks."[90] The inability of the West and its Arab allies to kill him, for almost a decade after 9/11, and their continuing failure to eliminate the group's media or financial operations after nearly sixteen years of war speaks to bin Laden's successes in maintaining organizational and operational security.

Patience

The improvement of bin Laden's fighters between Jaji in 1987 and Jalalabad in 1989 was the result of both experience gained in battle and patient training. Patience would, after Jalalabad, become a hallmark of al-Qaeda's operations. Small, harassing operations "would be easy to conduct," bin Laden would contend, but they would not defeat the enemy. What al-Qaeda would come to term a "qualitative operation"—one that would have major impact on the foe—"obviously requires good preparation" and, therefore, bin Laden concluded, his fighters needed to "be patient and pious, for that is the provision and weapon of he who hopes for victory."[91]

Bankruptcy

Bin Laden believed the USSR was defeated in Afghanistan because of the economic damage it suffered rather than from military attrition. "Gorbachev explained to them [the politburo]," bin Laden wrote, "that the [Afghan] war had bled the Russian economy dry and they could no longer afford to fund this expensive war, which they could see no end to."[92] He also believed that not only was the Red Army "smashed and pulverized" but that the "huge economic drain that the Jihad placed on the Soviet economy" was "a magnificent blow to the morale of the Communist mindset."[93] This belief—whether empirically accurate or not—guided bin Laden's military strategy from then on, especially against the United States. "We are continuing this policy [guerrilla warfare] in bleeding America to the point of bankruptcy, Allah willing, and nothing is too great for Allah."[94]

Management

Bin Laden brought the experience he acquired in working in his family's construction business to the task of organizing his fighters at Masadah al-Ansar and then in al-Qaeda. As in Saudi Arabia, he worked with the human material at hand, but quickly made the key determination that "we were not military persons, we were civilians."[95] He therefore ran his operations as civilian enterprises with a key military component that required an effective managerial hand. The journalist Ahmad Zaydan—who knew and observed bin Laden for twenty-plus years—wrote that during the Afghan jihad, bin Laden behaved every bit like a businessman. "He was very much organized and he was very much calculating things."[96]

Logistics

Bin Laden's Afghan experience as a benefactor, engineer, and fighter taught him that the mujahedin would always be under "continuous pressure" from a much more powerful enemy and so would be "in need of continuous logistical support." "You need to have ammunition at the right time," as he put it; "you need launchers for the rockets, you also need facilities to evacuate the dead persons, may God accept them as martyrs."[97] Determining that "the two elements of fighting are money and souls," bin Laden and his senior lieutenants would later build al-Qaeda into an organization that could amply and reliably supply both, for their own operations as well as for the Islamist insurgencies they chose to support in various parts of the world.[98]

Media

Near the end of the anti-Soviet jihad, bin Laden told Isam Darraz he was "convinced of the importance of the media in serving Islamic causes."[99] He also later recalled the deep impression made on him by the power of the official Saudi media to help the Afghans' cause. Across the Arabic-speaking world, he said, the Saudi media "would cover the topic [of the Afghan jihad] in its five daily broadcasts, speaking about the heroic stand of the Mujahedin fighters."[100] He came to see the media as not just a fundraising vehicle during a war but also as a means for teaching Muslims that jihad was a religious duty, one that they must be prepared to undertake whenever and wherever there was a threat to Islam. "It is obvious that the media war in this century is one of the strongest methods [of warfare]," bin Laden told Mullah Omar before 9/11. "In fact its ratio may reach 90 percent of the total preparation for battles."[101]

Jihad

Bin Laden and his colleagues learned in Afghanistan that Islam's only means of survival from foreign attacks was jihad. "Does the crocodile," he asks, "understand a conversation that doesn't include a weapon?"[102] He learned this in part from Shaykh Azzam, who wrote, "Anyone who looks into the state of the Muslims today will find their greatest misfortune in the abandonment of jihad."[103] As a practicality, he learned it by fighting Soviets who had no interest in negotiations and left Afghanistan only because victory was not in sight and their economy was being ravaged by the cost of war. "There can be no dialogue with [infidel] occupiers," bin Laden argued, because they sought to eliminate Muslims and the Islamic identity, and "to deter them by any other means than [jihad] we would be like going in circles."[104] From Moscow's withdrawal to this day, bin Laden and now his successor Ayman al-Zawahiri demands that Muslims recognize that there is but one relevant historical model to ensure their survival: that of Saladin and his use of jihad.[105] Whether the issue was ending infidel occupation of Palestine, Iraq, Afghanistan, or Saudi Arabia, there was just one remedy. "Palestine and its people have been suffering a great deal for almost a century at the hands of the

Christians and Jews," bin Laden wrote. "Both opponents have not captured it from us through negotiations and dialogue, but by iron and fire, which is the way to regain it. Iron can only be cut with iron."[106]

Al-Qaeda

Odd as it might seem, given how universally it has been spoken and written of, one issue that has arisen from work on Osama bin Laden is whether or not al-Qaeda actually exists. Given the documents captured in Afghanistan and Iraq and subsequently published; the testimony of the group's (reluctant) defectors Jamal al-Fadl and Abu Jandal; the words and actions of bin Laden and his lieutenants; and the ample media coverage of all the efforts to root it out, the questions seems silly. Yet asked it has been. In his useful book *Al-Qaeda: Casting a Shadow of Terror*, Jason Burke recounts every possible event in which al-Qaeda might have been involved, and yet wasn't. In general, of course, Burke is correct that al-Qaeda cannot possibly have done everything that has been attributed to it. But Burke continues to view al-Qaeda as a traditional terrorist organization, which it certainly is not. Flagg Miller, a professor of religion at the University of California Davis, has studied 1,459 audio tapes by two hundred "leading Islamists from around the world" and concluded there is "no indication that the term al-qaeda was used before 2001 to denote a specific group or organization."[107] Indeed, Miller haughtily berates Peter Bergen for denouncing as "nonsense" previous claims that there is no al-Qaeda organization, arguing that "Bergen's aggressive editorial interventions—not unusual for such trade books—prevent closer analysis."[108] Miller's smug and highly selective use of evidence represents a microcosm of the contribution social science has made to the study of bin Laden and al-Qaeda. Finally, Gilles Kepel, an expert on Islamism, has recently written that al-Qaeda is a "hypothetical organization."[109]

Does it or does it not exist? My conclusion is that al-Qaeda surely does exist, that it was founded by Osama bin Laden and his colleagues, and that to this day his remaining colleagues direct its operations. I also believe that many others—Burke, Flagg, and Kepel among them—have not found it because they are looking for a more conventional terrorist group, something al-Qaeda is not. Neither is it what

Steve Coll and Lawrence Wright, respectively, refer to as a "small incubating cult of martyrdom" or a "death cult."[110]

What did bin Laden and al-Qaeda's other founders intend when they first organized it in 1988? They were, first off, trying to maintain momentum for the nascent worldwide Islamist movement into the post-Afghan jihad era. The multinational nature of the Afghan jihad only began in the last years of the war against the Soviets, and al-Qaeda was meant to keep Muslim attention on the jihad project after it lost the focus provided by the Red Army. Al-Qaeda was also intended to provide support for jihad through its own media activities, military operations, and assistance to like-minded Muslims. It was to provide a base from which the ummah-wide Islamist movement and potential adherents could be organized, trained, paid, and generally inspired. Al-Qaeda, bin Laden would explain, was founded to give jihad "the status of worship."[111] Bin Laden stressed that it was an organization open to all Muslims, not only Arabs. He added, however, that in the contemporary Muslim world this was easier to say than accomplish. People often speak of Islam, he said, in "simple terms, but there are differences in terms of customs."[112] He argued that such differences must be made irrelevant because "in God's faith, people are treated as equals" and that "the crucial factor is not a person's mistakes but his good deeds and righteousness."[113] In al-Qaeda, bin Laden declared, "we [will] have no discrimination on the basis of color or race. We cooperate with people on the basis of piety and righteousness . . . because we are one nation and one qiblah."[114]

To accomplish these goals, bin Laden modeled al-Qaeda on the Afghan insurgent organizations with which he was most familiar. These happened to be the most militantly Islamist as well as the most militarily effective groups, including Yunis Khalis's Hizbi-Islami, Jalaluddin Haqqani's organization, Abdul Rasul Sayyaf's Islamic Union, and Gulbuddin Hekmatyar's Hizbi-Islami. A key point often lost on Western analysts is that neither bin Laden nor his colleagues ever intended to build a terrorist organization; they intended to construct an insurgent organization that could absorb substantial punishment from always far more powerful foes and endure.

Is it an insurgent organization or a terrorist group? This is not a mere matter of semantics but rather represents a fundamental difference.

Terrorist groups are small; obsessively secretive; aim at publicity, not victory; constitute a lethal nuisance, not a national security threat to the nation-state; and are subject to defeat by decapitation or attrition. Insurgent groups, on the other hand, are much larger; balance the need for secretiveness with the need for propaganda; aim at victory and define what constitutes victory; pose genuine security threats to nation-states; and put so much effort into succession-planning that neither decapitation nor attrition is likely. Bin Laden also brought a new dimension to insurgency. Whereas historically most insurgencies are specific to nation-states, al-Qaeda is the first to have a substantial international presence.

There were four basic components to the organization of "al-Qaeda" at its inception. The first was a military component, which would field fighters—as individuals or in small groups—for training, advising, and/or combat purposes to places where local Islamists were fighting insurgencies. The initial areas of interest were Kashmir, Tajikistan, and Mindanao; Chechnya would soon be added to the list. The military component also included a cadre of veterans to keep training non-Afghan Muslims at camps in Afghanistan. Interestingly, no decision had yet been made to use al-Qaeda fighters to attack targets of the group's choosing, be they Arab regimes, the United States, or Israel. Al-Qaeda was not looking for a war of its own in 1988–1989.

The second component was broadly administrative to deal with finances—acquiring, budgeting, and dispensing funds—arms procurement, documentation, and logistical matters. When al-Qaeda began operations in September 1988, Tawil noted, nine of the group's fifteen founders were administrative specialists.[115]

The third would deal with religious matters: issuing fatwas and developing religious training courses for members of the organization and those its camps trained.

The fourth was a media/propaganda wing that would build on the MK's propaganda programs.

All these components would be overseen by a Shura Council chaired by bin Laden. When it was later decided that al-Qaeda would run its own military operations—the first a 1992 attack on U.S. troops in Aden, Yemen—a higher military committee was formed to handle insurgency support, as well as to approve, support, and fund al-Qaeda operations whose "planning, execution, and method of attack were all undertaken by commanders in the operational field [geographic area]," as Abu Jandal told the journalist Khalid al-Hammadi.[116]

Al-Qaeda's method of operation has remained fairly constant since 1988. For example, its military component was not meant to foment insurgencies in the Muslim world, but to assist them. While instigating Muslims to jihad worldwide would be al-Qaeda's main task, the organization's primary military task would be to help local Islamic insurgencies become better trained, financed, and led. Based on the founders' experience in the anti-Soviet jihad—during which they found that Afghans reacted violently to Arab attempts to assume military or religious leadership—they concluded that any Islamic insurgency must be started and led by the nationals of the country in which it was to occur. The necessary corollary to the rule was that al-Qaeda members sent to offer assistance would be subordinate to the locals. This was a lesson al-Qaeda members took a long time to learn, but that they did is evident today in Afghanistan, Yemen, Saudi Arabia, the North Caucasus, southern Thailand, Palestine, and Somalia, where Islamist insurgent forces are overwhelmingly local and led by locals. Al-Qaeda's one major departure from this doctrine was in Iraq under Abu Musab al-Zarqawi. As will be discussed, the al-Zarqawi deviation yielded disaster for al-Qaeda and came nearer than anything else after 9/11 to destroying it. That al-Qaeda learned this lesson thoroughly is seen in the quiet, subordinate, and generally effective performance by al-Zarqawi's first successor, the late Abu Hamza al-Muhajir.

Revealing how al-Qaeda was patterned after Islamist Afghan insurgent groups gives an opportunity to refute what has become a common refrain from many who write about bin Laden, and one that I allude to above; that is, that he claimed that he and "his men" defeated the Red Army in Afghanistan, and that the Afghans played a supporting role. These writers have used this to reduce bin Laden to a windbag, braggart, and fantasist. I would agree wholeheartedly that such would be an apt description of bin Laden had he made such a claim—but he did not. In the twenty-some years after the Soviet defeat, bin Laden attributed the mujahedin victory first to Allah and then to the Afghans. When he spoke of "we" when discussing the Afghan war, he invariably spoke in terms of "Muslims."

There are two main reasons he did this. First, because it was true; the Afghans drove the Red Army out and they would be the first to publicly denounce anyone who made a contrary contention. To my knowledge, no credible Afghan called out bin Laden on this point, although many Western experts did. And second, because bin Laden viewed Afghanistan as a God-given opportunity for Islam to revitalize itself, and was grateful for the Afghans' heroism and for allowing Arabs and non-Arab Muslims to play a bit part in their epic saga. He believed that he and all Muslims needed the Afghans much more than the Afghans needed them. The Afghan mujahedin saved not only their country but also Muslim holy sites, the Arab Gulf states, and much of the Islamic world. When the world looked to the Afghans, bin Laden wrote, "they found a population whose morale was high and who were committed to fighting the Russians. The Afghans had in their possession the rifles their grandfathers and great-grandfathers had used to fight the British. The Afghans were even selling their sheep in order to buy ammunition for their rifles. . . . Therefore, Allah blessed the mujahedin leadership with the ability to raise the banner of Jihad. . . . The Afghans were able to repel the largest invasion of recent times by the forces of disbelief against Islam. We ask Allah to reward them with the best rewards. . . . Had it not been for the grace of Allah and the people of Afghanistan, the Arabian Gulf states would have fallen into the hands of Communism."[117]

Securing Victory

After Jalalabad, bin Laden turned to the task of uniting the major groups of Afghan mujahedin so that they could secure their victory. He became fully involved in brokering an arrangement among the seven main groups, one that would allow them to defeat the Afghan communists, consolidate countrywide political power, and govern the country. As will seen more fully in chapter 4, achieving unity was an extremely long shot, given the animosities that had built up among the groups during the war and the ongoing interference of both the Saudis and the Pakistanis in trying to put their favorites—Sayyaf and Hekmatyar, respectively—in a dominant position. Prince Turki and the Riyadh regime were particularly interested in making sure that Ahmad Shah

Massoud gained as little power as possible because they feared he would work with the Iranians to spread Shia Tehran's influence in both Afghanistan and Central Asia. Bin Laden would stay involved in these negotiations—to a greater or lesser degree—until late in 1991, and his efforts reflected the belief formed in his youth that Muslims must unite to defeat their enemies.[118] Over the next few years, bin Laden would find that it was much easier to defeat a superpower than to form his fractious coreligionists into "one rank."

Toward a Global Jihad

By 1989, Osama's experience in the Afghan jihad had deepened the militant Salifism with which he grew up and transformed him into an implacable opponent of those he deemed "the enemies of Islam," an assortment of foes he would itemize over the next seven years. The changes in Osama were noted by his mother. After he left for Afghanistan, Allia wrote, "the nightmare started."[119] Family members and friends noted Allia's growing fears for her son. "In the beginning of his path, being a mother, she was very concerned," her sister Laila Ghanem recalled in 2001. "But when she saw his conviction . . . she said, 'God protect him.'"[120]

Bin Laden himself was open about what the anti-Soviet jihad had meant to him and what he believed it should mean to all Muslims. "Thanks be to God for this great blessing," bin Laden said in 1988,

> the blessing of jihad in the cause of God—the peak of true Islam, which people in this age have forgotten is a religious duty. It is due to God's blessing that we are returning to jihad after long years of negligence and after the Islamic holy sites have been taken; Muslim women were taken prisoner; and their land and honor were violated. By God's blessing this banner is hoisted high as our Prophet, may God's peace and prayers be upon him, did earlier. God has blessed us with taking jihad in our hands in order to make up for our misdeeds when we abandoned religion in the past. Praise be to God for allowing us to perform jihad in Afghanistan as he did for the best of men, our Prophet, may God's peace and prayers be

> upon him. . . . I would like to advise my brother Muslims in all parts of the East and West to take the initiative and leave what they are doing to assist in raising the banner of jihad for the cause of God. This banner is the best banner and the mujahedin are the best people. . . . May God accept our and your prayers and our urging of believers to perform jihad in order to deter the infidel forces and be truthful.[121]

In but a few sentences, bin Laden sketched out several themes that would characterize his future rhetoric and actions. First, he made clear that the Muslim world's woes were the sole responsibility of Muslims who had "forgotten [jihad] is a religious duty." Yes, the Soviets, Jews, Zionists, Western Christians, and Arab tyrants had imposed themselves on Muslims through colonization, imperialism, economic exploitation, and repressive governance, but they had done so only because Muslims had not lived their faith and defended their ummah through jihad. Bin Laden's was a long way from the argument of Bernard Lewis and others who claimed Muslims blamed others for their failings. Bin Laden's message here and henceforth would always be "God helps those who help themselves," and he would return to this tenet again and again to oppose the Muslim world's defeatism.

The second theme was that it was a religious duty for all Muslims to join or contribute to a jihad to retake the holy places and lands occupied by Islam's enemies. Bin Laden was not calling on Muslims to wage an offensive jihad to add new territory to Islam, but, instead, to restore what now belonged or had once belonged to Islam and to exact retribution from those who had violated Muslim land and honor.

A third theme—attendant to the second—was the recovery of Palestine. Although he did not mention Palestine by name in the foregoing passage, there seems no doubt he was talking about Jerusalem when he referred to "Islamic holy sites" taken from Muslims. In 1988, the only holy site then perceived by Muslims as occupied by infidels would be Israel's occupation of Jerusalem (the U.S.-led coalition did not establish a base in Saudi Arabia, of course, until August 1990). Palestine and al-Aqsa, as noted in chapter 1, were in the forefront of the young bin Laden's religious concerns in the 1970s. This argues against those who claim bin Laden concerned himself with Palestine only after the 9/11 attacks.

The final theme here, one that would increasingly dominate bin Laden's thinking and public utterances, was the global nature of the struggle against Islam's enemies. When he called on Muslims "in all parts of the East and West," Osama revealed that he was thoroughly acquainted with Islam's diversity, particularly after his experience with the multinational group of non-Afghan Muslims who had helped defeat the Red Army. Bin Laden left Afghanistan with a global perspective, one he would use to assess what it would take to defeat "God's enemies." He was ready to engage a world that was itself globalizing and that therefore would provide him the tools he needed to incite a global jihad.

4

NOMAD, 1989–1996

Returning to Saudi Arabia after Jalalabad, Osama bin Laden found he had become famous. Najwa bin Laden wrote about her husband that "everyone was astonished that a wealthy bin Laden son actually risked death or injury on the front lines." The returning hero was in great demand—to give speeches and interviews.[1] There is no evidence this new celebrity went to his head, nor is there evidence he encouraged it.

He resumed work for the Bin Laden Company and was involved in constructing roads, tunnels, and buildings, especially in the areas of Taif and Abha in eastern Saudi Arabia.[2] Bin Laden proved to be more than the boss of a construction crew. He was adept at ironing out problems between the company and Saudi officials, and used his ability to speak English (fairly well, at any rate) to coordinate with European and American engineers working on projects in the Kingdom.[3] And while he was unhappy about the unhelpful role played by Prince Turki in the effort to build Afghan unity after Soviet withdrawal, bin Laden "was still a [Saudi] patriot in those days, loyal to his country and his king," as his wife put it, one who then believed, as he himself later said, that "the [Saudi] regime started under the flag of Islam and under this banner the people of Saudi Arabia came to help the Saudi family take power."[4]

For a young Saudi Salafist and loyalist like bin Laden, however, returning to the Kingdom was a disorienting experience. After being praised for fighting the atheist communists in Afghanistan, he found his efforts, for example, to fund, equip, and then use Yemenis with Afghan battle experience in a campaign to overthrow South Yemen's Marxist regime were opposed by the same Saudis who had praised him—both regime officials and religious scholars.[5] In 1991, bin Laden worked with two Yemeni Afghan veterans—Tariq al-Fadhli and Jamal al-Hadhi—and financed two insurgent training facilities in Yemen, one in the mountains of northern Yemen near the town of Sada' and the other in Yemen's southern Abayan Province.[6] Bin Laden also traveled to Yemen—mostly to Sana, Abyan, and Shabwah—where he delivered lectures urging Muslims to fight the Yemen Socialist Party.[7] He later said that Saudi officials asked him to stop this activity, but that "we continued to cooperate with them [Yemen's anti-communist mujahedin] against the leaders of atheism in the Socialist party."[8] The term "cooperation" was bin Laden's euphemism for sponsoring of a series of assassinations of Yemeni socialist leaders between 1990 and 1994.[9]

In the Kingdom, bin Laden maintained his relationship with the religious scholars and their supporters who had started Saudi Arabia's Islamic Awakening (Sahwa), which was a movement aimed at ending official corruption and bringing the regime into full compliance with Islamic law. In particular he befriended shaykhs Salman al-Awdah and Safar al-Hawali. The Sahwa leaders sent a "Declaration of Demands" to King Fahd in May 1991, and a "Memorandum of Advice" to Saudi Grand Mufti Shaykh Abdul Aziz bin Baz in September 1992. Neither recipient responded positively to the documents, and this hard-line response led to increased internal religious dissent.[10] This in turn spurred the regime to crack down on reformist scholars in 1994. Many Sahwa leaders, including al-Awdah and al-Hawali, were imprisoned. Ironically, the jailings silenced many advocates of peaceful change—which Osama bin Laden then supported—and created a vacuum that was filled by men favoring a more violent approach to purifying Islam in the Kingdom.[11] When bin Laden later adopted the more vocal and violent position, he would credit al-Awdah, al-Hawali, and their colleagues as the proper leaders of the reform effort, and maintain that he was stepping forward to act only because they were incarcerated.[12]

When later released, al-Hawali kept quiet on most issues that had earned him jail time, although he later issued a fatwa justifying the 9/11 attacks.[13] Al-Awdah, however, systematically recanted his earlier positions and found lucrative, regime-sponsored teaching and media posts open to him. He eventually publicly denounced bin Laden.[14]

While working for reform, bin Laden also began writing private letters to senior Saudi officials, such as interior minister Prince Nayef, about the threat posed to Saudi Arabia by Saddam Hussain's Iraq, predicting that it intended to attack the Kingdom. Receiving what he thought unsatisfactory answers, bin Laden was so convinced that, as his wife put it, "the Iraq Army would walk across the Kuwaiti border to Saudi Arabia that he gave speeches warning of the danger." Omar bin Laden recalls that his father never supported Saddam—always calling him a "nonbeliever"—and believed "the leader of such a strong army will never stop looking for war."[15] Bin Laden's warnings were validated when Saddam invaded Kuwait in August 1990, and indeed looked ready to move into Saudi Arabia. In response, bin Laden rallied to the al-Saud flag and offered his services to the regime through Prince Sultan, the defense minister. He proposed using the family's construction equipment to build a defensive line, and that he mobilize Afghan veterans to man it. His plan was turned down by the Saudi royal family, who then asked the United States for help and secured religious permission for Western militaries—that is, infidel militaries—to operate in the Arabian Peninsula.

Bin Laden was deeply shocked by the decision. Since the "very early eighties" he had said Islam's next battle would be against the United States, and now King Fahd had asked Washington to land forces in the Prophet's birthplace.[16] He warned his royal contacts that if the American military established a foothold on the Peninsula it would never leave. Bin Laden's Sahwa friend Shaykh al-Hawali agreed, and cited his and bin Laden's views when he said, "it is not the world against Iraq. It is the West against Islam. . . . The real enemy [of Islam] is not Iraq. It is the West."[17] To bin Laden's deepening dismay, "heavily armed Saudi troops" raided his farm near Jeddah and disarmed the nearly one hundred Afghan veterans employed there. Bin Laden's son remembers that his father was "so furious he could not speak"; that he called Crown Prince Abdullah to ask why his National Guard troops conducted the raid; and that Abdullah—an al-Saud then admired by bin Laden—promised to investigate and report back to him, but never did.[18]

Angry that the regime had turned down his offer, bin Laden could not get over that the al-Sauds and their grand mufti had welcomed infidel soldiers into the Kingdom to defend Muhammad's birthplace.[19] "My people or most of the [Saudi] people's sons," he would later recall, "were shocked by the fatwas issued by people [Saudi scholars] in whom they had full confidence, so we had to wait until this shock disappeared."[20] In response, bin Laden confronted senior regime scholars: "How can you issue a fatwa sanctioning the Americans' entry into the country? This is not permissible."[21] He asked Sahwa scholars to issue a fatwa against the deployment, and supported one issued by Saudi Shaykh bin Uthaymin that declared it obligatory for all Muslims, especially those on the Arabian Peninsula, to resist what he called "the invaders." He also used bin Uthaymin's fatwa to mobilize young Saudis to travel to Afghanistan for paramilitary training, and "a considerable number of Saudis heeded the call."[22]

None of this succeeded, and as in the campaign to destroy South Yemen's Marxist regime, the Saudi royal family and its scholars voluntarily aligned themselves with those whom a traditionally educated, young Saudi loyalist like bin Laden could only see as the enemies of God and Islam.

The contradictions in Riyadh—encouraging young men to fight communists in Afghanistan, but not in Yemen; inviting Western military forces into the Kingdom; jailing Sahwa scholars and Saudi mujahedin returning from Tajikistan, Bosnia-Herzegovina, and elsewhere; and convincing some Awakening scholars to recant and toe the regime's line in exchange for release from prison and salary, status, and position—may, in hindsight, amount to the beginning of the end of the Saudi monarchy. The focus here has been on these actions' impact on bin Laden, but he was not alone in feeling betrayed by the regime and its scholars. These people acted on their convictions. "What made the [Saudi] youths take up arms and carry out bombings in Saudi territories?" asked bin Laden's bodyguard, Abu Jandal; "I believe it is the Saudi Government's stupid policy toward these people [the youth]. Those who bombed the al-Muhayya complex spoke frankly in their audiotapes over the Internet that they went to jihad with the permission of the state and the instigation [of scholars like] Shaykh Sa'd al-Burayk,

Shaykh A'id al-Qarni, Shaykh Salman al-Awdah and many others who instigated the youth. But when the confrontation began between the government and these youths, the youths were surprised to find that the shaykhs had abandoned them. In fact, Shaykh Sa'd al-Burayk and Shaykh A'id al-Qarni began attacking these youths, who were the product of their lectures, sermons, lessons, and religious circles."[23]

Nonetheless, as I have argued, the Saudi narrative has generally been accepted and propagated by Western writers. In *Ghost Wars*, Steve Coll presents the foregoing events based on interviews with Khalil A. Khalil, who is identified as a pro-Saudi theologian, and Prince Turki. The bin Laden these men describe—swaggering, boastful, threatening, disrespectful toward both scholars and princes, offering outlandish figures of the mujahedin at his command, and demanding an interview with King Fahd—does not square with the portrait of bin Laden we have from others, either then or later.[24] Differing accounts are omitted and the Khalil-Turki description is accepted as gospel; also not cited are bin Laden's predictions of an Iraqi attack on Kuwait. After recounting the stories of two al-Saud loyalists, Coll endorses the Saudi narrative by quoting Prince Turki's view of the "radical changes" that had occurred in this heretofore good young Saudi. "He changed from a calm, peaceful and gentle man interested in assisting Muslims," Turki almost tearfully laments, "into a person who believed that he would be able to amass and command an army to liberate Iraq. It revealed his arrogance and haughtiness."[25]

Bin Laden left Saudi Arabia for Pakistan, using the intervention of his brothers to convince the Saudi officials to let him travel on the condition he would return to the Kingdom. Once there, he made it clear he had no intention of returning, writing to his wife, "Najwa, do not leave one dish in Saudi Arabia."[26] He then wrote a "tender letter of apology" to his brothers for misleading them by saying he would return to Saudi Arabia, thereby abusing their good offices.[27]

Peace Broker

Bin Laden returned to Peshawar and remained there for nearly a year, working to mediate the political chaos and violence that were intensifying among the Afghan insurgent groups. He cooperated with other Arabs who had been associated with Shaykh Azzam in wartime aid for the Afghans, and especially with a fellow Saudi named Wael Julaidan, who ran a council of the major Islamic NGOs working out of Peshawar. "We used to visit Afghan leaders to resolve disputes," Julaidan has said, "because at the time the disputes of the Afghan leaders were getting more serious. From time to time we went together to talk to the different Afghan leaders, to calm them."[28]

Their work was for naught, however, as bin Laden and his colleagues were pulling in the opposite direction from Prince Turki and the Pakistanis—bin Laden playing the "honest broker" and working for an inclusive accord—mediating between the bitter enemies Hekmatyar and Massoud, and only demanding that no Afghan communists be put in a new Afghan government—and Turki and the Pakistanis seeking a deal that looked inclusive but made Sayyaf and Hekmatyar primus inter pares.[29] Lawrence Wright's work has claimed that this episode made bin Laden and Turki "deadly antagonists," but this seems premature.[30] That antagonism would soon emerge, but the trigger would be bin Laden's public denunciation of Turki's masters in the royal family.

For the West, in fact, bin Laden's animosity toward the United States and Britain, which developed during this peacemaking effort, is more important than his anger at Turki. While the assertion that Washington and the West abandoned the Afghans after the Soviet withdrawal is now accepted as fact, it is in fact entirely inaccurate. From the exit of the last Red Army trooper in 1989 until well after the Afghan communists' defeat in 1992, the United States, Britain, Germany, and the UN worked diligently to install a regime in Kabul that would include representatives of all Afghan groups—so long as they were not Islamists and had not fought and bled to drive out the USSR. At one point, for example, Washington had three diplomats of ambassadorial rank and one special envoy—Peter Tomsen, Robert Oakley, Phyllis Oakley, and Zalmay Khalilizad—working to produce a regime that would include sophisticated, English-speaking, secular Afghans; Afghan technocrats; former communists—even former Afghan communist president Najibullah; supporters of the deposed Afghan king; and Afghans who had spent the war making money in America, Europe, Iran, or India. In other words, the West was ready to consider anyone save those who had carried AK-47s and killed Soviets. Indeed, a major reason a post-Soviet Afghan civil war began was because those who had fought saw their hard-won right to rule being handed by Westerners to Afghans who were nominal Muslims and had chosen to sit out the war. This situation, moreover, made Riyadh and Islamabad believe that support for the hardest-line Islamists—Sayyaf and Hekmatyar—was the only way to stop the formation of a pro-Western Kabul regime that would also be friendly to the anti-Sunni and/or anti-Pakistani governments of India, Iran, and Russia. (History is repeating itself. Today Riyadh and Islamabad face the same dilemma with the Karzai regime, which is antithetical to their interests and which is being bolstered by the United States and NATO.)

In this context, the "abandonment" mantra is easily dismantled by an Afghan who did fight the Soviets. "There were attempts [after the Afghan communists fell]," Islamic Union chief Abdul Rasul Sayyaf said, "by Russia and other atheist powers, led by the United States and Europe, to find groups of Afghans to succeed the Soviets after their departure, provided they would establish a non-Islamic government in Afghanistan."[31] Of all the culprits Sayyaf named, bin Laden most blamed the United States. "We were fighting against the communists [since 1979]," he later said, "and now the United States was pressuring us to cooperate with those very same communists. The United States has no principles. To achieve its own interests, it forgets every principle."[32]

The postwar intra-mujahedin disaster had a deep and lasting impact on bin Laden's approach to war-making. After the Afghans' crack-up, bin Laden concluded that any Islamist military victory would be lost unless followed quickly by the creation of a regime made up of all the elements that had played a substantive role in the war. Bin Laden later said his experience with the ethnically and tribally divided Afghans made it clear that wars could be fought and won by Muslims even when divided into factions; the threat of an infidel enemy's superior power would produce a workable if limited unity. Victory, on the other hand, could not be translated into a durable consolidation of political power unless the same or greater unity was present in the postwar era. Military victory in Afghanistan, he said, was accompanied by a relaxation of wartime pressure, and this easing removed the impetus for quasi unity and led each group to seek its own best interests. "The withdrawal of the Soviets from Afghanistan," he wrote, "was accompanied by an almost immediate break out of fighting amongst the Afghan factions. There existed differences between the various leaders. Political differences in Islam that divide Muslims are considered evil and it is not possible for Islam to be established in their midst. Defeating an enemy may be possible whilst differences exist, but Islam cannot be established on the land with these differences."[33]

Henceforth, bin Laden's concern for maintaining enough wartime unity to consolidate power and to create a workable government would become a dominant factor in his thinking and planning. It was reflected in the efforts he made to reconcile the Sudanese regime and its domestic opponents between 1991 and 1996; to narrow the differences between Mullah Omar and Hekmatyar and Sayyaf in post-1996 Afghanistan; and, most especially, in his advocacy of united mujahedin movements in Iraq and Somalia after 2003.

Putting down Stakes in Sudan

From Sudan, bin Laden prepared to use al-Qaeda to broaden the war on the United States. This started with a 1992 attack on U.S. forces in Yemen, and was followed by support for anti-U.S. forces in Somalia between 1992 and 1994. He also worked to increase his personal fortune with commercial construction and agricultural enterprises, the idea being to create reserves so he could offer funding where needed, such as to the economically troubled regime of National Islamic Front (NIF) leader Hasan al-Turabi, whom he assisted mostly through personal loans and by asking wealthy Saudis and other Gulf Arabs to invest in the country. His businesses maintained al-Qaeda, employing group members and other non-Afghan Muslims who fought in Afghanistan and supporting their families. And as his economic activities expanded, bin Laden sent his lieutenants into the Horn of Africa and elsewhere to sell products and reconnoiter likely locations for an al-Qaeda presence.

Bin Laden's familiarity with the Islamic world's diversity deepened in Sudan, more so than had he stayed in Afghanistan or Saudi Arabia.

In Khartoum, he also commanded an organization—with military and commercial arms—larger than ever before. When in his youth he had worked for his father's company, the financial risks had been the firm's. His personal responsibilities in Afghanistan had been greater, but while he funded some operations, the majority had operated on funds from others. In Sudan, he alone was responsible for success or failure. That experience ultimately proved hard, disappointing, and impoverishing, but it left bin Laden comfortable with command, able to make hard decisions and hold an organization together in times of turmoil, and removed the last naiveté of youth, especially his faith in the trustworthiness of all Islamic scholars. The Sudan years also saw bin Laden outline al-Qaeda's strategic priorities—potential targets and political, military, and media operations—which remained consistent to this day.

Life in Sudan

In December 1991, bin Laden began to settle his wives and children, and some of his followers, in a cluster of houses—to be used as both residences and offices—on the same street in al-Riyadh city, a wealthy Khartoum suburb. At least one was designated as a guest house for the large number of visitors who came from outside Sudan, especially from the Muslim world and Europe.[34] Bin Laden put his eldest sons into what his wife Najwa describes as "a very good school," and supplemented it by hiring "highly qualified" instructors to instruct those boys and his other sons at home in science, mathematics, history, and—of course—religion.[35] Bin Laden grew to enjoy Sudan and the Sudanese; in some of his poetry he calls Khartoum his favorite city.[36]

The reaction to bin Laden among his Sudanese neighbors was typical. They described him as a kind, humble man who lived a very modest life. He spoke little, was respectful to his neighbors, and walked to prayers five times a day at a nearby mosque. "We used to see bin Laden at prayer all the time," a fellow worshiper recalled. "His general appearance manifested he was a religious man."[37] His gardener, a Sudanese named Mahjub al-Aradi, told *Al-Quds al-Arabi* in late 2001 that bin Laden "would eat the leftovers from guests because he thought this was a blessing from the Prophet." Al-Aradi said that in the mornings bin Laden would go to the office, then to his guest house, staying there until 8 or 9 in the evening, at which point he would head home.[38]

Despite his low profile, the first major threat to his life took place in Sudan, with an attack on bin Laden and his eldest son, Abdullah, at their home by members of a takfiri group known as Al-Takfir wa al-Hijra, which believed bin Laden was "not sufficiently Muslim." "We used to meet with the brother guests at 1700 hours every evening," bin Laden recalled several years later. "On that day, and for a reason known to God, I was late [for the meeting], then I heard a barrage of bullets fired on the guest room. Some bullets were [fired] at me. So I took my weapon and went to a position overlooking the house to investigate the matter. I gave my eldest son a weapon and told him to take a position inside the house. I thought that an armed group had attacked the guards, and we prepared ourselves for a clash. But it was discovered that the attack was aimed directly at the guest room, which was stormed by three young men who opened fire on the place where I used to sit. One [guest] was hit in the abdomen, another in the thigh, and a third in the leg. There were Sudanese security forces near the house, so they clashed with them, killing two and wounding the third."[39]

Later, other takfiris would try to kill bin Laden when they thought he would be at prayers in the al-Thawrah mosque in Khartoum.[40] The attackers killed a number of worshipers, but bin Laden was not in attendance. And takfiris would take another crack at bin Laden's life after he returned to Afghanistan in 1996. Oddly, despite the long-standing record of takfiri hatred for bin Laden, several reputed al-Qaeda experts describe bin Laden, al-Qaeda, and the Taleban as adhering closely to takfiri doctrine.[41]

Sudanese Businesses

Bin Laden said he first visited Sudan in 1983 to investigate "its agricultural capabilities and investment opportunities." When he returned in late 1991, he began to work in both agriculture and road construction.[42] One of bin Laden's major goals was to increase his personal fortune as much as possible—"he concentrated on developing his wealth and enlarging the scope of his trading and investment activities," as a close al-Qaeda associate put it.[43] He built a variety of businesses, some focused on import-export opportunities, others on construction. The largest of the latter was called Al-Hijrah for Construction and Development and employed six hundred of the roughly seven hundred men who worked for bin Laden in Sudan. The company built the 500-mile highway called the "Challenge Road" linking Khartoum and Port Sudan, where it participated in building the city's new airport and several nearby dams.[44] He also convinced a fair number of Saudis to invest in Sudan.[45] He was still able to move funds out of the Kingdom and to purchase and import construction vehicles and machinery from his family's company. This would continue until King Fahd stripped him of Saudi citizenship in 1994.[46]

It was to agriculture that bin Laden devoted most of his personal attention in Sudan. As Lawrence Wright has written, it was "farming that captivated his imagination."[47] Bin Laden owned an enormous farm in the Damazin area of southeastern Sudan, on land he received from Sudan's regime in payment for some of his construction work. There he raised cows, cattle, and horses, and grew corn, soybeans, sorghum, and other vegetables; he also worked a salt farm located near Port Sudan.[48] As in Saudi Arabia, bin Laden seemed happiest when away from the city. Najwa recalled, "He had seriously overworked his mind to discover new ways of producing the largest sunflowers in the world. Nothing made my husband happier than showing off his huge sunflowers."[49] Their size was due to genetic improvements his employees had made in them, he did the same with cattle and perhaps trees.[50]

Growing al-Qaeda

Bin Laden brought al-Qaeda members to Sudan, leaving a skeletal staff in Afghanistan to look after the training camps and other facilities. His senior military lieutenants in Sudan were his overall military commander Abu Ubaydah al-Panshiri and Panshiri's deputy Abu Hafs al-Masri, both Egyptians. While bin Laden pursued business matters, dealt with Turabi and his regime, and worked to extend his contacts across the Muslim world, Abu-Ubaydah and Abu Hafs managed the small military force of Afghan veterans al-Qaeda kept in the Sudan, which was given refresher military training on bin Laden's agricultural properties.[51] His lieutenants also worked with Sudan's militia forces, and collaborated closely with Sudanese intelligence service chief Salah Abdallah Gosh, collecting information in Africa and abroad.[52] Bin Laden also sent al-Panshiri and al-Masri on a reconnaissance mission to Somalia. Al-Panshiri was later sent to contact Islamist organizations in Eritrea, delivering cash to that country's Jamaat-i Jihad group and helping it to build several training camps.[53]

There has been an endless debate over what role al-Qaeda played in Somalia during the U.S.-led UN operation Restore Hope. Estimates have gone from large to tiny to none at all. The truth seems to be that bin Laden's Afghan Arabs—as in Afghanistan—played a small role in the Somali conflict. Bin Laden had built several training camps in southern Somalia before the U.S.-led UN mission arrived, and al-Qaeda leaders were active there. Always concerned about safe havens, al-Qaeda saw the Somali camps as potential refuges were al-Qaeda members forced to flee Sudan, Saudi Arabia, or Yemen. Abu Jandal has explained, "They aspired to make Somalia a stronghold for them close to the Arab Peninsula because the brothers in al-Qaeda had an aim to liberate the Arab Peninsula later on. If al-Qaeda established a solid base in Somalia it also could be used to block the United States, which [will] certainly seek to control the Horn of Africa."[54] Al-Qaeda members provided weapons and training to Somali fighters in 1993–1994, but the role they played on the ground in Somalia is best described as minor.

More important was what bin Laden and his lieutenants learned from observing the U.S. performance. Bin Laden believed that "the American soldier was a paper tiger and [would] after a few blows run in defeat . . . dragging their corpses and shameful defeat." This view was summarized by Abu Jandal, who says al-Qaeda concluded that while the "U.S. arsenal is full of weapons, it does not have men."[55]

Al-Qaeda members were also working in other parts of Africa and the world to establish the organization's presence, to prepare for war, or both. In 1992, for example, bin Laden sent his friend the Afghan veteran Khalid Fawwaz to Nairobi, to build the Kenyan network that eventually prepared the 1998 attack on the U.S. embassy in that city. As cover for this work, Fawwaz opened an import-export company named Asma in 1993.[56] In 1994, bin Laden moved Fawwaz to London to handle al-Qaeda interests there, and replaced him in Nairobi with his secretary Wadih al-Hage, another Afghan veteran.[57] Wali Khan Amin Shah was bin Laden's advance man in places al-Qaeda was considering attacks, communicating by sending encoded messages via "mail drops and fax machines." In the Philippines, Khan worked with Ramzi Yousef—author of the 1993 World Trade Center bombing—to plan attacks on President Clinton and Pope John Paul II in Manila, develop plans for bombing U.S airliners flying Pacific routes, and assist Filipino Islamists to build training camps.[58]

In Sudan, bin Laden developed relations with EIJ leader Ayman al-Zawahiri. As noted, bin Laden first met al-Zawahiri during the Afghan jihad when both were involved with Shaykh Azzam. Al-Zawahiri was then fully focused on Egypt, and his influence on bin Laden was minimal. As we have seen, others have argued that al-Zawahiri skillfully inserted senior EIJ members, such as Abu-Ubaydah al-Panshiri and Abu Hafs al-Masri, into bin Laden's inner circle—and later into al-Qaeda—and by so doing set himself on the road to becoming bin Laden's éminence grise, or even "Osama's brain." Yet there is no evidence whatever that, for example, either Abu Ubaydah or Abu Hafs were less than totally loyal to bin Laden; and there is nothing to suggest that either acted to manipulate bin Laden on al-Zawahiri's behalf, paving the way for his taking over al-Qaeda. Indeed, there also is nothing to suggest that al-Zawahiri—from the time he met bin Laden until the al-Qaeda chief's death—has had much impact on his thinking; indeed, all the evidence points in exactly the opposite direction. The story of al-Zawahiri craftily brainwashing bin Laden and hijacking al-Qaeda is cut from whole cloth by the Saudis and others, as part of their "good-Saudi-boy-led-astray-by-evil-Egyptians" narrative.

Nowhere was the Saudi spin more evident than in Lawrence Wright's book *The Looming Tower*. Wright recounts a tale from Jamal Khashoggi, a Saudi journalist, that has him being sent to Sudan by the bin Laden family to obtain an interview from a war-weary and discouraged bin Laden, longing for nothing more than to be a farmer and almost ready to renounce violence. "That would be a very public signal to the [Saudi] government that he accepted its terms [to give up jihad]." After several meetings with Khashoggi, Wright says, bin Laden joined the journalist for dinner and "rhapsodized about how much he missed Medina and how he would like to go back and settle there."[59] Khashoggi inferred that bin Laden was ready to do the Saudi-appeasing interview, but he turned out to have been mistaken.

> Just then someone approached bin Laden and whispered in his ear. Osama stood up and went into the garden. In the shadows, Khashoggi could see two or three men quietly speaking in Egyptian accents. Five minutes later, bin Laden returned, and Khashoggi posed the question [would he renounce violence] again. "What will I get for that?" bin Laden asked. Khahsoggi was caught by surprise. Osama had never acted like a politician before, negotiating for personal advantage. "I don't know," Khashoggi admitted, "I'm not representing the [Saudi] government. . . ." Bin Laden smiled. "Yes, but a move like this had to be calculated." He [bin Laden] aired a couple of sweeteners: a full pardon for him, a timetable for the complete withdrawal of the American forces from the peninsula. Khashoggi had the feeling that his friend was losing his hold on reality.[60]

There you have the Saudi narrative in a nutshell. A good-but-erring Saudi boy (Osama) is approached by another still-good Saudi boy (Khashoggi) and given a chance to repent and return home. Tired and unhappy, Osama is about to accept the offer when at the last moment a mysterious person taps him on his shoulder and asks him to the garden to talk to two or three men with "Egyptian accents" (al-Zawahiri, Abu Hafs, and Abu Ubaydah?). Afterward, Osama returns to the table transformed, not as a good boy but as a recalcitrant renegade or even mentally unbalanced. Choosing to forego Kashoggi's offer, he continues down the Egyptian-paved road to perdition. On reading this passage, I recalled Mark Twain's comment after discussing the physics-defying transit of a cannonball in his essay about James Fenimore Cooper's *Leatherstocking Tales*. Having described the cannonball's utterly impossible flight, which Natty Bumppo is able to retrace in order to find the fort from which it was fired, Twain simply asks his readers "Isn't that a daisy?"

Supporting Saudi Reformers

Bin Laden's departure from Saudi Arabia did not mean withdrawing his support for the reform movement—or Islamic Awakening—under way in the Kingdom. He had been fully involved with the Awakening members since 1989 and probably before, given its members advocacy and aid for the Afghan jihad, and supported their two major initiatives with King Fahd and the grand mufti: the "Declaration of Demands" and the "Memorandum of Advice." The initiatives were phrased in what bin Laden described as a "kind, clear, and honest fashion," and urged the king to return to Shariah rule, end corruption, develop the economy, and become the champion—rather than the opponent—of Islamic causes from Yemen to Palestine to the Balkans. Bin Laden regarded the documents as an essential part of Islamic governance because giving advice to those who govern "is a necessary requirement in Islam."[61]

To continue pushing for change, bin Laden created the Advice and Reform Committee (ARC) early in 1994. The ARC's public office was in London, but its communiqués were prepared in Sudan. The trigger for the ARC's formation was the Saudi regime's 1993–1994 crackdowns on scholars who led the Islamic Awakening in the Kingdom. The suppression increased in scope and brutality as it proceeded, and among the imprisoned were, as noted earlier, the two scholars bin Laden most admired, Salman al-Awdah and Safar al-Hawali. With the leading reform scholars in prison, bin Laden decided to begin speaking publicly in their place and moved his friend Khalid al-Fawwaz from Nairobi to the UK to run the ARC office while he managed the committee's publications from Sudan. In so doing, bin Laden's demonstrated his ability to reach into the Kingdom for religious guidance from sympathetic scholars. The ARC was created "with consultation with our brothers in the Arabian Peninsula," he wrote in explaining his motivation for speaking out.[62] "After the Saudi government harassed the ulema, dismissed them from their jobs in universities and mosques, and prevented the distribution of their tapes," bin Laden told *Al-Quds al-Arabi*, "I decided that if it [the Saudi regime] was going to prevent them from speaking, I would begin to promote virtue and repudiate vice, something which had been suspended [in the Kingdom]."[63]

The ARC published communiqués criticizing the al-Saud family's behavior and its economic, domestic, and foreign policies. The communiqués used in this study cover the period 1994 to 1998. They focus on the issues just noted, and also reflect bin Laden's intensifying criticism, eventually leading to his denunciation of King Fahd as un-Islamic, senior royal family members, and the Saudi religious establishment. The communiqués clearly got under the royals' skin—the family was described as "obdurate in its hatred of Islam"—but presumably were approved by the Kingdom's reformist scholars.[64] They are most valuable, however, as our first extended look at bin Laden's written thought. They also merit attention because they underscore bin Laden's decision not to run al-Qaeda strictly as a traditional terrorist group, one that by definition is a lethal nuisance to its foes but not a national-security threat. The communiqués prove that bin Laden had concluded that he and al-Qaeda would help Muslims achieve victory over the entities oppressing them rather than bother them with pinprick attacks in the manner of such terrorist groups as Abu Nidal, the Irish Republican Army, the Palestine Liberation Organization, and Czarist Russia's socialist revolutionaries.

The ARC communiqués laid out the themes from which all bin Laden's future public presentations and private planning would flow. The first focus was the al-Saud family's corruption, and in particular its failure to use oil revenue to improve the people's lives. Bin Laden's deep and abiding concern for "good governance" is clear. The ARC's second focus involved the increasingly bitter confrontation between the Saudi regime and young scholars demanding reforms to make Islamic law apply to every aspect of the Kingdom's affairs. Its third focus—the one that came to dominate its publications—was the al-Sauds' foreign policy, which bin Laden and his ARC colleagues viewed as not only un-Islamic but also anti-Islamic.

In the ARC communiqués, bin Laden argued that the Saudi economy was a shambles because "of the personal wastefulness" of government officials who "squander the country's money and resources on their appetites."[65] Royal family members used their positions to skim funds from government purchases, especially from "the astronomical amounts spent on the military."[66] Defense spending, bin Laden argued, was nothing more than a "source of income for influential princes"; the spending was not only excessive but failed to ready the Saudi army for war, as was proven in 1990–1991, when U.S. and Western forces were called to defend the Kingdom against Iraq.[67] So greedy were the al-Sauds that they even diverted donations from private Saudi citizens for Bosnian relief to their own accounts and then "dissolved charitable organizations" and replaced them with "organizations and foundations subservient to royal family members."[68] For these crimes, the communiqués assigned responsibility to the royal family, especially to King Fahd, Prince Sultan, Prince Nayef, and the governor of Riyadh.[69] These men led the way in the "plundering of the public wealth."[70]

Pervasive royal greed and corruption had made the country an economic disaster, dooming the average Saudi to live in a "contemptible social condition." Government-provided social services had significantly deteriorated, and people were especially hurt by the decline of a reliable water service, water being "the most important element of life."[71] In addition, the royals' uncontrolled spending was "affecting their basic necessities," such as food, medicine, gas, electricity, fuel, and education. Riyadh was vastly increasing the national debt, and the interest thereon not only caused people to suffer but was worsening unemployment, which "has been rampant in the country among college graduates and youth for the past ten years."[72]

"The basis of the problem," bin Laden told King Fahd, "is that you and your regime have strayed from the requisites of monotheism and its obligations . . . you and your regime have legislated and governed by positive law . . . the scum of human positivist thoughts."[73] The use of man-made law amounted to the "attribution of partners to God" and results in laws "that make forbidden things permissible," such as usury, which is "one of the greatest mortal sins."[74] The sole solution to these ills, bin Laden wrote, was abolition of man-made laws and a return to a Shariah-only environment. This was the obvious rectifying action, and yet, bin Laden then asked the Saudi grand mufti, Shaykh bin Baz, why was it not being taken? Answering his own question, bin Laden explained that for the rulers' sake bin Baz and his colleagues issued rulings in which the "truth is twisted" to please the rulers.[75] Such decisions hurt the country and stimulated popular distrust in the regime's official scholars. This was a dangerous situation, he reminded bin Baz, because the citizens' duty to obey the scholars was tied directly to their demonstrating a "commitment of defending the truth."[76] The disintegration of religion stemmed from the combination of bad rulers and bad scholars, and, in the al-Sauds, the Kingdom already had rulers who were dajjals (the Muslim Antichrist).[77] He therefore beseeched the grand mufti to "fear God and to keep your distance from these tyrants and wrong-doers who have proclaimed war on God and His messenger."[78]

The increasing harshness of Riyadh's crackdown on the Awakening scholars led the ARC to redouble its attacks on the royal family and its official scholars. By mid-1994, bin Laden identified the arrest and detention of the reformers as "King Fahd's policy of turning the people away from the path of God." The worst arrests, he said, were those of the "two venerable shaykhs" al-Awdah and al-Hawali.[79] This was an "evil crime" perpetrated by "the servants of the dinar and the ones who sold their religion."[80] Bin Laden also claimed that the U.S. government had ordered King Fahd "to arrest prominent scholars and preachers" as part of a "comprehensive Jewish campaign [to humiliate] the Muslim people."[81]

As bad as the al-Sauds' actions were, the silence of most of the Kingdom's official scholars during the crackdown was worse. "You are required to stand by your fighting scholar brothers in their defense," bin Laden seethed. Instead these scholars had stood silent as the al-Sauds imprisoned "the best of the ummah, its mujahid ulema."[82] Bin Laden initially cut Shaykh bin Baz some slack because he spoke favorably of the arrested scholars. But when bin Baz issued a fatwa authorizing the arrests, he denounced the grand mufti and his colleagues for showing that they preferred "earthly things and materials" to their religion, and were far from being heirs of the Prophet, whose duty is to appear in public "speaking the truth and not being afraid of an unjust king or infidel rulers."[83] Just as he had told the al-Sauds, when the arrests began, "be cheerfully advised of a war with God," bin Laden now told bin Baz and his colleagues that their credibility was gone.[84] "We cannot excuse the scholars and other influential people of this standing," he wrote, "who could have assisted and defended the victims of injustice with a statement of truth about them."[85] Official scholars should henceforth be deemed as much "a stranger to our religion" as the al-Sauds, because "there is still no obedience to a creature who is in disobedience to the Creator."[86]

Having denounced the al-Sauds for their handling of the economy, national defense, and social services, as well as for arresting "true scholars" and turning official scholars into deceiving civil servants,[87] bin Laden turned his vitriol on Riyadh's foreign policy and the scholars who supported it, especially Shaykh bin Baz. "The most significant characteristic of your regime's foreign policy," he told King Fahd in August, 1995, "is that it is tied to the interests of the Western and Crusader nations and to those Muslim countries governed by tyrants. Proving this does not require too much effort."[88] In a series of messages, bin Laden savaged Riyadh's anti-Islamic external policy on several fronts.

Yemen

It was in Yemen, bin Laden wrote, that the al-Sauds began "a habit of supporting the enemies of Islam." The Yemeni people led by their ulema sought to overthrow the Yemeni Socialist Party, which "had enslaved the Yemeni people . . . killed innocent ulema . . . [and] spread apostasy and corruption." Shockingly, bin Laden wrote, the al-Sauds—especially King Fahd and Prince Sultan—supported Yemen's socialists against the Muslims, and exactly as they had in the Kingdom, Riyadh and its official scholars tried to ensure that the Yemeni socialists "shackled the Islamic Awakening in Yemen."[89]

United Nations

The ARC communiqués paid limited attention to the UN, but they did define the main theme bin Laden and al-Qaeda would later use toward the organization. "The UN," bin Laden explained, was little more than "a tool to implement the Crusaders' plans to kill the causes of the nation of Islam and its peoples." Though this was obvious to Muslims, the Saudi regime still cooperated with UN initiatives in Palestine and, worse, abided by UN plans in the Balkans which allowed Bosnian Muslims to be "surrendered to the Serbian monster," showing that the human rights and equality slogans the West raised through the UN "are nothing but dead slogans when it comes to Muslim matters." In supporting the UN, the ARC concluded, the al-Saud regime was "no different from the secular governments that publicly war on Islam . . . [and] secularism amounts to atheism."[90]

United States

"In reality," bin Laden told King Fahd, "Saudi Arabia is no more than an American protectorate subject to American laws."[91] After the U.S. and Western militaries arrived in the Kingdom in 1990, he wrote, Riyadh had "filled it with American army bases," even while "America and its allies steal and loot from the wealth and riches of the country."[92] And, speaking of those forces, bin Laden asked the king, "don't we [Saudis] have a right to ask about the reason they have stayed so long?"[93] Bin Laden argued that Fahd, his ministers, and their scholars had permitted infidels to enter on the basis of an "arbitrary" fatwa which "insulted the honor of the ummah."[94] As a result of the decision, Riyadh had become Washington's dependable surrogate: "If Islamic causes conflict with Western interests you have always stood up for Western interests" in such places as Palestine, Somalia, Algeria, Yemen, and Sudan. "Western and Crusader countries dictate your policies from the outside," bin Laden claimed, and you respond "by protecting the interests of the infidel Western countries that encounter these Islamic causes." If this was not the case, bin Laden asked, why was it that Riyadh and its scholars had pushed young Saudis to go and fight communists in Afghanistan, but stopped them from doing the same in Yemen? The answer, he said, was the United States wanted Soviet and Afghan communists killed, but preferred the stability provided by the Marxist regime in Yemen.[95] This foreign policy shattered the al-Sauds' Islamic credibility, bin Laden concluded.[96]

Palestine

With regard to this "mother of all Islamic issues,"[97] the Saudi royal family and their scholars traitorously approved opening relations with the Zionists who were "usurping sacred Muslim land that God blessed."[98] Bin Laden condemned Shaykh bin Baz for his fatwa permitting peace with the Jews, claiming it gave "a veneer of legitimacy to the surrender [peace with Israel] that the treacherous cowardly Arab tyrants signed."[99] Bin Baz's fatwa not only contradicted his earlier Palestine fatwas—which called for jihad until Jerusalem's recovery and "Jewish foreigners return to their country"[100]—but was "a necessary step leading to the establishment of Greater Israel, extending from the Nile to the Euphrates and through large portions of the Arab Peninsula."[101] With the fatwa, bin Laden said, bin Baz proved he was not satisfied with having surrendered Mecca and Medina to U.S. occupation in 1990, but was now eager to please "a band of occupying Zionists in Palestine" by surrendering al-Aqsa Mosque.[102] "The surrender peace with the Jews" signed by Riyadh and sanctioned by its scholars, bin Laden wrote, "inflicted harm on the ummah and defied reality." "Who among the experts," bin Laden asked, "said that more than a billion Muslims who own the largest natural resources on earth with strategic locations are unable to defeat 5 million Jews in Palestine?"[103]

In these ARC communiqués, bin Laden established that he was far from ready to give up on jihad, and, indeed, that he saw himself as fighting far more than the U.S. military's presence on the Arabian Peninsula. In fact, he had mapped out his future jihad's parameters. He had not fully sorted out which target—the Saudis, the West, or the United States—should be hit first. He had, however, focused on Washington's interference with and control over the al-Saud regime in a way suggesting that the United States was both a far *and* a near enemy, one all Muslims had an interest in evicting from their world. Moreover, bin Laden had clearly crossed his own personal Rubicon. By damning the Saudi royal family, publicly defaming and questioning the faith of King Fahd, Grand Mufti bin Baz, and other senior royals and scholars, and declaring that all of them were at war with God—and that he was taking God's side—bin Laden made it clear that his commitment to jihad was for the long haul. The communiqués also made it clear that his motivation and that of al-Qaeda at the time—as it is today—was the belief that Islam was under attack by apostates from within and from U.S.-led Crusaders and Jews from without. The only proper response was defensive jihad.

Hardening Attitudes

Lawrence Wright's work argues that during the Sudan years bin Laden was on the cusp of shelving the jihad to become simply a family man and a businessman. "Bin Laden explained that he was through with warfare. He said he was resolved to quit al-Qaeda altogether and become a farmer." Wright even added that before Friday prayers bin Laden "would sometimes speak in the main Khartoum mosque, urging his fellow Muslims to discover the blessings of peace."[104]

The ARC communiqués yield no hint of any such diminishing commitment to jihad, and bin Laden told *Al-Quds al-Arabi* in early 1994, on the eve of founding the ARC, that the West did "not accept the natural right of Muslims to defend themselves. Our [al-Qaeda's] position in Afghanistan caused some of Islam's enemies to try to obstruct our cooperation with Muslims. The world tends to prefer to overlook the oppression and persecution in Bosnia and occupied Palestine and then hasten to accuse Muslims of terrorism if they defend themselves. It wants to keep Muslims weak and unable to defend themselves. We also know that there are contacts among diplomats, all resigned to curb our movement and stop our contact with our brothers. But we say that cooperation in piety is continuing among Muslims."[105]

Wright also argues that the only thing that kept bin Laden from retiring was the continuing presence of U.S. forces on the Arabian Peninsula.[106] This, too, seems palpably false, given the evidence. In fact, his attention was focused on problems across the Islamic world, in part because "his contacts with Sudanese officials allowed him to keep his finger on the pulse of events in the region, especially the Gulf, East Africa, Egypt, and the Maghreb,"[107] and in part because of the large number of Islamic scholars from various backgrounds who visited him as his guests in Sudan or as delegates to al-Turabi's Arab Islamic People's Congress. These meetings, bin Laden told Abdel Bari Atwan, made his time there "the most important and fruitful of his life."[108] Under the NIF regime, Sudan also welcomed mujahedin who faced incarceration or execution if they returned to their countries. Islamist fighters fleeing Algeria, Libya, Egypt, Yemen, and other Muslim states found a home in Sudan, and bin Laden added to the expatriate population by bringing al-Qaeda fighters from Afghanistan and the Gulf and giving them "jobs, salaries, and homes."[109] He also strengthened al-Qaeda's corps of theological experts and advisers. In the ARC's first communiqué, bin Laden announced the arrival of Saudi "brothers and scholars" into Sudan. "They will offer knowledgeable advice and they will ban all prohibited activities."[110] Finally, after the 1995 Dayton Accords for the Balkans were concluded, bin Laden funded the relocation to Sudan of some mujahedin who had fought in Bosnia.[111]

From Khartoum, bin Laden also began taking a harder look at increasing the number of al-Qaeda attacks on U.S. interests. The ones in Yemen and Somalia had done little to remove the U.S. military from the Arabian Peninsula. Bin Laden was still driven by the hadith describing the Prophet's death-bed demand that all infidels be evicted. The U.S. presence on the Peninsula may have presented an opportunity to blur or even eliminate that aforementioned distinction between Islam's "far" and "near" enemies, the latter by historical tradition to be fought first. The journalist Ahmad Zaydan wrote that in Sudan bin Laden "deliberately focused on the [the United States as the] common and clear enemy rather than the nearest enemy." Thus, he defined a common enemy that was both near and far and by thus blurring the distinction between the two appealed to Islamist groups, like al-Zawahiri's, that wanted Islam's near enemies engaged first.[112] Al-Qaeda's late military commander Abu Hafs al-Masri told Abdel Bari Atwan that in 1994 bin Laden moved to link military and ARC political activities. "He began to concentrate on building a considerable military organization to carry out operations against U.S. military, administrative, and business targets, initially on the Arabian Peninsula."[113] Al-Masri's words are backed by the vitriolic condemnation of the United States in ARC communiqués of the period; by al-Qaeda-inspired attacks on the U.S. military in Saudi Arabia in November 1995; and by Abu Jandal's claim that bin Laden had initially intended to declare war on the United States from Sudan.[114]

Given the foregoing, one is hard pressed even to imagine bin Laden was thinking about ending his mujahedin career while in Sudan. Indeed, much closer to the mark is Mark Huband's conclusion that "bin Laden *always* intended to infiltrate the body politic of Sudan and use the country as the launching pad for jihad."[115]

Played for a Fool and Time to Go

Though but thirty-two years old on his arrival in Sudan, bin Laden had nonetheless already had experience some men do not acquire in a lifetime. He had enjoyed an enviable upbringing as the child of a billionaire who hobnobbed with royals and Islamic scholars; worked as a manual laborer; managed construction projects; married and fathered a growing family; risked his life as a combat engineer; fought, led his own forces, and been wounded; returned to his country as a hero; and, finally, alienated its government and been forced into exile. Given this, one would expect bin Laden, by 1992, to be a thoroughly toughened character, not easily fooled. And mostly he was—with the disastrous exception of a still largely unshaken faith in the altruism of Islamist scholars.

Bin Laden would be neither the first nor the last person—Muslim and non-Muslim—to be made a fool of by the leader of the regime in Sudan, Dr. Hasan al-Turabi. Educated at Kings College in London and the Sorbonne, al-Turabi was a brilliant, multilingual scholar who talked of expanding the sway of Islam through the Horn of Africa and eventually around the world. This was music to bin Laden's ears, of course, and it at least temporarily deafened him to the reality that al-Turabi was a lying, self-serving windbag who saw in bin Laden what some observers called a "mobile emergency bank."[116] Al-Turabi provided a warm welcome for bin Laden, staging "a lavish reception in his honor" at which he told attendees that bin Laden had been named a member and adviser to the NIF. Bin Laden responded with thanks and a five-million-dollar donation to the party.[117] Bin Laden's son Omar claims his father soon "became enthralled with a goal of bringing the impoverished country up to modern standards."[118] The goal was fantasy, however, and the money bin Laden donated was just the start of a fund-draining exercise al-Turabi would lead him through.

Bin Laden, as noted, pursued his own economic interests in the Sudan and simultaneously contributed heavily to al-Turabi's efforts to build a viable Islamic state. Bin Laden, a friend said, bought into the idea that Sudan could be an Islamic state, and thought "he could offer something to this state by means of his trade and construction services and his relations to the [Saudi] kingdom and the Gulf."[119] On arriving, bin Laden provided two million dollars to the NIF, to care for Afghan Arabs already living in Sudan. He then gave the regime another loan to cover emergency importation of wheat, and he later guaranteed payments for purchases of gas, helicopters, and artillery pieces. He also agreed on several occasions to buy Sudan's entire cotton crop with hard currency and recoup costs by selling it abroad. His construction outfit built major roadways—including one 350-mile highway—and, as we have seen, helped build Port Sudan's airport, for the operation of which he contributed another $2.5 million dollars. The construction done for the NIF regime was paid for with huge land grants in eastern Sudan—one consisting of a million-plus acres—where bin Laden raised livestock and grew sesame seeds, gum Arabic, and those amazing sunflowers.[120]

It seems fair to say that al-Turabi got what he wanted out of bin Laden, which was enough funding to keep the regime limping along. Bin Laden's own investments were mostly unsuccessful, and he was asked to leave the country—by al-Turabi and Sudan's President Omar al-Bashir, so they could dodge U.S. and UN sanctions—before he could determine if his enormous land holdings could turn a profit. In his rushed departure from Sudan, he lost a great deal. He sold his businesses, land, houses, and construction and agricultural machinery at fire-sale rates or simply abandoned them. There is, moreover, no evidence that his loans to al-Turabi's regime were repaid. In sum, bin Laden got well and truly clipped by al-Turabi; as Lawrence Wright has written, his assets in Sudan were "essentially stolen from him."[121] He would arrive in Afghanistan with his personal fortune greatly reduced. Later, according to Jonathan Randall, al-Turabi would mock him as a fool, saying "all Osama could say was jihad, jihad, jihad."[122]

Bin Laden did not publicly denounce al-Turabi's betrayal. "The Sudanese government at the highest level informed me of its difficult position and the scale of Saudi pressure on it," bin Laden told Abdel Bari Atwan, referring to the effect the ARC communiqués were having. "They asked me to stop issuing statements. On the day I was told to stop issuing statements I sought to find an alternative land capable of bearing the word of truth."[123] Bin Laden more or less kept his silence about Sudan, merely noting that it "has not completed the required steps of the application of Shariah" and warning al-Turabi and al-Bashir that U.S. and Saudi guarantees were worthless.[124] "The U.S. promised Sudan," bin Laden said in 1997, "that, in return for my expulsion, they would restore economic aid to Sudan . . . but Sudan's economic aid was not restored."[125] Despite it all, bin Laden maintained cordial relations with Sudanese leaders, sending a letter of condolence, for example, to President al-Bashir after the death of the Sudanese vice president in 1998. "This tragedy has come at a time," bin Laden wrote, "when the international Christian crusade is rushing madly against our country Sudan and the heart of the Muslim world."[126]

Despite his hurried departure, bin Laden had not been entirely unprepared to leave Sudan. As noted, he had left behind operating training camps in Afghanistan with al-Qaeda members managing them.[127] And while deeply frustrated with the Afghans' apparent inability to consolidate power in a post-Soviet government, he refrained from publicly criticizing any leader, pointing out to *Al-Quds al-Arabi* that he had always focused "on helping our brothers in Afghanistan since 1985, and cooperating with anyone who might "help Muslims defend themselves and their religion." "We harbor no hostility toward anyone or any Afghan groups."[128] He also never claimed that the Arab mujahedin had defeated the Soviets in Afghanistan, often saying that "credit must be given where it is due" and congratulating the leaders of the seven main Afghan insurgent groups for their "ability to raise the banner of jihad."[129] As noted, not only did he know such a claim would have been untrue, he knew with how much vitriol the Afghans would have rejected it.[130] Bin Laden's own conclusion was that "God helped me and we come to the land of Khorasan [Afghanistan] again" and that he and al-Qaeda were stronger for the move. "We are in an invincible land which enjoys security, pride, and immunity against the humiliation and subjugation which our brothers are subject in our own country."[131]

5

ORGANIZER, 1996–2001

Bin Laden returned to Afghanistan on May 18, 1996. He landed in a small jet at Jalalabad airport, and was followed in the ensuing days by his wives, children, and a number of his followers. They were all welcomed by the "old mujahedin," the Afghans with whom bin Laden had fought against the Red Army. He was met at the airport by Islamic Union Commander Saznur—who in the mid-1980s had wanted nothing to do with those Arab fighters intent on "racing to death"—and Engineer Mahmoud, a veteran Hisbi Islami-Khalis commander. Although his return had been approved by Afghan president Burhanuddin Rabbani and Prime Minister Hekmatyar, bin Laden gave most credit to Yunis Khalis for facilitating his return, because of the major Afghan leaders he alone stayed clear of post-Soviet factional fighting. "Allah blessed Shaykh Muhammad Yunis Khalis, by keeping him clear from this difference and infighting," bin Laden wrote. "The Arabs left Afghanistan during the problems of factional infighting, but Shaykh Yunis Khalis welcomed them back."[1] The warm reception of bin Laden and his followers, Abu Jandal explained, "was a kind of payback for Shaykh Usama for everything he had offered the Afghan warriors during their war against the Soviet troops."[2]

The depth of affection and respect they showed for bin Laden on his return was significant, and perhaps an early sign that no Afghan Pashtun tribesman—Taleban or not—would surrender bin Laden to his enemies. The now-jailed al-Qaeda theorist Abu Musab al-Suri, for example, was present when bin Laden arrived and has written on his reception. "I heard something incredible from Yunis Khalis . . . during a meeting," al-Suri stated. "He said to Abu Abdallah [bin Laden], in his thickly accented but proficient Arabic, 'I have nothing but myself, and it is very dear to me. However, you are more precious to me, and your well-being is more important than my own. You are our guest, and no one can get to you. If anything happens with the Taleban, tell me. Though there is little I can do after they reach you, I will do all I can.'"[3] Khalis need not have worried about the Taleban. Soon after Mullah Omar's forces occupied Jalalabad in July 1996, al-Suri reported that Taleban officials likewise pledged to protect bin Laden, though they knew him only by reputation and had not invited him to Afghanistan, and so had no obligation to him. Bin Laden was in Jalalabad when the Taleban entered the city, according to al-Suri. "And I personally witnessed a meeting [between the Taleban and Arab mujahedin]. I was a guest visiting Shaykh Abu Abdallah, 'Usama,' when some high-level Taleban figures came in, including a minister and officials. One said 'you are the Muhajarin [the early followers of the Prophet Muhammad] and we are the Ansar [those who sheltered Muhammad and his followers],' causing the eyes to well up with tears. At the very end of the meeting, the minister said, 'You are not just our guests and we your servants, rather we serve the very ground you walk on.'"[4]

Settling In

While living near Jalalabad in Nangarhar Province from May 1996 until the following May, when he moved to Kandahar, bin Laden, his family, and an assortment of al-Qaeda fighters and their families lived in several locations. They first inhabited a large guest house once used by the Soviet military in Jalalabad; then, as their numbers expanded, they moved to a compound called Hadda Farm, which was under the jurisdiction of Yunis Khalis; and, finally, to camps in the Tora Bora mountains that the mujahedin had used in the anti-Soviet jihad.[5]

Throughout this year, an Egyptian-Canadian named Ahmed Said Khadr (killed in October 2003) and his family lived near the bin Ladens. Khadr's wife, Maha, and children have said the bin Ladens were "social" within strict limits bin Laden imposed, and that in these months he behaved as "a normal human being," one who dealt well with his dual role as a family man and as al-Qaeda's chief. Khadr's second eldest son, Abdurahman, recalled that bin Laden had "issues" with his wife and kids. "Financial issues, you know." The kids wouldn't listen, or do what he wanted them to do. "So it really comes down to it—he's a father and he's a person."[6] The pictures of Osama given by Maha, Abdurrahman, and Zaynab Khadr mesh well with others of him as a youth, during his first tour in Afghanistan, and in Sudan. As Abdurrahman has said, "it was very important for [bin Laden] to sit with his kids every day at least for two hours after their Islamic prayer. They sat and read a book. It didn't have to be something religious. He loved poetry very much. So he tried to encourage them to read, memorize, and write poetry. So every once in a while it would be a different book, sometimes poetry, sometimes history or sometimes it's about grammar, language, sometimes a religious book. . . . Yeah he [also] loved volleyball and loved horse riding. And he'd do it. I mean among the people he was not Osama bin Laden. He was just Osama—and kids played around him. Kids would go shake his hand. He played volleyball with them or just horse raced with them. He was just a person."[7]

Bin Laden's ascetic side, however, was never absent. "He was against using ice and he actually forbade it to the people that lived around him," Abdurrahman claimed, adding that he also forbade them from using electricity for fear that they would get spoiled, "even though he knew they needed it." Bin Laden kept cows and horses and wanted his family and followers to be prepared, so "they'd be able to survive." For bin Laden, Abdurrahman says, the important thing was the "cause," not himself or his family or where they lived; he quotes bin Laden as saying, "I can live anywhere, I'll live anywhere."[8] The Khadr family's bottom line was expressed by Abdurrahman's brother Abdullah, who said that bin Laden was "something like a saint." "I see him as a very peaceful man."[9]

In May 1997, Mullah Omar invited him to reside in the Taleban capital, Kandahar. Bin Laden accepted and moved his family and some of his lieutenants and fighters; he ordered others, including the Khadrs, to stay in Jalalabad and Kabul.[10] In Kandahar, he began a more peripatetic life. He now had al-Qaeda members in three major Afghan cities, as well as training facilities in Khowst, Kandahar, Helmand, and Nangarhar provinces.[11] He participated not only in personnel and organizational matters, but—as in Sudan—spent time with ordinary Afghans, offering prayers with Mullah Omar at a mosque in Kandahar, for example, and visiting wounded Taleban and al-Qaeda fighters recovering in Kabul's hospitals.[12] This travel was not curtailed after Washington replied to al-Qaeda's attacks on two U.S. embassies in East Africa with a cruise missile attack on mujahedin training camps at Khowst on August 20, 1998, though the security detail accompanying him did get larger.[13] Some things did not change with the move to Kandahar, however. On arriving, bin Laden's bodyguard Abu Jandal noted, "Mullah Omar gave him [Osama] the choice either to stay at the Electricity Company housing complex, where there are all the services, or to stay at the Qandahar Airport housing complex, which did not have such utilities. He selected the airport complex because he wanted his followers to live an austere and modest life in this world. There were no utilities in the complex and there was no running water. Shaykh Usama bin Laden used to say: 'We want a simple life.'"[14]

Bin Laden also was married for the fifth time on July 25, 2000, to an eighteen-year-old Yemeni woman named Amal al-Sadab.[15] The marriage was arranged between Osama bin Laden and the woman's family. Abu Jandal delivered funds for the dowry, to cover the cost of the wedding, and travel money—a total of $5,000—to the bride's family in Yemen.[16] A few weeks after the wedding, bin Laden told an interviewer Afghanistan was a good place to raise his family. "It is my desire," he said, "that my children grow up in an atmosphere of jihad and absorb Islam in its true spirit. Believe me, when your children and your wife become part of your struggle, life becomes very enjoyable."[17]

More than in Sudan, however, bin Laden was the target of assassination attempts in Afghanistan. During the year he lived near Jalalabad, he was subjected to several clumsy attacks, which have been attributed to the Saudi intelligence service. It was after one of these attempts that Mullah Omar invited bin Laden to move to Khandahar, where the Taleban could better protect them.

The change in venue did not, however, stop the attempts on bin Laden's life. Just after the American air strike on Khowst in August 1998, according to the Pakistani journalist Rahimullah Yusufzai, "three men financed by the Saudi government" were arrested by the Taleban before they could attack bin Laden.[18] From his talks with bin Laden and al-Zawahiri, Yusufzai learned that the team's leader was a man named Siddiq Ahmed, a member of a Turkestani family that had immigrated to Saudi Arabia. Ahmed's family had not been granted citizenship, and Saudi intelligence offered him that status, and a million riyals, if he would kill bin Laden. Bin Laden told Yusufzai that Siddiq confessed that the attempt was ordered by Saudi Prince Salman bin Abdula Aziz, Riyadh's governor and King Fahd's brother.[19] Then, in October 1998, using data from al-Qaeda intelligence officers, Taleban security apprehended a Saudi and three Pakistanis who were plotting to kill "the wealthy Saudi national Osama bin Ladin." The Taleban executed the Saudi; it is not clear what happened to the Pakistanis.[20] And in July 1999, yet another plot was foiled when Taleban security arrested four men wearing Taleban security uniforms as they tried to drive a jeep through a checkpoint into Kandahar city. The Taleban found explosives and weapons in the vehicle, and said the would-be assassins were Tajiks who confessed to being members of Massoud's forces and to having a network of informers in the city.[21] Finally, the Palestinian journalist Jamal Abd-al-Latif Ismail clearly inferred that in 1999—after his late-1998 interview of bin Laden in Kandahar—the Saudi intelligence service had tried to bribe him to carry a small signaling device and to switch it on before his next session with bin Laden. Ismail turned the Saudis down, telling them he had no wish to be killed with the al-Qaeda chief, and moreover did not want his children to remember "their father as a low and despicable person" who helped kill bin Laden.[22]

Another set of failed assassination attempts on bin Laden were conducted by a group of takfiris, the same sect that had tried to kill bin Laden and his son Abdallah in Khartoum. In March 1999, the group's leaders met in Peshawar to discuss bin Laden and afterward issued a fatwa "calling for the death of the infidel," and then "launched a campaign" to kill bin Laden and other al-Qaeda members, according to an article in the *Sunday Times*.[23] They "declared Usama bin Ladin a non-Muslim and an agent of the United States, adding that he was staying in Afghanistan to further 'his master's interests.'"[24] Pakistani police officials claimed that the takfiris attacked bin Laden at least three times, and that there were other shootouts between takfiris and al-Qaeda fighters.[25] Although the attacks failed, they reflected takfiri hatred for bin Laden, notwithstanding some Western experts who have branded bin Laden, al-Qaeda, and—at times—the Taleban as takfiris.

Finally, bin Laden's second Afghan sojourn saw the West—especially its governments, media, and intelligence services—develop an obsession with his health. Hoping bin Laden would die so they could avoid risky military operations against the man who twice declared war on them, Westerners conjured various ailments—from kidney disease to Marfan's syndrome—from which he was dying. Kidney disease was the particular favorite. Stories had him sneaking into a Pakistani military hospital in Rawalpindi or an American one in Dubai for dialysis, or having portable dialysis machines brought into his stronghold in the Afghan mountains to keep himself alive. There is no evidence for any of these claims, and bin Laden himself said, "I am in very good health, thank God."[26] This judgment was backed by others. Omar bin Laden claimed that "grueling treks" through Afghan mountains "seemed the most pleasant of outings to our father." Abu Jandal recalled that bin Laden had "an iron constitution." "Before 9/11 he exercised a lot. In the morning, he would read and study, and in the afternoon, if he did not have anything else to do, he would engage in sports: shooting his AK-47, horseback riding, playing volleyball. With his height, close to the net he was unbeatable. He could ride his horse 70 kilometers [35 miles] without the slightest problem. He fell only once, in 2000, and broke a couple of ribs. Every Friday he organized soccer matches, and obviously his position was that of center forward."[27]

Declaring War

Bin Laden's August 23, 1996, declaration of war on the United States was published in the London-based *Al-Quds al-Arabi* and, to ensure wide distribution in Saudi Arabia, on the UK-based Saudi dissident Web site *Al-Islah* on September 2.[28] The statement marked a sharp shift in his assessment of why Islam's main enemies had proven so hard to defeat. In the 1994–1996 ARC communiqués discussed earlier, bin Laden's main focus had been on reforming or defeating the corruption, misrule, and un-Islamic behavior—especially in matters relating to foreign policy—of the Saudi royal family. To be sure, bin Laden used the communiqués to indict Riyadh's kowtowing to the United States and following Washington's orders, but his main target clearly was the Saudi regime. The August declaration, however, showed that bin Laden had rethought his position. While he still regarded the Saudi regime as corrupt and un-Islamic and used much of the declaration to outline the king's misrule, he concluded that the al-Sauds and Islam's other major enemies—Israel and the tyrannical governments in Egypt, Algeria, Jordan, and so on—were capable of oppressing Muslims because of the monetary, military, and political support they received from the United States. By shifting attention to the United States, bin Laden implemented an idea he had broached a year earlier: that al-Qaeda's focus in the Kingdom should be on the American occupiers, "the sponsor not the sponsored"; the al-Sauds, after all, were merely the "shadow of the U.S. presence."[29] The details of the 1996 declaration have been amply examined,[30] but the gist of it was well captured in bin Laden's rather homespun explanation to his son of why it was wisest to identify and then attack the enemy's weakest link. Although he was talking here about giving priority to attacks on the United States before Israel, his rationale was the same for attacking America before going after the Muslim tyrannies. Omar bin Laden had asked why not attack Israel before America, given that Israel was a "small country near to us," while America was a "huge country far away from our shores."

> My father paused before explaining it this way. "Omar, try to imagine a two-wheeled bicycle. One wheel is made of steel. The other wheel is made of wood. Now, my son, if you wanted to destroy the bicycle, would you destroy the wooded or the steel wheel?"
>
> "The wooden wheel of course," I replied.
>
> "You are correct my son. Remember this: America and Israel are one bicycle with two wheels. The wooden wheel

represents the United States. The steel wheel represents Israel. Omar, Israel is the stronger power of the two. Does a general attack the strongest line when in battle? No, he concentrates on the weakest part of the line. The Americans are weak. It is best to attack the weakest point first. Once we take out the weak wooden wheel, the steel wheel will automatically fail. Who can ride a bicycle with only one wheel?"

He patted my knee with his hand. "First we obliterate America. By that I don't mean militarily. We can destroy America from within by making it economically weak, until its markets collapse. When that happens, they will have no interest in supplying Israel with arms, for they will not have extra funds to do so. At that time, the steel wheel will corrode and be destroyed by lack of attention.

"That's what we [Muslims] did to the Russians. We bled blood from their body in Afghanistan. The Russians spent all of their wealth on the war in Afghanistan. When they could no longer finance the war, they fled. After fleeing their whole system collapsed. Holy Warriors defending Afghanistan are the ones responsible for bringing a huge nation to its knees. We can do the same thing with America and Israel. We only have to be patient."[31]

And so the United States would henceforth be al-Qaeda's fixed objective, with bin Laden arguing that the victory God promised Muslims could be achieved if they pursued three war aims: (a) drive the United States from as much of the Muslim world as possible; (b) destroy Israel and the oppressive Muslim tyrannies; and (c) settle accounts with the heretical Shia. Bin Laden insisted, moreover, that the three goals be pursued seriatim and not in parallel, for reasons more fully explored in chapter 6. This strategy was clearly laid out in the twelve-page declaration—which some Westerners claim to find turgid—and from the day of its issue to today, no one, whether in the United States, the West, or the Muslim world, can justifiably profess doubt that U.S. policies motivated bin Laden, and have inspired other Muslims to support that struggle by picking up arms, donating funds, or offering prayers. An anti-U.S. defensive jihad was mandatory for six reasons:

1. The U.S. military and civilian presence in the Prophet's homeland on the Arabian Peninsula
2. Washington's protection and support for tyrannical Muslim governments
3. Washington's unquestioning and unqualified support for Israel
4. Washington's support for countries that oppress Muslims, especially Russia, China, and India
5. U.S. and Western exploitation of Muslim energy resources at below-market prices
6. The U.S. military presence in the Muslim world outside the Arab Peninsula[illegible]

Bin Laden would sharpen and refine these points in future public statements, but they would otherwise remain unchanged. They would, moreover, gradually be adopted as casus belli by Islamist groups from Nigeria to Pakistan to the Pacific, as well as among individuals and groups in the Sunni Muslim diasporas in Europe and North America. Bin Laden supplanted in a swoop the appeals by Muslim leaders for an anti-U.S. jihad based on America's "debauched and degenerate" lifestyle. To be sure, bin Laden and his followers deemed the West degenerate and debauched; no country they governed would look like Canada. But the Islamists had witnessed two decades of failure by Iran's leaders to ignite a jihad against Western decadence. The reality was that as long as the West did not try to impose its decadence—for which many Muslims considered "democracy" a synonym—in the Islamic world, Muslims would live and let live; few were or are willing to die in a jihad against congressional elections, gender equality, R-rated movies, or Budweiser. Cultural-political considerations were not part of bin Laden's jihadist rhetoric; indeed, only others—particularly U.S. and Western political, military, and media leaders—have tried to persuade people that al-Qaeda and its allies are motivated by such factors. This is the main reason the West is losing to the Islamists.

Bin Laden's declaration of war was followed eighteen months later by a fatwa ordering and authorizing "jihad against the Crusaders and Jews" and announcing the creation of the "World Islamic Front against Crusaders and Jews," an organization composed of al-Qaeda, al-Zawahiri's EIJ, and four other Islamist groups. Unlike the declaration of war, the February 23, 1998, fatwa was signed by several fully credentialed Islamic scholars, thus giving it religious authority. In addition, assemblies of Islamic scholars in Afghanistan and Pakistan gave the fatwa "confirmation and authorization" shortly after its publication.[33] This authorization may be the document's central importance, one long ignored in the West. While the evidence at hand suggests that the World Front never gelled as an organization, the fatwa gave the call for defensive jihad theological gravitas.[34] Henceforth, other Islamic scholars could denigrate the document and issue counter-fatwas, but the result has simply been an unending debate about whose fatwa was bigger, a debate that has not repealed the World Front's mandate. The core of the 1998 fatwa read, "The ruling to kill the Americans and their allies—civilians and military—is an individual duty for every Muslim who can do it in any country in which it is possible to do it, in order to liberate the al-Aqsa Mosque and the holy mosque [in Mecca] from their grip, and in order for their armies to move out of the lands of Islam, defeated and unable to threaten any Muslim. . . . We—with God's help—call on every Muslim who believes in God and wishes to be rewarded to comply with God's order to kill Americans and plunder their money whenever they find it."[35]

This, then, gave the necessary religious grounding to bin Laden's defensive jihad—making it an "individual duty for every Muslim"—and permitting the targeting of U.S. civilian as well as military personnel in Saudi Arabia and around the world. The fatwa was both theologically valid, bin Laden argued, and commonsensical. "If the Israelis are killing the small children in Palestine and Americans are killing innocent people in Iraq [via sanctions], and if a majority of the American people support their dissolute president [Clinton]," he explained, "this means the American people are fighting us and we have the right to target them."[36] The fatwa's call for "plundering" U.S. money would eventually give priority to attacks meant to damage the U.S. economy.

After the fatwa's publication, bin Laden argued assiduously for a defensive jihad based on the principle of reciprocity that went to the core of Islamic war-making and the West's idea of just war. A human life is a human life, he said, and the lives of Muslims and all other people were of equal worth and equally worth defending. "There are two sides in this conflict," bin Laden said in late 1998:

> world crusaders allied to Jewish Zionists [and] led by the United States, Britain, and Israel, and on the other side the Islamic world. In such a conflict, it is unacceptable for the first side to launch an aggression, enter my land, property, and sanctities, and plunder the Muslims' oil, and then say the Muslims are terrorists when it faces any resistance from them. This is stupid, or they think others are stupid. We think it is our Shariah duty to resist occupation with all our strength and punish it by the same means it uses against us.[37]

> The killing of innocent civilians, as Americans and some intellectuals claim, is really very strange talk. Who said our children and civilians are not innocent, and that shedding their blood is justified? That it is lesser in degree? When we kill their innocents, the entire world from west to east screams at us, and America rallies its allies and agents, and the sons of its agents. Who said our blood is not blood, but theirs is? Who made this pronouncement? Who has been getting killed in our countries for decades? More than one million children, more than one million children have died in Iraq and others are dying [due to sanctions]. Why do we not hear someone screaming or condemning, or even someone's words of consolation or condolence?[38]

Polemicist

As we have seen, bin Laden was heavily involved in producing Shaykh Azzam's magazine *al-Jihad* in the 1980s, and in 1994 created the ARC to issue communiqués to oppose the al-Sauds and support reformist Saudi scholars. Only after returning to Afghanistan, however, did he launch a dedicated effort to build an al-Qaeda media arm, one whose coverage and sophistication would prove mostly impervious to the countermedia capabilities of the West and Arab regimes. As Bruce B. Williams has said, bin Laden and al-Qaeda "adroitly mastered" the wireless communication techniques of the Information Age, crafting "a series of carefully staged statements designed for the new media."[39]

Bin Laden's intensive, and thoroughly up-to-date, use of media-related technology was nonetheless primarily based on lessons he drew from Muhammad's sunnah and the behavior of Muslim heroes, such as Saladin and Shakyh Azzam. All three recognized that victory could never be won without exploiting contemporary media to inform, instruct, shame, warn, incite, and propagandize. When Abu Musa al-Suri and al-Zawahiri condemned bin Laden as an egotistical media hound—as noted above—they merely showed that bin Laden had more closely read and better absorbed Islamic history. Like Thomas Paine, bin Laden used polemics to denigrate and bait the enemy, while bracing compatriots for the long, hard struggle ahead.

Luring America

Afghanistan was far better than Sudan as a place from which to run a war against the United States. Sudan's terrain, first of all, was more easily covered by U.S. satellites than was Afghanistan's maddening mix of deserts, mountains, higher mountains, and even higher mountains. Sudan also suffered from a surplus of hostile neighbors—opposed to al-Turabi's regime and bin Laden—and foreign espionage services are always at work there. Finally, Sudan's security and military services are capable of controlling domestic foes and any foreign Islamists settled in Khartoum. This, of course, was not the case with the Taleban any time before 9/11. While it is clear that bin Laden would not have chosen to leave Sudan until forced to in May 1996, it is likely that he would have eventually done so for a better fighting position from which to launch major anti-U.S. attacks.

Between 1996 and 2001, bin Laden would attack U.S. interests at home and abroad on three occasions. "He [bin Laden] would always say that we must hit America on a front it never expects," recalled Abu Jandal. "He kept saying that he wanted to fight America on a battlefield it cannot control."[40] These recollections mesh with bin Laden's own rhetoric, which he designed to complement al-Qaeda's military efforts to lure America into a fight on Muslim territory. "I am told," he said in early 1997, "that if I desist from voicing my protests against [Saudi King] Fahd and the U.S., I will be pardoned. I do not ask for the mercy of America. If America has the courage, it should come here and arrest me."[41] Abdel Bari Atwan also made this point, maintaining that bin Laden told him in late 1996 that he was trying to "bring the U.S. to fight on Muslim soil."[42]

Why was bin Laden so eager to lure U.S. forces into Muslim lands? As Michael Vlahos writes, "America was a means to an end for al-Qaeda," and to exploit it bin Laden needed it close to hand for several reasons.[43] First, the historical resonance of an infidel invader on Muslim land would be profound in the Islamic world, stimulating recruitment and funding among extremist, moderate, and nominal Muslims. Second, U.S. personnel would be easier to kill in the Afghan barrens than in North America, and a steady flow of casualties, bin Laden believed, would spur political dissent in the United States, break Washington's will to fight, and result in American withdrawal, as had happened in Lebanon (1983) and Somalia (1994). Third, al-Qaeda's strategy was to drive America as far as possible from the Muslim world before progressing to phases two and three: destroying Israel and the Arab regimes, and dealing with the Shia. Fourth, bin Laden was aware that al-Qaeda could not defeat the United States unless it helped create a scenario in which much of the Muslim world joined or sympathized with an anti-U.S. jihad. Manpower, financial, and logistical limits required drawing the United States into "a confrontation with all the Islamic peoples," as bin Laden put it before 9/11. "We are working for a big operation," one that will "drag the United States into a large-scale front which it cannot control.[44] Luring U.S. forces to Afghanistan, therefore, was the way to start al-Qaeda's strategic ball rolling. According to Vlahos, it was al-Qaeda's "vehicle for advancing history" toward restoring the Islamic order envisioned by bin Laden and other Salafis, and the first lures were cast in Kenya, Tanzania, and Yemen.[45]

East Africa

The August 7, 1998, bombings of U.S. embassies in Kenya and Tanzania—bin Laden called them the "two mighty smashes"—were the first major effort to lure Washington into sending forces to Afghanistan.[46] A year earlier, bin Laden had begun the campaign by ridiculing U.S.

attempts to capture him, saying that the Americans were "cowards and cannot confront me. If they even think of confronting me, I will teach them a lesson similar to the lesson they were taught in Somalia a few years ago."[47] And seven weeks before the bombings, he again taunted Washington's impotence, arguing that "if God protected me from dying at the hands of the Russians, I will certainly not die at the hands of the Americans."[48] The August attacks, however, came and went, earning only an ineffective barrage of Cruise missiles fired at al-Qaeda's Afghan training camps and a pharmaceutical plant in Khartoum. A year after, bin Laden was still goading Washington. He marked the anniversary by claiming the 1998 U.S. air strikes "rang the bell of war with Muslims" and that he had "no fear" of waging war against cowardly Americans.[49]

USS *Cole*

After al-Qaeda bombed the USS *Cole* in Aden's harbor on October 12, 2000, bin Laden told Ahmad Zaydan, "I knelt to thank God for this heroic operation that damaged the prestige of the United States and served as a warning for them to leave the Arab world and the [Arabian] peninsula according to the Prophet's hadith."[50] A month later he sent a messenger—Mullah Omar had banned him from speaking face-to-face to the media—to the Pakistani journalist Rahimullah Yusufzai, who said bin Laden "endorsed the action of those who bombed the U.S. warship in the Yemeni port of Aden."[51] Bin Laden also told Zaydan that he and his lieutenants hoped the Aden strike would draw U.S. forces to Afghanistan, but expected an American air strike on al-Qaeda interests there. He said they anticipated a more powerful and prolonged U.S. response than after the 1998 bombings and thought that would occur in January 2001. During the interview, Zaydan saw al-Qaeda members and families in Kandahar "moving their belongings from one house to another" in anticipation of the air strike that never came.[52] Bin Laden even sent al-Zawahiri to Kabul and Abu-Hafs al-Masri elsewhere to ensure al-Qaeda's leadership stayed functional were he killed.[53] At day's end, this lure also failed, but al-Qaeda did not suffer the damage it had expected the attack to cost its Afghan infrastructure, and, as former al-Qaeda theorist Hashim al-Makki has said, the stunning attack on the *Cole* greatly increased the flow of volunteers and funding to al-Qaeda from across the Muslim world.[54]

Shaping Jihad's Battle Space

While unleashing military and rhetorical anti-U.S. attacks, bin Laden conducted a media campaign—following the American model of "shaping the battle space"—in South Asia, one designed to build durable support for al-Qaeda's presence. His specific targets were the Taleban; the Afghan and Pakistani peoples; Pakistan's army; Kashmiri insurgents; student groups; and the Afghan and Pakistani ulema. Until 9/11, al-Qaeda's media operators seized every possible chance to address these audiences. For example, when Mullah Omar and his lieutenants refused the demands of Bill Richardson, America's ambassador to the U.N., in 1998—demands focused on human rights, especially women's rights, and the cessation of opium production—bin Laden praised the Taleban's decision, saying Richardson had come to "thwart the Islamic state project in Afghanistan." Citing the refusal as proving the Taleban's "adherence to its principles, and decision not to bargain over these principles," bin Laden said Mullah Omar spoke for the proud Afghan people, "who have given millions of martyrs in order to establish their Islamic state [and] will not relinquish this goal or sell it at any price."[55] No U.S.-led effort would succeed against the Taleban, bin Laden said in mid-2000, using words that by 2011 would be painfully haunting to Western ears.

> The United States and the United Nations have already imposed sanctions on Afghanistan. The have enclosed Afghanistan's borders as much as they could. The have put restrictions on the types of imports by Afghanistan. They have attempted to incite unrest, civil war, and bloodshed over here. What else do they want to try? They may try anything. The target is not Usama, as there are thousands of Usamas in the world. Their real target is to eliminate the Islamic identity of Afghanistan. The United States should understand that

> Afghanistan cannot be intimidated. In the last century, two of the world's superpowers faced defeat here; first the British Empire and then [the] Soviet Union. Countries that do not take a lesson from history face destruction. Afghanistan is a land of self-respecting Muslims. It cannot be pressured, allured, or intimidated into submission. Personally, I am extremely grateful to the people of Afghanistan and the Taleban that they have allowed me to live here despite facing difficulties. They have entertained me as a guest and taken care of me. It is true that only Afghans could take this burden. God has blessed them with power and ability.[56]

Al-Qaeda's media voiced support for those who opposed or were condemned by the United States. When Washington put the Taleban on its list of state sponsors of terrorism, for example, bin Laden told the media Mullah Omar should be congratulated for showing the world Afghans would not bend to the United States, while mocking U.S. officials for failing to see that the action inferred the Taleban was a legitimate government regime despite Washington's refusal to recognize it.[57] He also stressed what he described as the Islamophobic nature of anti-Taleban sanctions. The UN sanctions on the Taleban, bin Laden told Muslims, were imposed because Washington controls the UN.[58] Bin Laden defended the Kashmiri insurgent group Harakat al-Unsar when it was put on the U.S. list of terrorist groups, offering al-Qaeda's full support and appealing "to the Muslim world to provide assistance to the Kashmiri fighters." Harakat was a mujahid organization that "played a commendable role in Afghanistan and in Kashmir, also it's playing [an] important role in Islamic jihad."[59]

Al-Qaeda's media paid particularly close attention to supporting and cultivating religious fervor in Pakistan. In September 1998, for example, bin Laden sent a communiqué to the convention of the "Organization of Arabic Students in the Sindh," which was being held to condemn U.S. Cruise missile attacks on Afghanistan and Sudan. Praising the Arabic students for meeting, he urged them to follow the "youths of the Islamic Republic of Pakistan" who were "taking part in the Islamic jihad in Afghanistan, Kashmir, and other places in the world."[60] In all statements to Pakistani audiences, bin Laden stressed that the "Pakistani people have great love for Islam and they always have offered sacrifices for the cause of religion."[61]

In general, bin Laden seized upon every opportunity to align al-Qaeda with Pakistan and its army vis-à-vis the Kashmir issue and the overall threat from India. "Whatever Pakistan does in the matter of Kashmir we support it," bin Laden announced in 2000.[62] While the West was siding with India in ignoring "the dishonoring of thousands of Kashmiri Muslim women by India's security forces," Pakistan supported those seeking to avenge these women.[63] Pakistan's position had to be supported by all religious scholars, who should "shun differences and unite until the oppressed people of Kashmir are free from the Indian occupation and atrocities with the help of God."[64] Claiming Pakistan to be "the heart of the Muslim world and jihad is its heartbeat," he saluted its army and urged its generals "to strengthen their nuclear power and demonstrate it with full strength."[65] The Islamic world must support Pakistan and its army, Bin Laden said, because of the alliance between India and Israel and because "India's animosity toward Islam and Muslims is increasing with the passage of time."[66] Noting that al-Qaeda's fighters could "create problems" not only on the borders or in Kashmir but within India itself, bin Laden reminded his readers that it was "the duty of all Muslims to carry out jihad against India."[67]

Afghan and Pakistani Islamist scholars were among the last but not the least of the audiences targeted by al-Qaeda media. In Kandahar, bin Laden welcomed individual scholars or clerical delegations from Afghanistan and abroad, and likewise asked to meet Afghan scholars as he traveled the country. He also sought, received, and publicly praised scholarly support for his positions. In May 1998, for example, the "Ulema Union of Afghanistan" issued a fatwa demanding withdrawal of U.S. forces from the Arabian Peninsula. The Union said the forces were "spreading apostasy among the young people" and that their presence "violated the Koranic verses, the Prophet's hadith, and the views of the ummah's ulema." Bin Laden thanked the Afghan ulema and praised their "great fatwa" for proving "with irrefutable evidence that it is impermissible for these forces to enter these countries" and that there is "a necessity to expel them from there."[68] He emphasized that the Afghan ulema cited the authoritative hadith of the Prophet's demand "to expel the infidels from the Peninsula." The responsibility for acting upon the hadith lay with the "entire nation of Islam" and not just the peninsula's people.[69] In 1999, he sent a message to a Peshawar conclave of Sunni Deobandi scholars from Pakistan, India, the Gulf, and the Far East, congratulating them for publishing a statement condemning the United States on the first anniversary of its August 1998 strike on Khowst.[70]

Al-Qaeda media activities operated at three levels: the local audience, the Muslim world audience, and the Western and other non-Muslim audience, often addressing all three in one message. Each of the statements discussed had an international angle—terrorism, U.S. policy toward Muslims, India's aggression, and so on—but their main audiences were Afghans and Pakistanis, and they were meant to build a local constituency to stand by al-Qaeda if it succeeded in luring Washington into a military invasion of Afghanistan. It is hard to estimate the media's impact, but two things are clear: bin Laden believed it was a key element of al-Qaeda's jihad, and it stood him in good stead with the Afghan and Pakistani ulema after the 9/11 attacks.

Discrediting the King's Scholars

The most dramatic shift in bin Laden's thinking before his death involved the deterioration of his reverence for Islamic scholars, a deterioration that started during the 1990–1991 Gulf War, increased in Sudan, and then accelerated in Afghanistan. The change was manifested in increasingly vitriolic rhetorical attacks on those he referred to as "king's scholars," the Islamic scholars and jurists employed by Arab rulers to deliver religious justifications for anything they wanted to do.

As we have seen, bin Laden's disillusion with leading Saudi scholars first became public in the ARC's communiqués. As time passed, his disdain for the official scholars of the Arab regimes' grew more acerbic. He said it should not be up to him to declare a defensive jihad. "I am a humble and weak Muslim," he wrote from Kandahar, in a high dudgeon, and "giving the call to holy war is not my responsibility but it is the responsibility of the real leaders of the Muslim world, the religious leaders, and they understand their responsibility well, when and what they have to do."[71] But they had not done so, bin Laden said, and Muslims were beginning to recognize that this failure had hurt them as much as "the most ardent enemies of the nation."[72]

In particular, bin Laden emphasized, Muslims around the world were starting to see the American presence in Saudi Arabia was not "temporary." The al-Saud family's treason in this regard was bad enough, bin Laden said, but "what is worse is that this is what is being done by the [royal] court's ulema who have aggrandized themselves with the sultan's money, who have become arrogant with the sultan's status, and who sought the protection of the sultan's oppression, and have thus proceeded to trade the hereafter for the world of others and have written fatwas that permit what Allah has proscribed in order to entrench the infidels in the Arabian Peninsula. They have agreed with falsehood to defeat what is right."[73]

Living with and Assisting the Taleban

Simply having bin Laden agree to live under Mullah Omar's authority and protection increased the Taleban regime's standing in the Muslim world. Indeed, it is fair to argue that the decision to host bin Laden put the Taleban on the Islamic world's radar and led to the Taleban leaders' first glimmer of recognition that there might be a role for them beyond local Afghan affairs. Bin Laden is a "great Mujahid," editorialized the Pakistani paper *Jang* in late 1998, and "by sheltering and protecting" him the Taleban government had done "great work."[74] A Jordan-based Salafi scholar, Dr. Ibrahim Zayd al-Kilani, praised the Taleban's "strong and sincere" stance in the same way, but added a pointed warning: "We say the judgment of the Shariah is as follows: 'Whoever delivers the mujahid leader, Usamah bin Ladin, to God's enemies shall be considered a non-Muslim and supporter of U.S. policy in striking God's religion.'"[75] And one of the best analysts of Islamism, the Egyptian lawyer Muntasir al-Zayyat, wrote in July 1999 that there would be high political costs to the Taleban if it abandoned bin Laden, for by so doing it would "lose its unique character of commitment to Shariah and the protection of Islamic movements' leaders."[76]

Besides taking pride in their rising status among Muslims for sheltering "the great Arab mujahid," Mullah Omar and his lieutenants, as

Pashtun tribesmen, were bound by the code of Pashtunwali and thus, as the journalist Rahimullah Yusufzai argued, could not conceive of betraying anyone who had "taken refuge with them and sought their protection."[77] Al-Qaeda saw things the same way. Abu Musab al-Suri wrote, for example, "the Taleban have until now fulfilled the duty of the neighbor toward him who seeks refuge. They have fulfilled the duty of the Ansar toward the Muhajarin, and they have been the best of neighbors."[78] Well before 2001, therefore, there were two powerful reasons—Islamic obligations and Pashtun tribal mores—to believe the Taleban would choose war with the United States over surrendering bin Laden.

In more measurable terms, bin Laden substantially aided the Taleban. In the 1996–1997 period, he lent Mullah Omar veteran al-Qaeda insurgents who provided a leaven of combat experience and leadership to undertrained Taleban units. He also supplied funding for the Taleban's successful bribing of some of Massoud's commanders around Kabul to either switch sides or stand down as the Taleban moved toward the city. Further, bin Laden persuaded Jalaluddin Haqqani, Yunis Khalis's most senior and powerful commander, to send veteran fighters to join the Taleban's Kabul campaign. After the capital fell, moreover, to help the "student militia" (Taleban means "students") in the north, where they had "recently suffered some major military setbacks," he formed a unit of al-Qaeda mujahedin. The unit saw heavy fighting against Massoud's Northern Alliance in the northern provinces as the latter sought to regain lost territory. Bin Laden also tried, through intermediaries, to bridge differences between Mullah Omar and Abdul Rasul Sayyaf and Gulbuddin Hekmatyar and to bring the latter two men and their forces over to the Taleban.[79] Bin Laden failed in this effort, but his relationship with Sayyaf and Gulbuddin stayed cordial, so much so that Gulbuddin told the media that bin Laden was "my brother." About the al-Qaeda force, Roy Gutman has written in his excellent book *How We Missed the Story* that bin Laden's men were "ready to fight to the death and were the most feared by Massoud's commanders."[80] In fact, Massoud said his men could handle Taleban units, but found it much harder to take on the same units if they contained al-Qaeda fighters or al-Qaeda units alone.

There also is some evidence that just as he had in Sudan, bin Laden spent funds on construction in Afghanistan. In Kandahar, for example, he financed a new market facility in the main bazaar, and paid for a center for Taleban administrators and a new mosque on the site of an old movie theater.[81] The journalist Ahmad Zaydan has said that by 2000 bin Laden's men were welcome in Kandahar and were becoming part of society there because they helped the Taleban and spent money. "I never sensed the Kandaharis were uncomfortable about the Arab presence," Zaydan wrote. "I know for certain that everyone in Kandahar was pleased with the high rents paid by the Arabs and the revenue generated by Arab spending in the city, which moved the stagnant Kandahari economy."[82]

Finally, bin Laden deftly used rhetoric to praise the Taleban and all Afghans, and to reinforce their status as Muslims who refused to cower before foreign threats and defended guests with their lives. "Afghanistan," bin Laden told the Pakistani journalist Rahimullah Yusufzai in 1999, "[is] the only state in this age which has started to apply Islam and all Muslims should support it. . . . All Muslims should focus their efforts, in terms of relief, the call for God's path, and in terms of knowledge in support of this state. . . . Thank God, our relationship with the Taleban is very strong and close. It is an ideological friendship based on faith and not on political and commercial interests. Many countries have tried to exert pressure on the Taleban through enticements and threats, but the Almighty God entrenched them."[83]

Piping Days of Peace

During the eleven months between al-Qaeda's attack on the USS *Cole* and the 9/11 attacks, bin Laden solidified his ties to Mullah Omar, while preparing his forces for war with the United States. Mullah Omar's anger about the U.S. pressure he was under stemming from the *Cole* attack and bin Laden's media appearances remained points of friction in their relations, but bin Laden worked to calm Mullah Omar, using a contrite manner and public praise. The Taleban leader, he said, had built a "strong fort for Islam" in Afghanistan and had "saved the jihad of the nation [ummah]."[84] He also publicly pledged personal allegiance to the "Commander of the Faithful" and regularly urged others to do so. Bin Laden asked the scholars "to encourage people to wage jihad, to mobilize people in Afghanistan, and to issue fatwas on the legitimacy of the Emirate of Afghanistan."[85] Bin Laden called on the scholars to

> teach the Islamic nation that there is no Islam without a congregation, no congregation without an emirate, and no emirate without obedience. You are aware that at these difficult days, God has bestowed on the Islamic nation the rise of an Islamic state that applies God's sharia and raises the banner of monotheism, praise be to God, namely the establishment of the Islamic Emirate of Afghanistan led by the prince of the faithful Mullah Muhammad Omar, may God protect him. It is your duty to call on the people to adhere to this emirate, to support it with souls and resources, and to back it in resisting the overwhelming currents of the world's infidelism. . . . I take this opportunity to assert that it is God's desire that I pledge allegiance to the prince of the faithful Mullah Muhammad Omar, that I have indeed given him my word of allegiance. I hope my action will serve only God the Almighty.[86]

Bin Laden did not, however, pledge to abstain from attacks or from using the media, and, in fact, was aggressively trying to force Omar into a public reconfirmation of al-Qaeda's license to stay in Afghanistan by repeatedly offering to take his men and leave the country. "Usama bin Laden," one newspaper reported in late 2000, "has once again offered to Mullah Omar that he is ready to move to another country to save Afghanistan from foreign conspiracies and attack."[87] The offers embarrassed Mullah Omar and his ministers on several counts, for they implied that bin Laden did not think Mullah Omar could be trusted to handle U.S. pressure; that he doubted the Taleban's commitment to the Pashtun tribal duty of protecting guests; and that he questioned whether the Afghan citizenship he was granted would be honored if it came to war with America.[88] Omar had no choice but to reject bin Laden's offer each time it was made. In reaffirming his welcome to bin Laden, he announced that for all Taleban members "it was an issue of their [Afghan] honor and that they would sacrifice their lives to save their honor," and added that it is clear "the

United States was looking to attack Afghanistan" whether or not bin Laden was there.[89]

Checked by religious principle, tribal mores, nascent aspirations as leaders of Islam's only Islamic emirate, and bin Laden's clever tactics, Mullah Omar and his Shura Council settled down to solve their major problem, Ahmed Shah Massoud's Northern Alliance. By the spring of 2001, al-Qaeda-supported Taleban forces had driven Massoud's fighters into a pocket of territory in the northeast, amounting to less than 20 percent of Afghanistan. But his fighters were not defeated, and Massoud was masterfully securing financial and military aid from Iran, Russia, the United States, India, Uzbekistan, and some NATO countries, aid that might enable him to extend the war indefinitely.

At this point the interests of Mullah Omar and Osama bin Laden were fully aligned. Both knew that with his military talent, skill as a unifying leader among Afghanistan's ethnic minorities, and charisma, Massoud could stop the Taleban from countrywide consolidation of power. For Mullah Omar and his advisers, the one way to avoid a long, bloody, and unpredictable battle with the Northern Alliance was to kill Massoud. He was the Alliance's brain, heart, and soul and had prepared no successor. Bin Laden wanted to help the Taleban solve its Massoud problem, but not simply to please his hosts. By mid-2001, he knew what Mullah Omar did not: al-Qaeda attacks were scheduled for later in the year in the United States. Banking on them to lure the United States into Afghanistan, at long last, bin Laden and his lieutenants decided Massoud's demise would leave the Alliance leaderless and susceptible to defeat by the Taleban before al-Qaeda struck in the United States. Should al-Qaeda kill Massoud and the Taleban eliminate the Alliance before the attacks, Washington would have no effective Afghan ally to assist its forces—making the Afghan campaign harder, longer, and more costly. Killing Massoud was therefore a win-win scenario, and Mullah Omar and bin Laden knew the act was religiously permissible because Salafi scholars in Saudi Arabia and elsewhere had long since named Massoud Islam's enemy. "Unfortunately," Shaykh Musa al-Qarni said in 2006, "most of the so-called ulema in the Islamic resurgence in our country [Saudi Arabia] here were against Massoud and on Hekmatyar's side."[90]

Massoud was killed by an al-Qaeda-sponsored suicide bomber on September 9, 2001, much later in the year than bin Laden intended, and a telling object lesson for anyone foolish enough to expect things to happen on time in Afghanistan. The al-Qaeda raids in New York and Washington struck on September 11, and George W. Bush's administration swallowed bin Laden's lure lustily. Massoud was gone, but the Americans and their unlimited supply of greenbacks held the Northern Alliance together long enough to help the minimal U.S. forces deployed to take the major Afghan cities, and then loudly declare complete victory over al-Qaeda and the Taleban. The assertion was premature.

6

SURVIVOR AND PLANNER, 2001–2010

With smoke still rising from lower Manhattan, the Pentagon, and a Pennsylvania pasture, bin Laden had little time for celebration. He had sought to lure the United States into invading Afghanistan since at least 1997 and was pretty sure the 9/11 attacks would do the trick.[1] Still, he took no chances. On September 19, 2001, bin Laden announced that while cowardice and fear might yet prevail, if it did launch an invasion "the United States would face a crushing defeat."[2]

While continuing to goad Washington, bin Laden acted as if sure the fish was hooked. He later said he'd had six days' notice of the attacks—learning of the actual date on September 5—but had of course known for far longer that they were coming. He and his lieutenants probably began moving archives, ordnance, communications gear, and fighters into Afghanistan's mountains or into Pakistan much earlier. Indeed, Ahmad Zaydan has written, based on observations when interviewing bin Laden before 9/11, that "Usama and al-Qaeda in general were prepared for the worst Western and U.S. strike on Afghanistan"; such readiness helped them avoid getting killed or arrested after the fall of the Taleban.[3] Washington, moreover, gave al-Qaeda twenty-six more days to disperse its resources by not attacking until October 7; the delay was due to the Pentagon's lack of planning for Afghanistan and the Bush administration's fear of casualties or captured servicemen—especially pilots—before enough search-and-rescue units could be deployed to the war zone.[4] Given the quantity of al-Qaeda documents found by journalists and by U.S. and UK militaries, it is clear that evacuation was not completed by October 7. Nonetheless, the operation had been given priority, and was well planned and executed: nothing that could fatally compromise al-Qaeda, pinpoint its leaders, sketch its worldwide network, detail or locate its financial assets and transfer mechanisms, or outline its intentions, targets, or timetables was left behind.

The post-9/11 analysis of bin Laden's life and al-Qaeda was distorted. Indeed, the bin Laden–related literature was littered with assumptions ranging from plausible (a few) to wishful thinking (the majority). Conventional wisdom had it that while bin Laden, some of his senior lieutenants, and many fighters survived the U.S. onslaught, al-Qaeda as an organization was essentially destroyed. This tended to ignore the fact that bin Laden worked hard to lure U.S. forces into Afghanistan, which he would not have wanted to do had it meant al-Qaeda's annihilation. It also ignored that the "small military footprint" Washington had mandated was sufficient to win battles, not a war. Could al-Qaeda not have survived because it was a flexible and resilient organization that simply relocated to the tribal zone straddling the Pakistan-Afghanistan border before and after 9/11? In an incisive essay, the British journalist Mark Huband persuasively argues for this case, given what we know of bin Laden's managerial style. "Bin Laden believes in structures and organization," he wrote, "and the hierarchy he created is both al-Qaeda's main organizational strength as well as its source of credibility among Muslims. Al-Qaeda is not haphazard; there is a chain of command, orders are given, and plans are developed over time and distance."[5]

Huband's conclusion counters the common wisdom that al-Qaeda's organization was so weakened, and its leaders so isolated, by U.S. attacks that all it could do was issue statements and watch groups operate as its independent—in a command-and-control sense—"franchises" outside South Asia. These were a few of the many "assumptions" currently underpinning analyses of bin Laden and al-Qaeda. They may be true, but may not be. If not, the greater assumption that bin Laden posed little threat to the continental United States has been quite dangerous. What if the now bin Laden-less al-Qaeda remains a functioning organization and the so-called franchises—such as al-Qaeda in the Islamic-Maghreb (AQIM), AQI, and al-Qaeda on the Arabian Peninsula (AQAP)—are evidence of growth in vitality, size, and geographic reach?

Luck or Planning?

There is a good deal of solid analysis of the escape of bin Laden and his fighters from the Tora Bora Mountains to Pakistan in December 2001, so there is no need to rehearse the entire episode.[6] But it is worth evaluating what we did and did not know about bin Laden's knowledge of the region he had to cross to reach safety. It began in early November in or near Kabul, where bin Laden gave an interview to the Pakistani journalist Hamid Mir just days before the capital fell on November 12, 2001. He then traveled to Jalalabad and on to his base in Tora Bora. "Tora Bora had a special significance for him," Abdel Bari Atwan learned from an interview with bin Laden in 1996. "During the jihad against the Soviet Union it had been his main military base, but now he used it as a retreat—a place to think, plan, and relax."[7] Similarly, the journalist Muhammad al-Shafi'i has written that bin Laden went to Tora Bora in the summer of 1996 to complete work on his declaration of war on the United States.[8]

As Atwan said, bin Laden and his fighters had fought the Soviets in the Tora Bora area. They had built bases, caves, and tunnels there; and they had close ties to Yunis Khalis—the area's principal mujahedin leader in the anti-Soviet jihad—and to his military commanders. Moreover, because of his experience with Azzam's NGO and as a jihadi engineer and fighter, bin Laden was known and respected by Pashtuns on both sides of the border and could rely on their help. Finally, he knew that the force guarding Pakistan's border—the Frontier Corps—was led by a Pakistan army general, but that the troopers were drawn from local tribes and in reality took orders from tribal chiefs. If the latter wanted bin Laden to escape, the Frontier Corps would not stop him. In 1998 bin Laden said that he and al-Qaeda had found "a sympathetic and giving people in Pakistan who exceed all our expectations by their sympathy with us."[9]

Many in the West believed that bin Laden's first inclination would not be to save his own skin. From youth, as has been shown, he aspired to martyrdom. He also spent an arduous apprenticeship learning insurgency skills and was extremely unlikely to forego using them. He also calculated that his men had the advantage in the coming fight. Having seen Washington panic after the bombing of the Marines' barracks in Beirut in 1983, run after the loss of a few troops in Somalia in 1993 and the bombing of two U.S. embassies in East Africa in 1998, and fail to respond at all after the suicide attack on the USS *Cole* in 2000, bin Laden thought his mujahedin could outlast its offensive here, particularly on terrain he now knew well. Omar bin Laden said that while he and his father were in Tora Bora in 1996–1997, his father frequently hiked over the border into Pakistan. "Much to my dismay, he decided I should accompany him, telling me, 'Omar, we never know when war will strike. We must know our way out of these mountains.' Discontented unless he knew every inch of the path, he insisted 'We must memorize every rock. Nothing is more important than knowing secret escape routes.'"[10] Omar added that when he learned after 9/11 that his father went to Tora Bora, he concluded that, given his father's knowledge of the area and ability to speak fluent Pashtu, he would be hard to find there. "No one knows those mountains like my father."[11]

Bin Laden got away to fight another decade. Beyond mere concrete fact, however, bin Laden's survival was important in a less measurable but probably more profound way. In Islamic history, heroes who prevail in wars to defend the faith often succeed against long odds, so long in fact that observers and chroniclers have seen signs of "divine help."[12] Muhammad's victories at Badr and the Trench were over far larger and better-armed enemies. Khalid bin Walid's defeat of a bigger Byzantine force at Yarmuk in Syria was enabled by a sudden wind shift that blew sand in the Byzantines' eyes, blinding them as the battle began. Saladin's besting of Richard the Lionheart in the Third Crusade provides another example. And, of course, the Afghans' victory over the Soviet superpower's forces is commonly described as an instance of God aiding those who fight in His name, proving "true faith can overcome godless power."[13]

Bin Laden's survival after 9/11—while owing much to luck, his sense of geography, and his ability to take advantage of enemy lapses—seemed to many, many Muslims a tale of divine intervention. At Tora Bora, after all, the fight was not between a small but determined nation defending itself against a superpower; it was but one man and a few hundred companions taking on the West's military forces, incompetently led though they were. For millions of Muslims, bin Laden's escape represented unquestioned evidence of God's love for mujahedin who defended Islam. And this was not the first time God seemed to have weighed in on his side. Bin Laden and a small Arab band turned back a large Soviet force at Jaji; he had fought and been wounded at Jalalabad, but survived; a Soviet shell once landed near him but did not explode; he evaded assassination attempts in Afghanistan and Sudan; he lived through a 1998 U.S. Cruise missile barrage; and now he had emerged unscathed despite all that the U.S. and NATO forces could throw at or drop on him. The bin Laden who survived Tora Bora, therefore, was not just a brave man, but a brave man whom God seemed to have destined for greater things. This belief only deepened in the post–Tora Bora decade as bin Laden battled and baffled those he deemed God's enemies. And as each year passed, his status as a contemporary Islamic hero grew, as did the Saladin-like legend he would eventually leave in the annals of Islam's history.

Reasserting Control

Once in Pakistan, bin Laden had to count noses—who survived and who did not—and undertake substantial organizational reordering. He had some sizable advantages to exploit. The U.S. government and military, for example, simply shrugged their collective shoulders at bin Laden's escape, believing that the capture of major Afghan cities meant the war had been won and al-Qaeda and the Taleban broken forever. As noted, bin Laden had strong ties to the tribes straddling the Pakistan-Afghanistan border, as well as with Pakistan's Border Forces. His conduct in the anti-Soviet jihad also had yielded enduring friendships with Afghan mujahedin and with officers in Pakistan's military and intelligence services. While the United States and NATO indulged in premature self-congratulation, bin Laden and al-Qaeda began regrouping, refitting, and planning for war.[14]

In several late-2001 speeches and interviews, bin Laden announced to his audience that due to the war's exigencies he would not be speaking publicly as often. He added, however, that it would be hearing of Taleban-led resistance to the U.S.-NATO occupation, assuring it that al-Qaeda would aid that effort.[15] Once again, U.S. and Western officials failed to examine the substance of bin Laden's words. The depth of their analysis was something like "There is an attack threat in this message"; or "There is an attack threat in this message, but we have heard it before"; or "There is an attack threat in this message, but no specifics about its location or timing." Western media tended to follow suit, dismissing each new message as "another rambling diatribe."

Three questions arise from this: (1) Did Western officials expect bin Laden not to issue threats after twice declaring war on us? (2) Did they expect bin Laden to reveal the date, place, and type of weapon to be used in al-Qaeda's next attack? and (3) Did it occur to them that the words of al-Qaeda's leaders might have a purpose beyond threatening us? I know of no official who argued that bin Laden's messages might be part of a coherent campaign, one designed to give theological justification for al-Qaeda's next attack *in* the United States by letting Muslims know that he and al-Qaeda have adhered to the letter of the Koran, the Sunnah, and the traditions of Islamic history.

These speeches reveal bin Laden's continued mastery of the rhetorical power of silence. "We have many other things to do," bin Laden told his audience. "Our silence is our real propaganda. Rejections, explanations, or corrigendum only waste your time, and through them, the enemy wants you to engage in things which are not of use to you. These things are pulling you away from your cause. The Western media is unleashing such baseless propaganda, which makes us surprise[d], but it reflects on what is in their hearts and gradually they themselves will be captive of this propaganda. They become afraid of it and begin to cause harm to themselves. Terror is the most dreaded weapon in the modern age and the Western media is mercilessly using it against their own people. . . . You can understand what the performance in war [will be] of the nation which suffers from fear and helplessness."[16]

For nearly a decade, bin Laden spoke only when he wanted to and only on subjects he chose. The result was to drive his enemy—who long ago lost all ability to stay silent about anything—to distraction and into making and broadcasting foolish, unsubstantiated assumptions. Due to his extended silences, the West repeatedly concluded that bin Laden was dead; that he was running from rock to rock and cave to cave; that he was isolated and could not command al-Qaeda; that he was wasting away from a terminal disease (usually, as noted, kidney failure); that he was retired, turning over al-Qaeda to his sons or to al-Zawahiri; that there was an irreparable al-Qaeda/Taleban split and the latter would give bin Laden to NATO; or—the cream of an inane crop—that he was killed right after 9/11 and that all messages since then were pre-recorded or spoken by a double. None of these assumptions were based upon a lick of supporting evidence. They were purely the product of minds unable to tolerate silence and so create reasons for it. And then bin Laden would suddenly and without warning issue an audiotape showing that all the assumptions were nonsense. "These recordings," Professor Andrew Hill wrote, "place before bin Laden's opponents the spectacle of their most wanted enemy, accusing, threatening, and goading them, having harmed them already and declaring that he will do so again, having resisted the attempts to capture and destroy him, and continuing his capacity to play a role in the War on Terror. . . . It is almost as if bin Laden's image has metamorphosed into a form of weaponry . . . [and] the form bin Laden has come to present to the United States—namely of a being that is *haunting* them. This sense of haunting at once evokes both the uncertainties surrounding bin Laden's location, movements, and current activities; and his identification as a malevolent force, the fear of which persists in preoccupying the West. . . . In these recordings," Hill concluded, the very "absence of bin Laden's visible presence can itself be said to have functioned as a source of anxiety."[17]

After 2001, bin Laden ran a vigorous and sophisticated media war, one that built on the media operations he mounted during and after the Afghan jihad. Today it still focuses on four main areas.

Religious justification for more war

The 9/11 attacks' success in terms of casualties, economic cost, property destruction, and psychological impact surpassed bin Laden's expectations.[18] While clearly believing that they were authorized by the February 1998 fatwa, he nonetheless faced strong criticism from

Islamists who argued—in effect—that he had not played by the rules laid out in the Koran and the hadith. These included provisions that the enemy be warned; that he be offered a chance to convert to Islam; that truces be proposed to make war the last resort; and that if the foe tended toward peace so must Muslims. In short, bin Laden had lacked religious authority for that much success.[19]

Bin Laden took this criticism seriously. He had publicly and repeatedly said that the war was "fundamentally religious," and followed the "book of God Almighty and in the teachings of our messenger." "Under no circumstances should we forget this enmity between us and the infidels," he urged. "For the enmity is based on creed."[20] After al-Qaeda was repositioned in Pakistan, bin Laden began a series of statements aimed at meeting his religious obligations and placating his Islamist critics—and all Muslims, really—before al-Qaeda next struck in America. In late 2002, he began issuing a stream of warnings whose themes continued in virtually all subsequent messages.[21] "I am an honest adviser to you," he informed Westerners, and "I urge you to become Muslims." "We call you to Islam," he added, informing them that embracing Islam would prove "a dividend for you in life and the hereafter."[22]

He also offered long-term truces to Westerners, pointing out that Allah and Muhammad instructed Muslims to incline to peace if their enemies did.[23] To Americans he said that if their government "escalates or deescalates this conflict, we will reply to it in kind, God willing." To Europeans, he said that for those "who reject peace and want war we are ready. As for those who want peace, we have given them a chance."[24] This media campaign was specifically designed for bin Laden's theological critics, and constituted the most important aspect of al-Qaeda's preparation for its next attack on the United States.

Scourging apostasy

Since 9/11, Muslim regimes from North Africa to the Indian Ocean have been easy targets for bin Laden. Most supported the U.S.-led invasion of Afghanistan, and while all damned the U.S.-led invasion of Iraq, Egypt, Jordan, Saudi Arabia, and other Gulf states opened ports, airfields, military bases, and airspace. "The rulers of the region," while loudly opposing U.S. plans for Iraq, bin Laden wrote, "finally submitted and succumbed to U.S. pressure and opened their land, sea, and air bases." Offering "obvious support for the infidels against an Islamic country," they committed "a cardinal sin that renders one an infidel."[25] Pakistan took a place beside these Arab regimes as yet another state that had "fallen under the banner of the cross," and Karzai's Afghan regime was denounced as Satan-run from its start.[26] Under Musharraf, Zidari, and Karzai, moreover, the Pakistani and Afghan regimes "broke the back of the Islamic Emirate in Afghanistan" and stood "in the same trench against Islam."[27]

Bin Laden also denounced Saudi Crown Prince Abdullah's 2002 plan for Israel-Palestine peace as the work of a "Zio-American." Later, in a poem, he damned Arab regimes—while calling their rulers "Arab Zionists"—for not destroying Israel and liberating Palestine. "It is a world of crimes in which children are slaughtered like cows / Zion is killing my brothers, and the Arabs are holding a conference."[28] On the Palestine issue, he also took a rare public swipe at the Shia, identifying Lebanese Hizballah leader Hasan Nasrallah as standing in the same anti-Islam camp as Hosni Mubarak and "the rest of the Arab idol-kings" because Hizballah had dealt with the UN and the "Zionist entity" and approved UN Resolution 1701, which had "welcomed the Crusader forces to protect the Jews."[29] No collaborator, bin Laden warned, would be exempt from retribution "at the appropriate time."[30]

Discrediting the king's scholars

Those bin Laden called "king's scholars" were also easy targets. Calling them part of the "ulema of vice," bin Laden focused on the fact that almost no scholar had publicly attacked Arab regimes for aiding the U.S. invasion of Iraq. Instead of opposing aid, bin Laden said, these scholars convinced their followers that "treacherous rulers" were their "righteous guardians" and that it was necessary to support them.[31] The scholars' support for Arab tyrants; their acquiescing to infidel attacks on Muslim states; and their discouraging eager young Muslims from going to the jihad fronts to fight was evidence that "great evil is spreading throughout the Islamic world: the imams calling the people to hell are those who appear more than others at the side of the rulers of the region, the rulers of the Arab and Islamic worlds. Through the media and their own apparatuses . . . from morning to evening they call people to the gates of hell. . . . They all, except for those upon whom Allah had mercy, are busy handing out praise and words of glory to the despotic imams who disbelieved Allah and His prophet. They send telegrams praising those rulers who disbelieve Allah and His prophet. The newspapers and media spread heresy against Allah and His prophet. Other telegrams are sent from the rulers to these clerics, praising them for deceiving the nation."[32]

Since 9/11, official Islamic scholars had sanctioned their regimes' support for infidel war-making on Muslims; contradicted themselves by arguing that it was theologically permissible for men to wage jihad on the Soviets in Afghanistan but not on U.S.-led coalitions in Iraq and Afghanistan; and stood by while their employers let Israel invade Lebanon (2006) and Gaza (2008), build a wall to stop supplies flowing from Muslim Egypt into Gaza, and open a "dialogue of faiths" with infidels. The scholars' declining influence with Muslims had become clear lately. Their words had done nothing to deter the 9/11 attack or any of the insurgencies that had started up or been rekindled after it.[33] "Praise God," bin Laden told the Pakistani paper *Ausaf* in regard to several official clerics who denounced him and al-Qaeda. "The statements of court scholars have no importance for me," he announced. "They are supporting everything which has been forbidden by Islam."[34]

Focusing on U.S. policy

Of all who played into bin Laden's hands post-9/11, none did so as completely and mindlessly as the U.S. government. "Yes, America has primarily served Shaykh Usama bin Ladin and the al-Qaida organization," Abu Jandal said in 2005. "When Shaykh Usama attacked America [on 9/11] he wanted to expose it to the Islamic world. He sought to expose its evil. This is what really happened."[35] The United States invaded Afghanistan to defeat the Taleban and al-Qaeda and failed, stayed to westernize Afghans, and has been losing to those it swaggeringly came to conquer. It next invaded Iraq and created a Shia-run regime and society, empowering Iran and alienating all Sunnis, radical, conservative, or moderate. In both places, it has fielded a slow-moving, over-equipped, and casualty-averse army that failed to win under careerist generals drawing advice from New Age social scientists bent on pursuing hearts and minds and avoiding blood and iron. This had continued during the Obama administration, under which Washington expanded its military and civilian presence in Afghanistan, increased attacks in Pakistan, undertaken new political-military initiatives in Yemen and Somalia, ingratiated itself further with the Saudi and Egyptian police states, and allowed Israel's prime minister to defy its peace plans and whip up anti-Obama sentiment at pro-Israel rallies in the United States. And as Muslims have watched this go on, senior leaders in both U.S. parties have kept deceiving Americans by insisting that bin Laden, al-Qaeda, their Islamist allies, and Muslims generally hate American freedom, elections, liberties, and lifestyles, not Washington's actions in the Muslim world.

Since 9/11, then, U.S. officials have been laboring to do bin Laden's work. They have urged that school curricula in Muslim states be altered to defang jihad and boost secularism, reinforced foreign policies that polls show Muslims hate, and generally created a better and blinder antagonist for bin Laden than any he could have built to meet his needs. "This also shows that the struggle is an ideological and religious struggle and that the clash is a clash of civilizations."[36]

A Gift Bungled, Then Redeemed

The 2003 invasion and occupation of Iraq was a godsend for bin Laden, al-Qaeda, and the Sunni Islamist movement. It retains that status today, and will for the foreseeable future, not least because in the Muslim world's eyes the U.S. military left Iraq in defeat. The war provided the perfect Koranic predicate for a defensive jihad: an infidel power had attacked a Muslim country without provocation, occupied it, built a regime based on man's not God's law, and given rule to the heretical Shia. Thus, the Iraq war provided irrefutable justification for Muslims—not just Islamists—to join the cause bin Laden had called for since 1996, universalizing jihad. "Do not think that the war will be between the United States and Iraq or between Bush and Saddam," bin Laden told Muslims four months before the invasion. "It is between you, all our Muslim brothers, and us on the one side and the Crusaders and the Jews on the other."[37]

Furthermore, the invasion did for bin Laden what he had not done for himself: it vetted him in Muslim eyes as an acute analyst of American intentions. Since August 1996, bin Laden had warned Muslims that Washington intended to destroy strong Muslim states; topple any Muslim regime threatening Israel or blocking the creation of "Greater Israel" from the Nile to the Euphrates rivers; and seek to control oil-rich Muslim states. In Iraq, it did all of these things. Iraq proved that the U.S. government intended to rid the Muslim world of God's law and substitute man-made law, constitutions, elections, and parliaments.[38] Perception is always reality, and many Muslims now perceive that bin Laden's warnings were correct, lending him stature.

This was especially true about the U.S.-Israel relationship. As the role pro-Israel neoconservatives had played in causing the Iraq war became known to Muslims, bin Laden's earlier words became prescient. "I have already said that we are not hostile to the people of the United States," bin Laden had said in 2001. "We are against the system, which makes other nations slaves of the United States, or forces them to mortgage their political and economic freedom. The system is totally in the control of the American Jews, whose first priority is Israel, not the United States. It is simply that the American people themselves are the slaves of the Jews and are forced to live according to the principles and laws laid down by them. So, the punishment should reach Israel. In fact it is Israel which is giving a bloodbath to Muslims and the United States is not uttering a single word."[39]

As noted, the Iraq war advanced bin Laden's offensive against Muslim rulers and their Islamic scholars. The invasion could not have occurred without the help of Saudi Arabia, Egypt, Jordan, Kuwait, Qatar, and Bahrain. The U.S. occupation also was not viable without their help. In Islamic terms, there is no other way to see this than as Muslims aiding infidels to kill other Muslims, making them an enemy of Islam. The Arab regimes' support for the war proved again that Muslim rulers would always side with infidels to kill Muslims, and this popular perception undermined their religious justification for holding power. The "king's scholars" were not men of wisdom but rather men who were willing to accede to their secular rulers in return for wealth and position—or simply to avoid jail. And if the clerics' early acquiescence did not fully discredit them, their later decree that non-Iraqi Muslims need not fight infidels in Iraq shredded what remained of their credibility.

Confronted by Allah's gift of the U.S. war on Iraq, bin Laden and his lieutenants had to decide how to exploit it fully. This required that bin Laden's words match al-Qaeda's deeds; merely cheerleading Iraq's Sunni fighters from the Afghan sidelines would not suffice. Al-Qaeda's leaders named two goals in Iraq, one which might be called Islamic, the other organizational. Each could be achieved independently but pursued simultaneously. The Islamic goal was to join and assist the anti-U.S. Sunni insurgency, with the aim of beating the infidel occupiers, denying Iraq's Shias countrywide control, and building a Sunni Islamist regime. At the time of the invasion, however, bin Laden had few assets in Iraq beyond the ties al-Qaeda had made in 1999 to the Sunni Kurd group Ansar al-Sunnah in the north, and to Abu Musab al-Zarqawi's group, which worked with al-Qaeda in Afghanistan before 9/11 and afterward left for Iraq. On leaving, al-Zarqawi had not pledged loyalty to bin Laden.

Bungling the Islamic Goal

From the start, Iraq presented the kind of situation bin Laden least liked: it had afforded too little time for planning and placing assets. Therefore Iraq's insurgency—and al-Qaeda's part in it—had to be conceived and managed on the fly. After the invasion, bin Laden and his lieutenants negotiated with al-Zarqawi over whether and on what terms he would join al-Qaeda.[40] They were wary of the prickly disposition al-Zarqawi had showed in Afghanistan, as well as his virulent anti-Shia beliefs.[41] In the end—in my belief—they accepted al-Zarqawi's loyalty pledge and named him chief of "Al-Qaeda in the Land of the Two Rivers [Iraq]" to make the best of a bad situation. Al-Qaeda "warmly" welcomed union with al-Zarqawi's group, bin Laden announced, but then issued an implicit order to him to abide by his "responsibility to the orders of God and His prophet."[42] Bin Laden's wariness proved justified, for al-Zarqawi soon made himself the most potent strategic threat al-Qaeda faced after 9/11. While the Taleban's temporary loss of Afghanistan was a substantive tactical defeat, al-Zarqawi, his rhetoric, and actions would come close to destroying al-Qaeda as a credible international Islamist entity.

We have seen that from 1996 bin Laden made clear that al-Qaeda's three war aims were to drive the United States from the Muslim world, to destroy Muslim tyrannies and Israel, and to settle scores with Shias. He also made clear that the goals had to be pursued seriatim, not in parallel. Why? First, because bin Laden believed that a Sunni-Shia war would undermine his ability to focus Sunni militants on going after U.S. interests. As much as they hate those interests, the militants—especially Wahhabis and Salafis—loathe Shia more. And so al-Qaeda's best fighters and those of its allies would join a war on Shiism. Bin Laden's view was not ecumenical. However, he argued that the greater threats to Islam—America, the Arab regimes, and Israel—had to be beaten before settling the Shias' hash.

Were the Shias dealt with first, bin Laden believed, three things would occur. First, as noted, the militants' U.S. focus would be broken. Second, the Sunni rulers and their oil wealth would be the only prop for Iraq's Sunni minority in a fight against the Iran-backed Shia majority. The Sunni kings, dictators, and generals al-Qaeda identified as un-Islamic would be transformed into indispensable purveyors of arms and funds to Sunni mujahedin in Iraq. In addition, the rulers' scholars would issue fatwas making the Iraqi Sunnis' war against Iraqi Shias the holiest of holy wars, eternally damning any Sunni male who did not join the jihad against heretics in Iraq. So strong would be this sectarian pull, in fact, that al-Qaeda would be forced to side with Iraq's tyrant-backed Sunnis to fight the Shia. Third, Arab regimes would blame AQI for the sectarian war, thereby costing al-Qaeda popular support in the Muslim world.

But al-Zarqawi paid almost no heed to bin Laden's strategy regarding Iraqi Shia. From the day he pledged loyalty and was named its Iraq commander, he made it seem as if he meant to destroy al-Qaeda. He attacked coalition and Iraq regime targets regularly and effectively, but his men also behaved as takfiris, killing non-combatant Shias and Sunnis for not taking direction on religious and other issues. He bombed mosques, killed local mullahs and tribal chiefs, slaughtered civilians, and beheaded captives on television. In addition, he ignored al-Qaeda's two cardinal rules for fighters sent to aid Islamist insurgencies: first, that country-specific insurgencies must be led by the country's nationals, and second, that while al-Qaeda offers advice and aid as requested, it does not tell local fighters how to run their war.[42A] In a short time, al-Zarqawi managed to kill already slim chances of al-Qaeda's helping Sunnis to a victory that would allow formation of a Sunni Islamist state in Iraq. In so doing, he also very nearly mortally wounded al-Qaeda's standing both in Iraq and in the Muslim world.

While al-Zarqawi's campaign in Iraq had success—killing coalition and Iraqi soldiers in what bin Laden himself called "daring operations"—it was a train running full speed at al-Qaeda. By mid-2005, Muslim and Western leaders opposed to bin Laden started to label al-Zarqawi and, by extension, al-Qaeda, as takfiris.[43] True to his management style, bin Laden avoided public debate with al-Zarqawi, instead using his deputy Ayman al-Zawahiri and the late senior al-Qaeda leader Atiyah Abd al-Rahaman to press al-Zarqawi to stop killing civilians; to help him understand how he and Iraq fit in al-Qaeda's overall strategy; and to explain how al-Zarqawi's behavior undermined al-Qaeda's efforts in Iraq and worldwide.[44]

In pressuring al-Qaeda's Iraq chief, however, bin Laden had to walk a fine line. He not only needed to avoid publicly condemning al-Zarqawi—who was popular among the young. He knew that al-Zarqawi was not theologically wrong in killing some Sunni and Shia civilians in Iraq. Muslims of either sect who voluntarily worked for U.S.-led forces or the coalition-installed regime were legitimate targets. Cooperation with infidels against Muslims negated their Islam. The problem was not with killing Muslims in this category, but with al-Zarqawi's refusal to discriminate between them and innocent Muslims. He should have been focusing only on Muslims who aligned themselves with the occupiers. In trying to insulate al-Qaeda from the takfiri label, therefore, bin Laden could not concede the point that no Muslim was a legitimate target, for that position was theologically untenable; it would defame al-Zarqawi; and it would make the conduct of war by Muslims all but impossible. "Those Iraqis who get killed," bin Laden argued in late 2004, "and who belong to [Prime Minister] Allawi's renegade government—such as members of the Army, the security agencies, and the National Guard—are like Abu Jahl, the

Qureshi Arab [who opposed and fought the Prophet Muhammad]. Their killing is sanctioned and they are infidels. Muslims should not pray for them. . . . Religious scholars have unanimously agreed that supporting the infidels against the Muslims is one of the major causes for departure from the Muslim faith, and is considered one of the ten major violators of Islam. This is the case if the infidel is foreign or Arab, ruled or ruler."[45] Bin Laden took it upon himself to handle the problem in public and assigned lieutenants to work privately with al-Zarqawi to fix what was becoming an intolerable threat to al-Qaeda.

In an October 2005 letter, al-Zawahiri used the tone of a wise old uncle to give al-Zarqawi a clear but relatively gentle upbraiding. Throughout his ten-page missive, al-Zawahiri cited four issues al-Zarqawi needed to address to improve prospects for himself, for Iraq's Sunni resistance, and for al-Qaeda. First, al-Zawahiri said, the mujahedin in Iraq needed to see their mission did not end "with the expulsion of the Americans from Iraq." They needed to do political "fieldwork," to help gather all the mujahedin groups into "a nucleus around which would gather the tribes and their elders . . . and all the distinguished ones who were not sullied by [working with] the [U.S.] occupation." If the fighters were not united by the time the coalition left, al-Zawahiri warned, "secularists and traitors" would hold sway over them. Second, al-Qaeda's deputy chief wrote that videotaped beheadings were costing Iraq's Sunni mujahedin public support. "Among the things which the feelings of the Muslim populace who love and support you will never find palatable," al-Zawahiri said, "are the scenes of slaughtering hostages." They alienated people. If captives had to be killed it would be better to do it "by bullet." Third, al-Zawahiri wondered whether al-Zarqawi, who wanted to lead Iraq's Sunni insurgency, was not stirring up "sensitivities" by "the assumption of leadership for the mujahedin or a group of the mujahedin by non-Iraqis." Telling al-Zarqawi to look into this, al-Zawahiri asked what impact the sensitivities would have and how they might be eliminated "while preserving the commitment of the jihadist work and without exposing it to any shocks." Fourth, al-Zawahiri explained that random attacks on Shiites and their shrines were—like beheadings—harming the Sunni cause. Yes, al-Zawahiri conceded, Shiites were heretics and needed to be brought to heel. But for now the attacks not only kept insurgents from killing Americans but alienated the majority of Muslims, who could not "imagine" the need to kill Shiites.[46]

Bin Laden remained dissatisfied with al-Zarqawi's actions after al-Zawahiri's letter. In December 2005, another, much harsher letter was sent to al-Zarqawi from Atiyah. Atiyah—like al-Zawahiri—expressed al-Qaeda leaders' love and respect for al-Zarqawi and his followers and praised their military accomplishments. "After all, you are truly mujahedin against God's enemies. . . . You are the ones who have spited America . . . and you have broken its prestige and thrown it to the ground." Atiyah also praised al-Zarqawi for advancing al-Qaeda's task of inciting Muslims to jihad with "vast good work of awakening the generation and resurrecting the Muslim nation." But here ended the soft soap. Atiyah proceeded to excoriate al-Zarqawi. Al-Qaeda's aim in Iraq was not just killing the enemy. Echoing Clausewitz, Atiyah told al-Zarqawi that policy "must be dominant over militarism . . . [this is] one of the pillars of war that is agreed upon by all nations, whether they are Muslims or unbelievers." "Therefore, unless our military actions are servant to our judicious shari'a policy, and unless our short-term goals and successes are servant to our ultimate goals and highest aims, then they will be akin to exhaustion, strain, and illusion."[47]

Atiyah next focused on the obvious "shortcomings," "flaws," and "errors" in al-Zarqawi's thinking and behavior, citing his need to hear "opinion, advice, and instruction" on remedying these faults from those outside his circle of advisers.[48] Atiyah's thinking exactly reflects bin Laden's. His main points fall under traditionally bin-Ladenesque subheadings.

Muslims are watching

You represent al-Qaeda, Atiyah told al-Zarqawi, "a man of the public" whose "actions, decisions, and behavior result in gains and loses that are not yours alone." They were, rather, "for Islam." "Your actions have come to impact the entire world, and they are monitored and analyzed." Al-Zarqawi's actions in Iraq, Atiyah informed him, had to be taken with a view to his "integration" with the worldwide "jihad enterprise."[49]

Follow orders

Because al-Zarqawi's acts were having worldwide impact, his decisions were not his alone. "You need to keep in mind," Atiyah wrote, "that you are a leader in the field that is under greater leadership that is more potent and able to lead the Muslim nation." Al-Zarqawi should henceforth make no decisions "on a comprehensive issue" until he had consulted with "Shaykh Usamah and the Doctor, and their brothers there [in Afghanistan and Pakistan]."[50]

Get along with everyone

Atiyah stressed bin Laden's mantra that pan-Muslim support was essential and that al-Qaeda had to work with—"embrace"—less-than-perfect Muslims to achieve its ends. Local tribal shaykhs and especially "Islamic theologians" must be won to al-Qaeda's side because only they could bring the Muslim masses. "The long and the short of the matter is that Islamic theologians are the keys to the Muslim communities, and they are its leaders. For this reason, we should win them over by keeping quiet, overlooking things, and saying nice things, in spite of disagreement with them in most things both theoretical and practical." This would involve winning over the population in Iraq, calling upon them to fulfill their obligation to wage jihad, "lauding them for the good they do," and remaining quiet about "their shortcomings." Among the most crucial things involved was exercising all caution against attempting to kill any religious scholar or tribal leader who was obeyed, and of good repute in Iraq, from among the Sunnis, no matter what. Per bin Laden's guidance, Atiyah told al-Zarqawi that if he killed those he knew to be corrupt and treasonous "but who are respected and beloved by the people," it would "act against all the fundamentals of politics and leadership." Finally, Atiyah ordered al-Zarqawi to get along "with the brothers from other sects." Killing them was "not appropriate," fighting them now "is not good, indeed harmful, as God knows best."[51]

Be patient

Atiyah referred to al-Zarqawi's very un-al-Qaeda-like impatience. "Do not act alone and do not be overzealous," he advised. "Do not be hasty in reforming and mending the Muslim nation. Do not rush victory over the enemy, for the war and our journey are truly long. The important thing is to keep your reputation and that of the mujahedin pure." Patience was vital in the military area, Atiyah noted, and attacking hotels in Jordan, for example, without consulting al-Qaeda's leaders yielded "the mistake of lack of precision."[52]

Always consolidate

Reflecting bin Laden's desperate desire to avoid in Iraq the Afghan debacle of winning but not consolidating power, Atiyah warned al-Zarqawi that his behavior could cost Islam the fruits of evicting the infidels. Writing of his experience in 1994–1995 Algeria, Atiyah noted that although the regime "was on the verge of downfall," the mujahedin "destroyed themselves with their own hands," by alienating people with "oppression, deviance, and severity, coupled with a lack of kindness, sympathy and friendliness." The enemy did not defeat them. Rather, they "defeated themselves."[53] Atiyah also made clear that al-Zarqawi's position was not secure. When a subordinate did not take orders, and acted in a way that drove people "away from us and our faith and our jihad," Atiyah said, al-Qaeda's leaders would have to "replace him."[54]

Atiyah's letter disproves and discredits those Western writers who have claimed that after 9/11 al-Qaeda dissolved as a centralized organization and now existed mainly as a figurehead for multiple, uncontrolled affiliates. It made explicit, for example, that al-Qaeda was a centralized organization, and that its leaders outside South Asia were not independent actors but subordinates whose actions affected the whole organization and therefore had to accept the orders from al-Qaeda's senior leaders. Atiyah's letter was later validated by papers taken from bin Laden's residence at the time of his death. These showed that bin Laden and other South Asia-based al-Qaeda leaders were still influencing the affairs of the organization's widely dispersed branches.

At day's end, neither al-Zawahiri nor Atiyah succeeded, but, as often happened, the United States came to al-Qaeda's aid. On June 7, 2006, a U.S. air strike killed al-Zarqawi. At a stroke, al-Qaeda's biggest headache in Iraq was gone, giving it a chance to recover. Bin Laden sent longtime al-Qaeda member Abu Hamza al-Muhajir, an Egyptian, to replace al-Zarqawi. Al-Muhajir's first task was, per Atiyah's orders to al-Zarqawi, to make clear to Sunnis that al-Qaeda was in Iraq to help fight the U.S.-led coalition and those Iraqis—Sunnis and Shia—who supported it, not to take over the war effort or teach them their faith. Al-Muhajir was told "to take caution against being zealous about the name 'al-Qaida,' or any name or organization." He was to work quietly and to act as if "all the mujahedin are our brothers, the Sunni are our brothers and our friends, as long as they are Muslims, even if they are disobedient or insolent, whether they come into the [al-Qaeda] organization or not."[55]

In public, Bin Laden's first post-al-Zarqawi step was to issue a eulogy celebrating his attacks on the coalition and on Iraqis working for the infidels, and asking God to accept him as a martyr. Al-Zarqawi thus became a lamented Islamic knight, a hero in death as in life to his followers, but no longer a mortal threat to al-Qaeda.[56] Next, bin Laden began arguing that al-Qaeda's organization in Iraq had a shot at success. First, he apologized for al-Zarqawi's excesses—his takfirism—and declared henceforth that al-Qaeda's performance in Iraq would be acceptable to all Muslims. Second, given al-Zarqawi's popularity with young Muslims, he found ways to praise the fallen mujahid without endorsing his indiscriminate slaughter of Muslims. He sought to do this by driving home the Koranic truth that Muslims helping infidels against Muslims equaled apostasy and that the punishment for apostasy was death.[57]

Bin Laden also announced he was sending Abu Hamza al-Muhajir and Abu Umar al-Baghdadi to replace al-Zarqawi, assuring his listeners that both men were respected for "patience and steadfastness" during the U.S./NATO air raids in the Hindu Kush Mountains. Because experience fighting U.S. forces in Afghanistan still has cachet among Muslims, bin Laden added that both were "well known by your brothers in Afghanistan."[58] Bin Laden then turned to the pressing need for unity among Iraq's Sunni mujahedin. "But some of you have been tardy in another duty which is also among the greatest of duties," he chided Sunnis, and that is "combining your ranks to make one rank, as loved by Allah."[59] Citing Ibn Taymiyyah that "unity is mercy, disunity is torture," bin Laden urged Sunni Iraqis—he called them "grandchildren of Saladin"—to unite with—not under—al-Qaeda.[60] He told Iraqis and especially al-Qaeda fighters in Iraq that al-Zarqawi's fanaticism had been an error.

> I advise myself and the Muslims in general, and the brothers in the al-Qaeda organization everywhere in particular, to beware of fanatical partiality to men, groups, and homelands. . . . So the brotherhood of faith is what ties Muslims together, not belonging to tribe, homeland, or organization. And the interest of the groups takes priority over the interest of the individual, and the interests of the Muslim state take priority over the interests of the group, and the interests of the Ummah take priority over the interests of the state. These concepts must be practically implemented in ourselves. . . . We repeat their statements [those of the Prophet's successors] to them [the Muslims] to remove the exaggeration which has grown among some of them, through their exalting the orders of their group and the orders of its commanders.[61]

Looking to the future, bin Laden defined God's enemies as not just the United States and the West, but Muslims who—whether as individuals, groups, or governments—were helping them, including the many Shia who aided the infidels and whose al-Sadr Army, Badr Brigades, and al-Da'wah Party were delivering "fierce shocks" to Iraq's Sunnis.[62] He praised al-Zarqawi for being "the first to hoist the banner of opposing these criminals, fighting them, and stopping their expansion," and claimed that George Bush had caused the "so called civil war," by working with the leaders of the Shia against the Sunnis, "in the belief that this will quickly settle the war in his favor."[63] American forces had fueled this civil war by using money to "tempt" Sunnis and to "buy their allegiance." These Sunnis and all Muslims aligned with infidels "lost life in this world and in the hereafter."[64] They had stepped outside Islam and declared apostasy by their behavior, and thus it was "permissible to spill their blood and take their property."[65] Finally, bin

Laden spoke then and later in words meant both to (again) apologize for al-Zarqawi's sectarian extremism and to underline the duty to kill apostates. "I assure Muslims in general and our people in the neighboring states in particular, that they will see nothing from the mujahedin [in Iraq] but all that is good, God willing. We are your sons. The Muslim victims who fall during the operations against the infidel Crusaders or their usurper agents [the apostates] are not the intended targets. God knows that we are deeply saddened when some Muslims fall victim. Yet we hold ourselves responsible and seek God's forgiveness for that. We beseech God to have mercy on them and let Paradise be their final abode and to compensate their families and relatives."[66]

The message reveals how al-Qaeda's headquarters worked with subordinates in the field. In April 2008, al-Zawahiri and al-Muhajir described in three follow-up statements the dangerous splits among Iraq's Sunni fighters—many due to al-Zarqawi—and pressed for setting aside differences and unifying under the Islamic State of Iraq (ISI), an al-Qaeda-sponsored organization intended to unite Iraqi Sunni insurgent groups. Speaking on the occasion of the fifth anniversary of the invasion, al-Zawahiri repeated bin Laden's earlier assurance to the Iraqi mujahedin that the future of U.S. and coalition forces in Iraq was one of "failure and defeat." He derided General Petraeus's call for a "pause" in reducing U.S. troops as a "ridiculous farce to cover up the failure in Iraq and to help Bush dodge the decision to withdraw forces," which was nothing less than a declaration of defeat for the "Crusaders' invasion of Iraq," and simply transferred "the problem to the new president." Al-Zawahiri also said the end was near for U.S.-paid Sunni Awakening groups. The mujahedin were hunting them, and the "pause" was based on the groups' need for U.S. protection.[67]

Less pointed, but equally important, was al-Zawahiri's argument that as the military crisis ebbed, much work had to be done to prepare the Sunni insurgents to govern Iraq and stop Iran's aggression. "The people of Islam and jihad in Iraq have only to be persistent and remain firm" to exploit their success. While the Americans were "routed" and squabbling over a date for withdrawal, al-Zawahiri urged all groups to rally to the ISI. By uniting, Sunni fighters would keep Iraqi Shiites and their Iranian masters from achieving Tehran's goal of "annexing" southern

Iraq and the eastern parts of al-Jazirah, a region of northwest Iraq between the Tigris and Euphrates rivers, and "expanding to establish contacts with its followers in Lebanon." Iran and the West had criticized al-Zarqawi for being a foreigner bent on usurping the Sunni insurgency's leadership. Now al-Zawahiri dismissed Muqtada al-Sadr as a "naïve boy" who could not decide whether to fight or to demonstrate, adding that al-Sadr was being used by Iranian Intelligence "as a puppet."[68]

Al-Muhajir next issued a statement meant to promote the unity of Sunni fighters under the ISI's banner. Echoing al-Zawahiri, he wanted to let all Muslims know that "complete victory" over the U.S.-led coalition was "imminent," and that "with our omnipotent God's help" Sunni Islam would control the future. The insurgents were not fighting "the Crusader occupiers or Arab apostates" for the "sake of land," but "to exalt God's word on earth." Sunnis' "sincere adherence to God is the most important factor of victory and consolidation" and only genuine unity provides "pride, victory, and consolidation." And yet, al-Muhajir lamented, the Sunnis were disunited. Some turned from jihad, and others had proven by their actions that without unity there would be no victory "even if our commander is the best creation of God and the most courageous of men."[69]

To forge Sunni power, al-Muhajir said that the Prophet Muhammad's example should be summoned and all Sunni fighters—even those who fled from battle or deserted jihad or who either joined or stopped fighting the so-called Awakening Councils—would be welcomed under the ISI's flag: "the Prophet did not rebuke those who fled or use [their flight] as justification for vituperation. On the contrary, he invoked their pride in their clans after reminding them of their precedence in jihad and embracing monotheism. It is useful at times of hardship for a commander after turning to God to turn to those who had precedence in jihad, and to follow that by turning to the good sons of the clans, and he should never discredit any of them. If we leave them, then we leave them to the devil and his party, which is a loss to jihad and its soldiers. No sane person would advocate that."[70]

Al-Zawahiri completed this trio of pleas on behalf of Sunni unity by responding to questions he had solicited on the Internet. In his responses, al-Zawahiri focused on Iraq, especially one questioner's assertion that Iraq's Sunni minority could not prevail and that forming the ISI caused acrimony among the mujahedin. "I differ with what he said," al-Zawahiri responded, because "the Sunni community is not a minority in Iraq but they are a majority because the Kurds as well as the Turkomens are also Sunnis."[71] Regarding the ISI, he argued it was a force for unity, not factionalism. "The brothers in the mujahedin shura council [of the ISI] have exerted their utmost to absorb all the jihad resources in Iraq and they delayed the declaration of the state for several months in order to contact all the mujahid leaderships in Iraq." This declaration would not cause division but indeed keep the mujahedin from falling into the sedition of infighting, as happened in Afghanistan. He called upon any group, faction, or "body of people" who advocated for "the Islamic State of Iraq in its pure line, which is distant from nationalist fanaticism and secularism, and which endeavors to establish the Islamic Caliphate and liberate all the Muslim lands from the Crusaders and Jews," to unite into "one entity and hold talks."[72]

The foregoing is one of the few instances in the history of bin Laden and al-Qaeda in which their handling of a problem, from recognition of its existence to its resolution, can be confidently tracked. It makes several things apparent: that Bin Laden's was the guiding hand; that al-Qaeda is a functioning, hierarchical organization with clear command-and-control capabilities; that communication from al-Qaeda headquarters to the field may be challenging but is not impossible; that patience, perseverance, and reserves of skilled cadre remain organizational hallmarks; and that there is no trace of takfirism in either rhetoric or operations.

But did the process described yield some success in Iraq? The answer seems to be yes. In the last half of 2009, AQI became more militarily active, focusing attacks on such legitimate targets as Muslims working for the coalition or for the Iraqi regime and its military and security services; on foreign embassies in Baghdad; and on Western soldiers and Marines in particular.[73] In addition, AQI expanded its presence in the Anbar, Salah al-Din, and Diyala provinces, as well as in Kurdistan and Baghdad. In each place it infiltrated police and security organizations.[74] Most important, AQI's random attacks on Muslims dropped to nearly zero; in the March 2010 parliamentary elections, for example, AQI fighters were ordered to try to stop the voting but without violence.[75]

In April 2010, however, U.S. and Iraqi forces killed al-Baghdadi and al-Muhajir near Tikrit, disrupting the recovery of AQI and the ISI of which it is part.[76] But it now seems clear that al-Qaeda has reestablished significant military capabilities in Iraq—especially in terms of suicide bombings and raids on regime facilities—and is actively attacking the Shia tyranny that the United States allowed to be installed in Baghdad. In coming years, al-Qaeda will play a key role in the armed resistance of Iraq's Sunnis to the Iran-backed Shia domination of the country. This reality seems to validate the distinctly upbeat message contained in the ISI Shariah minister's eulogy for the two men. Minister Abu-al-Walid al-Mashadani assured mujahedin around the world that the ISI was "in good and strong hands," explaining that the two dead shaykhs and their shura council "were well prepared for this day, and settled all the expected issues in advance."[77]

Having survived if not fully recovered from al-Zarqawi's impact, al-Qaeda had achieved greater success in securing its organizational goal in Iraq. This second goal, as noted, was to build safe havens in Iraq contiguous to regions to which it had had little or no access, namely, the Levant, Turkey, and the Arabian Peninsula. In this, al-Qaeda was unquestionably successful, especially in opening a gateway for Salafi fighters moving from South Asia through Iraq to the Levant states and Gaza. With the end of the U.S. occupation of Iraq in late 2011, it is already clear that Prime Minister Maliki's regime is incapable of controlling the entire country. Whether the Iraqi provinces are given substantial autonomy or a Shiite-Sunni civil war starts, Iraq's border regions will be imperfectly policed, and al-Qaeda will be there. A civil war, in fact, would ensure that al-Qaeda would keep its safe havens. Iraq's outnumbered Sunnis would accept aid and manpower from any source and—even if reluctantly—would temporarily ignore grievances against al-Qaeda.

As in Afghanistan, the West knew of bin Laden's intentions and al-Qaeda capabilities regarding Palestine before the Iraq war. Bin Laden believed Palestine to be a key Islamic issue; he had failed—and was embarrassed by the failure—to place fighters near Palestine, and so had to hit Israeli targets outside the Levant. He also harbored hatred for the Egyptian, Lebanese, and Jordanian regimes for shielding Israel by closing their borders to the mujahedin. Bin Laden's quandary of how to help Palestinians destroy Israel, however, was partly resolved by Saddam's demise. While in power, Saddam was the best ally of Israel and the United States when it came to Israel's security. He dabbled with supporting Palestinian insurgents, but he also performed yeoman service in preventing the westward flow of Sunni fighters from South Asia to the Levant. Without Saddam, Israel has more than the marginally effective, easily intimidated, and always bribable Palestinians to contend with. Non-Palestinian Sunni fighters are moving through Iraq into the states of the Levant, and the 2011 fall of the police state in Egypt, together with the West's ongoing efforts to destroy Bashir al-Assad's regime in Syria has weakened Israel's border security.

Bin Laden believed that liberating Palestine—like evicting Westerners from the Arabian Peninsula—was Islam's cause, not just the Palestinians'. Every Muslim, he argued, "bears responsibility for the death of our oppressed kinfolk in the Gaza Strip." The Iraq war was "a rare and valuable opportunity for those honest in their desire to deliver al-Aqsa."[78] The key lay in building a mujahedin presence in Iraq that could move fighters across Iraqi borders to the Levant and onward to Gaza. Turning the tide would involve introducing some al-Qaeda but mostly other Salafi fighters into the Palestinians' war against Israel, which remained nothing more than a Crusader outpost that subsisted on U.S. support and the Arab regimes' cowardice. "I assure you," bin Laden told Muslims, "that the Zionist entity on the land of Palestine is very weak and abounds in weaknesses. It knows full well that it lacks the elements of survival in a large Islamic surrounding [area] without a cord of support from the West and their agents, the rulers of the region.[79]

By late 2007, bin Laden was confident that al-Qaeda had built a durable base in Iraq, one that could spread its influence, organization, and support for insurgency to adjacent states. This, he claimed, was especially true for the Levant states. In a statement, he spoke more frankly and ominously about Lebanon and Palestine than before, explicitly claiming that al-Qaeda could and would champion Palestine's liberation because Hizballah and Hamas had failed.[80] In a bit of revisionism, bin Laden revoked the support al-Qaeda had given Lebanese Hizballah and its Secretary General Nasrallah during their summer 2006 war with Israel.[81] He now accused Hizballah of turning its back on Palestine and of doing the bidding of Washington and its agent Arab rulers. "The [Muslim] people have openly witnessed this thing happening in Lebanon," bin Laden said, and they knew that UN Resolution 1701, which ended the war between Hizballah and Israel and called for a peacekeeping force, was a sham. "Are people unaware that these armies are the other face of the U.S.-Zionist alliance? Nonetheless, Secretary General Hasan Nasrallah is deceiving people. He welcomed these armies in public and promised to facilitate their mission even though he knows they were coming to protect the Jews and seal off the borders in the face of the honest mujahedin." Nasrallah had acted in this manner "to accommodate the wishes of the states that [are] backing him"—that is, Syria and Iran—and preferred to protect his own organization rather than make sacrifices for Palestine's freedom. Bin Laden described Nasrallah's actions as hypocrisy equal to the "traitors"—Egyptian President Anwar Sadat and Jordan's King Hussein—who signed "treaties that stipulate the closure of [their] borders" to prevent mujahedin from conducting "operations against the Jews."[82] Indeed, Bin Laden later said that Palestinians now faced a situation where all Levant states and Egypt were "cordon states."[83]

After damning Nasrallah, bin Laden accused Hamas's leaders of "cooperating indirectly" with "America's agents in the region" and said they were therefore "guilty of high treason against the ummah." Some Hamas leaders had been successfully "tempted" by the "ruler of the land of the two holy mosques" to damage their organization and betray Palestinians. Muslims should learn "a lesson from the fate of the Hamas movement's leadership, which had "relinquished its religion and did not achieve worldly gains when it obeyed the ruler of Riyadh and others by entering the national unity state and respecting the unjust international charters." At the Saudis' insistence, and to please Washington and Israel, Hamas had decided to "sell Jerusalem, al-Aqsa Mosque, and the blood of the martyrs."[84]

Bin Laden then unleashed an attack on the "agent rulers," meaning compliant Arab regimes, reminding them that al-Qaeda and its allies remained committed to toppling them and referring them "to the Islamic judiciary." In particular, he said the Levant's Arab rulers had to be destroyed so "the path to the broadest front for the liberation of Palestine" could be built "through the lands under their control," noting that Jordan offered "the best and widest of fronts," particularly given that "half of its residents are from the people of Palestine." Then, speaking not just to Palestinians but to all Muslims, bin Laden declared in an unprecedented way that al-Qaeda would directly aid Palestinians in their anti-Israel jihad, clearly implying that it had the military and logistical capabilities to do so. "I assure our kinfolk in Palestine in particular that we will expand our jihad, God willing, and we will not recognize the [Anglo-French] Sykes-Picot [Treaty] borders or the rulers appointed by the colonialists. By God, we have not forgotten you after the 9/11 events. Will anyone forget his own family? . . . We will not recognize a state for the Jews, not even on one inch of the land of Palestine, as did all the rulers of the Arabs when they adopted the initiative of the ruler of Riyadh years ago."[85]

Bin Laden concluded by prescribing the same martial reciprocity against Israel and the Arab rulers that he had against the United States. "Blood calls for more blood and demolishing calls for further demolishing." Al-Qaeda would fight beside Palestinians to "restore Hittin to us."[86] Hittin is the site in Palestine of Saladin's decisive victory over Frankish forces in July, 1187, that preceded his capture of Jerusalem that October.

Past tended to be prologue for bin Laden: if he said al-Qaeda would do something, odds were that it would happen. He did not say that major al-Qaeda attacks in the Levant and Israel were imminent; he stressed, rather, that the mujahedin were busy fighting the United States and its agents "in Iraq, Afghanistan, the Islamic Maghreb and Somalia." But as was the case after al-Zarqawi's death, instructions to the Palestinians arrived from other al-Qaeda spokesmen as to how to receive arriving al-Qaeda or al-Qaeda-assisted Salafi fighters in Gaza—men who, as bin Laden put it, "will not recognize a state for the Jews, not even one inch of the land of Palestine."[87]

In early 2008, al-Qaeda spokesmen said that following "the graduation of the largest class in Iraq's history of world-class jihad officers," Palestine would be their first destination. In an article by a well-known al-Qaeda essayist using the pseudonym "AsadAl-Jihad2," Palestinians were reminded of bin Laden's promise of aid and told that al-Qaeda had long been preparing to attack Israel, even if did not speak of it publicly. He announced that al-Qaeda was now in the midst of a three-year period of preparing attacks on Israel that began in 2007 and would "conclude at the end of 2009," when al-Qaeda will be positioned "for direct confrontation with the Jews in occupied Palestine." The author warned that after 2009, the attacks against the Israelis would not be limited to occupied Palestine but would "continue to reach all the areas in which Jews have a strong influence."[88]

Imploring Palestinians to be patient, AsadAl-Jihad2 said that "the opening of a branch or a front of al-Qaeda in Palestine cannot happen overnight" and would not be declared before the end of the 2008 [U.S. presidential] election." He then cited tasks Palestinians had to complete to be ready for al-Qaeda's arrival:

> Train in martial arts, assembling bombs and making explosives and rockets. In particular, "fighting and scientific skills" should be taught quickly to "committed Palestinian youth."
> Create routes for bringing muhajirun (foreign fighters) into Palestine and "protect them at the beginning and provide them with housing." This request was addressed to the "proud people of Gaza," where, if only 350 mujahedin "could train and prepare and learn the skills of war and join al-Qaeda," they would "shake the Zionist entity."
> Acquire as many weapons as possible, store them safely, and draw "encrypted maps" of cache sites.
> Learn to store essential foods for long periods and identify those foods most needed during wartime.
> Form groups of five or fewer, which would meet only once a week. Give each group a specific task. For example, to build explosives or distribute messages from al-Qaeda's leaders, especially Zawahiri's videos and lectures by "the beloved al-Zarqawi."
> Palestinian Salafist preachers must teach in "a lenient and merciful manner," and there must be no "fighting with the mujahedin brothers in Hamas."[89]

Two local al-Qaeda allies validated bin Laden's pledge to send weapons and fighters to Gaza. In February 2008, Abu Abd al-Rahman al-Ghazzawi, Fatah al-Islam's leader in Palestine, declared his group "has realized and understood God's purpose for us and that is the need to offer our support" to the Palestinians." Like AsadAl-Jihad2, al-Ghazzawi endorsed bin Laden's 2007 pledge to support Palestinians and agreed that the Palestinian cause was central to "the global jihad," a cause for all Muslims so "borders and languages cannot come between." Al-Ghazzawi also stressed his intent to "begin our war from Palestine" because Shiite Hezbollah—which he calls "the protectors of the Jews, the hizb [party] of Satan has blocked Fatah al-Islam from basing in southern Lebanon." Given this obstruction, al-Ghawazzi said he would bring "immigrants," foreign fighters, into Palestine. Uniting with fighters there, all would fight members of Fatah—the Palestinian National Liberation Movement—Hamas, or Shiites, or anyone who would "restrain us from the Jews."[90]

Later that February, AQI chief Abu-Umar al-Baghdadi declared Israel to be a religious state in which there was no difference between Judaism and Zionism. Both were "the core and origin of corruption." Israel was "a malignant germ that has been planted in the body of the ummah that must be extracted." Going farther than AsadAl-Jihad2 and al-Ghazzawi, al-Baghdadi decreed President Mahmoud Abbas's Fatah and the Hamas political leadership were as much the enemy of Islam as Israel, claiming, for example, that there was "no difference" between Israeli prime minister Olmert and "his criminals" and Abbas and his gang—indeed the latter deserved "more to be fought." Like bin Laden and other al-Qaeda leaders, however, al-Baghdadi did not condemn "those sincere people in the al-Qassam Brigades [of Hamas fighters]."[91]

Al-Baghdadi advised Palestinians much as had AsadAl-Jihad2: to preach Salafism more broadly and to teach young men to love jihad; to encourage the Hamas military wing to join al-Qaeda and its allies; to prepare to help "immigrant" mujahedin coming from Syria, Jordan, and Lebanon; and to devote more effort to disseminating jihadist media products. Finally, al-Baghdadi announced that "the cause of the al-Aqsa Mosque" was "of interest to every Muslim" and emphasized the part that mujahedin from Iraq would play in freeing Palestine. "As for the role of the Islamic state in the Land of the Two Rivers in the liberation of Palestine," he declared, "We trust in God and pray to Him and hope that just as the state of Nur al-Din the martyr was the foundation stone in the return of the al-Aqsa Mosque to the nation—and it was later entered by his student Saladin as a conqueror in the Battle of Hittin, just as the Caliph Umar entered it—the Islamic state of Iraq will be the foundation stone for the return of Jerusalem."[92]

Following bin Laden's lead, each al-Qaeda spokesman has openly threatened Israel and Fatah; differentiated "traitorous" Hamas politicians from noble al-Qassam Brigade fighters; highlighted the importance of Iraq and the Levant countries as bases for sending military aid to Palestinians; implicitly asserted that Palestinians would not defeat Israel without the muhajirun; advised patience as immigrant fighters were inserted and local ones were trained; and called for Palestinian media to teach young men Salafism and military skills. Overall, bin Laden and his lieutenants showed that al-Qaeda believed it had won a durable strategic victory in Iraq by securing contiguous safe haven; that Israel would have a higher priority as a target for al-Qaeda and its allies than before; and that even from the war-torn Pakistan-Afghanistan border, al-Qaeda was confident it could get fighters to Palestine.

Was this confidence justified? In Palestine there is currently a minor Salafi presence in the West Bank but a steadily growing military and proselytizing one in Gaza. Several Salafi organizations built training facilities in Gaza and displayed them to the media, defiantly proclaiming, "We are coming, Jews!"[93] They attacked Israeli army units raiding Gaza, as well as Christian and American targets there.[94] The Salafi groups claimed that their funding was local and that they "are linked to the brothers of the al-Qaeda organization only from an ideological point of view."[95] That said, Salafi fighters chant pro–bin Laden slogans while training, and Salafi spokesman Abdallah al-Ghazzi maintains that there is contact with al-Qaeda "on specific issues." "We are proud of him [bin Laden], because he is an honorable Shaykh, who defends Islam, and fights whomever is hostile to Islam and Muslims. We urge people to support him."[96] The Salafi leaders in Palestine reaffirmed their admiration for bin Laden as well as their allegiance to his anti-Irsaeli goals in eulogies published after his death.

Salafists in Gaza are fundamentally opposed to Hamas, and firefights have occurred between Salafi fighters and Hamas security during the latter's raids on Salafi mosques; on one occasion, Hamas police killed nine members of the Salafist Army of Islam.[97] This acrimony will continue because Gaza-based Salafi leaders—with al-Qaeda's blessing—are slowly recruiting fighters from the al-Qassam

Brigades. A number of Hamas fighters are "exasperated" with the fact that their leaders deal with Israeli officials, as well as with the on-again, off-again military "calm" between Hamas and Israel. In 2008, for example, three fighters publicly asked al-Qaeda to rebuke their leaders for "drifting away from the path of jihad and engaging in the political process with the Western-backed Palestinian authority that has resulted in the further tightening of the noose around Palestinian necks." They pledged support for "global jihad" and asked that "al-Qaeda lend its support [to] their military effort."[98] In separate Internet comments, writers who claimed to be Hamas fighters argued that no one was better suited than al-Qaeda "to offer salvation" to the Palestinian people." Whoever loved "Shaykh Usama bin Ladin" was a "believer," and "whoever hates him is a disbeliever."[99] While Salafist progress in Gaza is slow and contested, an Arab writer points out that the inflow of Salafis from Iraq will have a negative impact across the Levant. "Salafis have not yet taken root in Palestine," Urayb al-Rintawi wrote in late 2008. "However, who had expected to see demonstrations in Beirut of men and women whose appearance is similar to their coreligionists in Qandahar and Peshawar? If the Salafi tide is possible in Lebanon it is likely it will not be impossible in the hungry and blockaded Gaza Strip."[100] Al-Rintawi's warning was made particularly prescient by the collapse of Hosni Mubarak's regime in Egypt and the subsequent uptick in the flow of weapons and Sunni fighters across the border from Egypt into Gaza.

Israeli authorities claimed that al-Qaeda set up in Lebanon's Palestinian refugee camps, especially in Ayn al-Hilwah, in 2003. That same year, the media reported Mossad or its surrogates killed al-Qaeda's leader, an Egyptian named Abd-al-Sattar al-Masri, in the camp. Eight years ago it was hard to assess Israel's claims. Were they factual, or simply intended to hype terrorist threats to get more U.S. aid? Today, there is no reason to doubt. As noted, Gaza-based Salafist groups have publicly declared their presence, and in late 2008 the *Jerusalem Post* reported that "al-Qaida affiliates" had fired twenty-one rockets and eighteen mortar rounds into Israel, and had laid explosive charges near the security fence.[101] There is therefore clear evidence of rising Salafist militancy in the Levant, and no reason to think it will slow. Egypt's police state has fallen, Syria is under siege by the West, and Jordan and Lebanon face a growing Islamist militancy. All of this comes after Israel's security had been damaged by the destruction of Saddam's reliable, anti-Salafi bulwark. Indeed, Israel faces a larger Salafi threat now that U.S. forces have left Iraq. The Shia regime in Baghdad now has no incentive to stop Salafis from crossing its western border into the Levant; indeed, Iraqi security will improve as the Salafis leave. Given this scenario, the Israeli writer Amos Harel's depiction of al-Qaeda's success in securing its organizational goal in Iraq seems plausible. He has noted that the Arab Israelis and Palestinians have become more inclined to carry out terrorist attacks. "No less troubling is the growing identification they sense with the agenda of al-Qaeda, which is more extremist than that of Hamas or of the extremist wing of the Islamic Movement in Israel. For some years now the public declarations of Bin-Laden and his aides have increasingly focused on Israel and Jewish communities around the world as targets for terrorist attacks. It is also known that cells linked with al-Qaeda operate with relative ease in the Gaza Strip."

In Israel, he has pointed out, al-Qaeda has been finding "fertile ground."[102]

7

THE BIN LADEN ERA

New Year's is a time for reflection, and when champagne corks popped in some parts of the world to welcome in 2011, Osama bin Laden, like so many others, might have used the moment to take stock of his life. He had labored hard to emulate models he chose as a youth, especially the Prophet Muhammad, Saladin, and his father, Muhammad bin Laden. Like them, he had consistently matched words and deeds, and done so while leading a hard, dangerous, devoutly religious, and ascetic life. As 2011 began, he, al-Qaeda, and their allies were still at war with the United States, and they would surely have thought the mere fact of their continued military viability was validation of God's promise of victory to Muslims fighting in His cause. After such reflection and then prayer, bin Laden might have retired to think of new ways to destroy Islam's enemies in a struggle with no end in sight. In the West, outside of the U.S. Special Forces and CIA, most of the cork poppers would have given thought to neither him nor the war they were losing, or the coming morning's hangover.

The foregoing is cut from whole cloth; Western and Muslim calendars do not coincide. But in an era in which celebrity and spectacle are so prized, Western leaders, pundits, and generals have demonstrated a nearly complete disinterest in one of its most spectacular celebrities.[1] Though it would be a disastrous mistake to dismiss Osama bin Laden as only a celebrity—akin to various Hollywood, political, or sports vacuities—he continues to be one, and of epic proportions. Perhaps this disinterest reflects the fact that most contemporary celebrities are at best mediocrities. Perhaps it is because Western and especially U.S. leaders consigned bin Laden to being merely a kind of gangster, an Arab Al Capone, one of the "bad guys." This slotting also is, after all, natural and comfortable for Americans bred on the idea that criminals can be dealt with by Law and Order. It is likewise a neat fit for Americans who are taught that history is made by great, impersonal economic and social forces, and that individuals are carried by such forces. Those once thought of, in the days of a worthwhile education, as history makers—Great Men, if you will—were really villains or frauds, like the dead, white, misogynist, and slave-holding men who are said to have created the American republic.

Though a celebrity, bin Laden also is one of those "Great Men." It is fair to say that he has had a greater impact on how Americans view their society, government, and security than any other individual in the past fifty years. His actions have caused Americans to doubt their government's ability, and at times its desire, to defend them; he has made them wary of growing police powers at all government levels; he has made them suspicious of neighbors, immigrants, and tourists; he has recast the military they might have once admired as the world's best as an enormously expensive entity that can do anything but win wars; and he has waged a religious conflict against them that utterly confounds Westerners.

All this, I would suggest, flows from the abject failure of American leadership to understand bin Laden and therefore to understand how he has motivated increasing numbers of Muslims to wage jihad on America, a war his successors intend to bring to its cities and towns. If the leaders did understand, they could begin to teach Americans that bin Laden and those he has led and inspired have brought U.S. power to a standstill; that they are grossly miscast as a limited number of criminal, un-Islamic, and mass-murdering nihilists; and that defeating them, while a matter of survival, is anything but assured.

In what can be called the "bin Laden era," our misperception of the man has given a false sense of comfort, an unfounded belief that the West has the whip hand in the war against his organization. The best way to measure our misperception is to look at several working assumptions on which Western authorities have based their estimate of the foe. For example, they have always derived a sense of security from the fact of bin Laden not being a trained Islamic scholar. Indeed, many have dismissed him as a fraud because his education showed, as the scholar Michael Collins Dunn put it, that "his right to claim to be a religious scholar is highly questionable."[2] In 2005, Steve Coll identified bin Laden as an aspiring "activist theologian" along the lines of Abdullah Azzam.[3] Professor Khaled Abou El Fadl wrote that bin Laden "fancies himself a theologian and jurist," though never trained as either.[4] As recently as late 2006, West Point's Combating Terrorism Center published a study declaring, "Osama bin Laden may be the leading symbol of global Islamist militancy but the al-Qaeda leader wields less influence over Islamist theology than more obscure religious thinkers."[5] The consensus argument has held that bin Laden has been unable to speak authoritatively about Islam and its duties and therefore that Muslims will not listen to or follow his guidance.

This is a comforting but wholly false assumption. Bin Laden never claimed to be an Islamic scholar; indeed, in one form or another he often repeated a statement he made in August 2000: "My job is not to lead but to follow. . . . I always seek guidance from many great religious scholars."[6] Bin Laden's own estimate of his theological credentials has been echoed by others. "He had some knowledge of shariah and liked to listen to Muslim jurists whom he trusted," Shaykh al-Qarni has claimed, "but he was never an expert jurist." "Usama bin Laden," al-Qarni added, "does not see himself as more proficient in religious knowledge than the Islamic world's illustrious scholars."[7] In fact, bin Laden repeatedly denied being a scholar, claiming only to be a "humble slave of God" forced to public speaking because the Islamic world's "illustrious scholars" had been silenced. "He knows his theological limitations," wrote Cherif Ouazai, one of the first journalists to sketch the al-Qaeda's chief's life, "and that is why he surrounds himself with imams and ulema."[8] Underscoring this is the fact that al-Qaeda has a religious affairs committee as well as an official and appropriately trained theological spokesman, first Sulieman Abu Gaeyth—who recently was released from Iranian custody—and now Abu Yaha al-Libi. And from the 1990s, bin Laden clandestinely sought out advice from scholars still residing in Saudi Arabia, and presumably other Muslim countries as well.[9]

If this one assumption about bin Laden can be undermined by a quick review of facts, what other assumptions can also be? Nearly every Western expert and Muslim critic who has written on bin Laden has denigrated him for not being an original thinker (as we have seen, a key element of the Saudi narrative). Steve Coll claimed that bin Laden's "gifts of foresight and political analysis had always been limited"; Hashim al-Makki cited the "weakness" of bin Laden's political capabilities; Lawrence Wright argued that bin Laden "had never shown himself to be an interesting or original thinker"; the late, former Pakistani intelligence officer Khalid Khawaja bluntly assessed bin Laden as not only "not a genius" but also "not very intelligent"; Khaled Abou El Fadl added that bin Laden "is not the most systematic or consistent thinker"; and Bruce Lawrence, editor of one of the best anthologies of bin Laden's oeuvre, concurred: bin Laden was not "an original thinker" or "an outstanding Koranic scholar."[10] Saudi interior minister Prince Nayef said that bin Laden was not merely a "silly person" but actually an agent of foreign intelligence, an enemy of Islam like the separatist Khawarij, who, after the Prophet's death, "opened fronts against the Muslim ummah, weakening its capabilities and supporting its enemies."[11] And Prince Bandar bin Sultan—now Riyadh's national security adviser—described Osama bin Laden as a simple man who "didn't impress me as somebody who could be the leader of anything." "I thought he couldn't lead eight ducks across the road."[12]

It would seem to me a miracle if someone of that description had waged a decade-and-a-half war on the world's only superpower, and not only survived but helped push it toward bankruptcy. But that would be flip and unpatriotic, casting into doubt the idea that America is proceeding toward inevitable victory at the pace it desires. A more cogent response to allegations that bin Laden lacked an original mind would be "So what?" How many truly original minds are there? And do you need such a mind to accomplish great things? Jefferson maintained that he had not produced anything original in the Declaration of Independence, but, rather, reworked older ideas and theories. Oliver Wendell Holmes assessed Franklin Roosevelt as having a second-class mind but a first-rate temperament.

In bin Laden's case, not having an original mind proved a strength. Original minds produce original ideas, but these are not always ideas that inspire or inform the average person. Few can understand or appreciate Einstein's originality. Bin Laden's mind, however, was ideally suited for what he wanted to do. He had a thorough knowledge of the Koran and the hadith, and as a skilled polemicist nimbly used both to communicate effectively with 1.3 billion Muslims, providing them with familiar frame of reference in which to assess his words and actions.[13] Bin Laden's broad support among Salafis in Saudi Arabia and across the Muslim world, argues Saudi dissident Abdallah al-Rashid, has been due precisely to his lack of originality. Instead, that support has been "the result of his adoption of the same traditional religious message on which successive Salafi generations have been reared."[14]

The unoriginal bin Laden also brought other talents to bear. He was a skilled speaker, fluent in a lyrical and "at times even poetic"—as Bernard Lewis put it—brand of classical Arabic, long deemed an indispensable tool for effective leadership in the Arab world.[15] He had a firm command of contemporary world affairs, kept updated, and used the latest information to guide his decisions. He also used his management skills to run a multiethnic, multinational, and multilingual organization that is unique in the Muslim world. He displayed the cool reasoning of a cost-benefit-calculating businessman, and the sophistication of a media mogul.

His patience, steadiness under pressure, and perseverance were likewise remarkable, not only for keeping him alive and in the fight for so long, but for allowing him to survive his own nearly fatal mistakes: leading men against Soviets at Jaji before they were fully trained; expecting Prince Turki and Saudi intelligence to put Islam's interests ahead of the al-Sauds'; leaving large financial holdings in Saudi Arabia to be frozen or confiscated; trusting the promises of Sudan's self-serving leader, Hasan al-Turabi; prematurely trying to force Islamist unity by creating the World Islamic Front against Crusaders and Jews; and naming Abu-Musab al-Zarqawi as al-Qaeda's chief in Iraq.

As important, and perhaps even more important, bin Laden's personal life and comportment are reminiscent of Muslim heroes throughout Islamic history, and particularly Saladin's, the man whose actions, as James Reston, Jr., has written, "seemed to define what it meant to be a good Muslim."[16] Indeed, bin Laden is the stuff legends are made of in all cultures. He gave up a billionaire's lifestyle to fight for his faith, most of the time in some of the most rugged places on earth. He was a pious, generous, and personally brave man, who behaved with integrity and spoke with an eloquence that could alternately comfort and inspire his listeners. He dressed with modesty, behaved deferentially, and was as comfortable with the poor and the indigent as he was with the rich and the powerful. "One can build a legend around Osama, even a bigger legend than that of Robin [Hood]," University of Wichita law professor Liaquat Ali Khan wrote—from the perspective of being a foe of bin Laden but one who respected a man whose story "goes far beyond the confines of Nottingham, [and] cuts across cultures, religions, and civilizations. If the genius of an outlaw is to find law beyond law and to place justice at the core of criminality, Osama's claims that he is fighting foreign occupation, neo-colonialism and alien domination sound credible to Marxists, Palestinians, war critics, and imperialists. And if the genius of an outlaw is to establish a popular constituency that roots for his breaches of the law, Osama has done that, too."[17]

Bin Laden was fully conscious of the historical resonance of his activities, and the importance of Islamic history and its heroes in his rhetoric cannot be overestimated. Although largely illiterate, the Muslim masses know their faith's history—particularly military—and its heroes far better than Westerners know theirs. Through sermons, storytelling, and oral histories, passed from one generation to the next down the centuries, Muslims are intimately familiar with the Islamic past and tend to talk about it in their daily lives.

Bin Laden managed to insert himself into that history, and at the same time made it urgently relevant. His rhetoric and his actions addressed the current grievances Muslims have against Western intervention and the cruelty, hypocrisy, incompetence, and corruption of their own regimes. In addition, bin Laden's eluding the world's greatest military power for so many years has convinced many Muslims that he was the man, as one writer put it, whom God chose from his ummah "to raise the banner of jihad at a time when all Muslims have forsaken themselves and their religion."[18] For America and the West it would have been far better had Allah blessed bin Laden with a more original mind, one that produced rhetoric few could easily understand.

A third operating assumption is that bin Laden had no sense of what he and the Islamists would do after winning the war, no plan for governance. Jonathan Randall, an early bin Laden biographer, for example, argued that bin Laden "was not interested in the mundane business of running a government."[19] And even Michael Vlahos argued wrongly that, in terms of governance, bin Laden and al-Qaeda were "not addressing what people are actually looking for." Muslims were therefore "turning against al-Qaeda [and] looking for new models and practical outcomes."[20]

The truth is quite the opposite. It is precisely the issue of postwar governance that came to hold a dominant place in the minds of bin Laden and his senior lieutenants. "It is known that al-Qaida is laying down the foundation for a new order," Abdullah al-Rashid has written, although the evidence shows that bin Laden believed—pace Western experts—the enemy's definitive defeat to be the mandatory prerequisite to creating a viable government.[21] In January 2003, al-Rashid reminded his readers that bin Laden had "called for the establishment of a legitimate political and religious leadership to replace the existing corrupt Arab governments. He said the sincere people who pay attention to this matter—such as the ulema who are obeyed by the people, important figures and notables, and merchants—should assemble and meet somewhere safe and remote from the despotic regimes and establish a council of influential people in order to fill the vacuum resulting from these regimes' religious shortcomings and intellectual sterility."[22] The documentary record bears Rashid out. In the communiqués published by the ARC and other statements and interviews, bin Laden consistently condemns the al-Saudis and most Muslim rulers for not ensuring adequate supplies of water and electricity, and generally allowing social services to deteriorate. Even in that 1996 declaration of war on America, bin Laden devoted substantial space to explaining how the war would be a means to bring better governance to the Islamic world. "Today we begin to talk, work, and discuss," he wrote,

> what has befallen the Islamic world in general and the land of the two holy mosques in particular. We want to study the ways which could be used to rectify and restore rights to their

> owners as people have been subjected to grave harm and danger to their religion and their lives, people of all walks of life, civilians, military, security men, employees, merchants, people big and small, school and university students, and unemployed university graduates, in fact hundreds of thousands who constitute a broad sector of society. The same thing has befallen the people in industry and agriculture, the cities and the villages, and the people in the desert in the rural areas. . . . People have been greatly preoccupied with matters of their livelihood. Talk of economic decline, high prices, massive debts, and overcrowded prisons is widespread and endless in society.[23]

Pious, talented men must begin to plan for a return to the Shariah-based governance that will improve the lot of all Muslims. "Kings and rulers have lost their power legally and realistically," bin Laden told Muslims in the spring of 1998, and it was therefore incumbent on Islam's best and brightest to form a council to "run the jihad-for-God's-cause battalions in order to expel the occupying powers," as well as to take over and run national regimes.[24] This task, he said, was not up to him to accomplish; it had to be the subject of wider consultation. "The honest people who are concerned about this situation," bin Laden told Muslims, "such as ulema, leaders who are obeyed among their peoples, dignitaries, notables, and merchants should get together and meet in a safe place away from the shadow of these suppressive regimes and form a council of Ahl al-Hall wa al-Aqd [honest, wise, and righteous people who can appoint or remove a ruler in Islamic tradition] to fill the vacuum caused by the religious invalidation of the regimes and their mental deficiency. The right to appoint an imam is for the nation. The nation also has the right to change course if he deviates from it and remove him if he does something that warrants this, such as apostasy or treason."[25]

Once convened, the distinguished members of this council would begin assembling lists of "honest scholars, preachers, thinkers, and writers who can advise the ummah" and discuss how to reorganize government and rectify the "huge leadership failure" with which the ummah has been handicapped. Muslims must have "real, honest, independent, strong, trustworthy leaders" who are "well versed in the Fiqh of current affairs and the Fiqh of the Sharia." Only then would Muslim tyrannies and infidel occupation be eliminated and the "spread of poverty, ignorance, and disease" stemmed. Bin Laden also urged the broadest possible participation in this work. Everyone involved need not agree with each other, and doctrinal "errors" must not be an "obstacle," he wrote. "These errors should be noted and advice given." Here again, bin Laden emphasizes that only Allah is perfect. Men make mistakes, and are advised as to how to correct them, but work must proceed and not await consensus. To wait for all to agree would mean there would be "no scholars left," not to mention those who were "less than scholars."[26]

Bin Laden also advised Muslims to start thinking about how to order their relations with the non-Islamic world after the infidel occupiers were forced to withdraw and Arab tyrants deposed—confirming that he is not planning an endless offensive war to make all the world Islamic. Muslims were part of a larger world and must interact with it politically. Isolation might be the right option culturally and religiously, but not in terms of trade and commerce. He urged "honest people, especially ulema, preachers, and merchants," for example, to take advantage of "opinion polls which indicate most European peoples want peace." Muslim leaders should form committees "to enlighten European peoples of the justice of our causes, firstly Palestine . . . [and to exploit] the huge potential of the media."[27] Similar work, he added, needed to be done in the economic realm. "We are in the fifteenth century of this great religion," bin Laden reminded his listeners, and "it has clarified the dealing between an individual and another, the duties of the believer toward God, praise and glory be to Him, and the relationship between the Muslim country and other countries in time of war and peace. If we look back at our history, we will find that there were many types of dealings between the Muslim nation and the other nations in time of peace and war, including treaties and matters to do with commerce. As for oil, it will be a commodity subject to the price of the market. We believe that current prices are not realistic due to the Saudi regime playing the part of the U.S. agent and flooding the market which caused a sharp decrease in oil prices."[28]

So contrary to what passes for common wisdom, bin Laden, al-Qaeda, and other Islamists have been trying to lay the groundwork for a new Islamic society. Western commentators look about and see in the Islamists' hands no constitutions, no books of parliamentary procedure, no Magna Carta or Federalist Papers or Bills of Rights. In other words, they see nothing they deem essential for building a government and its laws. But what are the Koran and Sunnah if not the Muslim's world's indispensable tools for structuring and governing a society? As the world's most respected Salafi scholar, Abu-Muhammad al-Maqdisi, has said, Bin Laden wanted "esteem for his ummah by turning to the holy Koran in governance."[29] In support of al-Maqdisi's contention, Bernard Lewis has noted that the Koran is laid out in two parts: the first, to structure successful war-making against the status quo, and the second, to advise on how to consolidate power and form an Islamic state. Referring to the Meccan period, Lewis writes that "the verses in the Koran carry a message of opposition—of rebellion, one might even say of revolution, against the existing order," while the verses Muhammad received in the post-hijra Medina period focus "on how to conduct governance."[30] There is, then, in the Koran and the Sunnah ample principles for post-tyranny, post-occupation governance in Muslim states, principles that were successfully used in Islam's history to govern guided by the salaf—that is, Muhammad, his companions, and Muhammad's immediate successors as Islam's leader—those bin Laden and most Muslims have believed were "the best of men." We in the West would not like the governing edifice built from applying what bin Laden called the "sources of learning," but we should not deceive ourselves: bin Laden and his allies have had a postwar plan of governance, and it is one that would give them credibility with many Muslims.[31]

Finally, the most potentially lethal consensus assumption is that bin Laden and al-Qaeda have been losing the war because they kill more Muslims than infidels. Writers such as David Kilcullen, Mary Habeck, and Lawrence Wright have helped form this consensus, explaining that al-Qaeda—and at times the Taleban and other Islamist groups—are following takfirism, which, as we have seen, means the "pronouncement of unbelief against someone."[32] Those who abide by this doctrine take it upon themselves to decide who is and who is not a "good Muslim"; those not passing muster can be killed and their property taken. This consensus view is enormously important to U.S. interests because it is the basic operating assumption for the U.S. military's Afghan strategy, largely thanks to David Kilcullen's widely read book *The Accidental Guerrilla*.

The consensus received a patina of qualitative support in late 2009, when West Point's Combating Terrorism Center published a study entitled "Deadly Vanguards: A Study of al-Qaeda Violence against Muslims." The study showed that between 2004 and 2008, a mere 15 percent of the 3,010 victims in al-Qaeda's attacks were Westerners. From 2006 to 2008, only 2 percent (or 12 of 661) of the victims were Westerners. The other 98 percent were inhabitants of countries in which there is a Muslim majority.[33] Many in the media took this report to be a sure sign of al-Qaeda's demise, proof that its war really was against other Muslims.

No doubt there have been more Muslim than Western casualties from al-Qaeda attacks. The war is being fought, for now, only on Muslim territory. More pertinent, however, would be to ask about the casualty count among Muslims across the Islamic world—or simply in Afghanistan and Iraq—from attacks by U.S. forces and their allies between 2004 and 2008. Is it even remotely conceivable that there were been fewer than the 450 Muslims the West Point study claims al-Qaeda has killed? Additionally, how many Muslims were killed by Israel in Lebanon (2006) and Gaza (2008)? Most important, does anyone really believe Muslims are ignorant of this discrepancy or ambivalent about who is defending them—al-Qaeda and its allies or President Mubarak, the Algerian generals, and the al-Sauds?

The core of the problem here is that Western experts have latched on to a tenet of Shariah law that says something akin to "it is forbidden for one Muslim to kill another," made it an absolute across all times and all situations, and described any Muslim deviating from it a "takfiri." This contention, of course, is self-evidently absurd; it makes as much sense as saying the West should not have resisted and utterly destroyed German and Japanese fascism because "love thy neighbor," "turn the other cheek," and "thou shall not kill" are absolutes in all times and places. Were that the case, there is no way al-Qaeda or any Muslim could legally make war, even in self-defense. Indeed, the Prophet and his companions would have been unable to defend themselves and Islam would have died at birth. This clearly is not what the Koran or the hadith intend. At the very moment the West Point study was published, for example, the Saudi and Yemeni regimes were busy slaughtering Sunnis and Shias in Yemen with artillery, fixed-wing aircraft, and helicopter gunships; no complaints came from either country's official scholars or from the West. Likewise, Muslim militaries fought alongside infidel forces to kill Iraqi Muslims in the 1990–1991 Gulf War after Riyadh had its clerics issue a fatwa making God's impermissible permissible. Finally, if the Koran and hadith banned one Muslim from killing another, why would Washington and NATO have engaged in the massively expensive effort to train 400,000 Afghan Muslims as military and police personnel for the job of killing other Afghan and non-Afghan Muslims?

Reading the materials available in English about what might be called the "Islamic way of war," I can't help but notice much similarity with the West's concept of just war. Good intentions are paramount in each, as are the idea of reciprocity, the possibility of victory, and proper authorization for war. It is not clear to me, however, that Islam shares anything close to the West's acute concern for proportionality; it especially does not share the West's post-1945 idea of proportionality which has, at least in the case of the United States, prevented victory in war since Japan's defeat. In each tradition there is deep concern for preventing unnecessary civilian casualties, but in neither—if rightly applied—does the certainty of civilian casualties prevent war from being declared or, having started, does it preclude pursuit of total victory. And in Islam's way of war, scholars all but universally agree that Muslims supporting or working for infidels, or who wage war with them against Muslims, can be killed. "If a scholar views them as explicitly assisting the American military in the occupation," writes the scholar of Salafism Quintan Wiktorowicz, "then the most relevant Qur'anic verses and hadiths are related to the status of those who assist in warfare against Muslims (and the vast majority of Islamic scholars concur that such individuals are legitimate targets)."[34]

As I have tried to establish, bin Laden and his lieutenants never pronounced a takfiri doctrine and always publicly denounced allegations that they abided by the doctrine. "We do not make general takfir," bin Laden told the Saudi rulers, "and we do not spill the blood of Muslims carelessly. But if some Muslims get killed during Mujahedin operations, this falls under what is permitted."[35] In addition, as we have seen, bin Laden was himself the repeated target of self-declared takfiri assassins in Sudan and Afghanistan.

There is no doubt, however, that bin Laden and his lieutenants have been extremely sensitive to charges of takfirism and have seldom allowed such allegations to stand without a stong public rebuttal. They have known that to be labeled as such by Muslims would undermine much of their popular support and appeal. Indeed, as discussed in chapter 6, the most serious post-9/11 strategic threat to al-Qaeda was Abu Musab al-Zarqawi and his takfiri beliefs and actions. It was al-Zarqawi's murderous behavior toward Sunni and Shia Muslims in Anbar Province and elsewhere in Iraq that gave U.S. military forces the chance to bribe, train, and arm Sunni Iraqis. One of al-Qaeda's own all but mortally wounded the organization and helped save Washington and its allies from even greater disaster in Iraq. The even greater irony is that the U.S. military's killing of al-Zarqawi slowed al-Qaeda's decline in Iraq, giving it the chance to rebuild its organization there.

If bin Laden and his like are not takfiris, what, then, are they? The terms Wahhabi and Salafi have been of course most often applied to bin Laden, and I would argue Salafi is the better. Bin Laden clearly reflected what Professor El Fadl identifies as the pivotal difference between Wahhabism and Salafism, which is that "Wahhabism is far less tolerant of diversity and differences of opinion."[36] Saudi Wahhabism, for example, features a pervasive attitude of superiority, disdain, and intolerance for non-Wahhabi, non-Arab Muslims, which would prevent any unity among al-Qaeda's diverse membership. Bin Laden's bore-sighted focus on the Koran, the hadith, the words and examples of the first three Muslim generations, and a few later jurists and scholars is documented and puts him squarely into the Salafi category. This doctrine, though not Sunni Islam's most popular, is respected for its piety. In no way is it seen as outside the faith's legitimate parameters; it constitutes one of "the largest Islamist movement[s] in the Muslim world"; and it attracts men and women in Europe, the Middle East, Central Asia, Southeast Asia, and Africa.[37] For Americans it is useful to think of bin Laden's attitude toward Islam's founding leaders and documents as akin to that of their fellow citizens who believe governance must be based on the Founders' "original intent."

Fortunately, several scholars—Quintan Wiktorowicz foremost among them—have done excellent post-9/11 work on Salafism, defining the doctrine more precisely and detailing a pattern of Salafi behavior that best fits bin Laden. Dr. Wiktorowicz argues there are three categories of Salafis:

First, "Salafi purists," who are scholars who study the Koran, hadith, and other materials; publish tracts to spread Islam and help Muslims understand their faith and behave accordingly; and generally keep a monkish distance from the public. In dealing with Muslim rulers, they prefer giving advice in private, are opposed to offering public advice or encouraging antiregime agitation, and adamantly oppose violence. Purists dominate the Saudi religious establishment, and are the most aged of the Salafi population.[38]

Second, "Salafi politicos," who believe that academic studies and behind-the-scenes advising fall far short of fulfilling a scholar's responsibilities. They believe that nonviolent public agitation is needed to purify Islam. Politicos arose after Saudi Grand Mufti bin Baz's 1990 fatwa allowing U.S. and Western military units into the Kingdom, a decree bin Laden's friend Shaykh Safar al-Hawali said was official approval for infidel colonization of the Arabian Peninsula.[39]

Third, "Salafi jihadists," who argue that purists are too loyal and subservient to corrupt Muslim regimes, and while politicos have a better grip on current events, they are too timid in responding thereto.[40] These men emerged during the Afghan-Soviet war (1979–1992). They support purist teachings and writings meant to spread Islam, as well as the politicos' public proreform agitation. The jihadis, however, believe that to purify Islam and bring Muslims back under God's rule, a defensive jihad must be waged on Islam's foes, be they infidels or nominal Muslims. In essence, they seek to make jihad a form of worship and Islam's sixth pillar, what bin Laden called "the peak of true

> Islam."[41] Salafi jihadis also see their role to be one of aiding and advising, but not replacing, mujahedin leaders. They give jihadi military leaders substantial discretion when making decisions about weapons, targets, methods of operation, and noncombatant casualties. Bin Laden referred to this approach as the "jurisprudence of reality."[42]

Although the three categories of Salafis have major differences in approach, they all share complete agreement on four key issues. First, the beliefs of all three are based nearly exclusively on the Koran and hadith, and they see the latter as an indispensable complement to the Koran because it depicts "the perfection of Islamic practice" as "applied to concrete, real world problems."[43] Wiktorowicz points out that some Salafi scholars spend their entire careers validating hadiths.[44] Second, most members of each group believe Washington is waging an aggressive war on Islam, intending its destruction, and that Americans and Israelis are "people of war."[45] Third, all Salafis believe a defensive jihad to resist infidel aggression or invasion is a "just cause par excellence."[46] And fourth, all share a strong inclination toward isolation, thinking first, last, and always in terms of what is best for Islam and Muslims. Given the broad agreement on vital issues, the splits among Salafis are not about belief—on that there is strong consensus. Their differences lie in how each group assesses contemporary international events; how those events impact Islam and Muslims; and how creed should be applied to deal with the events for Islam's benefit.[47]

Why is this rather esoteric summary of Salafism's three trends important vis-à-vis Osama bin Laden? Because bin Laden easily fits into the third category, Salafi jihadis. As a result, the starting point for the West's understanding of bin Laden, and its debate about how to use public diplomacy to cope with his leadership and example, must not be the fatuous and dead-end idea that their ideology is a takfiri and outside any legitimate form of Islam. It is true that as a Salafi jihadi bin Laden is not in the mainstreams of Islam or Salafism, but it is more important to understand—and vital if the West plans to counter his influence—that bin Laden was, and continues to be seen as, a legitimate and good Muslim by his coreligionists. Many disagree with al-Qaeda's martial acts, but that bin Laden was a good Muslim they have no doubt. Even his purist and politico rivals in the Salafi movement (and recall that many are paid and controlled by Muslim regimes) do not disown him. They have given him the benefit of the doubt and called on him to repent.[48]

To underscore that bin Laden is in the fold of Islam and must be seen as such, it is worth looking more fully then heretofore at the views of Shaykh Abu Muhammad al-Maqdisi, a man widely deemed to be one of the most respected and most influential living jihadist theorists, who is sometimes referred to as "the mufti or godfather" of Salafi jihadis.[49] Al-Maqdisi was born in 1959 near Nablus in the West Bank, and from an early age was influenced by Salafi scholars. He later moved to Jordan, Kuwait, and Saudi Arabia, in turn. In the Kingdom, he was influenced by followers of Juhayman al-Utaybi—who led the seizure of the Grand Mosque in Mecca in November 1979—before moving to Pakistan during the anti-Soviet jihad. There he became a prolific author and met Abu Musab al-Zaraqwi. Al-Maqdisi later became al-Zarqawi's mentor when both were imprisoned in Jordan. During the current Iraq War, al-Maqdisi condemned al-Zarqawi's takfiri beliefs and methods, and later lost a son who was fighting the U.S.-led coalition in Iraq. He was released from prison by Jordanian authorities in March 2008, but as this is being written the media report that he is again being held and questioned by Jordanian police.

Al-Maqdisi's views are widely accepted among Salafi jihadis, as well as by many Salafi purists and politicos. These views include the rejection of democracy as an infidel religion; the need to explicitly and publicly denounce Arab rulers as Western "agents" who have made themselves objects of worship; the categorization of Muslim rulers not ruling only by Shariah as unbelievers; the identification of Saudi Arabia as an infidel state; approval of applying the concept of takfir to individuals whose actions—such as working for infidels against Muslims—nullify their Islam, but not to whole peoples or nations; a preference for attacking Islam's near enemies but no ban on attacking its far enemies; the termination of treaties or alliances between Muslim states and infidel countries—especially the United States—because they are a disavowal of Islam; the goal of jihad fighting in order to unite the ummah, not simply to damage to the enemy; and, finally, that jihad's central goal is to create an Islamic state rather than the "apocalyptic triumph of good over evil."[50]

Readers might note that the foregoing list of al-Maqdisi's theologically legitimate views—that is, they are not beyond accepted Islamic beliefs—pretty much match the reasons bin Laden consistently used to describe his justification for calling for a defensive jihad. And so what does al-Maqdisi think of bin Laden, not as a scholar, of course—al-Maqdisi does not regard him as such—but as a pious applier of the creed? Two passages from al-Maqdisi's 2009 writings speak volumes.

> Shaykh Usama bin Laden is the imam of the mujahedin in this era and only a nonbeliever or a self-serving hypocrite, loyal to the oppressive [Muslim] regimes, can deny what this man has brought forth in support of his religion. Only an ignorant coward, unaware of his religion and the absoluteness of jihad within it, or a spiteful and envious man, jealous of what God has bestowed on bin Laden in terms of stature and victory for his support of the faith, can deny such a fact. I have not had the honor of ever meeting him, although I took part in the lectures at the al-Qa'ida camps in Afghanistan, as well as in its jurisprudence institute in Peshawar, when it was first established.[51]

> Shaykh Osama bin Ladin, God protect him, wants to apply the Shari'ah of God, and combat the infidels who occupied our country [the umma] and looted our wealth. Shaykh Osama wants to defend the children and women who were enslaved by the oppressors and wants to free the detainees. He wants esteem for his ummah by turning to the holy Koran in governance. Shaykh Osama wants to raise the banner that reads "there is no God but God" over the White House. He wants to fight the Zio-Crusader plan that took al-Aqsa away from Muslims, made the inhuman Jews kill babies and kneeling chiefs, and violated the honor of our women and daughters. In short, Shaykh Osama holds in one hand the Koran and in the other hand a weapon, in order to establish a righteous caliphate following the prophetic path.[52]

All this puts paid to the notion that bin Laden and al-Qaeda have been rogue takfiris. Afghans, for example, overwhelmingly follow the least severe school of Sunni Islam—they are "a population that adheres fanatically to the sect of Hanafism in Islam," according to Abdullah Anas. And yet bin Laden and his men have thrived in Afghanistan, even though they are not only Salafis but adherents to the strictest of Sunni Islam's four schools, as formulated by Ahmed Ibn Hanbal in the eighth century.[53] But once again it is Abdel Bari Atwan who can help Western experts tumble to the obvious. "What makes al-Qaeda different to other Islamist organizations such as the Muslim Brotherhood," Atwan explains,

> is the flexibility of its ideology and its wide range of aims. While the leadership's own theological platform is essentially Salafi, the organization's umbrella is sufficiently wide to encompass various schools of thought and political leanings. Al-Qaeda counts among its members and supporters people associated with Wahhabism, Shafi'ism, Malikism and Hanafism. There are even some whose practices and beliefs are directly at odds with Salafism, such as Yunis Khalis, one of the leaders of the Afghan mujahedin. He is a mystic who visits tombs of saints and seeks their blessings—practices inimical to bin Laden's Wahhabi-Salafi schools of thought. The only exception to this pan-Islamic policy is Shi'ism. Al-Qaeda seems implacably opposed to it, as it holds Shi'ism to be heresy.[54]

Today and Tomorrow

At his death, bin Laden was in the prime of his life, though he doubtless a hard existence and the West's constant pursuit made his existence precarious. It is impossible to measure what he might have done had his life span not been cut short. His plans and behavior, however, which his successors will attempt to carry forward are measurable. The United States will continue to be al-Qaeda's main target, but its priority job will be inciting Muslims to jihad. Once America is defeated, al-Qaeda will turn to toppling Arab tyrannies, destroying Israel, and, eventually, to fighting Shia. Bin laden gave no indication that he expected to live long enough to finish the job.

From when he founded al-Qaeda, bin Laden anticipated a war of attrition, one that might last decades; he therefore planned ahead. Describing the jihad as multigenerational, bin Laden indicated shortly after 9/11 that the torch was being passed. "We have been struggling right from our youth," he wrote, and, in turn, the "whole of the Muslim Ummah is depending (after Allah) upon the Muslim youth" to make the same sacrifices. Indeed, one reason for bin Laden's often lengthy post-9/11 silences might well be that he was giving the next generation of al-Qaeda leaders—men such as Abu Yaha al-Libi and Azzam al-Amriki—the chance to become familiar faces and voices to al-Qaeda's audience. [55]

The question is, of course, what threat will a new generation pose? It comprises those who learned their trade in insurgencies in Iraq, Chechnya, the north Caucasus, southern Thailand, Mindanao, Kashmir, and Afghanistan, as well as in the ongoing Talebanization of Bangladesh, Pakistan, and northern Nigeria. The available data suggests three discernible trends. This rising generation will be, first, no less devout, more professional (and brutal), and less visible; second, larger, with more adherents and potential recruits; and third, better educated and more adept at using modern tools, especially weapons and communications. Easily accessible satellite television and Internet streaming video are deepening and broadening Muslim perceptions of an anti-Islamic West; neither Western diplomacy nor military/intelligence forces can negate the power of real-time video of the wars brought by Western invaders to Iraq, Palestine, and Afghanistan. New, harsher antiterror laws in North America and Europe, along with lurid tales from Guantanamo Bay, Abu Ghraib, and Bagram prisons are hardening perceptions. And the fundamentalization of the two great, evangelizing monotheist faiths is fueling a milieu already conducive to radical Islam. Militant Catholicism in Africa, especially, is revitalizing the historic Islam versus Christianity confrontation, creating a sense of threat and defensiveness on each side.

How big is this new generation? That's very hard to judge, though we need to keep in mind that Western authorities probably underestimated its predecessor's size. Estimates of al-Qaeda casualties range between 5,000 and 7,000 fighters, and the organization is thought to have lost two-thirds of its leadership. (For an organization that is sometimes said not to exist, those are impressive figures.)

In addition to good U.S. intelligence work, much of al-Qaeda's early loss of leadership was due to carelessness, a phenomenon that contributed to bin Laden's own death when an al-Qaeda fighter disclosed under interrogation the name of a courier who ultimately led U.S. forces to bin laden's residence in Abbotabad. Wali Khan, Khalid Sheikh Muhammed, and Ibn Shaykh al-Libi, for example, were as much swashbucklers as Islamists—flamboyant, cosmopolitan, and eager for notoriety. Their actions were tinged with arrogance—as if no bullet or jail was made for them—and they were captured in part because of their indifference to danger. Today, al-Qaeda teaches young mujahedin to study the failures of the previous generation and to be aware that "the security issue" will be predominant in the conflict with the West. "As long as the Islamic movement does not take this aspect seriously, the promised victory will continue to lack the most important means for its realization."[56]

Increasingly, al-Qaeda and its allies have been drawing members mainly from the educated middle and uppe-rmiddle classes, those who are comfortable accommodating their categorical rejection of Western culture with a willingness to embrace the latest technology.[57] Insurgent technicians continue to build improvised explosive devices (IEDs) and car bombs that can defeat U.S. detection/jamming technology; indeed, each new defensive technology is soon trumped by better insurgent weapons. In addition, al-Qaeda logisticians and trainers have diffused IED-building techniques to fighters in Yemen, Thailand, Somalia, and Pakistan. Al-Qaeda's media also are the most sophisticated, flexible, and omnipresent that U.S. forces face. They produce nearly real-time video of mujahedin attacks on coalition targets, interviews with insurgent leaders, and a flow of news to 24/7 Arab satellite networks.

Finally, the new generation has the advantage of following the modern Saladin, Osama bin Laden. He is their inspiration, whether or not he serves as their model. Indeed, though we have had a potent foe in bin Laden, the West may face a post–bin Laden era generation that is both less visible and more violent. "From what I know of my father and the people around him," Omar bin Laden told the media in early 2010, "I believe he is the most kind among them, because some are much, much worse."[58]

EPILOGUE

My aim in this book has been to portray Osama bin Laden—his thinking, behavior, and actions—in a way that accurately reflects the primary sources. I have not tried to make him seem like an admirable man (though, as might have become clear, I respect his piety, integrity, and skills) but instead like a formidable enemy, one whom we almost willfully misunderstood. I believe that in a war to defend America, operating on transparently false assumptions about bin Laden and al-Qaeda will prove to have been fatally inadequate, particularly in that political, military, and media leaders have used these assumptions to misinform Americans about him and the threat he has posed. As this book has tried to show, this method of operation is costing America the war that bin Laden, al-Qaeda, and their allies started, and we severely underestimate the chances of its reaching our shores. We are, I believe, fighting a war for survival; if we do not win outright and irrefutably, we will surely lose in the same manner.

And whether or not readers agree with my conclusions, I hope that the book has demonstrated that there is no either plausible or acceptable reason for Americans—whoever they are—to misunderstand bin Laden, the forces he commands and continues to inspire, and the threat they pose to America and its allies. Unlike a decade ago, the materials for correcting this misunderstanding are now available in

English and easily accessible. In fact, bin Laden has provided a mass of material for our use and education, though so far most Western leaders have validated his view that Americans in particular "do not like those who give [them] advice."[1]

Osama bin Laden has given Americans no excuse for ignorance about who he was, what he believed, or what he has intended to do to win. Something Abraham Lincoln once said about Confederate President Jefferson Davis—whom he often called an "insurgent leader"—seems equally true of bin Laden. "On careful consideration of all the evidence accessible," Lincoln told Congress in December 1861, "it seems to me that no attempt to negotiate with the insurgent leader could result in any good. He would accept nothing short of severance of the Union, precisely what we will not and can not give. His declarations to this effect are explicit and oft-repeated. He does not attempt to deceive us. He affords us no excuse to deceive ourselves. He cannot voluntarily reaccept the Union; we cannot voluntarily yield it. Between him and us the issue is distinct, simple, and inflexible. If we yield we are beaten; if the Southern people fail him he is beaten. Either way, it would be the victory or defeat following war."[2]

It is, I think, fair to paraphrase Lincoln and say if Muslims fail al-Qaeda then they are beaten. We should work to make that happen. However, most of the assumptions we have about bin Laden—whether born of comfort, boredom, laziness, or self-justification—have been dead wrong. He has afforded us no excuse to deceive ourselves.

ACKNOWLEDGMENTS

Writing this book, I have incurred three debts I must acknowledge. First, I wish to thank my literary agent, Stuart Krichevsky, and his staff for doing far more than an author has any right to expect. In seeking opportunities, negotiating contracts, making the mysteries of book-making and -selling intelligible, and keeping me fully informed on all fronts, Stuart and his team are all aces. I am proud and very fortunate to be associated with them.

Next, I want to thank Timothy Bent, my editor at Oxford University Press. Tim worked through the manuscript carefully and his changes made for a better book. This was a particularly difficult book to take on because it makes a detailed argument that not only challenges but—I think—negates much of what today is accepted as common wisdom about bin Laden. As a result, thorough documentation was vital. Tim consistently found ways to shorten quotations without obscuring arguments and supported a very evidence heavy set of endnotes. He also has a happy talent for using a prose rapier in places where my original weapon was a less effective polemical broadsword.

Finally, there are two groups whose extraordinary, underappreciated, and often maligned work in America's defense spurred me to try again to explain the nature of the foe against which we are fighting. As noted throughout this book, my view of bin Laden is far out of the mainstream. I have long seen him as America's greatest mortal enemy; I have never thought it enough simply to curse and condemn him simply because his views and faith are antithetical to our values. In 1996, therefore, I was fortunate to join a small company of CIA officers, at home and overseas, who came to hate bin Laden but who also knew that hate was not enough to defend America. These officers believed it their mission to understand bin Laden's motivation, to respect and measure his talents, and to explain it clearly to those who could capture or kill him and destroy al-Qaeda. They accomplished this mission, many times over, risking their lives and careers in the process. They were thwarted—and thousands of Americans have suffered for it—by self-seeking cowardice and by the ideological obsessions rife in the senior levels of the intelligence community and consecutive presidential administrations.

A decade later, many of these same officers continue to hunt al-Qaeda's continued, more geographically dispersed existence, and now loyally serve a third administration—Barack Obama's—that has deluded itself into believing that name-calling and self-imagined moral superiority will win the day against a lightly armed, religiously zealous, and—in their minds—completely un-modern Islamist enemy. Today, in addition, they are burdened not only by bin Laden's continued existence but also by the maddening reality that the very former CIA officer who stopped plans to capture bin Laden in 1998–1999 is now President Obama's senior adviser on "extremism," a word whose substitution for more accurate Islamic terms is emblematic of both ignorance and an eagerness to deceive. At a time when Washington minimizes the threat, these officers' common sense about bin Laden, al-Qaeda, and its Islamist allies, as well as their unrelenting efforts to destroy them, merits America's respect and gratitude.

But CIA efforts, even when combined with Special Forces' operations, drone attacks, and law enforcement activity, will not be enough to defeat the Islamist movement bin Laden and al-Qaeda have inspired. That must be done by conventional units of the U.S. Marines Corps and the U.S. Army. Since resigning from the CIA in late 2004, I have had the great good fortune to help train young Marine and Army NCOs and junior officers on how al-Qaeda and its allies perceive the world. Some of these individuals had not been to war, but most had been to Iraq or Afghanistan or both, some for multiple tours. As a group, I have found them decent, smart, tough, and funny, though also cynical and angry: cynical because those who had fought overseas did not encounter the freedom-hating nihilists their senior commanders had told them to expect, but hard-fighting, brave, and intelligent men who meant to drive them from the Muslim world, rather than to rob them of their liberties or stop their elections; and anger because they had been shackled with rules of engagement that favored the enemy and so increased their chances of not coming home. Prepared for an enemy that did not exist, and restrained from doing all they could to defeat the one that did, these young men and women have nonetheless excelled in an environment where this status quo U.S. foreign policy generates Islamist insurgents faster than they can be killed. All Americans should support and honor these young people, and remember them as lions led by self-serving moral cowards.

NOTES

CHAPTER 1

1. Abdel Bari Atwan, *The Secret History of al-Qaeda* (Berkeley: University of California Press), p. 220.
2. Mary Habeck, *Knowing the Enemy: Jihadist Ideology and the War on Terror* (New Haven: Yale University Press, 2006), pp. 176–177; Marc Sageman, *Understanding Terror Networks* (Philadelphia: University of Pennsylvania Press, 2004), p. 182; Jonathan Randall, *Osama: The Making of a Terrorist* (New York: Knopf, 2004), p. 39; Bruce Riedel, *The Search for al-Qaeda: Its Leadership, Ideology, and Future* (Washington, D.C.: Brookings Institution, 2008), pp. 136–147; David Kilcullen, *The Accidental Guerrilla: Fighting Small Wars in the Midst of a Big One* (New York: Oxford University Press, 2009), p. 289; Louise Richardson, *What Terrorists Want: Understanding the Enemy, Containing the Threat* (New York: Random House, 2006).
3. Lawrence Wright, *The Looming Tower: Al-Qaeda and the Road to 9/11* (New York: Knopf, 2006), p. 135. In a quirk of fate, Omar bin Laden claimed that, as a child, Osama lost nearly all vision in his right eye because a shard of metal from an object he was hammering flew up into his eye. "Over the years my father sought to conceal the problem, thinking it better for people to believe him to be left-handed rather than allow them knowledge that his right eye barely functioned. The only reason my father aims his weapon from the left side is because he is virtually blind in the right eye." Najwa bin Laden, Omar bin Laden, and Jean Sasson, *Growing Up bin Laden: Osama's Wife and Son Take Us inside Their Secret World* (New York: St. Martin's Press, 2009), p. 160.
4. Muhammad al-Shafi'i, "Arab Afghan says Usama bin Ladin's force strength overblown," *Al-Sharq al-Awsat* (Internet version), 6 October 2001.
5. Steve Coll, *Ghost Wars: The Secret History of the CIA, Afghanistan, and bin Laden, from the Soviet Invasion to September 10, 2001* (New York: Penguin, 2005), p. 204.
6. Al-Shafi'i, "Arab Afghan says Usama bin Ladin's force strength overblown."
7. Ibid.; Wright, *The Looming Tower*, p. 130.
8. Al-Shafi'i, "Arab Afghan says Usama bin Ladin's force strength overblown."

9. Peter L. Bergen, *The Osama bin Laden I Know* (New York: Free Press, 2006), p. 105.
10. Al-Shafi'i, "Arab Afghan says Usama bin Ladin's force strength overblown."
11. "Hotline to jihad," Leah Farrall, *Australian* (Internet version), 7 December 2009, and Sally Neighbor, *Australian* (Internet version), 11 December 2009.
12. Muhammad al-Shafi'i, "'Arab Afghans' theorist writes in book found by U.S. forces after Taleban's fall, part 1," *Al-Sharq al-Awsat* (Internet version), 24 October 2006.
13. Muhammad al-Shafi'i, "The story of Abu Walid al-Masri," *Al-Sharq al-Awsat* (Internet version), 11 February 2007.
14. "The Arab Afghans, part 3," www.aawsat.com, 9 July 2005; Farrall, "Hotline to jihad."
15. "Welcome in Yemen, bin Ladin, but!" *Al-Mahrusah* (Internet), 6 December 2002; and al-Shafi'i, "The story of Abu Walid al-Masri."
16. "The Arab Afghans, part 2," www.aawsat.com, 1 July 2005.
17. "The Arab Afghans, part 1," www.aawsat.com, 29 June 2005, and "The Arab Afghans, Part 3."
18. Farrall, "Hotline to jihad," and al-Shafi'i, "Al-Qaeda fundamentalist: Bin Laden believed the media exaggerations about him."
19. "The Arab Afghans, part 1."
20. "Welcome in Yemen, bin Ladin, but!"
21. The best study of al-Suri, which also contributes significantly to understanding bin Laden and al-Qaeda, is Brynjar Lia, *Architect of Global Jihad: The Life of al-Qaeda Strategist Abu Musab al-Suri* (New York: Columbia University Press, 2008).
22. Ibid., p. 7.
23. Ibid., pp. 76–77.
24. Ibid., p. 283.
25. Ibid., pp. 279, 290.
26. Ibid., p. 238.
27. Alan Culinson, "Inside al-Qaeda's hard drive," *Atlantic Monthly*, September 2004, pp. 60–61.
28. Ibid.
29. Al-Suri reportedly was captured by Pakistani police in Quetta in October 2005, and is now being held by Syria. See William Maclean, "Al-Qaeda ideologue in Syrian detention," http://www.reuters.com, 10 June 2009.
30. "Welcome in Yemen, bin Ladin, but!" and al-Shafi'i, "Al-Qaeda fundamentalist: bin Laden believed the media exaggerations about him," p. 4.
31. Farrall, "Hotline to jihad."
32. Lia, *Architect of Global Jihad*, pp. 286 and 314. The journalist Camille Tawil has noted that in breaks between bin Laden and other jihadis "their decision to strike out on their own did not sour their relationships with bin Laden, with him they were to remain on cordial terms." Tawil, *Brothers in Arms: The Story of al-Qaida and the Arab Jihadists* (London: Saqi Books, 2010), p. 32.
33. Jane Mayer, "The house of bin Laden," *New Yorker* (Internet version), 12 September 2002.
34. "White House responds calling Bin Laden a 'murderous thug,'" http://www.therichmarksentinel.com, 24 January 2010; and Bin Laden, bin Laden, and Sasson, *Growing Up bin Laden*, pp. 129, 130, and 132.
35. Bergen, *The Osama bin Laden I Know*, p. 95.
36. Jamil al-Dhiyabi, "Interview with Shaykh Musa al-Qarni, part 2," *Al-Hayah* (Internet version), 9 March 2006.
37. Coll, *Ghost Wars*, p. 153.

38. Wright, *The Looming Tower*, p. 129. On Darraz's status as a former Egyptian officer and the ten-year ban on overseas travel he received on returning from Afghanistan, see Tawil, *Brothers in Arms*, p. 21, and Muhammad al-Shafi'i, "Interview with Isam Darraz," *Al-Sharq al-Awsat*, 17 June 2002, p. 13.
39. Quoted in Wright, *The Looming Tower*, p. 131. See also Mark Huband, *Brutal Truths, Fragile Myths: Power Politics and Western Adventurism in the Arab World* (Boulder: Westview, 2004), p. 110.
40. Stéphane Lacroix, "Ayman al-Zawahiri. Veteran of the jihad," in Gilles Kepel and Jean-Pierre Milelli, eds., *Al-Qaeda in Its Own Words* (Cambridge, Mass.: Harvard University Press, 2008), p. 130.
41. Wright, *The Looming Tower*, p. 130.
42. As I was finishing the first rough draft of this work, a book appeared that must surely be considered a subset of the Saudi narrative, but one which is striking in its honesty and ample in the opportunities it gives the researcher to corroborate its story with other sources. The book—*Growing Up bin Laden*—was written by bin Laden's first wife, Najwa, and his fourth eldest son, Omar. It consists of alternating chapters written by Najwa and Omar. Najwa's story is detailed, personal, and insightful about her husband, and at times painfully poignant, while Omar's is sycophantically pro-Saudi, often whining, but nonetheless full of details and sharp insights about bin Laden, his personality, and piety. Together the memoirists have given the West a primary resource exceeded in value only by bin Laden's own writings and Peter Bergen's indispensable *The Osama bin Laden I Know*.

So the question is: Did the Saudis review the manuscript before publication and approve its publication? There are parts of the book that would have been useful to Riyadh. The Saudi-centric reasons for publication, I think, are clear: (a) Omar is effusive in his praise for the just, beneficent al-Saud family and so emphasizes his father's unjust condemnation of the Saudi royals and the rest of the bin Laden family's loyalty to the regime (pp. 85, 85, 126–127); (b) it serves the Saudi narrative for Westerners via Omar's claims that he and his brothers were routinely beaten by their father *after* they left the Kingdom and fell under the sway of evil Egyptians; and (c) it appeals to Western sympathies, not only by suggesting child abuse at bin Laden's hands (pp. 45, 107, 122) but also by describing Najwa's confinement to the home and domestic sphere (pp. 13, 186); the teenage Omar's love of peace (pp. 215, 221); the family's deprivation of the good things in life (pp. 43, 71); Omar's struggle to be free of his tyrannical father (pp. 136, 200); Omar's horror when his dad's men took his little dogs to use in chemical-weapons experiments (pp. 133–134, 229–230); and—essential for the Saudi narrative—Omar-the-good-Saudi-boy's immediate recognition of Ayman al-Zawahiri as an evil man who corrupted and controlled his father (pp. 129, 130, 132, and 212). On these issues, the book serves the Saudi state: Omar says his dad is wrong and the Saudis are okay, and paints a portrait of child abuse—physical and psychological, including his dad's denial of creature comforts for his family and willingness to kill his kid's pets—that would be sure to build hatred for bin Laden in the West. It should be noted that Omar's claim that he and his brothers were beaten is refuted by every other person who has written on bin Laden's behavior with his children—including bin Laden's bodyguard Abu Jandal, Abdullah Azzam's son Hudhayfah, Abdel Bari Atwan, and the family of Ahmed Said Khadr—and that, in any event, corporal punishment is still the norm in much of the Muslim world. Also, the loathsome doggie murder Omar relates would have no traction in a Muslim world that regards dogs as filthy and expendable.

The book serves Saudi propaganda purposes, but after filtering out the foregoing it seems clear that Riyadh made a mistake if they did not seek a prepublication copy for review and amendment. Najwa and Omar have written a book that portrays Osama bin Laden as a genuine Islamic hero, an Islamic Robin Hood. They confirm a host of other sources by describing bin Laden as pious, devout, without affectation, brave in battle, and willing to sacrifice to near-bankruptcy his and his family's well-being to fight in God's cause and help others to do the same. For Muslims steeped in their Prophet's story, Najwa and Omar trace a Prophet-like life for bin Laden: leaving his homeland and traveling to foreign countries to be able to practice his faith and battle those who attack it; an absolute faith in God's promise of victory if Muslims act to help themselves; a genuine egalitarianism in his dealings with those he has led; a belief that war is a last resort, but when fought should be won conclusively; and a tolerance for the foibles of humans as long as people repent and come back to God. *Growing Up bin Laden* is a romantic and heroic tale written by two people who—even given Omar's whining—love and respect Osama bin Laden and recognize the resonance of his words and deeds among Muslims who have, even if illiterate, an extraordinary knowledge of the Koran, their Prophet's life and sayings, and Islamic history. It will be interesting to see if *Growing Up bin Laden* is published in Arabic, as it would be an engine for winning bin Laden's memory even more love and respect across the Muslim world.

43. See Davis's introduction to Raymond Ibrahim, ed. and trans., *The al-Qaeda Reader* (New York: Broadway Books, 2007), p. xxx. The book itself is a highly selective and very limited collection of statements by bin Laden and al-Zawahiri, mostly the latter. Professor Ibrahim says his book "proves once and for all that, despite the propaganda of al-Qaeda and its sympathizers radical Islam's war against the West is not finite and limited to political grievances—real or imagined—but is existential, transcending time and space, and deeply rooted in faith" (ibid., p. xii). In my own research, I too have found the one instance of the sort of apocalyptic vision that Mr. Ibrahim considered the core motivation of bin Laden, al-Qaeda, and their Islamist allies. "The time has come when all the Muslims of the earth, especially the youth," bin Laden wrote in mid-December 2001, as al-Qaeda was evacuating Afghanistan and trying to keep up its followers' morale, "should unite and soar against Kufr and continue Jihad until these forces are crushed to naught, all the anti-Islamic forces are wiped from the face of the earth, and Islam takes over the whole world and all the other false religions." This is the one exception to the rule that apocalyptic rhetoric is almost entirely absent from bin Laden's oeuvre. At day's end, Professor Ibrahim's book proves that a few of several hundred pertinent bin Laden–authored documents is plenty to support a piece of analysis-by-assertion, but not nearly enough to prove anything "once and for all." Ibid., p. 269, and OBL, "Message to the youth of the Muslim ummah," *Markaz al-Dawa* (Internet), 13 December 2001.
44. Ibrahim, *The al-Qaeda Reader*, pp. xxxi and xxii.
45. Efraim Karsh, *Islamic Imperialism: A History* (New Haven: Yale University Press, 2007), p. 239.
46. Ibid., p. 240. Italics are the author's emphasis.
47. Ibid., pp. 84 and 87.
48. Lenn Evan Goodman, "Ibn Khaldun and Thucydides," *Journal of the American Oriental Society*, Vol. 92, No. 2 (April/June 1972), p. 261.
49. Michael Vlahos, "Examining the War of Ideas," *Washington Times* (Internet version), 19–22 July 2004.

50. OBL, "Address to the American People," Al-Sahab Media Production Organization, 14 September 2009.
51. Bergen, *The Osama bin Laden I Know*; Atwan, *The Secret History of al-Qaeda*; Steve Coll, *The Bin Ladens: An Arabian Family in the American Century* (New York: Penguin, 2008); and Lia, *Architect of Global Jihad*.
52. I did not, of course, have access to electronic versions of these books. My count of their use of primary bin Laden documents was reached by reading the endnotes line by line and keeping score as I went. I do not claim these counts are precise, but they are very close to the mark.
53. Rohan Gunaratna, *Inside al-Qaeda: Global Network of Terror* (New York: Columbia University Press, 2002); Jason Burke, *Al-Qaeda: Casting a Shadow of Terror* (London: I. B. Tauris, 2003); Randall, *Osama*; Sageman, *Understanding Terror Networks*; Coll, *Ghost Wars*; Fawaz A. Gerges, *The Far Enemy: Why Jihad Went Global* (New York: Cambridge University Press, 2005); Habeck, *Knowing the Enemy*; Wright, *The Looming Tower*; Coll, *The Bin Ladens*; Riedel, *The Search for al-Qaeda*; Roy Gutman, *How We Missed the Story: Osama bin Laden, the Taliban, and the Hijacking of Afghanistan* (Washington, D.C.: United States Institute of Peace, 2008).
54. It must be said that Messrs. Gutman and Coll are far from alone in their Massoud worship and in believing he could have been the tool for establishing a peaceful, pro-Western Afghanistan. American, British, UN, and French diplomats, politicians, intelligence officers, and journalists have long been entranced with the shambling, French-speaking, wispy-whiskered, Dylan-like Tajik commander, who Peter Bergen has argued had a "playful sense of humor" and was "a moderate Islamist and a brilliant general"; and the obvious alternative to Hekmatyar, Sayyaf, and other Afghans as the proper recipient of U.S. and Saudi political, military, and financial support. "Clearly, American money should have been funneled to Massoud," Bergen has written, "who was not only the best general in the Afghan war but the man whose policies were much more in keeping with American interests." Mr. Bergen, of course, is partially correct. Of all the major Afghan field commanders, Massoud behaved more like a Westerner and spoke more about implementing quasi-Western values than any other, which is precisely why—if he was sincere (a big if)—he had no future as an unifying national leader in Afghanistan. And while in strictly military terms Massoud was one of history's great insurgent commanders, the necessary steps for building that reputation negated his political future as anything more than leader of Afghanistan's minorities. Moreover, Massoud appeared less an Islamist only because he had the charisma and guile to play Westerners and some Islamists—Abudullah Anas and to a lesser extent Abduallah Azzam, for example—like violins. Most important, Massoud was from a disliked ethnic minority group that other Afghan ethnic groups—especially the majority Pashtuns—would not allow to rule the country. In the eyes of many Afghan and non-Afghan Muslim mujahedin, he also was a rank traitor to Islam. He had aligned himself—during the anti-Soviet jihad and after—with those seen by Afghans of all ethnicities as their country's atheist, heretical, historic, or polytheist enemies—the USSR and later Russia, Uzbekistan, Iran, India, the United States, the UK, and other NATO countries. Finally, he possessed a powerful enduring enemy in Pakistan. Without denigrating Massoud's talents, it is clear that, with this record of non-Islamic and anti-Islamic associates and a powerful assortment of foes, the only answer the West could have gotten if he survived into the post-9/11 era would have been more of what it has now—endless war in Afghanistan. See Peter L. Bergen, *Holy War, Inc.*:

Inside the Secret World of Osama bin Laden (New York: Free Press, 2001), pp.71–73, and for the one journalist whose admiration for Massoud did not prevent him from seeing through Massoud's "moderate Islamic" pose, see the fine essay by Sebastian Junger, "The lion in winter," *National Geographic Adventure*, March/April, 2001.

55. The bin Laden literature is replete with this sort of "if only he was more like us" sentiment. The most harmful version of this tack is the one that reinforces the false notion that bin Laden and other Islamists have nothing to do with the "real" Islam, and that young Muslims join al-Qaeda and other Islamist groups because of economic reasons, a lack of Westernization, and a shortage of libertinism, and not because of an ambition to defend their faith and brethren. Thus, we have Lawrence Wright claiming that "Radicalism usually prospers in the gap between rising expectations and declining opportunities. This is especially true where the population is young, idle, and bored, where art is impoverished, where entertainment—movies, theater, music—is policed or absent altogether; and where young men are set apart from the consoling and socializing presence of women. Adult illiteracy remained the norm in many Arab countries. Unemployment was among the highest in the developing world. Anger, resentment, and humiliation spurred young Arabs to search for dramatic remedies. . . . Martyrdom promised such men an ideal alternative to a life that was so sparing in rewards." This would be laughable stuff if it was not so widely and tragically believed by Americans, Europeans, and their governments. Bin Laden and al-Qaeda demonstrably have attracted the Muslim world's most devout, who also are often its best and brightest—does Wright think bin Laden's massive use of the Internet is aimed at the illiterate? One of the reasons America and the West are losing their battle with the Islamists is because they refuse to even accept the possibility that this is true, and so seek to push down Muslim throats a batch of Westernization and secularism that drives even more of the smart and devout to pick up Kalashnikovs. See Wright, *The Looming Tower*, p. 107.
56. Interestingly, Osama bin Laden held Saudi King Faisal in high regard. Steve Coll has described Faisal as an "austere and enigmatic man"; a pious Muslim who spoke of a jihad to retake Jerusalem; a workaholic; and a champion of modernization but not Westernization. He also was a fervent anti-communist, anti-Zionist, and—Coll says—an anti-Semite, although the latter term is given by most authors to anyone with the temerity to criticize Israel. Coll points out correctly that in all of these particulars Faisal was much like Muhammad bin Laden, and I would add that Osama bin Laden was much like both men. Regarding Faisal, Osama bin Laden said that the Saudi royal family should take a lesson from the king who, when he ruled, was "prepared to fight the Yemeni communists" and crafted a respectable leadership role for Saudi Arabia in defending Islamic interests. Needless to say, bin Laden also was highly positive toward King Faisal's support for the 1973 oil embargo. Coll, *The Bin Ladens*, pp. 71, 153, and 155; and OBL, "ARC communiques. Banishing communism from the Arabian Peninsula: The episode and the proof," and "Open message to King Fahd," 11 July 1994 and 3 August 1995, http://ctc.usma.edu, AFGP-2002–003345.

CHAPTER 2

1. Rahimullah Yusufzai, "Interview with Osama bin Laden," www.ABCNEWS.com, 4 January 1999.
2. See Jamal Abd-al-Latif Ismail, "Interview with Usama bin Laden," 23 December 1998. This interview is included in al-Latif's book *Bin-Ladin, al-Jazirah, and I* (London:

Islamic Information Monitor, n.d. [but after December 23, 1998, the date the interview was conducted in Kandahar]). The date of March 10, 1957, now appears to have attained definitiveness among those studying bin Laden, although there are still claims that he was born in January or July 1957. Other outliers include his wife Najwa's claim he was born on February 15, 1957; Steve Coll's claim he was born in January 1958; and Khalid Khalil Asad's claim he was born in 1953. Notwithstanding these differences, all the suggested dates point to two important facts: first, Osama bin Laden was still a relatively young man when he died, and second, the chance of errors—especially on dates, places, and names—occurring in a study of bin Laden, al-Qaeda, and the Islamist movement is significant. Najwa and Omar bin Laden, for example, put the following caveat into their very useful book; it is one with which I fully concur. The authors, the two bin Ladens wrote, "acknowledge that the timing and dates of family events may not be exact, and ask readers consider that the information in this book is essentially an oral history, and therefore subject to the omissions of memory." See bin Laden, bin Laden, and Sasson, *Growing Up bin Laden*, pp. xiv and 73; Coll, *The Bin Ladens*, p. 74; and Khalid Khalil Asad, *Warrior from Mecca: The Complete Story of Usama bin Ladin* (London: Al-I'lam li al-Nashr, 2000), p. 8.

3. This information is from a new Web site for the bin Laden family firms at http://www.sbg.com.sa/aboutus.html.
4. Coll, *The Bin Ladens*, pp. 31 and 43.
5. Mayer, "The house of bin Laden."
6. For example, Abdel Bari Atwan, "Interview with Saudi oppositionist Osama bin Ladin," *Al-Quds al-Arabi*, 27 November 1996. For other studies, see especially the excellent study by Steve Coll, *The Bin Ladens*.
7. Bin Laden, bin Laden, and Sasson, *Growing Up bin Laden*, p. 40.
8. Carmen bin Laden, *Inside the Kingdom: My Life in Saudi Arabia* (New York: Grand Central Publishing, 2004), pp. 26–27, and Christopher Dickey, "Portrait of a family," *Newsweek*, 5 April 2004.
9. Professor Mohyuddin, "Something with Regard to Saudi Arabia, Syria, and Yemen," *Ausaf* (Internet version), 8 January 2010. This praise for Muhammad bin Laden, as well as that cited in the preceding note, also has been echoed by former Saudi intelligence chief Prince Turki al-Faisal. "He was truly a genuine hero in the eyes of many Saudis, including the royal family," Turki explained, "because of what he did for the kingdom. But he was always the construction man. When there was a job to be done [Muhammad] bin Laden would do it." See Coll, *Ghost Wars*, p. 84. Turki's phrase "he was always the construction man" suggests that as wealthy and powerful as the bin Ladens are, they are still Yemenis by origin and so a bit down the social ladder from native-born Saudis, and even more rungs down from the royal al-Sauds.
10. Bin Laden, bin Laden, and Sasson, *Growing Up bin Laden*, p. 9.
11. Jamal Abd al-Latif Ismail, *Bin Ladin, al-Jazirah, and I* (n.p., n.d.). Ismail's book is an account of his lengthy interviews with bin Laden and al-Zawahiri in Khandahar on 23 December 1998. It contains the full text of both interviews, as well as a fascinating description of internal political machinations at al-Jazirah that eventually resulted in neither interview being published in full. A severely truncated version of Ismail's work can be found in Salah Najm, "Usamah bin Ladin: The Destruction of the Base," Al-Jazirah Satellite Television, 10 June 1999.
12. Hamid Mir, "Interview with Osama bin Laden," *Pakistan*, 18 March 1997.

13. Atwan, *The Secret History of al-Qaeda*, p. 41, and bin Laden, bin Laden, and Sasson, *Growing Up bin Laden*, p. 190.
14. Coll, *Ghost Wars*, p. 85; Khalid al-Batarfi is quoted in Bergen, *The Osama bin Laden I Know*, p. 17.
15. Atwan, *The Secret History of al-Qaeda*, p. 41.
16. Cherif Ouazai, "The bin Laden mystery: An investigation into the man who has defied America," *Jeune Afrique*, 7 September 1998.
17. Coll, *The Bin Ladens*, p. 107.
18. "Unattributed Biography of Osama bin Laden," *Frontline Online*, April 1999, and Atwan, *The Secret History of al-Qaeda*, pp. 42–43.
19. "Biography of Usamah bin Laden," Islamic Observation Center (Internet), 22 April 2000; "Unattributed Biography of Osama bin Laden," *Frontline Online*.
20. "Unattributed Biography of Osama bin Laden," *Frontline Online*, and "Biography of Usamah bin Laden," Islamic Observation Center.
21. Mir, "Interview with Usama bin Ladin," *Pakistan*, 17 March 1997.
22. Mir quoted in Bergen, *The Osama bin Laden I Know*, pp. 7–8.
23. Rudolph Peters, *Jihad in Classical and Modern Islam* (Princeton, N.J.: Markus Wiener, 1996), p. 46.
24. Bin Laden, bin Laden, and Sasson, *Growing Up bin Laden*, p. 8.
25. Sami Kulayb, "Interview with Shaykh Abd al-Majid al-Zindani," Al-Jazirah Satellite Television, 23 February 2007, and "Muslim duty is to put Bin Ladin's words into 'practice'—Yemeni Islamist," ABC.es, 11 October 2009.
26. Khalid al-Batarfi, "Denying she is angry with him, saying she prays to God to guide him on the right path, mother of Usama bin Ladin says: 'I do not agree with my son,'" *Al-Madinah*, 8 December 2001, p. 1; and David Ensor et al., "Bin Laden family believes Osama is alive," *CNN Daybreak*, 19 March 2002.
27. Khalid al-Batarfi, "Osama is very sweet, very kind, very considerate," *Mail on Sunday* (Internet version), 23 December 2001. Khalid al-Batarfi is a Saudi journalist who was a close childhood friend of bin Laden and is among a small group of prominent Saudi citizens who have purveyed to the West a portrait of the young Osama as a kind and gentle individual who only became a terrorist after he left the benign and peaceful land of Saudi Arabia and fell in with bad Egyptian company. The testimony of these individuals—discussed more fully in chapter 1—is mostly accurate for the pre-1979 Osama, but it paints him a bit too much as an angel to be accepted without some skepticism.
28. Michael Slackman, "Bin Laden's mother tried to stop him, Syrian kin say," *Chicago Tribune*, 13 November 2001, p. 5; and bin Laden, bin Laden, and Sasson, *Growing Up bin Laden*, p. 4.
29. Randall, *Osama*, p. 57.
30. Coll, *The Bin Ladens*, p. 75.
31. Bin Laden, bin Laden, and Sasson, *Growing Up bin Laden*, p. 167.
32. Ensor et al., "Bin Laden family believes Osama is alive."
33. Slackman, "Bin Laden's mother tried to stop him, Syrian kin say."
34. Samir Awwad, "Umar, son of bin Ladin, says during an important interview 'The Americans are not serious about finding my father,'" *Al-Rayah* (Internet version), 20 August 2008.
35. Bin Laden, bin Laden, and Sasson, *Growing Up bin Laden*, p. 8.
36. Ibid., p. 25, and Bergen, *The Osama Bin Laden I Know*, p. 15.
37. Coll, *The Bin Ladens*, p. 13.
38. "Interview (written) with Usama bin Laden," *Ghazi*, August, 2000.

39. This is said with the author's knowledge that the family's current leader, Bakr bin Laden, has denounced and disowned Osama, and various other family members—especially those with lucrative U.S. and European business investments—have bewailed Osama's wayward actions. To accept these statements at face value, however, would be naïve. Saudi Arabia is an increasingly capable and brutal police state, and much of the bin Laden business is based therein. It would be bad for business and the longevity of some bin Ladens, therefore, to be found publicly praising al-Qaeda from the dunes of the Hejaz. The family's reputation and competitiveness for business opportunities in the West also would be severely degraded if it was proven to have maintained friendly contact with, let alone support of, al-Qaeda. The most recent evidence of the downside of carrying the bin Laden name is seen in the travails of Omar bin Laden, Osama's fourth eldest and only terminally adolescent son. He has been denied a UK visa, refused political asylum in Egypt and Spain, and believes his security requires him to keep moving. See Mehdi Hasan, "The NS Interview: Omar bin Laden," http://www.newstatesman.com, 19 November 2009, and Guy Lawson, "Osama's Prodigal Son," http://www.rollingstone.com, 20 January 2010. The estimate of the number of Muhammad bin Laden's descendants is in Isambard Wilkinson, "Profile: Osama bin Laden's family," http://www.telegraph.co.uk, 23 July 2009, and Martin Fletcher, "The impenetrable jungle of Osama bin Laden's family tree," http://www.timesonline.co.uk, 23 December 2009.
40. Ensor et al., "Bin Laden family believes Osama is alive."
41. Carmen bin Laden, *Inside the Kingdom*, pp. 70 and 72.
42. Bin Laden, bin Laden, and Sasson, *Growing Up bin Laden*, p. 25.
43. Marianne Macdonald, "O Brother, where art thou?" *Evening Standard*, 26 May 2006.
44. The 1994 statement and the bin Laden family's denunciation of the 9/11 attacks as actions that "violate Islam and are totally rejected by all religions and humanity at large" are in Muhammad Saddiq, "Bin Laden family statement," *Al-Sharq al-Awsat* (Internet version), 15 September 2001.
45. For Osama's "blood is thicker than water" remark, see Rahimullah Yusufzai, "In the way of Allah," *Pakistan* (Internet version), 15 June 1998. For the balancing statement, see Rahimullah Yusufzai, "I am not afraid of death," http://www.Newsweek.com, 4 January 2004.
46. Carmen bin Laden, *Inside the Kingdom*, pp. 133 and 200.
47. "Interview with Sa'd al-Faqih," *Frontline Online*, April 1999. This is a very useful compendium of the interviews on which PBS's *Frontline* based its April 1999 documentary about bin Laden. Another but anonymous view on the possibility that bin Laden continued to derive income from the family business in the compendium argues: "Most of the [bin Laden] brothers and sisters are observing Muslims and are very keen not to 'spoil' their income with money that is not theirs. They believe that it is their duty to let the owner of any riyal [Saudi currency] to have it. The only way they guarantee [this] is by letting [Usama] bin Laden's share reach him. Some of the brothers and sisters also believed it was their religious duty to support the distinguished brother from their own money. While many are very careful not to irritate the royal family, many more do not care and insist on letting the money reach Usama . . . some sisters are very religious and they believe even if your brother is a real criminal he is your brother. He's got to live comfortably."

An example of one bin Laden who may still support Osama is his half-sister Shaikha. "She is very close to Osama," said her late husband Muhammad Jamal Khalifah, "because she is religious and he is religious, and they are the two [most] religious [people] in the [bin Laden] family. And she is alone; she doesn't have a brother from her mother, so he [Osama] was really taking care of her." The late

Shaykh Azzam also remarked on the religiosity of Osama's sisters and their relationship with him. "He [Usama] once went to one of his sisters and presented her with Ibn Taymiyah's fatwa regarding Jihad with one's wealth," Azzam wrote. "So, she pulled out her checkbook and wrote a check for eight million riyals. All of a sudden, those who were around her came to talk her out of it, asking 'Are you insane? You give out eight million in one shot, while you live in a rented apartment? It will cost a least one million to build your own house!' So, she went back to Usamah and said to him: 'Usamah, my brother, I need one million of these riyals to build a house for myself.' So, he said to her: 'By Allah, I will not give you back a single riyal, as you live in an apartment, relaxed, while the [Afghan] people are dying and cannot even find a tent to shelter themselves in." Also suggesting Osama's siblings were not divvying up his money among themselves is the fact that a trust fund of nearly $10 million was set up in Saudi Arabia that contained the money owed to Osama by the two major bin Laden companies. The fund apparently will benefit bin Laden's children in the future. See Bergen, *The Osama bin Laden I Know*, p. 46; Mayer, "The house of bin Laden"; Abdullah Azzam, "I have never laid my eyes on a man like him," *Fi Dhilal Surat at-Tawbah*, p. 301, in English at http://forums.islamicawakening.com/f18/abdullah-azzam-usamah-bin-ladin-i-have-never-laid-my-eyes-man-like-him-1090/; and Steve Coll, "Osama's trust fund," *New Yorker* (Online version), 2 October 2008.

48. Bruce B. Lawrence, "In bin Laden's words," *Chronicle of Higher Education* (Internet version), 4 November 2005.
49. Malise Ruthven, "The eleventh of September and the Sudanese mahidya in the context of Ibn Khaldun's theory of Islamic history," *International Affairs*, Vol. 78, No. 2 (April 2002), p. 341.
50. Mark Long, "Ribat, al-Qaida and the Challenge for U.S. Foreign Policy," *Middle East Journal*, Vol. 63, No. 1 (Winter 2009), p. 36.
51. Abdul Sattar, "Osama urges ummah to continue jihad," *The News* (Internet version), 7 May 2001.
52. Steve Coll, "Young Osama," *New Yorker* (Internet version), 12 December 2005.
53. Ibid.; and bin Laden, bin Laden, and Sasson, *Growing Up bin Laden*, pp. 13 and 19. In this book, Najwa describes her religious beliefs in a way that suggests she and her husband were completely compatible in this realm. Later, Najwa's last-born son, Ladin, also spoke in words that showed Najwa and Osama were as one on the issue of jihad. "My mother taught and instilled in me," eight-year-old Ladin said in 2001, "an unending, everlasting feeling that I should always be motivated to fight and die for the glory of Islam. I stand for jihad and against Kufr today, and shall do so to [until] eternity. Jihad is in my mind, heart, and blood veins. No fear, no intimidation can ever take this feeling out of my mind." See Sattar, "Osama urges ummah to continue jihad." Sattar says these words were spoken at the wedding of bin Laden's eighteen-year-old son Osman. In his article, Sattar says the foregoing words were delivered by the eight-year-old "Osman," mistakenly using the groom's name rather than Ladin's, who was born in 1993.
54. Coll, "Young Osama"; bin Laden, bin Laden, and Sasson, *Growing Up bin Laden*, p. 19.
55. Bin Laden, bin Laden, and Sasson, *Growing Up bin Laden*, pp. 13, 19.
56. Bergen, *The Osama bin Laden I Know*, p. 5.
57. Ibid., pp. 8–9.
58. Coll, *The Bin Ladens*, p. 146.
59. Coll, "Young Osama."
60. It is interesting that Ahmed Badeeb—Osama's biology teacher at al-Thagher and later co-laborer in the vineyard of the Afghan jihad—says that during Osama's career at

al-Thagher he was "not an all an [Ismalic] extremist." I think Badeeb's recollection shows two things: first, bin Laden was receiving a religious education common in its severity with that received by all young Saudi men, and second, in the greater scheme of things, a person only becomes an Islamic extremist in the eyes of a Saudi official if he becomes an enemy of Saudi Arabia. See Coll, *The Bin Ladens*, p. 249.

61. Although I find his views one-sided and disingenuously pro-Israeli, the commentator Daniel Pipes has nonetheless given a well-deserved intellectual comeuppance to those in the U.S. government and academic community who have argued—with purposeful disingenuousness—that the civil-society interpretation of jihad is more prominent and influential than in the Koran and the hadith than the martial interpretation. See Daniel Pipes, "Jihad through history," *New York Sun*, 31 May 2005, http://www.danielpipes.org/2662/jihad-through-history.
62. See Peters, *Jihad in Classical and Modern Islam*, pp. 116 and 118. Professor Peters notes that many Islamists believe the frequent reference to this hadith by Muslim and Western writers is meant to "weaken Muslim combativeness." In addition, Shaykh Azzam quotes several eminent Islamic scholars who say the hadith ranges from weak to outright fabrication. Shaykh Ibn Taymiyyah, for example, wrote: "This hadith has no source and nobody whomsoever in the field of Islamic knowledge has narrated it. Jihad against the disbelievers is the most noble of actions and moreover it is the most important action for the sake of mankind." See note 71 in Shaykh Abdullah Azzam, "Join the caravan," http://www.islamistwatch.org.texts/azzam/caravan/reference.html.
63. Atwan, "Interview with Usama bin Ladin,"27 November 1996.
64. John L. Esposito and Dalia Mogahed, *Who Speaks for Islam? What a Billion Muslims Really Think* (New York: Gallup Press, 2007), p. 19.
65. Ibid., p. 21.
66. Coll, *The Bin Ladens*, p. 198.
67. Coll, *Ghost Wars*, p. 85.
68. Bin Laden, bin Laden, and Sasson, *Growing Up bin Laden*, p. 25.
69. Quoted in Bergen, *The Osama bin Laden I Know*, p. 19.
70. Coll, *The Bin Ladens*, p. 204; OBL, "Message to the Muslim nation," *Islamic Studies and Research Center* (Internet), 4 March 2004; and OBL, "Practical Steps to the Liberation of Palestine," Al-Sahab Media Production Organization, 14 March 2009.
71. Quintan Wiktorowicz, "Anatomy of the Salafi movement," *Studies in Conflict and Terrorism* (Internet version), Vol. 29, No. 3 (May 2006).
72. Bergen, *The Osama bin Laden I Know*, pp. 63 and 68–69.
73. Mir, "Interview with Osama bin Laden in Jalalabad," *Pakistan*, 18 March 1997, and Ismail, *Bin-Ladin, al-Jazirah, and I*. Osama's mother also says he supervised some construction work in the holy cities. See Khalid al-Batarfi, "Osama is very sweet, very kind, very considerate.
74. Khalid M. al-Batarfi, "Growing up with Osama: 2 youths took different paths," http://www.seatlletimes.nwsource.com, 6 January 2007.
75. Coll, *The Bin Ladens*, pp. 210–212.
76. Ibid., pp. 212 and 230.
77. Thirty years on, bin Laden's bodyguard from 1996 to 2000, Nasser al-Bahri, would say "The thing I remember most about the Shaykh is that he was very, very active." See Tim Butcher, "My life in al-Qaeda, by bin Laden's bodyguard," http://www.telegraph.co.uk, 26 March 2008.
78. Bin Laden, bin Laden, and Sasson, *Growing Up bin Laden*, p. 60.
79. Ibid., p. 4.

80. Bergen, *The Osama bin Laden I Know*, p. 22. Khalid al-Batarfi also said that bin Laden would "fast every Monday and Thursday. [Monday and Thursday] fasting is an extra thing [bin Laden did] because it's what the Prophet used to do." See ibid., p. 15.
81. Bin Laden, bin Laden, and Sasson, *Growing Up bin Laden*, pp. 9 and 61.
82. Bergen, *The Osama bin Laden I Know*, p. 14; and bin Laden, bin Laden, and Sasson, *Growing Up bin Laden*, p. 21.
83. Bin Laden, bin Laden, and Sasson, *Growing Up bin Laden*, p. 20. On the horse's name, see Bergen, *The Osama bin Laden I Know*, pp. 14, 17.
84. Bin Laden, bin Laden, and Sasson, *Growing Up bin Laden*, p. 16; Sadha Umar, "The Event," LBC Satellite Television, 12 September 2004.
85. Ibid., pp. 21–22.
86. Ibid., p. 43. This brief discussion of bin Laden's love of nature gives an opportunity for a comment on the marginal use generally made of bin Laden–authored materials. In my experience, three points stand out about the use of these materials by government officials, the media, and many terrorism experts: first, each is examined as if the words are from an average U.S. or Western politician and therefore are mere bloviating; second, each document is examined mainly to see if there is any "credible threat information"; and, third, each document is treated in isolation, as if bin Laden—or other senior al-Qaeda people—are not smart enough to build and then argue cumulative positions. In the case of bin Laden and nature, the first point is pertinent. In five statements since 2002, bin Laden has attacked the United States for not signing the Kyoto Protocol and has indicted Washington and Muslim governments for not doing enough to cope with climate change. The official and media reaction generally has ranged from dismissive to claims he will rant about anything that discredits America, to assertions that he is loosing his audience and so is using issues sexier than the average Koranic exegesis to win more listeners. In short, the reaction has been that he is behaving like a Western politician. But given his genuine love of the outdoors, bin Laden's use of the environmental issue can be seen to serve five purposes beyond personal concern: (1) to anger Muslims over Washington's failure to do "more" about the God-created environment by focusing on environmental damage in the Muslim world, including the desertification occurring in Mauritania, the long drought in East Africa, and the rising sea levels flooding the low-lying Maldives and Bangladesh; (2) to stress the lack of good governance in the Islamic world by citing the failure of wealthy Muslim regimes to help mitigate the impact of climate change on Muslims; (3) to fuel anger in the environmentally minded populations of America's NATO allies, which are already opposed to the U.S.-led wars in Iraq and Afghanistan; (4) to court all opposed to globalization's impact by claiming that all-out U.S. government and U.S. corporate support for the process damages the environment and further impoverishes the Third World; and (5) to assert that U.S. ability to pursue globalization at the environment's expense would be reduced if "peaceful" economic actions were taken against America, including boycotting its products, urging governments to stop lending to Washington, and linking oil prices to the euro rather than the dollar. The point here is not that bin Laden has been on the angels' side of this issue, but that he has never said anything without a reason—usually an anti-U.S. reason—for saying it. In the case of the environment, U.S. officials and media do Americans a disservice by claiming that bin Laden's words are no more than the typical, publicity-seeking ravings common to average Western politicians. Bin Laden's use of the environmental issue is found in "Usama bin Laden's letter to Americans,"

Observer (Internet version), 24 November 2002; OBL, "Message to the American people," Al-Fallujah Islamic Minbar (Internet), 8 September 2007; OBL, "The way to save the earth," Al-Sahab Media Production Organization, 29 January 2010; OBL, "Shedding light on relief activity methods," Al-Sahab Media Production Organization, 1 October 2010; and OBL, "Provide relief for your brothers in Pakistan," Al-Sahab Media Production Organization, 2 October 2010.

87. "Ibn Khaldun," http://www.oxfordislamicstudies.com; Malik Mufti, "Jihad as statecraft: Ibn Khaldun on the conduct of war and empire," *History of Political Thought*, Vol. 30, No. 3 (Autumn 2009), pp. 385–410; Goodman, "Ibn Khaldun and Thucydides"; and Akbar S. Ahmed, "Ibn Khaldun and anthropology: The failure of methodology in the post 9/11 world," *Contemporary Sociology*, Vol. 34, No. 6 (November 2005), pp. 591–596.
88. Ismail, "Interview with Usama bin Laden," 23 December 1998.
89. Atwan, "Interview with Usama bin Laden," 27 November 1996.
90. Yusufzai, "Interview with Usama bin Laden,"4 January 1999; Hamid Mir, "Interview with Usama bin Laden in Jalalabad,"18 March 1997; and Usama bin Laden, "Message to the Muslim nation."
91. Bin Laden, bin Laden, and Sasson, *Growing Up bin Laden*, and Khalid al-Hammadi, "Al-Qaeda from within, narrated by Abu Jandal, 11 parts," *Al-Quds al-Arabi*, 3 August 2004–29 March 2005.
92. Bin Laden's son Omar describes his father's thinking on the issue as follows: "From the time we [boys] were toddlers, he [bin Laden] demanded that we be given very little water. As we grew older, he reinforced the importance of drinking water only when absolutely necessary. He explained that his children should be "tough" and "patient," so we must set our minds to resist nourishment of any kind for as long as possible. . . . Bin Laden sons must learn to be physically immune to inhospitable desert heat, to make our bodies and minds strong and sturdy. We were repeatedly warned that we must be prepared to face desert warfare when the infidel West attacked the Muslim world, a belief that first developed in his mind when I was a baby [Omar was born in 1981] and grew with every passing year." See bin Laden, bin Laden, and Sasson, *Growing Up bin Laden*, 61.
93. Zaydan, *Usama bin Ladin without Mask*, p. 39.
94. OBL, "Lecture: The hadith of Ka'ab ibn Malik concerning the Tabuk expedition," Al-Sahab Media Production Organization, c. March 2006.
95. Ruthven, "The eleventh of September and the Sudanese mahdiya," p. 351.
96. Coll, *The Bin Ladens*, p. 15.
97. "Text of Usama Bin Laden poster calls for holy war against U.S.," *WAddmmhhmmyy* (Internet version), 19 August 1999.
98. Abdel Bari Atwan, editor in chief of *Al-Quds al-Arabi*, has said that he came away from his interview with bin Laden believing he was "a religious scholar as knowledgeable in discussing the Koran as any academic I have met." Abdel Bari Atwan, "Guns and fried eggs in a mountain cave," *Sunday Times* (Internet version), 16 September 2001. In addition, bin Laden's wife Najwa has said that bin Laden "was an expert regarding our faith"; that he acted as her religion teacher after their marriage; and that she "was surprised [that] my young husband could recite both sacred texts [the Koran and the Sunnah] without referencing a single page." On this issue, Omar bin Laden has said on occasion "he [Osama] would entertain those who would ask by reciting the Koran word for word. I would stand silently in the background, often with a Koran in my hand, checking his recitation carefully. My father never missed a word." Omar adds that his father told him he memorized the Koran when in "mental turmoil" after Muhammad bin Laden's death.

Finally, the excellent Pakistani journalist Rahimullah Yusufzai, who had semi-regular pre-9/11 access to bin Laden, has written that bin Laden "recited from the Holy Qur'an like a religious scholar" when seeking to support his arguments. See bin Laden, bin Laden, and Sasson, *Growing Up bin Laden*, pp. 17 and 42, and Rahimullah Yusufzai, "Taliban let bin Laden break his silence," *The News* (Internet version), 6 January 1999.

99. Coll, *The Bin Ladens*, p. 203.

100. OBL, "Lecture: The hadith of Ka'ab ibn Malik."

101. "Mujahid Usama bin Ladin talks exclusively to Nida'ul Islam about the new powder keg in the Middle East," *Nida'ul Islam* (Internet), 15 January 1997. The journal notes that the interview occurred in October/November 1996.

102. Ouazai, "The bin Laden mystery."

103. Al-Batarfi, "Osama is very sweet, very kind, very considerate." Bin Laden later recalled that "the call to jihad came into my mind for the first time when the Jews disgraced Baitul Muqdas." He is referring here to Israel occupying Jerusalem in the 1967 war. See Mir, "Interview with Usama bin Ladin in Jalalabad," 18 March 1997.

104. Quoted in Bergen, *The Osama bin Laden I Know*, p. 15.

105. Bin Laden, bin Laden, and Sasson, *Growing Up bin Laden*, p. 254. On this point, bin Laden later wrote, "We are now at the tail end of nations, and our rulers are the vassals of the Nazarenes [Christians]." See OBL, "The wills of the heroes of the raids on New York and Washington," Al-Sahab Media Production Organization, 11 September 2007.

106. Peters, *Jihad in Classical and Modern Islam*, p. 10.

107. Randall, *Osama*, pp. 60–61. Batarfi's recollection of how the teenage bin Laden dealt with religious differences between himself and others meshes fully with bin Laden's public approach to that issue throughout his adulthood. "A human being remains human; Satan can make him stumble," bin Laden said. "His status is not wretched because of an accidental mistake from which no one is infallible . . . the nature of man is to err. It is impossible for people not to make mistakes and when they happen, differences break out between them. Major sins are committed in the best of eras [meaning the era of the Prophet Muhammad and his companions]." Bin Laden even applied this force-as-a-last-resort approach to the Islamist Juhaymin al-Uteybi and his followers, who took over the Grand Mosque in Mecca in November 1979. While not arguing that the seizure was justified—though years later he said the radicals were "true Muslims . . . killed ruthlessly"—he condemned King Fahd for not exhausting all peaceful means to regain the mosque before using force. "Level-headed people at the time believed that the incident could have been resolved without bloodshed. All that was necessary was time, especially knowing that there were only a few dozen [*sic*—there were hundreds] inside the Mosque, who were surrounded [by Saudi troops] and were armed mostly with hunting rifles and only limited supplies of ammunition. But King Fahd . . . arrogantly refused to listen to any advice and ordered tanks and armored vehicles to enter the Sacred Mosque. The sight of scores of dead Muslims and the destruction of minarets, waifs, and pavement of a mosque that is supposed to be sacred is unforgivable." See OBL, "Lecture: The hadith of Ka'ab ibn Malik"; Muhammad al-Shafi'i, "New message from bin Ladin. . . " *Al-Sharq al-Awsat* (Internet version), 19 January 2003; Usama bin Laden, "Message to our people in Iraq," Al-Sahab Media Production Organization, 23 October 2007; Yaroslav Trofimov, *The Siege of Mecca. The Forgotten Uprising in Islam's Holiest Shrine and the Birth of al-Qaeda* (New York: Doubleday, 2007), pp. 246–247; and OBL, "Message to the Saudi rulers," http://www.jihadunpsun.com, 16 December 2004.

108. Evan R. Goldstein, "How just is Islam's just war tradition?" *Chronicle of Higher Education* (Internet version), Vol. 54, No. 32 (11 April 2008).
109. Khaled Abou El Fadl, "The Crusader," *Boston Review* (Internet version), Vol. 31, No. 2 (March/April 2006).
110. Husayn bin Mahmud, "This is al-Qaeda (1)," *Islamic Al-Fallujah Forums* (Internet), 6 August 2009.
111. Ismail, "Interview with Usama bin Laden," 23 December 1998, pp. 7–8.
112. Peters, *Jihad in Classical and Modern Islam*, pp. 7–8. As noted, bin Laden has always had a strong affinity for Ibn Taymiyyah. In late 1996, the editor in chief of *Al-Quds al-Arabi* visited bin Laden's base in Tora Bora and found a volume called *Ibn Taymiyah's Fatwas* prominently displayed in Osama's library. See Abdel Bari Atwan, "Story of infiltration across Pakistani border and minefields with Taliban forces 'help'; days in Afghan Arabs' base in Khorasan mountains," *Al-Quds al-Arabi*, 27 November 1996.
113. Christopher Henzel, "The origins of al-Qaeda's ideology: Implications for U.S. strategy," *Parameters*, Vol. 35 (Spring 2005), p. 71.
114. OBL, "Statement to the Saudi rulers," http://www.jihadunspun.com, 16 December 2004. Bin Laden likewise cited repentance as the means by which the al-Sauds could rehabilitate themselves in "Interview with Mujahid Usama bin Ladin," *Nida'al Islam* (Internet), 15 January 1997, and Yusufzai, "Interview with Osama bin Laden," 4 January 1999.
115. Bin Mahmud, "This is al-Qaeda (1)"; John L. Esposito, *The Oxford History of Islam* (New York: Oxford University Press, 1999, pp. 280–281.
116. Muhammad al-Uwayn, "Ideology of takfir," *Kingdom of Saudi Arabia TV 1*, 10 August 2004.
117. Bin Laden's apparent disdain for the untrained and self-proclaimed religious scholars may well extend to Muhammad Abd al-Salam Faraj, "an electrician and self-taught theologian for the underground jihad in Egypt." Faraj wrote a famous book called *The Neglected Duty* that supported Qutb's demand for a strategy focused on the near enemy before the far enemy. In the materials in my possession, bin Laden neither refers to nor quotes Faraj. He also does not quote from the work of Ayman al-Zawahiri. For some data on Faraj, see Henzel, "The origins of al-Qaeda's ideology," p. 75.
118. Al-Batarfi, "Osama is very sweet, very kind, very considerate."
119. Al-Batarfi, "Growing up with Osama."
120. Bin Laden, bin Laden, and Sasson, *Growing Up bin Laden*, p. 25.
121. Quoted in Bergen, *The Osama bin Laden I Know*, p. 14.
122. Ibid., pp. 6–7.
123. John Miller, "Talking with terror's banker: An exclusive interview with Osama bin Laden," http:///www.ABCnews.com, 28 May 1998.
124. Randall, *Osama*, p. 61.

CHAPTER 3

1. Tawil, *Brothers in Arms*, p. 20.
2. *The Arab Ansar in Afghanistan*, Islamic Muhajirun Network, 2006. This documentary's script says the film was produced in 1988 by Al-Muslim Recordings in Jeddah, Saudi Arabia. The 1988 date is clearly wrong, however; the documentary covers the battles around Jalalabad that began in March 1989. The Egyptian journalist Isam Darraz is prominent among those credited with making the documentary.
3. Carmen bin Ladin, *Inside the Kingdom*, p. 126.

4. Zaydan, *Usama bin Ladin without Mask*. Zaydan's valuable book contains two extensive interviews he conducted with bin Laden before 9/11, which the Taleban refused him permission to publish. In the book, Zaydan also records his impressions of al-Qaeda's military commander, Abu Hafs al-Masri, describing his ideas, plans, and relationship with bin Laden.
5. Abd-al-Karim and al-Nur, "Interview with Saudi businessman Usama bin Ladin."
6. Coll, *The Bin Ladens*, p. 251, and Weaver, "The Real bin Laden."
7. Weaver, "The Real Bin Laden."
8. Jamal Khashoggi, "Interview with Prince Turki al-Faisal, part 4," *Arab News* (Internet version), 7 November 2001. Here is the Saudi narrative working at full tilt with one of the principal players interviewing another, who, perhaps, is the key player. Coll, *The Bin Ladens*, p. 295.
9. Khashoggi, "Interview with Prince Turki al-Faisal, part 4," and "Biography of Usamah bin Laden."
10. Khashoggi, "Interview with Prince Turki al-Faisal, part 4."
11. Coll, *Ghost Wars*, pp. 87–88.
12. Ibid., p. 88, and Coll, *The Bin Ladens*, p. 291.
13. Coll, *Ghost Wars*, pp. 87–88.
14. The best work on the seizure and recapture of the Grand Mosque is Yaroslav Trofimov, *The Siege of Mecca*.
15. Bergen, *The Osama bin Laden I Know*, pp. 59–60. In the context of this statement, the extent of bin Laden's changed attitude toward the Saudi royal family can be seen in his 2001 words on the same issue. "When the ummah was on the brink of annihilation," bin Laden told a Pakistani reporter, "the Caliph of the Muslim ummah [sarcastic reference to King Fahd] reneged on his faith and endeared himself to Christianity. The Cross of Christ was seen hanging on his chest." See Abdul Sattar, "Usama urges ummah to continue jihad," *Pakistan* (Internet version), 7 May 2001.
16. Lia, *Architect of Global Jihad*, p. 93.
17. This information on Azzam was drawn from what I regard as the three best English-language works on the shaykh: Andrew McGregor, "'Jihad and the rifle alone': Abdullah Azzam and the Islamist Revolution," *Journal of Conflict Studies* (Internet version), Vol. 23, No. 2 (Fall 2003); Thomas Hagghammer, "Abdullah Azzam, Imam of the Jihad," in Gilles Kepel and Jean-Pierre Milelli, eds., *Al-Qaeda in Its Own Words* (Cambridge, Mass.: Harvard University Press, 2008), pp. 81–101; and Asaf Maliach, "Bin Ladin, Palestine, and al-Qaida's Operational Strategy," *Middle Eastern Studies*, Vol. 44, No. 3 (May 2008), pp. 353–375.
18. McGregor, "'Jihad and the rifle alone.'"
19. Usama bin Muhammad bin Laden, "Introduction to 'The battle of the Lion's Den, Afghanistan, 1987,'" in Shaykh Abdullah Azzam, *The Lofty Mountain*, 1st ed', http://www.maktabah.net/store/images/35/Lofty%20mountain.pdf, n.d., p. 85. Bin Laden's experience of the scarcity of Islamic scholars on the ground in Afghanistan during the anti-Soviet jihad started his animosity for the Saudi religious establishment. Certainly he returned to the Kingdom in 1989 with a still respectful but much more critical attitude toward official Saudi scholars, and by the time he moved to Sudan he was damning them regularly. Bin Laden's view of the importance of the role of what might be called "combat scholars" was shared at the time by Shaykh Abdullah Azzam and is championed today by Shaykh Abu Muhammad al-Maqdisi, who probably is the Muslim world's most respected Salaf-jihadi scholar. Shaykh Azzam, for

example, argued in 1987 that "mature propagators are still the talk of the hour in the Islamic jihad in Afghanistan, and the subject of pressing necessity and glaring need. . . . [The scholars] are not occupying the roles they should." And al-Maqdisi said in 2009 that the leaders of monotheism in Muslim countries must send the mujahedin "religious ideologues . . . [to] support their jihad and defend them against accusations and slanders from the rulers' clerics." Abdullah Azzam, "Join the caravan" (15 April 1987), and "Open interview with Shumukh al-Islam members and the esteemed Shaykh Abu-Muhammad al-Maqdisi," Islamic al-Fallujah Forums (Internet), 28 October 2009.

20. "No glory without jihad," Al-Ghurbah Establishment (Internet), 31 August 2009. This film shows speeches by several prominent Islamist and al-Qaeda leaders, including Azzam and bin Laden.
21. OBL, "Lecture: The hadith of Ka'ab ibn Malik."
22. Hagghammer, "Abdullah Azzam, imam of the jihad," p. 90.
23. Bergen, *The Osama bin Laden I Know*, p. 26. The starting date of the bin Laden–Azzam relationship is obviously of some consequence. As noted, some authors claim bin Laden was a student of Azzam at King Abdul Aziz University, while others argue that they met only after the Soviets invaded Afghanistan. Adding to the confusion is bin Laden's wife Najwa's claim that she and bin Laden traveled to the United States in summer 1979—that is, before the Soviet invasion—so bin Laden could meet in Los Angeles "with a man by the name of Abdullah Azzam." Khalid al-Batarfi also says bin Laden visited the United States to get medical attention for one of his sons but says nothing of Azzam or the trip's date. On the basis of Najwa bin Laden's claim, Steve Coll has argued that Najwa's story clinches the fact that bin Laden was in the United States in 1979 to meet Azzam. But does it? Although bin Laden does seem to have visited the United States at some point, why would he have to come to America to meet Azzam, who was then living and teaching in Jordan and was free to travel to Saudi Arabia for business or religious reasons? And what business would the men have had to discuss six months *before* Moscow invaded Afghanistan? That said, Azzam is reported to have traveled to the United States at some point between 1973 and 1980 at the invitation of the Muslim Student Association and "is said to have lectured in several states for the association's various branches." At day's end, bin Laden and Azzam may or may not have met in America in 1979, but it appears this is the best date at which to fix the start of the serious bin Laden–Azzam relationship. See bin Laden, bin Laden, and Sasson, *Growing Up bin Laden*, pp. 25–27; al-Batarfi is quoted in Bergen, *The Osama bin Laden I Know*, p. 22; Steve Coll, "Osama in America: The Final Answer," *New Yorker* (Internet version), 30 June 2009; and Azzam's visits to the United States are discussed in Andrew McGregor, "Jihad and the rifle alone," and in Thomas Hagghammer, "Abdullah Azzam, Imam of the jihad," in Kepel and Milelli, *Al-Qaeda in Its Own Words*, p. 89.
24. Al-Dhiyabi, "Interview with Shaykh Musa al-Qarni, part 2." Shaykh al-Qarni now criticizes bin Laden at the Saudi regime's direction, and so this portrait of bin Laden as a manipulative, headstrong, reckless leader is a bit overdrawn so as to support the Saudi's anti–bin Laden narrative. Bin Laden's practice of seeking advice from his lieutenants, allies, and trusted scholars, for example, is well documented. Still, al-Qarni is substantially correct; bin Laden ultimately intended to be in charge of whatever he was doing.
25. Zaydan, *Usama bin Ladin without Mask*.

26. Bergen, *The Osama bin Laden I Know*, p. 39.
27. Isam Darraz, "Impressions of an Arab journalist in Afghanistan," in Shaykh Abdullah Azzam, *The Lofty Mountain*, 1st ed. Also included is an unnamed Arab associate's description of bin Laden while living in 1980s Peshawar: "He was a very normal man. He had no bodyguards, would go shopping at the bazaars, and converse lightheartedly with his friends. Within the society of 10,000 Arabic people [in the Peshawar region] he was a well-known person, but he kept his lifestyle simple so as not to be conspicuous relative to the average Arabian."
28. Bergen, *The Osama bin Laden I Know*, p. 29.
29. McGregor, "Jihad and the rifle alone," and Bergen, *The Osama bin Laden I Know*, pp. 32–33.
30. Bin Laden, bin Laden, and Sasson, *Growing Up bin Laden*, p. 35.
31. Bergen, *The Osama bin Laden I Know*, pp. 32–33.
32. "Journal to publish bin Laden's poetry," *Australian Broadcasting Company News* (Internet), 23 September 2008, and Rick Salutin, "Why Osama is hooked on classics," http://www.theglobeandmail.com, 8 August 2008.
33. Richard A. Gabriel, *Muhammad. Islam's First Great General* (Norman: University of Oklahoma Press, 2007), p. xxvi. Muhammad also understood and feared the potential power of his enemies' propaganda and especially feared the power of attacks by poets. Professor Gabriel says that Muhammad directed the killing of "several poets and singers who had ridiculed him," and Martin Lings, in his biography of the Prophet, has him referring to one enemy poet and warning that "he did us injury and wrote poetry against us; and none of you shall do this but he shall be put to the sword." In the wake of the 2006 publication in Denmark of caricatures of the Prophet, bin Laden advocated the killing of the cartoonist and those who supported him by referring to the Prophet's decision to have the poet Ka'ab al-Ashraf killed because he wrote verses critical of Allah and Muhammad. Bin Laden said the only possible dialog with the West was with weapons, and hoped many Muslims would be eager to do the job of killing the cartoonist, just as Muhammad ibn Mallamah and his colleagues volunteered to kill Ka'ab al-Ashraf.

    Also in the manner of the Prophet, Nur al-Din, and Saladin, bin Laden made consistent use of poetry—his own and others'—in his public statements. After U.S. forces conquered Afghanistan, for example, several thousand al-Qaeda-related audio tapes were acquired, some of which are recordings of bin Laden reciting poetry. A U.S. scholar working on the tapes said they showed bin Laden to be a "skilled poet" whose work included "clever rhymes and meters." A former bodyguard of bin Laden has said that he often recited poetry to relax and entertain his companions. And in March 2001, bin Laden published a collection of his poems in Arabic and Pashtu in a volume entitled *Qasida* (Epic). The poems praised Afghan leaders who helped him return to Afghanistan—Yunis Khalis is singled out as a heroic, courageous "tiger." As a propaganda tool, bin Laden used poetry to celebrate al-Qaeda's attacks and martyrs, to criticize al-Turabi and al-Bashir for buckling to U.S. pressure to evict him, to memorialize the plight of the Palestinians, and to blend famous events of Islamic history with contemporary affairs in an effort to show Muslims their ancestors overcame greater challenges than they face today. He also used poetry as a means of questioning the "masculinity and sense of honor" of Muslim men who did not join the jihad. Though it may exist, I have seen no evidence that any Muslim regime or Western intelligence service tried to use Arabic poetry against bin Laden. See ibid., p. 65;

Martin Lings, *Muhammad: His Life Based on the Earliest Sources* (Rochester, Vt.: Inner Traditions International, 1983), p. 171; OBL, "O people of Islam," Al-Sahab Media Production Organization, 26 April 2006; Bernard Haykel, "Osama bin Laden, a purveyor of poetic terrorism," http://www.thedailystar.com.lb, 19 July 2008; Rod Norlund, "Bin Laden's former bodyguard speaks," http://www.msnbc.msn.com, 26 August 2007; Januulah Hashimzada, "I will continue jihad against the infidels," *Wahdat*, 27 March 2001, pp. 1 and 5; Hamid Mir, "My last question to Osama bin Laden," *Friday Times* (Internet verision), 22 September 2001; and John Harlow, "Pray silence for bin Laden the wedding poet," http://www.timesonline.co.uk, 21 September 2008.

34. Amin Maalouf, *The Crusades through Arab Eyes* (New York: Schocken Books, 1984), pp.143–144.
35. Ibid., p. 180.
36. Geoffrey Hindley, *Saladin: Hero of Islam* (Barnsley, UK: Pen and Sword Books, 1976), p. 11. Professor Hindley also devotes an entire chapter to describing how deftly Nur al-Din used his propaganda machine to support jihad. See, pp. 32–45.
37. Ismail, *Bin-Ladin, al-Jazirah, and I.*
38. "Interview with Mujahid Usama bin Ladin," *Nida'al Islam* (Internet), 15 January 1997. Bin Laden's hatred for media that work for Arab regimes grew over time and became part of his own triangle of evil: rulers–official scholars–rulers' media. Among the biggest and most potent foes of Islam, bin Laden claimed in 2004, were "the media persons who belittle the religious duties such as jihad and other rituals," adding that they were "atheists and renegades." OBL, "Message to the Islamic nation," *Islamic Studies and Research Center* (Internet), 4 March 2004.
39. Ismail, *Bin-Ladin, al-Jazirah, and I.*
40. "Speech by Usama bin Laden," Middle East Media Research Institute (MEMRI), Special Dispatch, No. 539, 18 July 2003.
41. OBL to Shaykh Abd-al-Raheen al-Tahan, n.d., http://ctc.usma.edu/AQ/PDF/AGFP-2002–800073-Trans-Meta.pdf. An al-Qaeda member of the Saudi generation following bin Laden's echoed the same sentiments, indicating the double-edged sword of modern communications in allowing both easier interpersonal communications and more sophisticated and comprehensive tools with which governments censor or block communications. "At that time we were not aware of the issue of ideological arguments against the unbelievers' deeds," Abu Jandal—born in 1973—explained to an interviewer.

> The youths did not have a clear idea about the various trends of the Islamic groups [outside Saudi Arabia] until we went out [of the country] for jihad. As soon as we left for jihad from the large prison called the Kingdom of Saudi Arabia, large horizons of knowledge opened for us. We began to feel that we were completely absented [when in the Kingdom] from what was going on in our world [ummah]. I recall that when we were in Saudi Arabia, the leaflets of [the London-based Saudi dissident] Dr. Muhammad al-Masri were distributed to us in complete secrecy for fear that they might get into the hands of the merciless Saudi security service. We were brought up in Saudi Arabia on the concept of eat and remain silent. This is the prevailing concept of the kingdom's motto [logo?] (two swords and a palm tree). This means eat from the palm tree and remain silent because the two swords are there to cut off the head of anyone that acts differently.

See Khalid al-Hammadi, "Al-Qaeda from within, narrated by Abu Jandal, part 8," *Al-Quds al-Arabi*, 26 March 2005, p. 17.

42. Michael Vlahos, "The Muslim renovatio and U.S. strategy," http://www.2techcentralstation.com, 27 April 2004.
43. Bergen, *The Osama bin Laden I Know*, pp. 48 and 62–63, and Zaydan, *Usama bin Ladin without Mask*. There are other points on which bin Laden disagreed with Azzam, but the evidence does not show they became sources of acrimony between the two men. In his excellent essay on Azzam, for example, Andrew McGregor points out that the shaykh refused to cooperate with the Palestine Liberation Organization because of its corruption and secularism, and that he believed a "small band of Arabs . . . changed the tide of battle [in Afghanistan]." Bin Laden bought neither of these ideas. He always believed that it was not only possible but essential to work temporarily with less-than-perfect Muslims, and even non-Muslims, as long as the combined efforts were directed against Islam's major enemy. "Under the circumstances," bin Laden said a month before the 2003 U.S.-led invasion of Iraq, "there will be no harm if the interests of the Muslims converge with the interests of the socialists in the fight against the Crusaders [in Iraq], despite our belief in the infidelity of the socialists." He also often said Arab participation in the Afghans' jihad was minor coda to and not a major factor in the war. "I start by reminding you [the Muslim world]," bin Laden wrote in early 2003, "of the defeat of the world's largest Superpower [the USSR] after ten years of fierce fighting by the sons of Afghans and whoever helped them from the sons of the Muslims, by God's grace." Bin Laden always claimed that the Arabs—because they learned to work together and gained combat experience—gained far more from their wartime activities than did the Afghans and their cause. See McGregor, "Jihad and the rifle alone"; OBL, "Message to our brothers in Iraq," Al-Jazirah Satellite Television, 11 February 2003; and OBL, "Exposing the new Crusader war in Iraq."
44. Jamil al-Dhiyabi, "Interview with Shaykh Musa al-Qarni, part 1," *Al-Hayah* (Internet version), 8 March 2006; and Bergen, *The Osama bin Laden I Know*, p. 93. Although not corroborated by other reporting, Abu Jandal argues that Shaykh Azzam turned against Massoud by the time of his [Azzam's] death in late 1989. Abu Jandal claims Azzam concluded that Massoud was an "agent" of the West, but argued against exposing Massoud at the time because that would "shake the trust between the Afghan jihad leadership and the Islamic peoples." Abu Jandal claims Azzam said: "Leave him [Massoud] now. Now is not the time. A time will come when he is exposed," adding that at the right time he "intended to publish a book exposing Ahmad Shah Massoud." See Khalid al-Hammadi, "Al-Qaeda from within, part 10."
45. Al-Dhiyabi, "Interview with Shaykh Musa al-Qarni, part 1."
46. Bergen, *The Osama bin Laden I Know*, p. 48.
47. Ibid., and OBL, "Remove the Apostate," Al-Sahab Media Production Organization, 20 September 2007. In the literature on bin Laden, there is much that disagrees with the view of Abdullah Anas regarding the unbroken friendship of bin Laden and Azzam. Much of it is based on the Saudi narrative discussed above; to wit, that Osama was brain-washed by al-Zawahiri and other radical Egyptians who took the good Saudi boy down the road toward Satan. Steve Coll, for example, reports Azzam was angry over Osama's decision to form Arab-only units and fretted over his radicalization. Coll cites unnamed "Arab activists and journalists" as claiming that Shaykh Azzam whined, "You see what Osama is doing—he is collecting and training young people. This is not our policy, our plan," and later said, "I am worried about his [bin Laden's] future if he stays with these people [the Egyptians]." That Coll's unnamed sources, and the unnamed sources of other writers, said this cannot be doubted, but in the three years Azzam lived after he and bin Laden parted ways I found nothing that was unquestionably

said by the shaykh that makes the point. Indeed, Azzam seems never to have shifted from the view of Osama that he recorded as follows.

> On this occasion, I would like to ask Allah—the Mighty and Majestic—to preserve our brother, Abu Abdullah, Usamah bin Ladin. I have never laid my eyes on a man like him on this Earth; he lives in his home like one who is in a state of poverty. I used to stay in his home in Jeddah when making Hajj or Umrah, and he did not have a single chair or table in his entire house! He had four wives, and not a single one of them had a chair or table in it. Despite this, if you ask him for a million riyals for the Mujahedin, he would pull out a check and write it for you in a matter of seconds. . . .
>
> If you were to sit with him, you would think that he was a servant from the servants, with his manners and his manhood. By Allah, I hold him to be like this. I asked [Afghan insurgent leader] Sayyaf to announce a decision to prevent him from moving here [in Peshawar], but he was always be eager to be in the midst of the battle. His blood pressure would drop often, so, he would fill his pockets with salt and carry a jug of water with him. He was unable to walk, as he would constantly have to swallow some salt and drink some water in order to raise his blood pressure.
>
> Believe me when I tell you that when he would visit me in my home, when he would hear the telephone ring, he would get up and bring it to me, so that I would not have to get up from my place! Such manners, humility, manhood . . . we ask Allah to preserve him, if He wills.

See Coll, *Ghost Wars*, pp. 163–164 and 204, and Abdullah Azzam, "I have never laid my eyes on a man like him," *Fi Dhilal Surat at-Tawbah*, p. 301, in English at http://forums.islamicawakening.com/f18/abdullah-azzam-usamah-bin-ladin-i-have-never-laid-my-eyes-man-like-him-1090/.

48. Ismail, *Bin-Ladin, al-Jazirah, and I*.
49. Azzam's assassination posed a difficult issue for the Saudi's good-Osama-gone-bad narrative. Needless to say, a good Saudi lad would never kill a highly educated Islamic scholar and selfless jihadi, but the assassination itself was too good a propaganda opportunity to pass up. In a 2006 interview, Shaykh Musa al-Qarni nicely halved the loaf. Asked whether bin Laden "was the one who assassinated Shaykh Abdullah Azzam," al-Qarni replied, "As to whether he was involved in Abduallah Azzam's assassination I would as soon accuse myself of the crime rather than bin Laden. I knew that he [Azzam] and bin Laden had a relationship of amity and mutual respect. . . . I cannot believe that bin Laden was involved in planning, financing, or even knowing about the assassination plan." Asked in a follow-up question if "Azzam was assassinated by bin Laden's 'followers' without bin Laden being aware of the matter," al-Qarni jumped at the chance to explain how the Egyptians had ruined the good Saudi boy. "It is possible, yes. It could have been done without his knowledge," al-Qarni said. "The changing circumstances [after the Soviet retreat] made bin Laden find only the [Egyptian] al-Jihad organization beside him. He found himself in circumstances that drove him to the other side and to adopt violence as a method. Many of the people who were acquainted with Shaykh Usama bin Ladin, and I was one of them, did not agree with his pursuit of this course. We opposed him on making this choice. When the signs began to appear he was going to cooperate with al-Jihad we opposed him and tried to show him that it was an erroneous course of action."

With al-Qarni's answer, the Saudi narrative had its cake and ate it too. Saudi society and its educational system had made Osama too good a boy to kill Azzam, but his personal character flaws—such as not being very smart—would have allowed him to be led to ruin by the crafty, evil Egyptians. See Jamil al-Dhiyabi, "Interview with Shaykh Musa al-Qarni, part 2."

50. Peter Arnett, "Osama bin Laden: The interview," CNN, 12 May 1997. On this subject, see also Rahimullah Yusufzai, "Osama bin Laden: Al-Qaeda," in Harenda Baweja, ed., *Most Wanted. Profiles of Terror* (New Delhi: Lotus Collection, Roli Books, 2002), p. 22.
51. Muhammad al-Sahi'i, "Chatter on the World's Rooftop," *Al-Sharq al-Awsat* (Internet version), 29 October 2006. Bin Laden would later take the lesson he learned at Jaji about using fieldworks to defeat superior Western military technology and apply it successfully against U.S.-NATO forces in 2001–2002, and then recommend it to his coreligionists in Iraq in 2003. "O mujahedin brothers in Iraq," he said a month before the U.S.-led invasion, "do not be afraid of what the U.S. is propagating in terms of their lies about their power and their smart, laser-guided missiles. The smart bombs will have no effect worth mentioning in the hills and in the trenches, on plains, and in forests. They must have apparent targets. The well-camouflaged trenches and targets will not be reached by either their smart or stupid missiles. There will only be haphazard strikes that dissipate the enemy ammunition and waste its money. Dig many trenches. The [Prophet's] companion and successor Umar, may God be pleased with him, stated: 'Take the ground as a shield because this will ensure the exhaustion of all the stored enemy missiles within months.' Their daily production is too little and can be dealt with, God willing." See OBL, "A message to our brothers in Iraq," Al-Jazirah Satellite Television, 11 February 2003.
52. Arnett, "Osama bin Laden: The interview."
53. John Miller, "Greetings America. My name is Osama bin Laden. Now that I have your attention . . . ," *Esquire*, February 1999.
54. Bergen, *The Osama bin Laden I Know*, p. 29.
55. "Biography of Usamah bin Laden"; Michael Scheuer, *Through Our Enemies' Eyes. Osama bin Laden, Radical Islam, and the Future of America*, rev. ed. (Dulles, Va.: Potomac Books, 2006), pp. 104–105; Asad, *Warrior from Mecca*, p. 31; and Coll, *Ghost Wars*, pp. 156–157.
56. Bergen, *The Osama bin Laden I Know*, p. 62, and Coll, *The Bin Ladens*, pp. 88 and 291.
57. Darraz, "Impressions of an Arab journalist in Afghanistan."
58. Ibid.
59. Ibid. Delay in the start of construction may have been due to the previous obligations; bin Laden's engineers had to build camps, roads, and buildings for Afghan leaders, Islamic NGOs, and Saudi intelligence. Bin Laden's builders were also much involved in building military-related facilities in and around Khowst in 1985–1986 for Jalaluddin Haqqani's forces.
60. Ibid. In an interview long after the event, bin Laden's brother-in-law Muhammad Jamal Khalifa takes a page from the Saudi narrative—the chapter on bin Laden being none too smart—and claims that he did his best to persuade bin Laden that the site he had chosen for al-Masadah al-Ansar was too dangerous and would cost many Arab lives. "Everyone is saying this is wrong," Khalifa says he shouted, "so Osama, please leave this place now." Khalifa claims bin Laden ignored him even though Abu-Ubaydah al-Panshiri—one of bin Laden's veteran military experts—agreed with Khalifa. See Bergen, *The Osama bin Laden I Know*, pp. 51–52. Khalifa's picture of a headstrong, unheeding bin Laden matches that outlined above by the anti-bin Laden Saudi Shaykh Musa al-Qarni.

61. Darraz, "Impressions of an Arab journalist in Afghanistan," and Bergen, *The Osama bin Laden I Know*, p. 56.
62. Darraz, "Impressions of an Arab journalist in Afghanistan."
63. *The Arab Ansar in Afghanistan*, Islamic Muhajirun Network, 2006.
64. Darraz, "Impressions of an Arab journalist in Afghanistan."
65. Ibid. Among those who worked as religious teachers and advisers in bin Laden's training camps were the highly respected Salafist scholar Abu Muhammad al-Maqdis, and the Salafist Saudi academic Shaykh Musa al-Qarni, once bin Laden's theological adviser and now a supporter of the Saudi regime. See "Open interview with Shumukh al-Islam members and the esteemed Shaykh Abu-Muhammad al-Maqdisi," *Islamic al-Fallujah Forums* (Internet), 28 October 2009, and al-Dhiyabi, "Interview with Shaykh Musa al-Qarni, part 1."
66. Darraz, "Impressions of an Arab journalist in Afghanistan."
67. *The Arab Ansar in Afghanistan*, Islamic Muhajirun Network, 2006.
68. Bergen, *The Osama bin Laden I Know*, pp. 13, 55.
69. Coll, *The Bin Ladens*, p. 302. Notwithstanding Coll's positive words here, he and, more subtly, Lawrence Wright made pointed comments clearly inferring bin Laden's lack of physical bravery and his desire to be any place except where guns are being fired. This is odd, because among the people who fought alongside bin Laden there is virtually unanimous testimony showing bin Laden to have been unflappable and fearless on the battlefield. That he suffered from low blood pressure at times and needed glucose is true, but none of his comrades—to my knowledge—have ever claimed this was a ruse to dodge combat. Part of the problem for Coll and Wright may have been their sources for this issue. Both authors interviewed a former senior CIA officer who is on record as saying that "he [bin Laden] was not a valiant warrior on the battlefield." This view is no more than an assertion, as I can vouch for the fact that there is nothing in the CIA files that discusses or describes bin Laden's performance during the anti-Soviet jihad in a negative light. Indeed, Coll, Wright, and other authors were led astray numerous times by a few former senior CIA officers and countless FBI officials, a reality that will become exquisitely and perhaps embarrassingly clear when the 9/11 Commission's archives are made available to the public. See ibid., pp. 256, 377, and 381; Wright, *The Looming Tower*, pp. 100, 116, and 138. The CIA official's comment is in Weaver, "The Real bin Laden."
70. Jamil al-Dhiyabi, "Interview with Shaykh Musa al-Qarni, part 2."
71. Bergen, *The Osama bin Laden I Know*, p. 55.
72. Usama bin Muhammad bin Laden, "Introduction," p. 77.
73. The literature on the fight at Jalalabad strongly suggests that there were Arab units there in addition to the one that included bin Laden. The high number of Arab casualties also suggests this, as does the increase of non-Afghan volunteers traveling to Afghanistan after the Jaji battle and the morale-boosting results of the mujahedin's use of U.S. Stinger missiles. Bin Laden describes the influx of young men—as well as the absence therein of known Islamist scholars—in Usama bin Muhammad bin Laden, "Introduction," p. 85. The ninety-day struggle around Jalalabad has yet to receive book-length treatment, but a feel for the battle can be gained from the following: Muhammad Yusaf and Mark Adkin, *The Bear Trap. Afghanistan's Untold Story* (Lahore: Jang Publishers, 1992), pp. 226–232; Coll, *Ghost Wars*, pp. 190–195; and David Loyn, *In Afghanistan: Two Hundred Years of British, Russian and American Occupation* (New York: Palgrave Macmillan, 2009), pp. 159–161.
74. The rudimentary military knowledge of bin Laden and many of his colleagues at this stage was apparent when bin Laden told Isam Darraz they had been surprised by the

enemy's tactic of advancing close behind a rolling artillery barrage. Darraz, "Impressions of an Arab journalist in Afghanistan."

75. Robert Fisk, "On finding Osama bin Laden," *Independent* (Internet version), 24 September 2005.
76. *The Arab Ansar in Afghanistan*, Islamic Muhajirun Network.
77. Bergen, *The Osama bin Laden I Know*, p. 56. Bin Laden's celebrity continued to grow so that by the early 1990s, according to Shaykh al-Qarni, "everyone knows [Osama] bin Laden." See al-Dhiyabi, "Interview with Shaykh Musa al-Qarni, part 1."
78. Darraz, "Impressions of an Arab journalist in Afghanistan," and Zaydan, *Usama bin Ladin without Mask*, p. 22.
79. Usama bin Muhammad bin Laden, "Introduction," p. 86.
80. *The Arab Ansar in Afghanistan*, Islamic Muhajirun Network.
81. Darraz, "Impressions of an Arab journalist in Afghanistan."
82. Bergen, *The Osama bin Laden I Know*, p. 59.
83. Yusufzai, "Interview with Osama bin Laden," 4 January 1999.
84. The emphasis bin Laden put on training was visible when he was asked in late 1998 about his contribution to the anti-Soviet jihad. He did not refer to his own or his Arab-only unit's activities but rather to the training camps he had funded, helped to build, and assisted managing. "What I know," he told the journalist Jamal Ismail, "is that God has been gracious to us by allowing us to contribute to the opening of jihad camps in Afghanistan during the jihad against the Soviet Union. Thanks be to the Almighty God, more than 15,000 men received training in these camps, most of them from the Arab countries and some were our brothers from the Islamic world." See Ismail, *Bin-Ladin, al-Jazirah, and I*.
85. The quality of the 9/11 attacks is self-evident, and for an excellent analysis of the unanticipated combat skills of al-Qaeda insurgent fighters in Iraq, see Stephen Biddle, "Afghanistan and the future of warfare: Implications for army and defense policy" (Carlisle, Pa.: Strategic Studies Institute, U.S. Army War College, 2002). For the high quality of bin Laden's Arab fighters before 9/11—as demonstrated in the Taleban-Massoud war—see the fine book by Roy Guttman, *How We Missed the Story*, pp. 188–190 and 218.
86. OBL, "Message to our people in Iraq." Bin Laden, at the same time, worried that his demand for thorough training might give some an excuse to delay starting jihad because training was not perfect. Once the "prerequisites of men and material become available for jihad," bin Laden said in 1998, as much preparatory training as possible must be provided. But training could not be used as an excuse to avoid jihad. "Perseverance is a virtue except when there is a chance for deliverance," he argued, and endless preparation that delayed the start of jihad only allowed the enemy to grow stronger and harder to defeat. See Ismail, *Bin-Ladin, al-Jazirah, and I*; OBL, "Abdallah's initiative—the great treason," http://www.cybcity.com/mnzmas/osam.htm, 1 March 2003; and Yusufzai, "Interview with Osama bin Laden," 4 January 1999.
87. Ismail, *Bin-Ladin, al-Jazirah, and I*.
88. Darraz, "Impressions of an Arab Journalist in Afghanistan."
89. Khalid al-Hammadi, "Al-Qaeda from within, narrated by Abu Jandal, part 4," *Al-Quds al-Arabi*, 22 March 2005, p. 19.
90. OBL, "Message to our people in Iraq."
91. Atwan, "Interview with Osama bin Laden," 27 November 1996, and OBL, "Message to our people in Iraq."

92. Usama bin Muhammad bin Laden, "Introduction," p. 86.
93. Ibid., p. 79.
94. OBL, "Message to the American people," Al-Jazirah Satellite Television, 30 October 2004. Bin Laden added that the U.S. and Soviet experiences in Afghanistan were also similar in the stubbornness of the leaders who ordered the invasions. "I would like to draw your [Americans'] attention to the fact," bin Laden said in a 2007 talk, "that the main reason for the collapse of the Soviet Union was that it was stricken by their leader, Brezhnev, who was vain and arrogant, refusing to recognize facts. Since the first year of the [Soviet] invasion of Afghanistan, reports indicated that the Russians are losing the war, but he refused to admit it so defeat would not be on his personal record. However, not admitting defeat does not change anything of the truth as far as any sensible people are concerned. Instead, it exacerbates the problem and increases the losses. Today, you are showing [in President George W. Bush's stubbornness] a striking resemblance to their situation almost twenty years ago." OBL, "Message to Americans," *Al-Fallujuh Islamic Minbar* (Internet), 8 September 2007.
95. Darraz, "Impressions of an Arab journalist in Afghanistan."
96. Bergen, *The Osama bin Laden I Know*, 53.
97. Darraz, "Impressions of an Arab journalist in Afghanistan"; "Statement by al-Qaeda leader Osama bin Laden in 'First war of the century' program," Al-Jazirah Satellite Television, 27 December 2001.
98. For a revealing look at the emphasis and professionalism al-Qaeda brings to logistics operations in the current Afghan war, see Ahmad Zaydan, "Interview with Mustafa Abu al-Yazid, supervisor general of al-Qaeda in Afghanistan," Al-Jazirah Satellite Television, 8 June 2009. It also worth noting that Abu al-Yazid—a career financier and logistician in al-Qaeda—was appointed al-Qaeda's commander in Afghanistan after the Taleban took over the bulk of combat operations against U.S.-NATO forces and al-Qaeda could resume its traditional role of supporting and not leading the combat side of an Islamist insurgency. In the June 2009 interview, for example, Abu al-Yazid gave an extensive outline of how al-Qaeda's role in Afghanistan had changed from combat to a focus on providing limited numbers of combat cadre, training, resupply, intelligence-gathering, and media operations. (Abu al-Yazid was killed in Afghanistan in 2010.)
99. Darraz, "Impressions of an Arab journalist in Afghanistan."
100. Usama bin Muhammad bin Laden, "Introduction," p. 84.
101. OBL to Mullah Omar, n.d. but before 9/11, AFGP-2002-600321, http://www.ctc.usma.edu.
102. OBL, "Message to the American people."
103. Azzam, "Join the caravan."
104. OBL, "Message to the Muslim nation," *Islamic Studies and Research Center* (Internet), 30 October 2004.
105. Ibid. Saladin is a key figure in that history and those discussions. "Until this day," James Reston, Jr., wrote in his *Warriors of God*, "Saladin remains a preeminent hero of the Islamic world. It is he who united the Arabs, who defeated the Crusaders in epic battles, who recaptured Jerusalem, and who threw the European invaders out of Arab lands. . . . Saladin lives vibrantly, as a symbol of hope and as the stuff of myth. In Damascus, Cairo, Amman, or East Jerusalem, one can easily fall into lengthy conversations about Saladin, for these ancient memories are central to the Arab sensibility and to their ideology of liberation. On the bars of the small, dimly lit cell in the Old

City of Jerusalem where Saladin lived humbly after his grand conquests is the inscription 'Allah, Muhammad, Saladin.' God, prophet, liberator. Such is Saladin's relation to the Muslim God."

Bin Laden made brilliant use of the intimacy of Muslims with Islamic history and their consequent ability to make easy analogies between struggles of the past and those of the present. He often used the figure of Saladin to stimulate such analogy making. "Is it not time," he asked Muslims in May 2008,

> to disavow Arab and non-Arab tyrants, from Indonesia to Mauritania, for the path to honor, glory, happiness and regaining Palestine is clear and manifest in the religion of Almighty God, and that path was taken by the heroic leader Salah-al-Din Ayyubi. When comparing some of his [Saladin's] deeds with some of the deeds of the Arab rulers during those decades [of the Crusades] we will see clearly the path to regain Palestine, God willing.

—Salah-al-Din abided by the teaching of Islam, and read the words of Almighty God. . . . Thus he realized the way to break the disbelievers' might is by fighting in God's way.
—Salah-al-Din used to consort with pious ulema and sought [religious] knowledge even in the field of jihad in order to apply it, and helped the ulema in urging the nation [ummah] to struggle against the Crusaders.
—Salah-al-Din fought the [Muslim] princes and their helpers who had fought alongside the Crusaders against the Muslims, even those princes used to say, 'There is no God but God,' because they knew they had violated those great words with their deeds.
—Salah-al-Din used to enlist volunteers for jihad without the approval of Richard [the Lionheart], the King of Britain, or his representatives, to start jihad against them [the Crusaders]. . . . [Today, ulema] led by the formerly Shaykh of the Awakening [Salman al-Awdah?] gets permission from America's agent in Riyadh [Saudi King Abdullah] as a condition to fight the Americans.

See Vlahos, *Fighting Identity: Sacred War and World Change* (Westport, CT: Praeger Security International, 2009), p. 55; James Reston, Jr., *Warriors of God: Richard the Lionheart and Saladin in the Third Crusade* (New York: Anchor Books, 2002), p. xiv; and OBL, "Message to the Muslim nation."

106. OBL, "The way of salvation for Palestine," Al-Sahab Media Production Organization, 21 March 2008. Bin Laden shared the view of Confederate Lieutenant-General Nathan Bedford Forrest that "war means fighting and fighting means killin'." Causing casualties was an essential part of bin Laden's war-making because it is historically part of the path to victory and because he believed that the United States and its allies were extraordinarily casualty-averse. This facet of his thinking is important to keep in mind when it comes to the use of nuclear and other unconventional weapons against the U.S. Bin Laden said it was a Muslim's duty to acquire nuclear weapons—al-Qaeda has been trying since 1991—and he had religious authorization to kill up to ten million Americans. If al-Qaeda acquires a nuclear device, they will use it in a first strike in the United States as a way to knock it out of the war, so that they can then focus on the main enemies—the Arab regimes and Israel. See John D. Wright, *The Oxford Dictionary of Civil War Quotations* (New York: Oxford University Press, 2006), p. 101; Rahimullah Yusufzai, "Conversations with terror," *Time*, January 11, 1999, p. 36; and Nasir bin Hamd al-Fahd, "A treatise on the legal status of using weapons of mass destruction against infidels" (Internet), May 2003.

107. Flagg Miller, "Al-Qaida as a 'pragmatic base': Contributions of area studies to sociolinguistics," *Language and Communications*, Vol. 28 (2008), p. 388.
108. Ibid. Bergen's extensive work, Omar Nasiri's compelling memoir, Abu Jandal's extensive commentary, the captured al-Qaeda materials published by West Point's invaluable Combating Terrorism Center, and literally dozens of other sources put paid to the idea that al-Qaeda is a figment of conspiratorial imaginations. The final word on this goes to Shaykh Musa al-Qarni, who was an adviser to bin Laden when al-Qaeda was formed. "As to whether it [al-Qaeda] is an organization," al-Qarni said, "it is certainly an organization." See Omar Nasiri, *Inside the Jihad: My Life with al-Qaeda: A Spy's Story* (New York: Basic Books, 2006); and al-Hammadi, "Al-Qaeda from within, 11 parts"; Combating Terrorism Center, http://ctc.uma.edu; and al-Dhiyabi, "Interview with Shaykh Musa al-Qarni, part 2."
109. Zaydan, *Usama bin Ladin without Mask*.
110. Coll, *The Bin Ladens*, p. 96, and Wright, *The Looming Tower*, p. 107.
111. "Exclusive Interview with Usama bin Ladin," *Ummat*, 28 September 2001, pp. 1 and 7.
112. Kiyohito Kokita and Yuji Moronaga, "Terrorist asks writer to compile a biography—Testimony of Pakistanis who have met with bin Ladin," *AERA*, 8 October 2001, pp. 18–20.
113. "Statement by Usama bin Ladin," Al-Jazirah Satellite Television, 10 September 2003, and Muhammad al-Shafi'i, "New message from Bin Ladin . . . ," *Al-Sharq al-Awsat* (Internet version), 19 January 2003.
114. Abu Shiraz, "Interview with Usama bin Laden," *Pakistan*, 20 February 1999, p. 10; "Bin Laden to the scholars of Deoband," 27 March 2002, http://ctc.usma.edu, AFGP-2002-901188; and Atwan, "Interview with Usama bin Ladin," 27 November 1996. The best of intentions, of course, seldom make things perfect. Despite bin Laden's words, al-Qaeda does suffer internal disharmony, just as any other multinational organization does. "Actually there were rivalries among al-Qaeda members," Abu Jandal has explained. "The Egyptians used to boast about being Egyptians. The Saudis, Yemenis, Sudanese, and Arab Maghreb citizens used to do the same things sometimes. This troubled Shaykh Usama and he used to send me to help eliminate these regional rivalries because the enemies of God, those who have sickness in their hearts, and informants would exploit these ignorant attitudes and try to sow divisions and disagreements among al-Qaida members." Bin Laden's goal, Abu Jandal stated, was to convince the disputants that "the issue of nationalism was [to be] put out of our minds, and we acquired a wider view than that, namely the issue of the ummah." The remarkable thing about al-Qaeda is not its internal squabbling between and among nationalities, but rather that those animosities have been limited and controlled and that the organization has now operated effectively for almost twenty-four years. Al-Hammadi, "Al-Qaeda from within, narrated by Abu Jandal, parts 1 and 6," *Al-Quds al-Arabi*, 18 March 2005, p. 17, and 24 March 2005, p. 19.
115. Tawil, *Brothers in Arms*, p. 29.
116. "Abu Jandal, Former Personal Bodyguard of Usama Bin Ladin and Leading al-Qaida Element in Yemen Reveals to Al-Quda Al-Arabi . . . ," *Al-Quds al-Arabi*, 3 August 2004, p. 4.
117. Usama bin Muhammad bin Laden, "Introduction," pp. 80–84.
118. OBL, "The way to foil plots," Al-Sahab Media Production Organization, 29 December 2007.
119. Khalid al-Batarfi, "Osama is very sweet, very kind, very considerate."
120. Michael Slackman, "Bin Laden's mother tried to stop him, Syrian kin say."

121. "The Arab Ansar in Afghanistan."

CHAPTER 4

1. Bin Laden, bin Laden, and Sasson, *Growing Up bin Laden*, p. 33, and Yusufzai, "Osama bin Laden: Al-Qaeda," p. 22.
2. Fisk, "On finding Osama."
3. Randall, *Osama*, p. 64.
4. Bin Laden, bin Laden, and Sasson, *Growing Up bin Laden*, p. 82, and Robert Fisk, "Interview with Saudi dissident Usama bin Ladin," *Independent*, 10 July 1996, p. 14.
5. Coll, *Ghost Wars*, p. 221, and al-Hammadi, "Al-Qaeda from within, part 8," p. 17.
6. Bergen, *Holy War, Inc.*, pp. 172–173.
7. Ibid. Tariq al-Fadhli told Steve Coll that bin Laden was the key to the Islamist resistance in Yemen. "He funded everything," al-Fadhli said. Steve Coll, *The Bin Ladens*, p. 374.
8. Atwan, "Interview with Usama bin Ladin," 27 November 1996.
9. Scheuer, *Through Our Enemies's Eyes*, p. 122.
10. R. Hrair Dekmejian, "The Rise of Political Islam in Saudi Arabia," *Middle East Journal*, Vol. 48, No. 4 (Autumn 1994), pp. 633–635.
11. Wiktorowicz, "Anatomy of the Salafi movement."
12. Bin Laden's respect and affection for al-Awdah and al-Hawali would remain strong until late in the 1990s. The two shaykhs are, for example, mentioned on ten separate occasions as the leaders and exemplars of the Saudi Awakening in West Point's selection of communiqués published by bin Laden's Advice and Reform Committee. See Advice and Reform Committee Communiques, http://ctc.usma.edu, AFGP-2002–003345.
13. Long, "Ribat, al-Qaida, and the Cahllenge for U.S. Foreign Policy," p. 42.
14. Safar al-Hawali does not seem to be a high-profile figure in the Saudi media, although his writings are posted on Salafi and other Islamist and jihadi Web sites. He was part of a group of Saudi scholars who in 2004 signed a letter urging Iraqis to fight the U.S.-led occupation, and has stridently warned Muslims that Christian fundamentalists are "complete in [their] support for Israel" and intend to "work relentlessly to undermine the Muslim world"; his views in regard to the United States appear to be identical to bin Laden's. Salman al-Awdah, on the other hand, is preeminently what bin Laden would describe as one of the "king's scholars." Al-Awdah leads the way in renouncing the tenets of jihad he is on record as identifying as God's law, denouncing bin Laden for following his earlier teachings to the letter, championing Islamist groups who give up the fight against Arab regimes, and praising the Saudi regime; he stresses the importance of all Saudis being proregime patriots. On al-Hawali, see *Atlas of Islamist Ideology*, http://ctc.usma.edu/atlas/Atlas-ResearchCompensium.pdf; Mamoun Fundy, "Safar al-Hawali: Saudi Islamist or Saudi Nationalist," *Islam and Christian-Muslim Relations*, Vol. 9, No. 1 (March 1998), pp. 5–21; and Safar ibn Abdur Rahman al-Hawali, "An Open Letter to President Bush," http://www.sunnahonline.com, 15 October 2001. On al-Awdah, see Shaykh Salman al-Awdah, "Letter to Usama bin Ladin," *IslamToday* (Internet), 17 September 2007; Turki al-Dakhil, "Interview with Saudi cleric Salman al-Awdah," *Al-Arabiyah Television*, 28 August 2009; and, Salman al-Awdah, "Revsions and Objections," *Ukaz* (Internet version), 22 August 2009.
15. Bin Laden, bin Laden, and Sasson, *Growing Up bin Laden*, pp. 73, 79.
16. Bergen, *Holy War, Inc.*, p. 64.

17. Coll, *Ghost Wars*, p. 229.
18. Bin Laden, bin Laden, and Sasson, *Growing Up bin Laden*, pp. 83, 84.
19. Scheuer, *Through Our Enemies' Eyes*, pp. 123–124.
20. Atwan, "Interview with Usama bin Ladin."
21. Al-Hammadi, "Al-Qaeda from within, part 8," p. 17.
22. Atwan, *The Secret History of al-Qaeda* p. 46.
23. Al-Hammadi, "Al-Qaeda from within, part 8," p. 17.
24. Coll, *Ghost Wars*, pp. 221–223.
25. Ibid., p. 223. A more likely scenario is that in regard to bin Laden's offer, the Saudis tried to have him and the United States on their team. In a 2001 interview with Hamid Mir, a Pakistani journalist, bin Laden said he refused a request from the Saudis to publicly support the joint U.S.-Saudi effort to evict Saddam from Kuwait. This makes perfect sense from the Saudi perspective. The Saudis, understandably, did not want to bring thousands of armed and trained mujahedin into the country—what do you do with them when Iraq is defeated?—but they certainly would have benefited among the Kingdom's populace if their deal with the United States was endorsed by a man many Saudis regarded as a devout and pious Muslim and an Islamic war hero. Many writers have doubts about bin Laden's brain power, but he clearly had enough smarts to dodge the Saudis' twofold plan to get his helpful immediate support while simultaneously neutering the religious credentials that are the foundation of his reputation. See Mir, "My last question to Osama bin Laden."

    I would note here that Coll is not alone in this whole-hog acceptance of the Saudi narrative. Lawrence Wright, as we shall see, is even more credulous when it comes to taking these spinning Saudis at face value. As an example the following will suffice. Although the overwhelming bulk of the evidence shows that bin Laden became increasingly anti U.S. during the anti-Soviet jihad (1979–1992), Wright prints the following—obviously provided by his official Saudi interlocutors—without any comment as the literal truth. "Privately, bin Laden approached members of the royal family during the Afghan jihad to express his gratitude for American participation in that war. Prince Bandar bin Sultan, the Saudi ambassador to the United States, remembered bin Laden coming to him and saying, 'Thank you. Thank you for bringing the Americans to help us get rid of the secularist, atheist Soviets.'" When reading this kind of stuff, the phrase *caveat emptor* comes to mind. See Wright, *The Looming Tower*, pp. 151–152.
26. Bin Laden, bin Laden, and Sasson, *Growing Up bin Laden*, p. 92.
27. Several stories have surfaced about how bin Laden managed to reacquire his passport travel documents, but I have seen nothing that seems as likely as the explanation I published in 2002. One or more of the bin Laden brothers intervened with Saudi interior ministry officials and persuaded them to release the necessary documents to their brother Osama so he could travel to Pakistan to close out his business holdings and then return. Since 2002, Abu Jandal has related roughly the same explanation for bin Laden's ability to travel. "Shaykh Usama himself was given a one-time passport, to be used to exit Saudi Arabia and return only once. He used this passport for a final exit from Saudi Arabia and never returned. He was given the passport because of his personal connections with some members of the royal family. He was given that passport to travel to Pakistan to liquidate his investments there and then return to Saudi Arabia and live under house arrest. But he used his permission to exit Saudi Arabia and never return." See Scheuer, *Through Our Enemies's Eyes*, p. 128, and al-Hammadi, "Al-Qaeda from within, part 3," p. 19.

28. Bergen, *The Osama bin Laden I Know*, p. 104. While he focused on trying to stop Afghan factionalism during this year, bin Laden also remained involved with several training camps in the country. In addition to training al-Qaeda and other fighters, bin Laden later told Mullah Omar, "we were successful in cooperating with our brothers in Tajikistan in various fields including training. We were able to train a good number of them, arm them, and deliver them to Tajikistan. Moreover, Allah facilitated to us delivering weapons and ammunition to them." See OBL to Mullah Omar, n.d. but before 9/11, http://www.ctc.usma.edu, AFGP-2002-600321.
29. Coll, *Ghost Wars*, p. 236; Mir, "Interview with Osama bin Laden," 18 March 1997, and Wright, *The Looming Tower*, p. 161.
30. Wright, *The Looming Tower*, p. 162.
31. Asad, *Warrior from Mecca*, p. 27.
32. Mir, "Interview with Usama bin Laden," 18 March 1997, and Shiraz, "Interview with Usama bin Ladin," 20 February 1999, p. 10.
33. Usama bin Muhammad bin Laden, "Introduction," p. 82.
34. "Part one of a series of reports on bin Ladin's life in Sudan," *Al-Quds al-Arabi* (Internet version), 24 November 2001; Januulah Hashimzada, "I will continue jihad against infidels, Usama bin Ladin," *Wahdat*, 27 March 2001, p. 5; and bin Laden, bin Laden, and Sasson, *Growing Up bin Laden*, p. 111.
35. Bin Laden, bin Laden, and Sasson, *Growing Up bin Laden*, pp. 95 and 111.
36. Hashimzada, "I will continue jihad against infidels."
37. "Bin Ladin loved Sudan, adored its people, adjusted to their customs; his life in Sudan was simple," *Al-Quds al-Arabi* (Internet version), 26 November 2001.
38. "Part one of a series of reports on bin Ladin's life in Sudan."
39. Bergen, *The Osama bin Laden I Know*, p. 135, and Abdel Bari Atwan, "Interview with Usamah bin Ladin," 27 November 1996, p. 5.
40. Abdel Bari Atwan, "Interview with Usamah bin Ladin," 27 November 1996, p. 5.
41. While based in Sudan, bin Laden cut ties with Algeria's Armed Islamic Group (GIA) because of its takfirism. Having invited the GIA to send a representative to Khartoum in late 1995 to discuss building al-Qaeda camps in Algeria and to "seek reassurances about the soundness of the GIA's doctrine," bin Laden was threatened with death by the GIA's Redouane Makudor—Makudor drew his finger across his throat to make the point—if al-Qaeda sought to act in Algeria without GIA approval. This was enough for bin Laden, who cut ties with the GIA, apparently agreeing with the Algerian mujahid Abdullah Anas's description of takfiris as "very crazy, very crazy. They kill everybody." Anas's is an accurate statement that explains why takfiris are hated with a passion throughout the Muslim world. If bin Laden, al-Qaeda, and the Taleban were takfiris in their beliefs and behavior they would pose a zero menace to the United States and the West because the Muslim world would be united in a determination to eradicate them wherever found. And yet several leading Western analysts of al-Qaeda and Islamism argue strongly that these are takfiri forces and will destroy themselves because of near-universal Muslim hatred for takfirism. Again, if this was true, the analysts would be correct. But they are not correct; there is nothing takfiri about al-Qaeda, the Taleban, and most of their allies. The sole exception to this statement was Abu Musab al-Zarqawi who, as al-Qaeda's uncontrollable chief in Iraq, proved in a relatively short period that takfirism will destroy its advocates by turning nearly all Muslims against it. As discussed later in this book, al-Zarqawi was the only strategic threat to al-Qaeda after 9/11—Iraqi Sunnis' hatred for his behavior facilitated the temporary success of the U.S. "surge"—and if the U.S. military had not killed him, al-Qaeda would have had to remove or kill

him to ensure the organization's survival. Incorrectly assigning the takfiri label to al-Qaeda and its allies will lead to disaster by making Western leaders underestimate their size, intellectual deftness, growth potential, and ability to form working, if not always permanent, cooperative relationships. For bin Laden's meeting with Makudor and Anas's remark, see Tawil, *Brothers in Arms*, pp. 95 and 104–105; Lia, *Architect of Global Jihad*, pp. 128–129; and Bergen, *The Osama bin Laden I Know*, p. 135. For three leading Western analysts who mistakenly fix the takfiri label on al-Qaeda, the Taleban, and other Islamist groups, see Kilcullen, *The Accidental Guerrilla*; Lawrence Wright, "The Rebellion within," *New Yorker* (Internet version), 2 June 2008; and Peter L. Bergen and Paul Cruickshank, "The unraveling," *New Republic* (Internet version), 11 June 2008.

42. Abd-al-Karim and al-Nur, "Interview with Saudi Businessman Usama bin Ladin," p. 4.
43. Al-Hammadi, "Al-Qaeda from within, part 3," p. 19.
44. Mark Huband, *Brutal Truths, Fragile Myths: Power Politics and Western Adventurism in the Arab World* (Boulder, Colo.: Westview, 2004), p. 79; Fisk, "On finding Osama"; and al-Hammadi, "Al-Qaeda from within, part 3," p. 19.
45. "Biography of Usamah bin Laden," Islamic Observation Center (Internet), 22 April 2000.
46. "Bin Ladin loved Sudan."
47. Wright, *The Looming Tower*, p. 168.
48. Coll, *The Bin Ladens*, p. 398.
49. Bin Laden, bin Laden, and Sasson, *Growing Up bin Laden*, pp. 96–97.
50. Huband, *Brutal Truths, Fragile Myths*, p. 79, and Bergen, *Holy War, Inc.*, p. 79.
51. Huband, *Brutal Truths, Fragile Myths*, p. 77.
52. "Part one of a series of reports on bin Ladin's life in Sudan," and John Prendergast and Don Cheadle, "Lose this friendship with bin Laden crony in Sudan," *Houston Chronicle* (Internet version), 20 February 2006.
53. Huband, *Brutal Truths, Fragile Myths*, p. 78; "Bin Ladin loved Sudan"; and Muhammad Salah, "Ali al-Rashidi: The Egyptian policeman who paved the way for 'Afghan Arabs' in Africa and prepared them to take revenge against the Americans," *Al-Hayah*, 30 September 1998, pp. 1, 6.
54. Al-Hammadi, "Al-Qaeda from within, narrated by Abu Jandal, parts 3 and 9," *Al-Quds al-Arabi*, 21 March 2005, p. 19, and 28 March 2005, p. 21.
55. Huband, *Brutal Truths, Fragile Myths*, p. 81; Mir, "Interview with Usama bin Ladin," 18 March 1997; and al-Hammadi, "Al-Qaeda from within, part 3," p. 19.
56. Huband, *Brutal Truths, Fragile Myths*, p. 78; and al-Hammadi, "Al-Qaeda from within, part 3," p. 19.
57. Khalid al-Hammadi, "Interview with Abu Jandal, former personal bodyguard of Usama bin Ladin," *Al-Quds al-Arabi*, 3 August 2006, p. 4; and Scheuer, *Through Our Enemies' Eyes*, p. 139.
58. Miller, "Greetings America. My name is Osama bin Laden," and Simon Reeve, *The New Jackals: Ramzi Yousef, Osama bin Laden, and the Future of Terrorism* (Boston: Northeastern University Press, 1999), pp. 71–93.
59. Wright, *The Looming Tower*, p. 199.
60. Ibid. One must also acknowledge that bin Laden was not stupid enough to think he could return to Saudi Arabia without paying a price. In April 1994, for example, he publicly refused King Fahd's request—made with "great insistence"—that he and his Saudi followers return to the Kingdom. In response, bin Laden said it is "necessary for us to remain in exile, knowing full well what is behind your desire [for our return]." Bin Laden reminded the king that his regime had seized their passports, frozen their

bank accounts, and systematically defamed them in the Kingdom and internationally. He said that they were not prepared to forget that "your actions indicate to us what your intentions are for us." See Advice and Reform Committee, "Our invitation to give advice and reform," http://ctc.usma.edu, 12 April 1994, AFGP-2002-003345. All Committee communiqués used herein are from this group of records. Hereafter, each is cited as ARC, title of communiqué, date. A communiqué's title is used only in its first citation; thereafter only the date is given.

61. ARC, 12 April 1994. Bin Laden's stress here on the "kind, clear, and honest fashion" in which the reformist documents were presented to the king was meant to highlight how far the reformers had gone to work within and not against the Saudi system of governance. As in Western just-war theory, Islamic tradition holds that war is a last resort, so underlining a record of peaceful but unanswered remonstrance to the ruler—as Thomas Jefferson clearly laid out in the Declaration of Independence—is part of being able to explain and justify a resort to war. Bin Laden would make this point again in his own 1996 Declaration of War. Writing of the reformers' peaceful campaign and submission of documents, bin Laden reminded his audience that "Although the memorandum submitted all that [advice] leniently and gently, as a reminder of God and as good advice in a gentle, objective, and sincere way, despite the necessity of advice for rulers in Islam, and despite the numbers and positions of the signatories of the memorandum and their sympathizers, it was of no avail. Its contents were rejected and its signatories and sympathizers were humiliated, punished, and imprisoned. The preachers' and reformers' eagerness to pursue peaceful reform methods in the interest of the country's unity was clearly demonstrated. So, why should the regime block all means of peaceful reform and drive people toward armed action? That was the only door left open to the public for ending injustice and upholding right and justice." See OBL, "Declaration of jihad against the Americans occupying the Land of the Two Holy Mosques; expel the heretics from the Arabian Peninsula," *Al-Quds al-Arabi*, 23 August 1996. Republished on the Internet by the Saudi dissident *Al-Islah* Website, London, 2 September 1996.
62. ARC, 12 April 1994.
63. Atwan, "Interview with Usama bin Laden," 27 November 1996. The Saudi regime's decision to stage a heavy-handed and then brutal crackdown on the Awakening scholars unwittingly also provided the opportunity for bin Laden to reluctantly assume a more prominent leadership role for Saudi youth and thereby begin his journey to being a figure of world historical importance. "The period during which the influential Saudi [Awakening] religious shaykhs were arrested, from 1993 to 1998," bin Laden's former chief bodyguard, Abu Jandal, has contended, "was sufficient for the youths to escape the influence of those religious shaykhs who represented a safety valve for the youths, because they [the shaykhs] used to rein them in and deter their recklessness. As soon as the head was severed from the body, those youths turned to another direction, and Usama bin Laden grabbed them into al-Qaeda, and the youths rushed toward jihad and the possession of weapons." See Khalid al-Hammadi, "Al-Qaida from within, as narrated by Abu Jandal, part 1," *Al-Quds al-Arabi*, 18 March 2005, p. 17.
64. ARC, "Higher Committee for Harm!" 15 October 1994.
65. ARC, 12 April 1994, and ARC, "Do not have vile actions in your religion," 16 September 1994.
66. ARC, 12 April 1994.
67. ARC, "An open message to King Fahd," 3 August 1995.
68. ARC, "Prince Salman and the Ramadan alms," 12 February 1995.

69. ARC, 3 August 1995.
70. ARC, "Prince Sultan and the aviation commissions," 11 July 1995.
71. ARC, 12 April 1994.
72. ARC, 11 July 1995.
73. ARC, 3 August 1995.
74. ARC, "Open letter to Shaykh bin Baz on the invalidity of his fatwa on peace with the Jews," 29 December 1994.
75. ARC, "The second letter to Shaykh bin Baz," 29 January 1995.
76. ARC, "Scholars are the Prophet's successors," 6 May 1995.
77. Ibid., and ARC, 16 September 1994.
78. ARC, 29 December 1994.
79. ARC, "Saudi Arabia unveils its war against Islam and its scholars," 12 September 1994.
80. Ibid., and ARC, "Quran scholars in the face of despotism," 19 July 1994.
81. ARC, 19 July 1994, and ARC, "Saudi Arabia continues its war against Islam and its scholars," 9 March 1995.
82. ARC, 16 March 1994.
83. ARC, 6 May 1995.
84. ARC, 12 September 1994. Bin Laden's claim that Saudi regime actions had started a war with God was soon accompanied by communiqués urging resistance and sedition by the Saudi security service and the Saudi army. Bin Laden reminded both that the jailed scholars were "the heirs of the prophet" and that to participate in the arrest of such men made "them accomplices in the [regime's] offense" and would "reduce you to a low and submissive rank." The regime, bin Laden said, intended to use them "as the spears that will pierce the chest of the ummah," and he said the al-Sauds deliberately shamed the army when they "imported women of the Christian armies to defend [the Kingdom]" and kept its strength at "a tenth of the size of the Zionist enemy." He concluded by telling the services "You are the servants of God, you are not the servants for the Saudi rulers . . . [and] the book of God bears witness to the punishment of those who stand by the tyrant." He urged the men to stand by the still-free scholars opposed to the regime and to "strive to release" the imprisoned scholars. See ARC communiques 12 September 1994 and 16 September 1994.
85. ARC communiqué, untitled, undated.
86. ARC, "The Saudi regime and the repeated tragedies of the pilgrims," 16 April 1997, and ARC communiqué, untitled, undated.
87. ARC, 6 May 1995 and ARC, 15 October 1994.
88. ARC, 3 August 1995.
89. ARC, "Saudi Arabia supports the communists in Yemen," 7 June 1994, and ARC, 29 December 1994. Bin Laden justified his call for Yemenis to overthrow their communist rulers by citing the hadith in which the Prophet says all unbelievers must be evicted from the Arabian Peninsula. Bin Laden made clear here and in later statements that this hadith referred to the entire Arabian Peninsula and not just the state known as Saudi Arabia, which of course did not exist in the Prophet's time. Many in the West have not seemed to grasp that moving U.S. military forces from the Kingdom to Qatar and Kuwait does not solve for Muslims the issue raised by bin Laden.
90. ARC, 11 August 1995; ARC, 12 September 1994; and ARC, 29 January 1995.
91. ARC, 3 August 1995.
92. ARC, 19 July 1994, and ARC, 16 April 1997.
93. ARC, 3 August 1995.

94. ARC, 29 December 1994.
95. ARC, 3 August 1995.
96. ARC, 11 August 1995, and ARC, 7 June 1994.
97. ARC, 11 August 1995; this communiqué again demonstrates that Palestine was central to bin Laden's thinking and public statements long before the 9/11 attacks.
98. ARC, 29 December 1994.
99. Ibid.
100. Ibid. This communiqué also includes bin Laden's exposition of the Salafi-jihadi tenet that scholars issuing fatwas about jihad must have—as did Ibn Taymiyyah and Shaykh Azzam—Islamic knowledge *and* jihad experience so their decisions reflect reality. He told bin Baz he lacked "awareness of the true nature of the situation [in Palestine], and urged him to follow Ibn Taymiyyah's guidance. "Obligation is to be considered in matters of jihad," Taymiyyah held, "according to the opinion of the upright men of religion who have experience in what people of this world do, rather than those who mainly look at the matter from the viewpoint of religion. Do not adopt their opinion—not the opinion of men of religion who have no experience in the world." Bin Laden's frustration with this situation continued, and while several leading contemporary Salafi-jihadi scholars—Shaykh Abu Muhammad al-Maqdisi and Shaykh Nasir bin Fahd, for example—seconded Ibn Taymiyyah, a decade later he would still be protesting the influence of scholars lacking jihad experience. "For how can you obey, when jihad becomes a duty," he asked, "those [scholars] who have never fought for the sake of God?" See Wiktorowicz, "Anatomy of the Salafi movement," and OBL, "Second message to our Iraqi brothers," Al-Jazirah Satellite Television, 18 October 2003.
101. ARC, 29 January 1995.
102. ARC, 16 April 1997.
103. ARC, 29 December 1994, and ARC, 29 January 1995.
104. Wright, *The Looming Tower*, p. 169. The imam of the mosque where bin Laden worshiped in Khartoum, however, has said he did not lead prayers or speak at services. "He used to come to the mosque five times a day," Shaykh Abdul Ghafar recalled, "and he came to the mosque always very calm. He was a very, very decent man, and the very wisest man. And really a good Muslim. I asked him to address the Muslims in the mosque. He refused. He would just come to do his prayers. No more than that. . . . A Good Muslim! 100 percent, you know?" See Bergen, *The Osama bin Laden I Know*, pp. 132–133.
105. Abd-al-Karim and al-Nur, "Interview with Saudi businessman Usama bin Ladin."
106. Tawil, *Brothers in Arms*, p. 101.
107. Wright, *The Looming Tower*, p. 169.
108. Atwan, *The Secret History of al-Qaeda*, p. 48.
109. Ibid., p. 49. For an excellent and groundbreaking analysis of Bin Laden's Sudan-era relationship with Islamist insurgent groups from Algeria, Libya, and Egypt, see Tawil, *Brothers in Arms*.
110. ARC, 14 September 1994.
111. Scheuer, *Through Our Enemies's Eyes*, p. 152.
112. Zaydan, *Usama bin Ladin without Mask*, pp. 6–7.
113. Atwan, *The Secret History of al-Qaeda*, p. 49.
114. Al-Hammadi, "Al-Qaeda from within, part 3," p. 19.
115. Huband, *Brutal Truths, Fragile Myths*, p. 75.

116. "Part one of a series of reports on bin Ladin's life in Sudan," and Asad, *Warrior from Mecca*, p. 48. Al-Turabi would later patronize and ridicule bin Laden. Bin Laden came to Sudan, al-Turabi said, "as a contractor. He built a road and then he became interested in agriculture. . . . The poor man . . . I saw him once or twice. He visited me here [al-Turabi's home] and then I met him once at his home. He's a very simple man." See David Blair, "Man who harboured bin Laden is lodestar for terrorists," http://www.telegraph.co.uk, 30 January 2006.
117. "Part one of a series of reports on bin Ladin's life in Sudan."
118. Bin Laden, bin Laden, and Sasson, *Growing Up bin Laden*, p. 113.
119. "Bin Ladin loved Sudan."
120. Ibid., and Cherif Ouazai, "The bin Laden Mystery."
121. Wright, *The Looming Tower*, p. 224. Estimates of how much money bin Laden lost in Afghanistan are all over the map. Wright says that the amount was more than $160 million, while the fine British journalist Mark Huband has written that the loss was about $92 million. In addition, bin Laden told Abdel Bari Atwan that he had helped Sudan with "$300 million dollars of his own money." Whatever number is closest to the mark, it was made worse by the freezing of bin Laden's bank accounts in Saudi Arabia when King Fahd stripped him of his Saudi citizenship in 1994, an act that Omar bin Laden has said cut his father off from "huge" bank accounts—a point also made by Mark Huband. Two points seem clear here: first, bin Laden lost a great deal of money while in Sudan; much more, for example, than author Steve Coll—who has made something of a personal cottage industry out of downgrading bin Laden's fortune, income, access to money, and so on—has argued that he ever had in his control, and second, bin Laden, after returning to Afghanistan in 1996, was able to recoup enough of a fortune to keep al-Qaeda chin-to-chin in a war against the world's only superpower. I have always thought that the United States and its allies put too much stress on stopping the flow of money to bin Laden as a war-winning measure, especially when they are constantly prompting new donations through such actions as invading Iraq, reinforcing NATO forces in Afghanistan, bombing oil-rich Muslim states like Libya, and targeting Muslim countries for full-body airport scanning for men and women. The sources of his money have been simply too redundant and beyond our reach to make the resources devoted to finding and stopping them anything more than the fuel for a fool's errand. See ibid., p. 222; Huband, *Brutal Truths, Fragile Myths*, pp. 72 and 83; Atwan, *The Secret History of al-Qaeda*, p. 31; and bin Laden, bin Laden, and Sasson, *Growing Up bin Laden*, p. 128. On Steve Coll's obsession with this issue—which is more important than Lawrence Wright's rather daft obsession with trying to prove bin Laden was not a tall man—see his index entries for Osama bin Laden's financial problems, income, and inheritance in *The Bin Ladens*, p. 653.
122. Randall, *Osama*.
123. Atwan, "Interview with Usamah bin Ladin."
124. Ibid.
125. Mir, "Interview with Osama bin Laden in Jalalabad," 18 March 1997. In conversation with Abdel Bari Atwan, bin Laden was more astringent, saying that al-Turabi and his lieutenants "were un-Islamic and had betrayed him." The Pakistani journalist Januulah Hashimzada also reported that bin Laden wrote poetry in which he criticized "Sudanese rulers General Umar al-Bashir and Dr. Hassan al-Turabi who shamelessly asked Usama bin Laden to leave Sudan because of a little pressure from the United States." As noted earlier, bin Laden's use of poetry to attack his

Muslim opponents was in keeping with one of the major roles of poetry in Islamic history. See Atwan, *The Secret history of al-Qaeda*, p. 31, and Hashimzada, "I will continue jihad against infidels."

126. "Rebels say attack on Juba imminent," *Al-Quds Al-Arabi*, 19 February 1998, p. 1.

127. Rahimullah Yusafzai, "World's most wanted terrorist: An interview with Osama bin Laden," www.abcnews.com, 4 January 1999.

128. Abd-al-Karim and al-Nur, "Interview with Saudi businessman Usama bin Ladin."

129. Usama bin Ladin, "Introduction."

130. For two of the many Western writers who have claimed that bin Laden asserted the Arabs beat the Red Army, see Randall, *Osama*, p. 11, and Wright, *The Looming Tower*, p. 145. Randall says that bin Laden "claims that his Arab volunteers all but single-handedly defeated the Soviet Red Army in the 1980s," while Wright maintains that bin Laden "actually believed the fable . . . that his Arab legion brought down the mighty [Soviet] superpower." I can find no record of bin Laden giving anyone but Allah and then the Afghans the major credit for beating the Soviets. Such a claim would have been denounced by the Afghans and ruined bin Laden's relations with them. The Afghans' absolute willingness to call a spade a spade—especially on issues pertaining to *their* jihad—is one way of vetting bin Laden's claims to have participated in the war as a combat engineer and a fighter. Were these claims lies, the Afghans would have called Usama's bluff. To date only Westerners who really have no way of knowing one way or another have accused bin Laden of lying about his battlefield experiences.

131. Atwan, "Interview with Usamah bin Ladin."

CHAPTER 5

1. Usama bin Muhammad bin Laden, "Introduction."
2. Al-Hammadi, "Al-Qaeda from within, part 3," p. 19.
3. Abu Musab al-Suri, "A drama of faith and jihad: The Mujahedin (Arabs-al-Qaida) and Ansar (Afghans-Taleban)," *OSC Summary*, 16–17 October 2009.
4. Ibid.
5. The expanded living area bin Laden required, according to his son Omar, was to accommodate "my father's [Afghan jihad] war veterans from Pakistan, Yemen, and other countries converging on Afghanistan, bringing their wives and daughters with them." See bin Laden, bin Laden, and Sasson, *Growing Up bin Laden*, p. 172.
6. Rauf Tahir, "Persecutions instead of comforts," *Fact*, 1–31 October 2007, and "Al-Qaeda family: At home with Osama bin Laden," *CBC News Online*, 3 March 2004. Abdurrahman Khadr's referral to "financial issues" as an area of concern for bin Laden in mid-1996 matches similar assertions by Omar bin Laden, who says that on returning to Afghanistan, "He [Osama] was without money for the first time in his life." Omar claims that the combination of his father's economic disaster in Sudan and the Saudi regime's freezing of his bank accounts in the Kingdom yielded near bankruptcy. "We all knew by that time that my father was no longer a wealthy man," Omar recalls. "Although a system was in place to procure funds from those who supported Jihad, for there were a number of friends, family, and royals who still offered financial support, there were times the cash coffers were bare." There is no doubt the economic problems Omar names depleted bin Laden's access to *his* money. In addition, the Saudi regime's anger toward bin Laden surely made some former donors stop contributing. But all that said, Omar's description seems overdrawn. Other accounts of the finances of bin Laden and al-Qaeda after returning to Afghanistan are less stark. Indeed, in

Abu Jandal's commentary and in the long, often multiple interviews and stories by reputable journalists with reliable pre-9/11 access to al-Qaeda—like Rahimullah Yusafzai, Robert Fisk, and Ahmad Muwaffaq Zaydan—financial difficulties rarely arise. In addition, al-Qaeda's significant contribution to the Taleban's war against Massoud; the high tempo of training in al-Qaeda's Afghan camps; the funding for al-Qaeda's strikes in East Africa, Aden, and the United States; the substantial growth in al-Qaeda media operations; and the ongoing requirement to arm, feed, clothe, transport, and shelter al-Qaeda fighters and their families tend to suggest that al-Qaeda's coffers were usually far enough above "bare" to permit smooth operation. See bin Laden, bin Laden, and Sasson, *Growing Up bin Laden*, pp. 215 and 223.

7. "Al-Qaeda family: At home with Osama bin Laden," CBC News Online, 3 March 2004. As in Sudan, bin Laden in Afghanistan ensured that his sons received instruction in such "modern topics" as math, electronics, computers, and engineering by bringing in tutors from Arab countries. See "The West at War: Bin Laden's Son [Abdullah]: Dad has become invisible; always on his guard," *Sunday Mirror* (Internet version), 14 October 2001.
8. "Al-Qaeda family: At home with Osama bin Laden," CBC News Online, 3 March 2004.
9. "Documentary on life with bin Laden," http://www.chinadaily.com, 7 March 2004. Abdullah's mother Maha takes this point and adds a thought that explains why much of the Muslim world has seen bin Laden as something of a Robin Hood. "For me," Maha said, "I use to admire them [bin Laden and his family] because I knew they were [a] very, very rich family and they live in a very, very, very simple way—I mean I was like a queen compared to them because I was living in a house with electricity and water. They did not have this in their compound." See "Al-Qaeda family."
10. Andrew Duffy, "Radicalized in Ottawa," *Ottawa Citizen* (Internet version), 11 May 2008.
11. "Bin Ladin building new bases in Kandahar area," *Sunday Telegraph* (Internet version), 4 October 1998; Behroz Khan, "Bin Ladin makes 'rare' public appearance in Kandahar," *News*, 22 January 1999; Rahimullah Yusufzai, "Myth and Man," *Newsline*, 1 September, 1998; and Ahmad Muwaffaq Zaydan, "Bin Ladin is in 'Tora Bora' south of Jalalabad," *Al-Hayah*, 17 February 1999, p. 16.
12. "Laden makes first appearance in Kandahar," *News*, 11 April 1998, p. 12, and Aimal Khan, "Usama bin Ladin steps up public appearances in Kabul," *Frontier Post*, 7 September 1999, p. 12.
13. "Usama bin Ladin steps up public appearances in Kabul."
14. Al-Hammadi, "Al-Qaeda from within, part 5," and bin Laden, bin Laden, and Sasson, *Growing Up bin Laden*, pp. 208–209.
15. Taysir Alwani, "Bin Ladin weds Yemeni girl in simple ceremony in the presence of his supporters," *Al-Quds al-Arabi* (Internet version), 1 August 2000. One of bin Laden's previous four marriages ended in divorce—upon that wife's request—and so he remained within Islam's four-marriage limit.
16. Al-Hammadi, "Interview with Abu Jandal,"
17. "Interview (written) with Usama bin Ladin," *Ghazi*, 20 August 2000. In this interview, bin Laden also maintained his refusal to criticize his family in Saudi Arabia for their public statements about his actions and their loyalty to the Saudi regime. "My personal life is always driven by my responsibilities as a Muslim," he said, "[and] I am immensely thankful to God that he enabled my family to understand this. My family members are pray[ing] for me and no doubt they have

gone through a lot of difficulties [because of me]. But God gave them courage to face all that."

18. Rahimullah Yusufzai, "Taleban foil attempt on bin Ladin's life by Saudis," *News*, 26 December 1998, and "U.S. aid for Ahmed Shah Massoud against Usamah," *Jang*, 29 December 1998, p. 10.
19. Yusufzai, "Taleban foil attempt on bin Ladin's life."
20. Ahmad Zaydan, "Taleban execute young Saudi for performing hostile activities against bin Ladin," *Al-Hayah*, 5 October 1998, p. 1, and Yusafzai, "World's most wanted terrorist."
21. "Taleban forces foil attempt to assassinate bin Ladin, uncover hireling network in Kandahar and Peshawar," *Al-Quds al-Arabi* (Internet version), 29 July 1999.
22. Ismail, *Bin-Ladin, al-Jazirah, and I.*
23. Aimal Khan, "Arab radicals declare Usama a non-Muslim," *Frontier Post*, 10 March 1999, p.1, and Cathy Scott-Clark and Adrian Levy, "Rebel cult in blood feud with 'infidel' bin Laden," *Sunday Times* (Internet version), 18 July 2009. Both articles also note that in the spring of 1999 the same group of takfiris kidnapped the thirteen-year-old grandson, Haris, of Shaykh Abduallah Azzam and held him for ransom. The journalists report that someone paid "a huge amount to the kidnappers" to free the boy, and later the chief of the kidnap team was found dead with bullet wounds to the head. Although it is only speculation, it is easy to imagine, given bin Laden's love for Shaykh Azzam, that al-Qaeda was responsible for the rescue and the execution.
24. Khan, "Arab radicals declare Usama a non-Muslim"; Scott-Clark and Levy, "Rebel cult in blood feud with 'infidel' bin Laden."
25. Scott-Clark and Levy, "Rebel cult in blood feud with 'infidel' bin Laden."
26. Ismail, *Bin Ladin, al-Jazirah, and I.*
27. Bin Laden, bin Laden, and Sasson, *Growing Up bin Laden*, p. 173, and Porzio, "Bin-Ladin: I will tell you about the super-terrorist seen from up close," *Panorama*, 11 February 2010, pp. 86–92. Bin Laden concluded that Washington and its allies used "tendentious rumors" about his health as a propaganda tool to either "lower the morale of Muslims who sympathize with us . . . [or] perhaps also to ease the fears of the Americans of Usama and say that he cannot do anything." He added that, either way, such propaganda showed that U.S. leaders still did not understand that "the matter does not depend on Usamah. . . . 1.25 billion Muslims cannot [in]definitely allow the ancient House of God [in Mecca] to be controlled by the Jewish and Christian criminals." Ismail, *Bin Ladin, al-Jazirah, and I.*
28. Usama bin Laden, "Declaration of war against the United States," *Al-Quds al-Arabi*, 23 August 1996. The Declaration of war clearly portended al-Qaeda attacks on U.S. interests worldwide. The document did not discuss fomenting a domestic jihad in the United States, but there are bits of fragmentary evidence that bin Laden was at least considering Intifadah-type violence inside the United States. In May 1997, for example, bin Laden told CNN that Ramzi Yousef—the February 1993 World Trade Center bomber—would serve as "a symbol and teacher" for those who wanted to "transfer the battle into the United States." He added that this would help balance the current situation where "everything is made possible to protect the blood of American children while the blood of Muslims is allowed everyplace." In a March 1998 interview, bin Laden said he believed that "in the future . . . the Americans will face destruction from collisions among themselves." And in 2000, he said that there would be "a holy war against the United States in the United States . . . there would be a holy war in every street of the United States." Then after 9/11, bin Laden calmly explained that

"the battle has moved to inside America . . . [and] I swear by Almighty God . . . that neither the United States nor he who lives in the United States will enjoy security before we can see it as a reality in Palestine, and before all the infidel armies leave the land of Muhammad, may God's peace and blessing be upon him." Three months later, bin Laden told the media that he believed that the United States was a "heedless enemy" and still "does not know the flames it has ignited [by invading Afghanistan] would reach its homeland."

While this is not as much evidence as one would like to have to hang an analytic hat on, these statements and al-Qaeda's recruitment of the Californian Adam Gadahn—aka Azzam al-Amriki—as a major spokesman; the travel of young U.S. Muslims to secure military training and then fight in Somalia, Afghanistan, and Yemen; the activities of the U.S.-born, al-Qaeda-related cleric Anwar al-Awlaki, which include a call for jihad in the United States and may include influencing Major Nabil Hassan, who in late 2009 killed thirteen U.S. soldiers at Forth Hood, Texas; the reportedly increased efforts by al-Qaeda and other Islamist groups to recruit U.S.-citizen Muslims; the multiple Islamist attacks that have been foiled since 2007 in New York and other U.S. cities; and the summer 2010 start of an English-language, al-Qaeda-in-the-Arab-Peninsula Internet journal called *Inspire* (which is edited by a native of North Carolina now resident in Yemen and urges U.S. Muslims to violence against government officials, journalists, and infrastructure targets) suggest efforts to implement bin Laden's plans for a domestic jihad in the United States have been perking slowly along since 1996 and may now be nearing a simmer. See Arnett, "Osama bin Laden: The interview"; Azeem Siddique, "Interview with Osama bin Ladin," *Al-Akhbar*, 31 March 1998, pp. 1 and 8; "Usama bin Ladin sees holy war in 'every street' in U.S.," *Pakistan*, 2 May 2000, p. 8; Taysir Alouni, "Interview with Usama bin Laden, October 2001," *Qoqaz* (Internet), 23 May 2002; "Speech by Osama bin Laden," Al-Jazirah Satellite Television, 7 October 2001; "Bin Ladin's letter to Pakistani journalists," *Nawa-iWaqt*, 12 December 2001, pp. 1 and 10; W. G. Dunlop, "First edition of al-Qaeda magazine published," Agence-France Presse, 12 July 2010.

29. Arnett, "Osama bin Laden: The interview," and ARC, 7 May 1998; and Catherine Herridge and Justin Fishel, "N. Carolina man appears to be top editor of Al-Qaeda Magazine, U.S. officials say," http:///www.foxnews.com, July 19, 2010.
30. The fullest discussion still seems to be Scheuer, *Through Our Enemies' Eyes*, pp. 10–14 and 46–50, but also well worth consulting are Bergen, *The Osama bin Laden I Know*; Atwan, *The Secret History of al-Qaeda*; and Lia, *Architect of Global Jihad*. While the Declaration of War constituted a clear warning of al-Qaeda's intentions toward the United States, bin Laden did not include an invitation to Americans to convert to Islam, nor did he offer a truce to the United States. Both omissions are deviations from Islam's way of making war, and their negative ramifications for bin Laden within his peer group will be more fully discussed in chapter 6.
31. Bin Laden, bin Laden, and Sasson, *Growing Up bin Laden*, p. 177.
32. OBL, "Declaration of jihad against the United States," *Al-Islah* (Internet), 2 September 1996.
33. Al-Hammadi, "Al-Qaeda from within, part 3," p. 19.
34. The failure of the World Front to become what it was intended to be is clear in several statements bin Laden made to Muslim journalists. "This front," bin Laden said, "has been established as the first step to pool together the energies and concentrate the efforts against the infidels represented in the Jewish-Crusader alliance, thus replacing splinters and subsidiary fronts. . . . We thought it might form the basis of global jihad

against Jews and Crusaders, particularly the Americans. We thought it might push Muslim movements, groups, and individuals to join this movement. However, it seems we overestimated its ability and resources. It might have been better not to declare it, but what has happened has happened." More bluntly, al-Qaeda's late military commander Abu Hafs al-Masri said that the World Front "has become a burden on him [bin Laden] and his companions." See Yusufzai, "Interview with Osama bin Laden," 4 January 1999, and Zaydan, *Usama bin Ladin without Mask*, p. 27.

35. "Bin Laden, others sign fatwa to 'kill Americans' everywhere," *Al-Quds al-Arabi*, 23 February 1998, p. 3. While speculative, this fatwa may be more important today than at any time since its issuance. With its clear call and religious authorization for indiscriminate attacks on Americans, the fatwa provides potential motivation and justification for what appears to be an increasing number of young U.S.-citizen Muslim males who are contemplating or planning violence inside the United States.
36. Yusufzai, "I am not afraid of death."
37. Ismail, *Bin Ladin, al-Jazirah, and I*.
38. Alouni, "Interview with Usama bin Laden," 23 May 2002.
39. Lawrence, "In bin Laden's words," *Chronicle of Higher Education*. Lawrence also has collected, edited, and annotated one of the two best collections of bin Laden's works, *Messages to the World: The Statements of Osama bin Laden* (London: Verso, 2005). The other outstanding collection is Randall B. Hamud, ed., *Osama bin Laden: America's Enemy in His Own Words* (San Diego: Nadeem, 2005). There are other such collections, but none remotely approaches the value of these two books in the range of the statements presented, the insightfulness of the editors' commentary, and the editors' relative lack of axes to grind.
40. Quoted in Butcher, "My life in al-Qaeda, by bin Laden's bodyguard." It is interesting to note that Abu Jandal's father and maternal grandfather worked for the bin Laden companies in Saudi Arabia. See Porzio, "Bin-Ladin: I will tell you about the superterrorist seen from up close."
41. Mir, "Interview with Usama bin Ladin," 18 March 1997.
42. Atwan, *The Secret History of al-Qaeda*, p. 221.
43. Michael Vlahos, "Terror's mask: Insurgency within Islam," published by Johns Hopkins University/Applied Physics Laboratory, Laurel, Maryland, November 2003.
44. Al-Hammadi, "Interview with Abu Jandal," p. 4, and al-Hammadi, "Al-Qaeda from within, part 5," p. 19.
45. Michael Vlahos, "Terror's mask: Insurgency within Islam."
46. OBL, "Exposing the new Crusader war in Iraq," *Waaqiah* (Internet), 14 February 2003.
47. "Exclusive [report]," *al-Majd*, 4 August 1997, p. 1.
48. Qari Naved Masood Hashmi, "Osama bin Laden—A man as strong as a rock," *Pakistan*, 10 June 1998, p. 10.
49. "Bin Laden message marking U.S. embassy bombing," *MENA*, 7 August 1999.
50. Zaydan, *Usama bin Ladin without Mask*. The type of U.S.-Western operation in Afghanistan that al-Qaeda expected after the *Cole* was described in late 2000 to Zaydan by bin Laden's military commander Abu Hafs al-Masri. "It will be similar to the attack on Kosovo and Serbia," Abu Hafs said. "International forces will be mobilized against Afghanistan. The attack will continue for quite some time, during which America will use airbases in central Asia, in Uzbekistan and Tajikistan in particular, and maybe Pakistan. We do not rule out the possibility of Russia supporting Ahmad Shah Masud's forces in terms of money, arms, and manpower, to take hold of Taleban controlled areas."

51. Rahimullah Yusufzai, "Bin Laden endorses attack on *USS Cole*, denies Kuwaiti daily's report," *News*, 15 November 2000, p. 18. This incident is also interesting in that it is one of the few instances in which bin Laden was driven to act prematurely. He did not claim responsibility for the attack; the endorsement he sent to Yusufzai was stimulated by a story in the Kuwaiti paper *Al-Rai al-Aam* claiming that bin Laden had publicly denied any links to the *Cole* bombers and that he had no intention of attacking U.S. military or civilian installations in Arab countries. Denouncing the last part of the claim, bin Laden's messenger told Yusufzai that "Shaykh Osama bin Laden" stood by his 1998 fatwa "declaring Jihad against the U.S. and Israel owing to their anti-Islamic actions. He said the Fatwa was still valid and binding on Muslims."
52. Zaydan, *Usama bin Ladin without Mask.*
53. Gutman, *How We Missed the Story*, pp. 212–213.
54. Al-Shafi'i, "Al-Qaeda fundamentalist: Bin Laden believed the media exaggerations about him."
55. "Bin Ladin warns against U.S. plan to eliminate Afghan Arabs," *Al-Quds al-Arabi*, 15 April 1998, p. 1, and "Bin Ladin: Afghanistan's inclusion on U.S. 'terror list' is 'certificate of good conduct' for the Taleban," *Al-Quds al-Arabi*, 18 May 1998, p. 3.
56. "Interview (written) with Usama bin Ladin," *Ghazi*, 20 August 2000.
57. "Bin Ladin warns against U.S. plan to eliminate Afghan Arabs."
58. Ismail, *Bin Ladin, al-Jazirah, and I.*
59. Zafar Mahmood Malik, "Bin Ladin backs Harakat-al-Ansar," *Jang*, 20 October 1997, pp. 7 and 8.
60. "Bin Ladin message to anti-U.S. Conference," *Al-Akhbar*, 12 September 1998, pp. 7 and 8.
61. "Bin Ladin praises Pakistanis," *Nation*, 2 September 1998, p. 16.
62. "Usama bin Ladin: Jihad against India 'duty' of all Muslims," *Pakistan*, 23 August 2006, pp. 3 and 6.
63. Ibid., and Hashmi, "Osama bin Laden—A man as strong as rock," p. 10.
64. "Usama bin Ladin pens letter in support of Kashmiri jihad," *Wahdat*, 8 June 1999, pp. 1 and 5.
65. "Usama bin Ladin: Jihad against India 'duty' of all Muslims," and Abu Shiraz, "Interview with Usama bin Laden," *Pakistan*, 20 February 1999, p. 10.
66. Shiraz, "Interview with Osama bin Laden," 20 February 1999, p. 10, and "Usama bin Ladin: Jihad against India 'duty' of all Muslims." It was perhaps a sign of al-Qaeda's ability to keep bin Laden fully informed of international affairs that he was able in February 1999 to warn about the dangers to Pakistan in the then very much nascent relationship between India and Israel, one that would explode in its dimensions later in the years after the undeclared 1999 Pakistan-India war in the Kargil area.
67. "Usama bin Ladin pens letter in support of Kashmiri jihad," pp. 1 and 5, and "Usama bin Ladin: Jihad against India 'duty' of all Muslims."
68. "Clerics in Afghanistan issue fatwa on necessity to move U.S. forces out of the Gulf; Saudi oppositionist Usamah bin Ladin supports it," *Al-Quds al-Arabi*, 14 May 1998, p. 4.
69. ARC, "Supporting the fatwa by the Afghan religious scholars of ejecting American forces from the Land of the Two Mosques," 7 May 1998.
70. Aimal Khan, "Usama bin Ladin steps up public appearances in Kabul," *Frontier Post*, 7 September 1999, p. 12. The importance that bin Laden and al-Qaeda attached to this localized outreach campaign was visible in their effort to keep it up even when they were still reeling and reconstituting from the impact of the U.S.-led invasion of Afghanistan. In March 2002, bin Laden sent a letter to the "scholars of Deoband" who were then holding a large conference in Peshawar. He did not ask for support for

al-Qaeda, but did urge the scholars' support for Mullah Omar and the Taleban. Bin Laden asked the conference to teach Muslims

> that there is no Islam without a group, and no group without an Emir [leader], and no leadership without listening and obedience. And you know that God sent to this nation [ummah] in these very hard days, the establishment of an Islamic nation [-state] that will follow the Shariah of Allah, and will hold the tahwid flag, and it is in the Islamic Afghanistan with the leadership of Mullah Omar, God bless him. Your duty is to invite people to stay in this Emirate and triumph it with most expensive (lives and money) and to stand up with this nation [Afghanistan] to confront this deadly current of universal disbelievers. . . . I insist that you pledge your allegiance to Mullah Omar, after doing so myself, and I hope that it [the scholars' pledging] is truthful for God's sake because he is your brother that follows and leads, according to the Shariah of God.

See "Osama bin Laden to the scholars of Deoband, Peshawar, Pakistan," 27 March 2002, http://www.ctc.usma.edu, AFGP-2002-901188. A fuller version of this letter, which also was apparently delivered in audiotape format, can be found in Zaydan, *Usama bin Ladin without Mask*, p. 62.

71. Usama bin Laden, "Letter from Khandahar," Associated Press, 16 March 1998.
72. "Interview with Mujahid Usama bin Laden," *Nida'al Islam* (Internet), 15 January 1997.
73. Usama bin Laden, "Letter from Khandahar."
74. "U.S. aid for Ahmed Shah Massoud against Usamah."
75. Ibrahim Zayd al-Kilani, "Usamah bin Ladin, the eagle of Islam," *Al-Sabil*, 19 October 1999, p. 20. It is worth noting that many in the Muslim world had no doubt about what Osama bin Laden was fighting for. While the Clinton administration in 1999 was still claiming that America was being attacked because of its freedoms and lifestyle, al-Kilani wrote: "The Muslim mujahid leader, Usamah bin Ladin, devoted his money and his life for the sake of God, liberating Afghanistan from communist imperialism, and clearing Muslim countries of U.S. bases and imperialist hegemony, which, through its bases, occupies the land of the [Arabian] peninsula unjustly and aggressively—thereby defying the order of the prophet, may the peace and blessings of God be upon him, which says 'there shall not be two religions in the Peninsula'—and fights Muslims and Islam everywhere on earth. This struggler leader deserves victory, honoring, and protection. Delivering him to the enemies of Islam is betrayal of God's religion, loyalty to His enemies, injustice, sedition, and big corruption." In the years after 1999, Bin Laden would stay steadily on message regarding his motivation—U.S. foreign policy—for attacking the United States and allies, and in late 2010, President Obama was still saying America was being attacked for what it is, not what it does.
76. "Interview with Egyptian Islamist lawyer Muntasir al-Zayyat," *Al-Sharq al-Awsat*, 12 July 1999, p. 2, Al-Zayyat's realpolitik assessment of Mullah Omar's need to continue protecting bin Laden was shared by al-Qaeda's military commander, Abu Hafs al-Masri. "Mullah Omar knows that remining in power is linked to Usama," al-Masri told the journalist Ahmad Zaydan before 9/11, "since the legitimacy of the Taleban movement as specified from the beginning had stemmed from the need to protect Usama. Abandoning him would have divided Taleban ranks. For one thing, many field [military] leaders were connected to Usama and fought for him, thus, extraditing or deporting Usama would have

meant the Taleban had submitted to the Christians, an expression the implications of which were well known to religious school goers [the bulk of the Taleban] who had studied ancient school texts and were not familiar with politics and its complications or international pressure." See Zaydan, *Usama Bin Ladin without Mask*, pp. 25–26.

77. "Have Taleban changed their stand about Osama," *Jang*, 17 February 1999, p. 4, and Yusufzai, "Myth and Man." Former al-Qaeda theorist Abu Musab al-Suri has written that after U.S. cruise missiles hit al-Qaeda's camps at Khowst on 20 August 1998, many Taleban and other Afghans believed that Mullah Omar would ask bin Laden and his men "to halt their activities and close their bases." Al-Suri notes, however, that Mullah Omar said he would not and added that "if nothing remains in Afghanistan but my blood, I will not turn over Usama bin Laden and the Arab mujahedin." A Taleban minister also told al-Suri that "The amir of the believers [Mullah Omar] reprimanded those of us who were overcome with fear and trepidation [of the Americans]. He gave them a lesson in trusting God and being unafraid of America. 'For God with their [the mujahedin's] hands defeated those who were stronger than America, and are closer [to Afghanistan] than America: the Russians! And He destroyed their state.'" See al-Suri, "A drama of faith and jihad."
78. Al-Suri, "A drama of faith and jihad."
79. Aimal Khan, "Osama said mediating between Hekmatyar, Sayyaf," *Frontier Post*, 29 December 1998, pp. 1, 12, and "Mullah Omar ready for dialogue with Hekmatyar," *Ausaf*, 21 March 2001, pp. 1, 7.
80. Gutman, *How We Missed the Story*, p. 189.
81. "Bin Ladin building new bases in Kandahar," *Sunday Telegraph* (Internet version), 4 October 1998, and Joachim Hoelzgen, "The rulers of Kandahar," *Der Spiegel*, 9 November 1998, pp. 216–220. Bin Laden also sought to play the role of a foreign policy adviser to Mullah Omar. He urged Omar, for example, to permit him to speak to the "many international media agencies requesting interviews" and focus on the Taleban's steady expansion of Shariah rule in Afghanistan so as to stimulate monetary support for the regime from donors across the Muslim world. He also suggested that Omar authorize a program to support Islamists in the Muslim states of Central Asia to ensure "Jihad continuation in the Islamic Republics [that] will keep the [Taleban's] enemies busy and divert them away from the Afghan issue and ease the pressure off. The enemies of Islam problem will [then] become how to stop the spreading of Islam into the Islamic Republics and not the Afghan issue." See OBL to Mullah Omar, n.d. but before 9/11, http://www.ctc.usma.edu, AFGP-2002-600321.
82. Zaydan, *Usama bin Ladin without Mask*. Zaydan also noted that bin Laden's men were readily accepted by the historically insular Pashtuns in the city and province of Kandahar. "It was normal to see Arab Afghans in the streets of Kandahar as if they were locals," Zaydan recalls. "The only thing that distinguished them from the Afghanis was the fact that some of them did not speak the local spoken language, Pashtu. As for other respects, including the way they walked, dressed, and moved freely, it all gave the impression that they had become Afghans, or more accurately Kandaharis, which is the stronghold of Pashtun Afghans." Bin Laden's chief bodyguard Abu Jandal made the same point about Kandahar, but also included the city of Kabul. "The Arab mujahedin in Kandahar and Kabul used to share with the Afghans their numerous occasions, their weddings, and their sad occasions. The Afghans used to visit us and we used to visit them. We used to visit them during Eid to congratulate them, and they reciprocated. We used to spend the month of Ramadan together. We [al-Qaeda members]

lived a normal social life, but in a society that was alien to us in language, environment, and way of life." Al-Hammadi, "Al-Qaeda from within, part 1," p. 17.

83. Rahimullah Yusufzai, "Interview with Osama bin Laden," 4 January 1999; "Interview (written) with Usama bin Ladin," and Ismail, "Interview with Usama bin Laden," 23 December 1998. Of the many differing analyses of the Mullah Omar–bin Laden relationship, perhaps none is better than that offered by the Pakistani journalist Rahimullah Yusufzai. "What Mullah Omar and bin Laden, share more than anything," Yusufzai wrote just after 9/11, "is an absolute certainty that Allah will stay with them no matter how great the superpower that attacks them." See Rahimullah Yusufzai, "Face to face with Usama," *Guardian* (Internet version), 26 September 2001.
84. Ismail, *Bin Ladin, al-Jazirah, and I*, and "Interview with Mujahid Usama bin Ladin," *Nida'al Islam*, 15 January 1997.
85. "Bin Ladin pledges allegiance to Mullah Omar," Al-Jazirah Satellite Television, 9 April 2001.
86. "Bin Ladin asks Muslim to support Afghanistan's 'Prince of the Faithful,'" Al-Jazirah Satellite Television, 12 April 2001.
87. "Mullah Omar declines bin Liden's offer to leave Afghanistan," *Ausaf*, 19 December 2000, pp. 1, 7.
88. On the Taleban granting protection and Afghan citizenship to bin Laden and his family, see "Taleban confirms its intention to try bin Ladin; Pakistan prevented him for attending an Islamic conference," *Al-Quds al-Arabi*, 28 October 1998, p. 1, and bin Laden, bin Laden, and Sasson, *Growing Up bin Laden*, p. 175.
89. "Mullah Omar declines bin Liden's offer to leave Afghanistan." My own guess, for what it is worth, is there was never a chance of Mullah Omar turning bin Laden over to the Saudis or the Americans, simply because he believed it was wrong to do so. Bin Laden worked to make sure this would be the case, but Mullah Omar is a Muslim and a Pashtun above all, and so his care for a guest to whom refuge has been granted is absolute. Second, Mullah Omar is the prototypical Pashtun tribesman in that, as was said about Ulysses S. Grant, "he don't scare worth a damn." Indeed, constant pressure on Omar from Washington, its allies, the UN, and Pakistan simply increased his obstinacy. In this vein, Abdul Salam Zaeef, the Taleban's ambassador in Pakistan around 9/11, has related a story about Mullah Omar that shows his lack of fear and complete unwillingness to follow a course he does not believe in. The story also is a useful anecdote for anyone who believes Pakistan can control the Afghans if it wants to. "First, [Pakistani President] Musharraf invited Amir ul-Mu'mineem [Prince of the Faithful, Mullah Omar] to Pakistan [c. 1999–2000]," Zaeef writes, "but Amir ul-Mu'mineem turned him down; he did not want to travel to Pakistan. Then Musharraf asked to be invited to Kandahar in order to meet Amir ul-Mu'mineem. He wanted to discuss a deal with the United States over a possible handover of Osama bin Laden. Amir ul-Mu'mineem did not favor the agenda of the talks, and sent a message to Musharraf telling him that he would be welcome to visit as the leader of a neighboring country to discuss security, the economy or other issues; bin Laden, though, was a matter that concerned Afghanistan and the USA, not Pakistan. We specifically did not want to discuss it with Pakistan because it could lead to a deterioration of the relationship between the two neighboring countries. Musharraf cancelled his trip to Afghanistan." See Abdul Salam Zaeef, *My Life with the Taliban* (New York: Columbia University Press, 2010), p. 119.

90. Jamil al-Dhiyabi, "Interview with Shaykh Musa al-Qarni, Part 3," *Al-Hayah* (Internet version), 10 March 2006.

CHAPTER 6

1. Arnett, "Osama bin Laden: The interview," 12 May 1997. I want to note here that at 9/11 the study of bin Laden loses several important first-hand sources. The memoir of Najwa and Omar bin Laden, for example, does not go into the post-9/11 era, and neither does Abu Jandal's long, valuable commentary. In addition, bin Laden made only recorded media statements after 2002. As a result, we do not have interviews by such excellent journalists as Rahimullah Yusufzai, Abdel Bari Atwan, and Ahmad Muwaffaq Zaydan, and so lose the spontaneity of his answers, their views of what bin Laden said and how it tracks with what he said to them previously, and their observations of the events around him. That said, the sources we do have are plentiful, key, and primary, and so we can still track bin Laden's thought and continue the effort to match his words and deeds. We do not, however, have many observations by people who have been close to bin Laden, physically and culturally. The major exceptions are the data presented in Peter L. Bergen's book, *The Osama bin Laden I Know*, and the informed speculations about bin Laden's thinking and how he is reacting to events made in writings by Yusufzai, Zaydan, Atwan, and others, as well as by Omar bin Laden in media interviews. In addition, we have abundant material from the post-2001 period that affords our first chance to track bin Laden and his lieutenants from the point at which they identify problems threatening al-Qaeda to their actions to resolve them, and to efforts to advance the organization after the problem is negated. Though these data have less to say about bin Laden as a person, they offer unprecedented insight into his skills as al-Qaeda's leader, manager, and key strategist.
2. Quoted in "It is impossible to arrest and hand me over to the United States," *Nawa i Waqt*, 19 September 2001, pp. 1, 7. Notwithstanding ample evidence showing that bin Laden worked to lure U.S. forces to Afghanistan, claims that he was surprised by the post-9/11 U.S. invasion are still heard and—because U.S. leaders want to believe them—get wide media coverage. In April 2010, for example, a former mujahedin and associate of al-Qaeda named Noman Benotman told the media "al-Qaeda was clueless" about U.S. retaliation after 9/11, expecting nothing more than a large Cruise missile attack. The claim was published around the world, but it does not wash with the evidence. Benotman, moreover, is an ex-member of the Libyan Islamic Fighting Group (LIFG), which fought the USSR in Afghanistan and tried to kill Colonel Qaddafi. He now claims to have seen the light, turned against jihadism, and persuaded his former LIFG colleagues in Libyan jails to reject violence and travels the world preaching against Islamism—all of which serves Qaddafi's interests and keeps Benotman out of a Libyan jail. See J. J. Green, "Al-Qaeda considered a 'joke' to jihadists," http://www.wtop.com, 29 April 2010.
3. Zaydan, *Usama bin Ladin without Mask*.
4. This delaying factor is cited fifteen times in the index to Bob Woodward, *Bush at War* (New York: Simon and Shuster, 2002), p. 368.
5. Huband, *Brutal Truths, Fragile Myths*, p. 76.
6. The two best are Philip Smucker, *Al-Qaeda's Great Escape. The Military and the Media on Terror's Trail* (Dulles, Va.: Brassey's, 2004), and Gary Bernsten, *Jawbreaker. The*

Attack on bin Laden and al-Qaeda: A Personal Account by the CIA's Key Field Commander (New York: Three Rivers, 2006).

7. Atwan, *The Secret History of al-Qaeda*, p. 28, and Peter L. Bergen, "The Battle for Tora Bora," *New Republic* (Internet version), 22 December 2009.
8. Muhammad al-Shafi'i, "Al-Qaeda ideologue recounts details of conflict between hawks and doves in organization on weapons of mass destruction," *Al-Sharq al-Awsat*, 12 September 2002, p. 7.
9. Ismail, *Bin Ladin, al-Jazirah, and I*.
10. Bin Laden, bin Laden, and Sasson, *Growing Up bin Laden*, p. 173.
11. Ibid., pp. 246, 271, and 286.
12. Peters, *Jihad in Classical and Modern Islam*, p. 14.
13. Long, "Ribat, al-Qaida, and the Challenge for U.S. Foreign Policy," p. 31. And conversely, Muslims tend to see defeats—even repeated defeats—as a sign that God is testing their faith and resolve. When asked if he was discouraged by his enemies forcing him to move frequently, for example, bin Laden replied, "As for being driven from one land to another, this is the nature of war. You win some and you lose some. . . . There is good for him [the Muslim] in both cases [win and lose]. When a Muslim migrates repeatedly he is doubly rewarded. We pray to God, Praise and Glory be to Him, to make our migration, a migration for His cause." The faith enabling this steady attitude also in part explains why there is so little visible war-weariness in bin Laden's al-Qaeda, some of whose members have been in the field and away from home and family for twenty years. See Yusufzai, "Interview with Osama bin Laden," 4 January 1999.
14. A researcher is hard pressed to find reliable data showing that bin Laden was anything but delighted with the U.S. invasion of Afghanistan. The common wisdom in the West is that the U.S.-NATO defeat of the Taleban regime and al-Qaeda's loss of Afghan safe haven shocked and devastated the latter. Well, perhaps, but that is not perfectly clear. Ahmad Zaydan wrote that when interviewing bin Laden in 2001 he sensed al-Qaeda expected and was prepared for the Taleban's fall if U.S. forces struck Afghanistan. Likewise, Roy Gutman clearly shows that both bin Laden and Abu Hafs al-Masri regarded Taleban troops as at most marginally effective during and after the war against Massoud. Finally, bin Laden said publicly in 2007 that "the fall of the [Taleban] state is not the end of the world, nor does it mean that the Islamic community and the Islamic Imam collapse . . . jihad against the infidels should continue, as is happening in Afghanistan, Iraq, and Somalia." To be sure, bin Laden would have preferred to keep his Afghan safe haven, but he found its loss less shocking and devastating than his enemies hoped. See Zaydan, *Usama bin Ladin without Mask*; Gutman, *How We Missed the Story*, pp. 188–189; and OBL, "The way to foil plots."
15. "Exclusive interview with Usama bin Ladin," *Ummat*, 28 September 2001, pp. 1 and 7; "Speech by Usama bin Ladin, leader of the al-Qaeda organization," Al-Jazirah Satellite Television, 3 November 2001; Hamid Mir, "The war has not yet begun: Detailed interview with Usama bin Laden," *Ausaf*, 16 November 2001, pp. 9, 11; "U.S. biggest terrorist and merchant of death: Usama," *Nawa-i-Waqt*, 12 December 2001, pp. 1, 10; and, "Statement by al-Qaida leader Usama bin Laden," Al-Jazirah Satellite Television, 27 December 2001.
16. "Exclusive interview with Usama bin Ladin," *Ummat*, 28 September 2001, pp. 1 and 7.
17. Andrew Hill, "The bin Laden Tapes," *Journal for Cultural Research*, Vol. 10, No. 1 (January 2006), pp. 38, 41, and 42.

18. "We calculated in advance," bin Laden said in late 2001, "the number of casualties from the enemy, who would be killed [on 9/11] based on the position of the tower. We calculated that the floors that would be hit would be three or four floors. I was the most optimistic of them all . . . due to my experience in the [construction] field, I was thinking that the fire from the gas in the plane would melt the iron structure of the building and collapse the area where the plane had hit and all the floors above it only. This is all we had hoped for." See "Transcript of Usama bin Laden video tape," http://www.defense.gov/news/Dec2001/d20011213ubl.pdf, 13 December 2001.
19. There is absolutely no indication that bin Laden regretted either the 9/11 attacks or their consequences. They provided exactly what he wanted by prompting the U.S. invasion of a Muslim land, a success that was far more than doubled by the U.S. invasion of Iraq. Professor Fawaz Gerges, though, has written a book that argues—and quotes numerous, often unnamed Islamists to the effect—that the 9/11 attacks were either a severe setback to the Islamist movement or destroyed it entirely. At the time of the attack and immediately thereafter, bin Laden took no heed of this kind of criticism; his words then advised whiners to "wait and see." Today, with the United States waging and losing wars in two Muslim countries, its economy on the ropes, its president frightened of the words "Islamist" and "jihad," and Islamist insurgencies more widespread and vigorous than in 2001, the argument made by Professor Gerges and his unnamed sources seems questionable. See Fawaz A. Gerges. *The Far Enemy: Why Jihad Went Global* (New York: Cambridge University Press, 2005).
20. "Statement by Usama bin Laden in 'The first war of the century' program," Al-Jazirah Satellite Television, 3 November 2001. For a good discussion of the post-9/11 religious criticisms of bin Laden by other Islamists, see Quintan Wiktorowicz and John Kaltner, "Killing in the name of Islam: Al-Qaeda's justification for September 11," *Middle East Policy*, Vol. 10, No. 2 (September 2003), pp. 76–92.
21. "Statement by Usama bin Ladin," *Al-Qala'ah* (Internet), 14 October 2002, and OBL, "Message to countries allied with the United States," Al-Jazirah Satellite Television, 12 November 2002.
22. "Bin Ladin audio message," Al-Jazirah Satellite Television, 6 October 2002; OBL, "Letter to the American people," *Waaqiah* (Internet), 12 November 2002; "Bin Laden's letter to Americans," *Observer* (Internet version), 24 November 2002; and OBL, "Message to the American people," *Al-Fallujah Islamic Minbar* (Internet), 8 September 2007.
23. OBL, "Message to the American people," Al-Jazirah Satellite Television, 19 January 2009, and OBL, "Message to our neighbors north of the Mediterranean," *Al-Arabiyah Television*, 14 April 2004. Bin Laden and al-Qaeda seem to have put particular stress on making sure Muslims know they have actively sought peace with the West. "You are aware of our recent response to their opinion polls [showing high opposition to war the Afghan and Iraq wars]," bin Laden said in a message meant for Muslims, "where we offered a truce between us and them after the pullout of their armies and their ending of their harassment of us. All of this was rejected by them, and they are bent on continuing their Crusades against us." See OBL, "O Muslim People," Al-Sahab Media Production Organization, 26 April 2006.
24. "Bin Ladin audio message," Al-Jazirah Satellite Television, 6 October 2002; OBL, "Message to our neighbors north of the Mediterranean," *Al-Arabiyah Television*, 14 April 2004; and OBL, "Message to the American people," Al-Sahab Media Production Organization, 14 September 2009.

25. OBL, "Message to the Muslim nation," *Islamic Research and Studies Center* (Internet), 4 March 2004.
26. OBL, "Message to Muslims in Pakistan," Al-Jazirah Satellite Television, 3 June 2009; OBL, "Message to the Pakistani people," Al-Jazirah Satellite Television, 1 November 2001, and OBL, "Exposing the new Crusader war in Iraq."
27. OBL, "Remove the apostate," Al-Sahab Media Production Organization, 20 September 2007, and OBL, "To Muslims in Pakistan," Al-Jazirah Satellite Television, 3 June 2009.
28. OBL, "Crown Prince Abdullah's initiative is high treason," *Al-Quds al-Arabi*, 28 March 2002, p. 3; OBL, "Practical steps to liberate Palestine," Al-Sahab Media Production Organization, 14 March 2009; and Muhammad al-Shafi'i, "A site close to al-Qa'idah posts a poem by bin Laden," *Al-Sharq al-Awsat*, 20 June 2002.
29. OBL, "Practical steps to liberate Palestine," and OBL, "A message to the Muslim nation," Al-Sahab Media Production Organization, 18 May 2008.
30. OBL, "Second Message to Iraqi people," Al-Jazirah Satellite Television, 18 October 2003.
31. OBL, "Message to Americans," *Al-Fallujah Islamic Minbar* (Internet), 8 September 2007; OBL, "Exposing the new Crusader war."
32. "Speech by Osama bin Laden," *MEMRI*, Special Dispatch, No. 539, 18 July 2003. Almost as if to intentionally validate bin Laden's contentions, the Saudi religious establishment is so far abiding by an August, 2010, decree from King Fahd announcing that henceforth only members of the 20-member "Senior Scholars Authority"—all of whom are paid by the Saudi regime—can issue fatwas. This ruling contravenes the Koran and the sunnah and, in doing so, proves bin Laden's contention that official Saudi scholars are no more then yes men for the al-Saud family. See, Souhail Karam, "Saudi fatwa ruling seeks to contain clergy," http://www.reuters.com, 23 August 2010
33. The official scholars' impotence is partly due to bin Laden's logical, increasingly strident post-1994 attacks. His words, combined with the scholars' prostitution of their principles to please Muslim rulers, may have ignited an Islamic reformation, which the West has long hoped would be *the tool* for ending Islam's martial tenets. Westerners have assumed Islam's reformation would end its refusal to "turn the other cheek," and that the "new Islam" would teach Muslims to accept secularism and see the Koran and Sunnah as providing loose guidelines—like those today's Christians ascribe to the Bible—that allow libertinism, blasphemy, and sexual deviation. The reformation also would eliminate the Muslim's duty to defend his faith or fear God if he did not. As with most assumptions, however, this one will take the assumers to perdition. "The goal shared by all Islamists is nonetheless a radical goal," Michael Vlahos has said about what he calls "a 'world-historical' movement" now under way in the Muslim world. "The Restoration of Islam would mean an end to Western-style secular civil society in the Muslim world, even if it led to an Islamic civil society that Westerners would not find comfortable. Rather, violent radical elements are only a small part of a much broader movement for Islamic 'restoration,' which speaks more directly to Islamist visions than words like 'revival,' which in the Western consciousness at least refer more narrowly to simpler religious 'awakenings.' For Muslims, at least, their vision is one of an entire order restored, of not simply religion but of an entirely 'rightly guided' way of life brought back as it should be. For a generation or more the drive for this Islamic restoration has been gathering strength and exerting itself."

    While this view is never voiced by U.S. or European political leaders, it is clear to their diplomatic, military, and intelligence officers. In 2005, for example, the U.S.

diplomat Christopher Henzel said his political superiors were wrong. "In contemporary Western discussions of the Muslim world it is common to hear calls for a 'reformation of Islam' as an antidote to al-Qaeda. In fact a Sunni 'reformation' has been underway for more than a century, and it works against Western security interests." Henzel also is right in saying "the Salafist movement in the Sunni world" is spearheading reform. Taking Henzel's point further, it is fair to say that bin Laden—by words, deeds, and attacks on the scholars—has hurried the reformation. He was not a Salafi theologian, but took their guidance, championed it, and used it to show the king's scholars' failings, compromises, and sellouts.

Bin Laden, moreover, helped drive Sunni Islam's reformation in the direction taken by the Protestant Reformation. As the revolt against Rome rejected intermediaries between man and God, bin Laden insisted Muslims needed no intermediaries with God, especially men more eager for lucre than paradise. "Bin Laden has been able to transfer Islam from the local to the international arena in an era that has its own peculiarities," the noted London-based Saudi scholar Madawi al-Rashid has written: and

> The most prominent of these peculiarities are information, media, intellectual, and economic communication. He also has been able to transfer Islam from the hands of the jurisprudence scholars and their monopoly to those of the simple ordinary Muslim.
>
> Only God knows, but perhaps bin Ladin will be the last nail in the coffin of the Muslim ulema. Bin Ladin's address [rhetoric] confronts the jurisprudence scholars wherever they are, particularly in Saudi Arabia. . . . Bin Ladin's address is popular in the Islamic world, even the Western experts themselves testify to this, because he has transferred Islam from the jurisprudence assembly to two domains: the first domain is the entire world, and the second domain is the private individual. . . . With bin Ladin, Islam has become an individual project beyond the restrictions of jurisprudential scholars or of the political authority; a project that this individual could carry with him and move during the current age of travel, and perhaps his travels could take him to the port of Aden or Mombasa, or to the noise of Bangkok or New York.

A world where Islamic scholars of Muslim regimes are unable to influence ordinary Muslims truly would signal an Islamic reformation as revolutionary and violent as its Protestant counterpart. And, to Western dismay, such reformation is likely to yield the same near-term result: a century of war and destruction that leaves much of the world a charnel house, an economic wreck, or both. At day's end, bin Laden's role in generating an Islamic reformation is a more powerful anti-Western tool than any conventional or unconventional weapon al-Qaeda might acquire. See Michael Vlahos, "The Muslim Renovatio and U.S. Strategy," http.//www.2techcentralstation.com, 27 April 2004; Henzel, "The origins of al-Qaeda's ideology: implications for U.S. strategy," p. 70; and Madawi al-Rashid, "Islam today: From the jurisprudence scholars to the men of the cave," *Al-Quds al-Arabi* (Internet version), 6 February 2006.

34. Hamid Mir, "The war has not yet begun—Detailed interview with Usama bin Laden," *Ausaf*, 16 November 2001, pp. 9 and 11. It is worth saying that bin Laden was not only a master of media but also a master of silence. He never publicly responded to criticism from an official Islamic scholar, apparently content that Muslims who heard the scholars' statements would see that they were saying round was square, and that such contradiction discredited them more than anything he could say.
35. Al-Hammadi, "Al-Qaeda from within, part 8," p. 17.

36. OBL, "Message to the ummah in general, and to our Muslim brothers in Iraq in particular," *Al-Qal'ah* (Internet), 6 May 2004.
37. OBL, "Message to the people of the [Arabian] Peninsula," *Al-Quds al-Arabi*, 28 November 2002, p. 1.
38. A month before the U.S.-led invasion, bin Laden made a speech that provided Muslims with something of a scorecard against which to check the accuracy of his long-standing predictions. "We are following up with great interest and extreme concern," he wrote, "the Crusaders' preparations for war to occupy a former capital of Islam [Baghdad], loot Muslim wealth, and install an agent government which would be a satellite for its masters in Washington and Tel Aviv, just like all the other treasonous and agent Arab governments. This would be in preparation for establishing the greater Israel." See OBL, "Message to our brothers in Iraq," Al-Jazirah Satellite Television, 11 February 2003.
39. "Exclusive interview with Usama bin Laden," *Ummat*, 28 September 2001, pp. 1 and 7.
40. Atwan, *The secret history of al-Qaeda*, p. 205.
41. Calvert Jones, "Al-Qaeda's innovative improvisers: Learning in a diffuse international network," *Cambridge Review of International Affairs*, Vol. 19, No. 4 (December 2006), p. 559.
42. Osama bin Laden, "Message to Muslims in Iraq in particular, and the ummah in general," Al-Sahab Media Production Organization, 28 December 2004.

42A. Bin Laden publicly laid out al-Qaeda's traditional modus operandi a month before the U.S. invasion of Iraq, and also stressed that all Sunni mujahedin must cooperate because unity was indispensable to victory. This was another set of guidelines that al-Zarqawi ignored. See Osama bin Laden, "Message to our brothers in Iraq," Al-Jazirah Satellite Television, 11 February 2003.

43. Ibid.; bin Laden focused on this issue early in 2004, saying the Arab regimes were "unjustly and wrongly accusing them [the mujahedin in Iraq] of being like the al-Khawarji sect who held Muslims to be infidels and went to the excess of killing them." OBL, "Message to the Muslim nation," *Islamic Studies and Research Center* (Internet), 4 March 2004.
44. There has been much nonsense written about the killing of civilians in Iraq, most of it by Western politicians, pundits, and academics who insist the Koran absolutely bans one Muslim killing another in any circumstance. This untenable position has been given cynical support by state-run Arab media and Arabic-language outlets in Europe, a good number of which are funded by Saudi Arabia. The killing of Muslims by Muslims in a capricious and indiscriminate way is of course religiously forbidden; this was al-Zarqawi's practice in Iraq. But the killing by Muslims of Muslims who have sided with the infidels against their brethren or with Muslim regimes that oppress their citizens is a different story. For a Salafist like bin Laden and many other Islamist leaders, religious authorization for killing Muslims who fall into one or both of these categories comes first from the medieval Islamic scholar Ibn Taymiyyah. In a useful essay, Professor Rosalind W. Gwynne has written that Ibn Taymiyyah held that the just-converted-to-Islam Mongols were not true Muslims because they mixed their customs with the Shariah and "in their camps one heard no call to prayer and saw no one pray." For Ibn Taymiyyah, "These reasons made the Mongols legitimate targets. [Moreover,] Muslims who fought at their side under duress would go to heaven if killed. Muslims who allied themselves with them voluntarily had thereby removed themselves from the ranks of believers—had become apostates—and the punishment for apostasy is death."

Ibn Taymiyyah's medieval finding was reconfirmed in the late twentieth century by the now deceased grand mufti of Saudi Arabia, Shaykh Abdul Aziz bin Baz. In a fatwa called "The nullifiers of Islam," Shaykh bin Baz lists ten actions that if taken by a Muslim would "cause his life and wealth to be permissible [for taking] and which causes him to leave from the fold of Islam." The eighth of the nullifiers reads: "Eighth: Supporting or assisting the polytheists against the Muslims. The proof for this is Allah's statement: 'And whoever amongst you takes them [i.e., the unbelievers] as allies and protectors then he is indeed from among them. Verily, Allah does not guide a wrong-doing people" (Surah al-Maa'idah 51). The answer for bin Laden and al-Qaeda in Iraq and around the world, then, is not to refrain from killing any Muslim, but rather to end Zarqawi's indiscriminate practice and replace it with one that follows the clear and common-sense—for Salafists—guidelines set down by Ibn Taymiyyah and Shaykh bin Baz. Under these strictures, Muslims working for or fighting alongside the United States and its allies in Iraq and Afghanistan are legitimate targets, as would be the members of military and security services of police states like Egypt and Saudi Arabia. See Rosalind W. Gwynne, "Usama bin Ladin, the Qur'an, and Jihad," *Religion*, Vol. 36 (2006), p. 63, and Shaykh Abdul Aziz bin Baz, "The nullifiers of Islam," http://theclearsunnah.wordpress.com/2007/05/05/10-nullifiers-of-Islam/.

45. OBL, "Message to Muslims in Iraq in particular, and the ummah in general," Al-Sahab Media Production Organization, 28 December 2004.
46. "Letter from al-Zawahiri to al-Zarqawi, 11 October 2005," released by the Office of the Director of National Intelligence on 9 July 2006, www.dni.gov. Of the many signs of how much more bin Laden changed al-Zawahiri's ideas and modus operandi than vice versa, few are more compelling than this letter. In it we find not the acerbic, dictatorial al-Zawahiri of times past, but rather a patient, reasonable, and instructive al-Zawahiri who sounds much more like al-Qaeda's chief than the former fire-breathing, near-takfiri leader of the EIJ.
47. Atiyah to Abu Musab al-Zarqawi, http://ctc.usma.edu, 11 December 2005. In the memo accompanying this letter, West Point's Combating Terrorism Center says Atiyah is an Algerian—probably operating outside Pakistan's tribal areas—and that his "authoritative tone, and insider knowledge [in this letter Atiyah confirms the authenticity of the al-Zawahiri-to-al-Zarqawi letter of June 2005], indicate he is among the highest ranking leaders in al-Qaeda." The last point disproves the widely accepted notion that bin Laden was only interested in military action and killing and disdained political activities to build popular support. The evidence of the premium bin Laden and his senior lieutenants put on nonmilitary activities—as did the Prophet, Saladin, and their lieutenants—is so abundant that to misunderstand the point can only be attributed to ignorance or duplicity. But still the miscasting of the priorities of bin Laden and al-Qaeda continues. In 2007, for example, Efraim Karsh described "bin Laden's perception of jihad as a predominantly military effort to facilitate the creation of the worldwide Islamic umma." Karsh, *Islamic Imperialism* p. 230.
48. Atiyah to Abu Musab al-Zarqawi, 11 December 2005.
49. Ibid. Atiyah's belaboring of the idea that all Muslims watch the mujahedin so their actions must be acceptable by that audience is a direct reflection of bin Laden's long-asserted insistence that "the situation Muslims are living in today requires the mobilization of everyone who belongs to the religion." Muhammad al-Shafi'i, "New message from bin Ladin," *Al-Sharq al-Awsat* (Internet version), 19 January 2003.
50. Atiyah to Abu Musab al-Zarqawi, 11 December 2005.

51. Ibid. Bin Laden laid out al-Qaeda's position on takfirism and takfiri-like actions in late 2002; that is, he banned them. "If it is axiomatic that a dispute and difference are one of the most important causes of the failure and loss of power from which our nation [ummah] is suffering today," he explained,

> then it is also axiomatic that unity, consensus, and holding fast to the rope of Allah is [*sic*] the key to victory and triumph and the door to sovereignty and leadership. . . . The unity to which we are calling the Muslims today does not necessarily need putting an end to disputes over all small questions and minor issues. An end cannot be put to such disputes and their existence is not damaging. The unity we are demanding is the unity of the constants of creed, the dogmatism of religion, and the schools of Shariah. . . . We realize that there are some differences in interpretations between those working for Islam that cannot be ignored. But it is neither acceptable nor reasonable for us to remain prisoners over small questions and minor issues, thus disrupting action [being undertaken] in accordance with the rules of religion and the schools of Shariah at such a critical time in the nation's [ummah's] history.

See "Statement by Shaykh Usama bin Ladin," *Al-Qal'ah* (Internet), 14 October 2002.

52. Atiyah to Abu Musab al-Zarqawi, 11 December 2005.
53. Ibid.
54. Ibid.
55. Ibid.
56. OBL, "Eulogy for Abu-Musab al-Zarqawi," Al-Sahab Media Production Organization, 30 June 2006.
57. OBL, "Practical Steps for the Liberation of Palestine," Al-Sahab Media Production Organization, 14 March 2009.
58. OBL, "The way to foil plots," Al-Sahab Media Production Organization, 27 December 2007.
59. OBL, "Message to our people in Iraq," Al-Sahab Media Production Organization, 23 October 2007.
60. OBL, "The way to foil plots"; and OBL, "Second message to the Iraqi people," *Al-Jazirah Satellite Televsion*, 18 October 2003.
61. OBL, "Message to our people in Iraq."
62. OBL, "The way to foil plots."
63. Ibid.; and OBL, "Message to the American people," *Al-Fallujah Islamic Minbar* (Internet), 8 September 2007.
64. OBL, "The way to foil plots."
65. OBL, "Message to our brothers in Iraq," *Al-Jazirah Satellite Televsion*, 11 February 2003.
66. OBL, "The way to foil plots."
67. Ayman al-Zawahiri, "Five years after the invasion of Iraq and decades of injustice by tyrants," Al-Sahab Media Production Organization, 18 April 2008.
68. Ibid.
69. Abu Hamza al-Muhajir, "The Paths of Victory," *Al-Fuqran Establishment for Media Production*, 19 April 2008.
70. Ibid.
71. Ayman al-Zawahiri, "Open Interview, 2," Al-Sahab Media Production Organization, 22 April 2008.
72. Ibid.

73. "Al-Qaeda in Iraq shifting its tactics," http://www.CNN.com. 16 December 2009; Muhammad Shamsaddin Megalommoatis, "Avert the founding of the al-Qaeda state 'Kurdistan' in northern Iraq," http://www.americanchronicle.com, 24 February 2010; "Renewed fear of al-Qaeda return to Anbar," http://www.nigash.org, 17 February 2010; "Islamic State of Iraq: A statement on the blessed Tikrit raid," *Al-Fajr Media Center* (Internet), 9 December 2009; "Islamic State of Iraq: A statement on the fifth wave of the prison raid in Baghdad," *Al-Fajr Media Center* (Internet), 8 April 2010; Martin Chulov, "Al-Qaeda bombs hit three Baghdad embassies," http://www.guardian.co.uk, 5 April 2010; and "Iraq in 'open war' with Qaeda after bombings," http://www.kuwait-times.com, 8 April 2010.
74. Marc Santora, "Attacks threaten fragile security gains in cradle of Iraq insurgency," http://www.ocala.com, 17 November 2009, and "String of bombs in Iraq follow leadership losses for insurgency," http://www.dallasnews.com, 23 April 2010.
75. Abu-Umar al-Baghdadi, "Stop them do not kill them," *Al-Fajr Media Center* (Internet), 23 March 2010.
76. Tim Arango, "Top Qaeda leaders in Iraq reported killed in raid," http://www.nytimes.com, 19 April 2010, and "Al-Qaeda in Iraq confirms death of two top commanders," *Agence-France Presse*, 18 April 2010.
77. "Statement by the Ministry of Shariah Commissions in the Islamic State of Iraq," *Al Fajr Media Center* (Internet), 25 April 2010. Six weeks after the two men were killed, the U.S. commander in Iraq, General Ray Odierno, told the media that AQI had been "broken" by the deaths of these two men and those of other group members. Days after Odierno's statement, AQI staged a daylight commando attack on the central bank of Iraq in the center of Baghdad. The attack was of "a complex nature" and resembled "the Taleban's success with similar operations in Afghanistan and Pakistan." By August 2010, Brigadier General Patrick M. Higgins, commander of U.S. Special Forces in Iraq, recanted a bit of Ordierno's claim, noting that despite the death of its two senior leaders, al-Qaeda-in-Iraq's "cellular structure" remained "pretty much intact." See Bill Roggio, "Al-Qaeda in Iraq is 'broken,' cut off from leaders in Pakistan, says top U.S. general," http://www.longwarjournal.org, 5 June 2010; Kim Gamel, "Al-Qaida in Iraq claims deadly central bank attack," Associated Press, 18 June 2010; and Ernesto Londono, "Extremist groups 'very much alive' in Iraq, U.S. Special Forces official says," http://www.washingtonpost.com, 9 August 2010.
78. OBL, "Message to the Muslim nation," Al-Sahab Media Production Organization, 18 May 2008, and OBL, "Practical steps to liberate Palestine," Al-Sahab Media Production Organization, 14 March 2009.
79. OBL, "Message to the Muslim nation," Al-Sahab Media Production Organization, 18 May 2008.
80. OBL, "The way to foil plots," Al-Sahab Media Production Organization, 29 December 2007.
81. Ayman al-Zawahiri, "The Zionist-Crusader aggression on Gaza and Lebanon," Al-Sahab Media Production Organization, 28 July 2006.
82. OBL, "The way to foil plots."
83. OBL, "Practical steps to liberate Palestine," Al-Sahab Media Production Organization, 14 March 2009.
84. OBL, "The way to foil plots."
85. Ibid.
86. Ibid.
87. Ibid.

88. AsadAl-Jihad2, "The timing of the entrance of the al-Qaeda organization to Palestine," http://www.al-boraq.info, 28 January 2008.
89. Ibid. AsadAl-Jihad2's assigning of "simple things" for Palestinians to do to prepare for a more intense war against Israel mirrors exactly the tasks assigned by bin Laden in 1996 to the Saudi population to help them prepare for a war against the United States and the al-Saud regime. See OBL, "Declaration of war on the United States," *Al-Quds al-Arabi*, 23 August 1996.
90. Abu Abd al-Rahman al-Ghazzawi, "An announcement and statement to the Islamic nation," *Media Division of Fatah al-Islam*, 13 February 2008.
91. Abu-Umar al-Baghdadi, "Religion is sincere advice," http://www.muslim.net, 14 February 2008.
92. Ibid. The noted Salafi scholar Husayn bin Mahmud commented at the time that bin Laden and his lieutenants were following a tradition familiar to all Muslims by using Iraq as the base for reconquering Jerusalem. "Shaykh Usama, may God protect him, knows history," bin Mahmud wrote. "The liberation of Palestine at the hands of Salah-al-din began from Iraq. . . . Salah-al-Din liberated Jerusalem and Iraq was the start point. The black banners coming from Khurassan [an ancient land that contained much of modern Afghanistan] necessarily had to pass through Iraq [on the way to Jerusalem]." See "Husayn bin-Mahmud comments on Bin Laden's message," *Sada al-Jihad* (Internet version), Issue 24, 12 April 2008; Abu-Umar al-Baghdadi, "Religion is sincere advice."
93. The large number of Salafi groups in Gaza are reviewed in "A call to Salafi groups in Gaza to join forces and confront Hamas," *MEMRI*, Special Dispatch, No. 1946, 3 June 2008, http://www.memri.org. By April 2010, four of the groups—Jund Ansar Allah, Jam'at Jaysh al-Islam, Al-Tahwid wal Jihad, and Jund Allah—had joined together in an umbrella organization called Jaljalat. See Ibrahim Qannan, "Exclusive: New Salafist Gaza faction numbers 11,000," http://www.maannews.net, 23 April 2010.
94. Nidal al-Mughrabi, "Pro-al-Qaeda fighters train in Gaza strip," http://www.alertnet.org, 1 September 2008, and Michael Freund, "The growing al-Qaeda threat to Israel," *Jerusalem Post* (Internet version), 21 October 2008.
95. "Middle East: New militant group emerges in Gaza," http://www.adnkronos.com, 2 September 2008.
96. "Al-Qaeda affiliated group in Gaza," *Al-Arabiyah Televsion*, 3 September 2008.
97. Ibid.; "A call to Salfi Groups in Gaza to Join Forces and Confront Hamas," *MEMRI*, Special Dispatch, No. 1946, 3 June 2008, http://www.memri.org, and "Jaysh al-Islam threatens Hamas," *Al-Arabiyah Televsion*, 26 September 2008.
98. Ubaidah al-Saif, "Qassam brigades in Gaza issue urgent appeal to leaders of al-Qaeda," http://www.jiahdunspun.com, 26 June 2008.
99. See, for example, Abu-Muadh al-Maqdisi, "To the lions of al-Qassam in the relentless den," *Bayt al-Maqdis Islamic Forums* (Internet), 22 February 2008.
100. Urayb al-Rintawi, "Gaza's Salafis and Takfiris," *Al-Dustur* (Internet version), 12 September 2008.
101. Freund, "The growing al-Qaeda threat to Israel."
102. Amos Harel, "Al-Qaeda in Israel: Fertile ground for terrorism," http://www.haaretz.com, 20 July 2008. Mr. Harel's prediction seems to be coming true. Al-Qaeda now has an affiliate named the "Abdullah Azzam Brigades" that is operating in the Levant. The group was created and swore allegiance to bin Laden in July, 2009. It is commanded by a man named Salih Bin-Abdallah al-Qarawi, who is on Saudi Arabia's most-wanted

list of al-Qaeda fighters. Al-Qarawi has told the media the Abdullah Azzam Brigades will attack Israel, but its operations would not be limited to the Levant. As of late September 2010, the Brigades had claimed responsibility for launching rockets into Israel, as well as for an August 2010 suicide attack on a Japanese oil tanker in the Strait of Hormuz near Oman. See "Terror blast hits Japanese tanker in Gulf Strait, says UAE," Agence France-Presse, 6 August 2010; Abdullah Azzam Brigades, "The Raid of Shaykh Umar Abd-al-Rahman—Claiming Responsibility for the Bombing of the Japanese Oil Tanker," Al-Fajr Media Center (Internet), 3 August 2010; and "Behind the News: Implications of attack on Japanese oil tanker," Al-Jazirah Satellite Television, 4 August 2010.

CHAPTER 7

1. This paragraph and the next are informed by the recent book by Chris Hedges which details the decline of American education and culture, as well as its apparently limitless appetite for what he calls spectacle; the Romans would have called it bread and circuses. The book is by turns passionate, poignant, scathing, sad, and nauseating, but in all parts it is needed reading for Americans trying to understand why their country faces so many lose-lose situations. See Chris Hedges, *Empire of Illusion: The End of Literacy and the Triumph of Spectacle* (New York: Nation Books, 2009).
2. Michael Collins Dunn, "Usama bin Laden: The nature of the challenge," *Middle East Policy*, Vol. 6, No. 2 (October 1998), p. 25.
3. Coll, *Ghost Wars*, p. 269.
4. Fadl, "The Crusader."
5. "Bin Laden not top Islamist thinker: Study," *Reuters*, 16 November 2006.
6. "Interview of Usama bin Ladin," *Ghazi Magazine*, 20 August 2000, and "Interview with Usama bin Laden," *Takbeer*, 5–12 August 1999, p. 22.
7. Al-Dhiyabi, "Interview with Shaykh Musa al-Qarni, Part 2."
8. Ouazai, "The bin Laden mystery."
9. Bin Laden's surreptitious effort to tap religious guidance from trustworthy scholars resident in Saudi Arabia can be seen in a letter he wrote to Shaykh Abd al-Raheen al-Tahan and his associates, probably between 1994 and 1996. "May Allah reward you all for your comments [that] we asked you to express in our [draft] letter entitled 'Enunciation of the atheism of the Saudi regime,'" bin Laden wrote. He went on to take note of Shaykh al-Tahan's request that the letter's advice not be used in public, and agreed to refrain from doing so. Bin Laden said that "we have taken the advice that it would not be suitable to quote any scholars still serving [in Saudi Arabia]. We have decided to omit those quotes from this letter [probably a pending publication of bin Laden's ARC] and only mention other available evidence." Bin Laden then went on to explain that he and his lieutenants were seeking advice from "some of our brothers inside [Saudi Arabia]; from the scholars and Du'att [Callers to Islam] and others who have the same interest in studying what has to be done [to combat al-Saud rule]. Those communications took quite some time." See Osama bin Laden to Shaykh Abd-al-Raheen al-Tahan, http://ctc.usma.edu/AQ/PDF/AGFP-2002–800073-Trans-Meta.pdf.
10. Coll, *The Bin Ladens*, p. 406; "Welcome in Yemen, bin Laden, but!"; Wright, *The Looming Tower*, p. 152; Bergen, *The Osama bin Laden I Know*, p. 55; Fadl, "The Crusader"; Lawrence, *Messages to the World*, p. xvi.

11. Raid Qusti, "Bin Laden an intelligence agent," http://www.arabnews.com, 21 September 2006, and "Naif calls al-Qaeda Khawarij," *Arab News* (Internet version), 17 March 2010.
12. Quoted in PBS *Frontline*, http://www.pbs.org, 11 October 2001. Ironically, Bandar's comment on bin Laden's ineptitude is a view that much of the rest of the Muslim world has about Bandar and Saudis generally. Muslims widely believe—as do, based on my experience, many in Western intelligence agencies—that the Saudis are self-centered and selfish talkers and spenders, and if there is hard work to do they will hire a Pakistani or a Bangladeshi to do it. Indeed, part of the reason bin Laden's talents and character have been—I think—underestimated was because he was a Saudi. When the Egyptian journalist Isaam Darraz first joined bin Laden and his Arab group, he noted that the idea of Saudis fighting was "a source of extreme surprise to me." Another journalist close to bin Laden, *al-Jazirah's* Ahmad Muwaffaq Zaydan, had similar ideas. Many Afghans and Arabs at first distrusted bin Laden "from the mere fact that he was a Saudi," Zaydan has said, because of "the stereotypical notion that a person from the Gulf and a Saudi in particular has no practical cause, merely providing financial support for Islamic movements without interfering in their internal affairs. Accordingly, any opinion they voice or attempt to interfere would have been construed as being acted upon the instructions of the Saudi government to serve its own purposes." Zaydan also says that after Azzam's death, bin Laden did not make an open, formal move to replace him because he knew "how sensitive some Arabs would have been about a Saudi leading them." On the upside, Abdel Bari Atwan notes that once bin Laden proved his bona fides as a mujahid in battle he was "doubly admired by his followers because, as a rich Saudi, he could have lived a life as pampered as that of a prince." See Darraz, "Impressions of an Arab journalist in Afghanistan"; Zaydan, *Usama bin Ladin without Mask*; and Atwan, "Guns and fried eggs in a mountain cave," *Sunday Times* (Internet version), 16 September 2001.
13. Lawrence, *Messages to the World*, p. xvi.
14. Abdallah al-Rashid, "Will option of containment succeed? Al-Qaida is dragging [the Saudi] government into a war of legitimacy," *Shu'un Sa'udiyah* (Internet version), 4 July 2004.
15. Bernard Lewis, "License to kill," *Foreign Affairs*, Vol. 77, No. 6 (November/December, 1998), p. 14.
16. Reston, Jr., *Warriors of God*, p. 95.
17. Liaquat Ali Khan, "Who is feeding the Bin Laden legend," http://www.thedailystar.net, 28 December 2004.
18. "11 September and some doubts," *Open Source Center*, 5 May 10.
19. Randall, *Osama*, p. 14.
20. Vlahos, *Fighting Identity*, pp. 69 and 127.
21. Al-Rashid, "Will option of containment succeed?"
22. Ibid.
23. OBL, "Declaration of war on the United States," *Al-Islah* (Internet), 2 September 1996.
24. OBL, "Letter from Kandahar," *Associated Press*, 16 March 1998; "Bin Ladin urges jihad and expulsion of U.S. forces from the Gulf," *Al-Quds al-Arabi*, 23 March 1998, p. 4.
25. OBL, "Message to the Muslim nation," *Islamic Studies and Research Center* (Internet), 4 March 2004. He made the same call for prominent Muslims to prepare to rule in the place of their tyrannical leaders in Ismail, "Interview with Usama bin Laden,"

23 December 1998; OBL, "Letter from Kandahar," *Associated Press*, 16 March 1998; and Yusufzai, "Interview with Osama bin Laden," 4 January 1999.

26. OBL, "Practical steps for the liberation of Palestine," Al-Sahab Media Production Organization, 14 March 2009. Bin Laden pushed this line of argument unsuccessfully with Mullah Omar before 9/11. "Bin Laden did not completely agree with the Taleban when it came to running the country," Ahmad Zaydan wrote after interviewing al-Qaeda's chief. "He had hoped that the Taleban would expand the base of political participation by including figures such as Hekmatyar who was popular in Afghanistan and had political experience and diverse Islamic and international relations that go back to the days of the [anti-Soviet] jihad in Afghanistan. During the interview, bin Laden also criticized the Taleban for failing to expand the base of leadership by including some Afghani figures in the media and legal fields and others from various fields whose religiousness and efficiency could be trusted." See Zaydan, *Usama Bin Ladin without Mask*, p. 24.
27. OBL, "Message to our neighbors north of the Mediterranean," *Al-Arabiyah Television*, 15 April 2004.
28. Arnett, "Osama bin Ladin: The interview," 12 May 1997.
29. Abu Muhammad al-Maqdisi, "Obama's speech versus Osama's speech," http://al-faloja.org/vb/, 12 June 2009.
30. Bernard Lewis, "Freedom and justice in the modern Middle East," *Foreign Affairs* (Internet version) (May/June 2005).
31. Ibrahim A. Karawan, "Takfir," *The Oxford Encyclopedia of the Islamic World*, http://www.oxfordislamicstudies.com.
32. OBL, "Message to the Muslim nation," Al-Sahab Media Production Organization, 18 May 2008.
33. Scott Helfstein, Nassir Adullah, and Muhammad al-Obaidi, "Deadly vanguards: A study of al-Qaida's violence against Muslims," http://www.ctc.usma.edu/Deadly%Vanguards _Complete_L.pdf (December 2009).
34. Wiktorowicz, "Anatomy of the Salafi movement." On this point, bin Laden repeatedly reminded his audiences of the hypocrisy of Sunni clerics who now claimed that no Muslim could be killed by the mujahedin. "By the grace of Allah, the Most High" he explained in 2007–2008, "we performed Jihad with the Afghan mujahedin against the Russians, and the Afghan army was a weapon in their hands against us. They would pray and fast, but despite that, the senior Ulema of the Islamic world, including the Ulema of Pakistan, ruled that they could be fought. . . . [Today,] many people will cry: How can you kill the one who says there is no God but Allah? Had such people had the power or a word at the time of Salah-al-Din and after him, they would have prevented him from taking practical steps to liberate Jerusalem, and al-Aqsa Mosque would have remained in captivity for ten centuries." OBL, "Remove the Apostate," Al-Sahab Media Production Organization, 20 September 2007, and OBL, "Message to the Muslim nation," Al-Sahab Media Production Organization, 18 May 2008.
35. OBL, "Statement to Saudi rulers," http://www.jihadunspun.com, 16 December 2004.
36. Khaled Abou El Fadl, "Islam and the theology of power," *Middle East Report* No. 221 (Winter 2001), p. 32.
37. Quintan Wiktorowicz, "Framing jihad: Intra-movement framing contests and al-Qaeda's struggle for sacred authority," *International Review of Social History*, Vol. 49 (2004), p. 159, and Assaf Moghadam, "Motives for Martyrdom," *International Security*, Vol. 33, No. 3 (Winter 2008/2009), p. 63. A commander from a Palestinian Salafi

group—Ma'sadat al-Mujahidin—recently provided a useful and concise summation of Salafism. "We are committed," Shaykh Abu-Ubaydah al-Ansari said, "to the Koran and the Sunnah as the predecessors of the ummah understood them, not as we or others understand them. All these [recent] concepts are put aside and neglected, except when we find a consensus over an issue by the scholars of the ummah. At that time, we stick to the thought of the people who lived in the first three centuries of Islam, as advised by the prophet, may God's peace and prayers be upon him, for there is no room for personal whims in religion." See "The Al-Tahadi Network exclusively interviews one of the commanders of the Ma'sadat al-Mujahein, Shaykh Abu-Ubaydah al-Ansari, may God protect him," *Al-Fallujah Islamic Forums* (Internet), 14 February 2010.

38. Wiktorowicz, "Anatomy of the Salafi movement."
39. Ibid.
40. Wiktorowicz, "Framing jihad: Intra-movement framing contests and al-Qaeda's struggle for sacred authority," p. 170, and *The Arab Ansar in Afghanistan*, Islamic Muhajirun Network, 2006.
41. Quintan Wiktorowicz and John Kaltner, "Killing in the name of Islam: Al-Qaeda's justification for September 11," *Middle East Policy*, Vol. 10, No. 2 (September 2003), p. 78; Joas Wagemakers, "A purist jihadi-Salafi: The ideology of Abu Muhammad al-Maqdisi," *British Journal of Middle Eastern Studies* (Internet version), Vol. 36, No. 2 (August 2009); Moghhhadam, "Motives for Martyrdom," pp. 47 and 63; and *The Arab Ansar in Afghanistan*, Islamic Muhajirun Network, 2006.
42. In a lengthy fall 2009 online interview, Shaykh al-Maqdisi explicitly spoke about the primacy of the jihad's military leaders. "As I always say," al-Maqdisi explained, "I am the servant of the mujahedin, wherever they are. I am their supporter. . . . I am a supporter first, then an adviser. I am a supporter who gives all he has to defend their jihad and present the proof of its legitimacy. I respond to the accusations of the doubters. I am advisor who wants jihad to progress. . . . At the helm are the mujahedin themselves (with the grace of God). This is enough for me. This is what I care about most, after the knowledge of God Almighty." Earlier, in 2003, another Salafi jihadi, Saudi Shaykh Nasir bin Hamd al-Fahd, made the same point in the treatise he wrote authorizing the mujahedins' use of nuclear weapons against the United States. After finding justification for using the weapons in the Koran, hadith, and all schools of Sunni Islam, Shaykh al-Fahd said, "If people of authority [the mujahedin commanders] determine that the evil of the infidels can be repelled only by their [nuclear weapons] means, they may be used." The decision to use the weapon, in other words, rests with the military commander. That this is not a new view among Islamist scholars is made clear by Professor John Kelsey in a very pertinent discussion of the famous, late eighth-century Iraqi scholar Shaykh Muhammad ibn al-Hassan al-Shaybani. Kelsay writes that al-Shaybani's decisions gave wide discretion to military commanders in choosing tactics and methods of attack, and made it clear that there were several situations in which it was permissible for those tactics and methods to cause non-combatant Muslim casualties. See "Open interview with Shumukh al-Islam members and the esteemed Shaykh Abu-Muhammad al-Maqdisi"; Shaykh Nasir bin Hamd al-Fahd, "A treatise on the legal status of using weapons of mass destruction against infidels," May 2003; and John Kelsay, *Arguing the Just War in Islam* (Cambridge: Harvard University Press, 2007), pp. 105–110. For bin Laden's "jurisprudence of reality" remark, see OBL, "Lecture: The hadith of Ka'ab ibn Malik concerning the Tabuk expedition," c. March 2006.

43. Wiktorowicz, "Anatomy of the Salafi movement."
44. Quintan Wiktorowicz and Karl Kaltenthaler, "The rationality of radical Islam," *Political Science Quarterly*, Vol. 121, No. 2 (2006), p. 312.
45. Wiktorowicz and Kaltner, "Killing in the name of Islam," pp. 80, 82, and 86; and Wiktorowicz, "Anatomy of the Salafi movement."
46. Wiktorowicz and Kaltner, "Killing in the name of Islam," p. 84.
47. Wiktorowicz, "Anatomy of the Salafi movement."
48. Ibid. In September 2007, Saudi Salafi scholar Sahykh Salman al-Awdah sent an open letter to bin Laden that was extremely critical of the number of Muslim casualties that had resulted from the jihad being waged by al-Qaeda and its allies. Because al-Awdah and bin Laden had been close friends in the late 1980s and early-to-mid 1990s, and because bin Laden had once said al-Awdah was his hero and the proper leader of a defensive jihad, Western governments and some Arab regimes celebrated the letter as a nail in bin Laden's coffin. It was no such thing. Al-Awdah addressed bin Laden as "My brother Osama" and in no part of the letter did he suggest that bin Laden's rhetoric or actions put him outside Islam. Al-Awdah bewailed Muslim casualties, urged bin Laden to repent, but otherwise did little more than give fodder for more bad Western analysis. Indeed, al-Awdah probably has more gravitas in the West than in the Muslim world, given that he renounced his earlier standing as a Salafi firebrand bent on purifying Islam in Saudi Arabia to get out of prison. He is now an employee of the al-Sauds as a prominent Saudi academic with his own television program and Web site. As always, bin Laden took the criticism without public response, probably believing that the betraying character of the writer spoke for itself. See Shaykh Salman al-Awdah, "Letter to Usama bin Ladin," *IslamToday* (Internet), 17 September 2007.
49. Wiktorowicz, "Anatomy of the Salafi movement," and Wagemakers, "A Purist jihadi-Salafi."
50. Wagemakers, "A Purist jihadi-Salafi."
51. "Response by Shaykh Abu Muhammad al-Maqdisi," http://www.alboraq.info, 3 April 2009.
52. Abu Muhammad al-Maqdisi, "Obama's speech versus Osama's speech," http://al-faloja.org/vb/, 12 June 2009.
53. "Arab Afghan says Usama bin Ladin's force strength overblown."
54. Atwan, *The secret history of al-Qaeda*, p. 233.
55. OBL, "Message to Muslim youth," *Markaz al-Dawa* (Internet), 13 December 2001.
56. Sayf-al-Din al-Ansari, "But take your precautions," *Al-Ansar* (Internet), 15 March 2002. Al-Ansari's guidance again underscores bin Laden's constant theme that Muslims were responsible for their own problems and that their failures facilitated infidel success.
57. See especially Sageman, *Understanding Terror Networks*, and Robert Pape, *Dying to Win. The Logic of Suicide Terrorism* (New York: Random House, 2005).
58. Lara Setrakian, "Exclusive: Osama bin Laden's son warns his sucessors will be worse," http://abcnews.go.com, 11 February 2001.

EPILOGUE

1. OBL, "Address to the American people," 14 September 2009.
2. Abraham Lincoln, "State of the Union message," 3 December 1861.

BIBLIOGRAPHY

The core of this biography is based on Osama bin Laden's own words and the words of commentary, reflection, and reminiscence of those closest to him. A great many of these words are used here for the first time, but it would be both churlish and unfair not to salute and thank the writers who have made essential contributions to our understanding of bin Laden, al-Qaeda, and their allies, movement, and jihad. Among a host, the following are, in my view, the most important, insightful contributors: Peter Bergen; Abdel Bari Atwan; Steve Cole; Ahmad Muwaffaq Zaydan; Rahimullah Yusufzai; Carmen, Najwa, and Omar bin Laden; Brynjar Lia; Randall Hamud; Roy Gutman, Jonathan Randall; Mark Huband; Bruce B. Lawrence; Camille Tawil; and Quintan Wiktorowicz. I hotly disagree with some of what they have written; they may disagree or scorn some or all of what I argue here. Be that as it may, their work helped make mine possible, and will benefit all who take time to read it.

PRIMARY SOURCES: OSAMA BIN LADEN (IN CHRONOLOGICAL ORDER)

Usama bin Muhammad bin Laden, "Introduction to 'The battle of the Lion's Den, Afghanistan, 1987,'" in Shaykh Abdullah Azzam, *The Lofty Mountain*, 1st edition,n.d. http://www.maktabah.net/store/images/35/Lofty%20mountain.pdf.

The Arab Ansar in Afghanistan, Islamic Muhajirun Network, 2006. Bin Laden is interviewed in this documentary filmed in 1989.

Ali Abd-al-Karim and al-Nur Ahmad al-Nur, "Interview with Saudi businessman Usama bin Ladin," *Al-Quds al-Arabi*, 9 March 1994, p. 4.

Advice and Reform Committee Communiques, 1994–1998, http://www.usama.edu, AFGP-2002–003345.

Letter from Osama bin Ladin to Shaykh Abd-al-Raheen al-Tahan, no date, but before May 1996, http://ctc.usma.edu/AQ/PDF/AGFP-2002–800073-Trans-Meta.pdf.

Robert Fisk, "Interview with Saudi dissident Usama bin Ladin," *Independent*, 10 July 1996, p. 14.

Osama bin Laden, "Declaration of jihad against the Americans occupying the land of the two holy mosques; Expel the heretics from the Arabian Peninsula," *Al-Quds al-Arabi*, 23 August 1996. [Republished on the Internet at the Saudi dissident *Al-Islah Website*, London, 2 September 1996.]

Abdel Bari Atwan, "Interview with Usama bin Laden," *Al-Quds al-Arabi*, 27 November 1996.

"Mujahid Usama bin Ladin talks exclusively to Nida'ul Islam about the new powder keg in the Middle East," *Nida'ul Islam* (Internet), 15 January 1997. [The journal notes that the interview occurred in October/November 1996.]

Hamid Mir, "Interview with Usama bin Ladin," *Pakistan*, 18 March 1997.

Peter Arnett, "Interview with Osama bin Laden," www.CNN.news, 12 May 1997.

Zafar Mahmood Malik, "Bin Ladin backs Harakat-al-Ansar," *Jang*, 20 October 1997, pp. 7 and 8.

"Rebels say attack on Juba imminent," *Al-Quds al-Arabi*, 19 February 1998, p. 1.

"Bin Laden, others sign fatwa to 'kill Americans' everywhere," *Al-Quds al-Arabi*, 23 February 1998, p. 3.

Usama bin Ladin, "Letter from Kandahar," *Associated Press*, 16 March 1998.

"Bin Ladin urges jihad and expulsion of U.S. forces from the Gulf," *Al-Quds al-Arabi*, 23 March 1998, p. 4.

Azeem Siddique, "Interview with Osama bin Ladin," *Al-Akhbar*, 31 March 1998, pp. 1 and 8.

"Bin Ladin warns against U.S. plan to eliminate Afghan Arabs," *Al-Quds al-Arabi*, 15 April 1998, p. 1.

"Bin Ladin: Afghanistan's inclusion on U.S. 'terror list' is 'certificate of good conduct' for the Taleban," *Al-Quds al-Arabi*, 18 May 1998, p. 3.

John Miller, "Talking with terror's banker: An exclusive interview with Osama bin Laden," http:///www.ABCnews.com, 28 May 1998.

Qari Naved Masood Hashmi, "Osama bin Laden—A man as strong as rock," *Pakistan*, 10 June 1998, p. 10.

"Bin Ladin praises Pakistanis," *The Nation*, 2 September 1998, p. 16.

"Bin Ladin message to anti-U.S. conference," *Al-Akhbar*, 12 September 1998, pp. 7 and 8.

Jamal Abd-al-Latif Ismail. *Bin Ladin, al-Jazirah, and I*. Islamic Information Monitor, n.p., n.d. [The book contains al-Latif's interview of bin Laden in Kandahar on 23 December 1998. A severely truncated version of Ismail's work is Salah Najm, "Usamah bin Ladin; the destruction of the base," *Al-Jazirah Satellite Television*, 10 June 1999.]

Rahimullah Yusufzai, "Interview with Osama bin Laden," www.ABCNEWS.com, 4 January 1999.

Rahimullah Yusufzai, "I am not afraid of death," www.Newsweek.com, 4 January 1999.

John Miller, "Greetings America. My name is Osama bin Laden. Now that I have your attention . . . ," *Esquire* (Internet version), February 1999.

Abu Shiraz, "Interview with Osama bin Laden," *Pakistan*, 20 February 1999, p. 10.

"Usama bin Ladin pens letter in support of Kashmiri jihad," *Wahdat*, 8 June 1999, pp. 1 and 5.

"Interview with Usama bin Laden," *Takbeer*, 5–12 August 1999, p. 22.

"Bin Laden message marking U.S. embassy bombing," Middle East News Agency, 7 August 1999.

"Text of UBL Poster calls for Holy War against U.S.," WAddmmhhmmyy (Internet), 19 August 1999.

"Usama bin Ladin sees holy war in 'every street' in U.S.," *Pakistan*, 2 May 2000, p. 8.
"Interview (written) of Usama bin Ladin," *Ghazi Magazine*, 20–27 August 2000.
Rahimullah Yusufzai, "Bin Laden endorses attack on *USS Cole*, denies Kuwaiti daily's report," *The News*, 15 November 2000, p. 18.
Januulah Hashimzada, "I will continue jihad against infidels, Usama bin Ladin," *Wahdat*, 27 March 2001, p. 5.
"Bin Ladin pledges allegiance to Mullah Omar," *Al-Jazirah Satellite Television*, 9 April 2001.
"Bin Ladin asks Muslim to support Afghanistan's 'Prince of the Faithful,'" *Al-Jazirah Satellite Television*, 12 April 2001.
Abdul Sattar, "Usama urges ummah to continue jihad," *Pakistan* (Internet version), 7 May 2001.
Letter from Osama bin Laden to Mullah Omar, n.d. but before 9/11, 2001, http://www.ctc.usma.edu, AFGP-2002–600321.
"It is impossible to arrest and hand me over to the United States," *Nawa-i-Waqt*, 19 September 2001, pp. 1, 7.
Hamid Mir, "My last question to Osama bin Laden," *Friday Times* (Internet version), 22 September 2001.
"Exclusive interview with Usama bin Laden," *Ummat*, 28 September 2001, pp. 1 and 7.
"Speech by Osama bin Laden," *Al-Jazirah Satellite Television*, 7 October 2001.
Usama bin Laden, "Message to the Pakistani people," *Al-Jazirah Satellite Television*, 1 November 2001.
"Speech by Usama bin Ladin, leader of the al-Qaeda organization," *Al-Jazirah Satellite Television*, 3 November 2001.
"Statement by Usama bin Laden in 'The first war of the century' program," *Al-Jazirah Satellite Television*, 3 November 2001.
Hamid Mir, "The war has not yet begun—detailed interview with Usama bin Laden," *Ausaf*, 16 November 2001, pp. 9 and 11.
"U.S. biggest terrorist and merchant of death: Usama," *Nawa-i-Waqt*, 12 December 01, pp. 1, 10.
"Bin Ladin's letter to Pakistani journalists," *Nawa-i-Waqt*, 12 December 2001, pp. 1 and 10.
"Transcript of Usama bin Laden video tape," http://www.defense.gov/news/Dec2001/d20011213ubl.pdf, 13 December 2001.
Osama bin Laden, "Message to the youth of the Muslim ummah," *Markaz al-Dawa* (Internet), 13 December 2001.
"Statement by al-Qaeda leader Osama bin Laden in 'First War of the century' program," *Al-Jazirah Satellite Television*, 27 December 2001.
Osama bin Ladin, "Crown Prince Abdullah's initiative is high treason," *Al-Quds al-Arabi*, 28 March 2002, p. 3.
Taysir Alouni, "Interview with Usama bin Laden," *Qoquz* (Internet), 23 May 2002. [Alouni conducted this interview in October 2001.]
Muhammad al-Shafi'i, "A site close to al-Qa'idah posts a poem by Bin Laden . . . ," *Al-Sharq al-Awsat*, 20 June 2002.
"Bin Ladin audio message," *Al-Jazirah Satellite Television*, 6 October 2002.
"Statement from Shaykh Usama bin Laden," *Al-Qal'ah* (Internet), 14 October 2002.
"Osama bin Laden to the scholars of Deoband, Peshawar, Pakistan," 27 March 2002, http://www.ctc.usma.edu, AFGP-2002–901188. [A fuller version of this letter, also sent in audiotape format, is in Ahmad Muwaffaq Zaydan, *Usama bin Ladin without Mask; Interviews the Taliban banned*. Beirut: World Book Publishing, 2003.]

Osama bin Ladin, "Letter to the American people," *Waaqiah* (Internet), 12 November 2002. [Parts of the letter are also in "Bin Laden's letter to Americans," *Observer* (Internet version), 24 November 2002.]

Osama bin Laden, "Message to countries allied with the United States," *Al-Jazirah Satellite Television*, 12 November 2002.

Osama bin Laden, "Message to the people of the [Arabian] Peninsula," *Al-Quds al-Arabi*, 28 November 2002, p. 1.

Muhammad al-Shafi'i, "New message from bin Ladin . . . ," *Al-Sharq al-Awsat* (Internet version), 19 January 2003.

Usama bin Ladin, "Message to our brothers in Iraq," *Al-Jazirah Satellite Television*, 11 February 2003.

Osama bin Laden, "Exposing the new Crusader war in Iraq," *Waaqiah* (Internet), 14 February 2003.

Osama bin Laden, "Abdallah's initiative—the great treason," http://www.cybcity.com/mnzmas/osam.htm, 1 March 2003.

"Speech by Osama bin Laden," Middle East Media Research Institute (MEMRI), Special Dispatch No. 539, 18 July 2003.

"Statement by Usama bin Ladin," *Al-Jazirah Satellite Television*, 10 September 2003.

Usama bin Ladin, "Second message to the Iraqi people," *Al-Jazirah Satellite Television*, 18 October 2003.

Usama bin Ladin, "Message to the Muslim nation," *Islamic Studies and Research Center* (Internet), 4 March 2004.

Usama bin Laden, "Message to our neighbors north of the Mediterranean," *Al-Arabiyah Television*, 15 April 2004.

"Osama bin Laden, "Message to the ummah in general, and our brothers in Iraq in particular," *Al-Qal'ah* (Internet), 6 May 2004.

Osama bin Laden, "Message to the Muslim nation," *Islamic Studies and Research Center* (Internet), 30 October 2004.

Osama bin Laden, "Message to the American people," *Al-Jazirah Satellite Television*, 30 October 2004.

Osama bin Laden, "Statement to Saudi Rulers," http://www.jihadunspun.com, 16 December 2004.

Usama bin Ladin, "Message to Muslims in Iraq in particular, and the ummah in general," *Al-Sahab Media Production Organization*, 28 December 2004.

Robert Fisk, "On finding Osama," *Independent* (Internet version), 24 September 2005.

Osama bin Laden, "Lecture: The hadith of Ka'ab ibn Malik concerning the Tabuk expedition," *Al-Sahab Media Production Organization*, c. March 2006.

Usama bin Ladin, "O Muslim people," *Al-Sahab Media Production Organization*, 26 April 2006.

Osama bin Laden, "Eulogy for Abu-Musab al-Zarqawi," *Al-Sahab Media Production Organization*, 30 June 2006.

"Usama bin Ladin: Jihad against India 'duty' of all Muslims," *Pakistan*, 23 August 2006, pp. 3 and 6.

Usama bin Ladin, "Message to the American people," *Al-Fallujah Islamic Minbar* (Internet), 8 September 2007.

Osama bin Laden, "The wills of the heroes of the raids on New York and Washington," *Al-Sahab Media Production Organization*, 11 September 2007.

Usama bin Ladin, "Remove the apostate," *Al-Sahab Media Production Organization*, 20 September 2007.

Usama bin Laden, "Message to our people in Iraq," *Al-Sahab Media Production Organization*, 23 October 2007.
Osama bin Laden, "The Way to Foil Plots," *al-Sahab Media Production Organization*, 29 December 2007.
Osama bin Laden, "The way of salvation for Palestine," *Al-Sahab Media Production Organization*, 21 March 2008.
Usama bin Ladin, "Message to the Muslim nation," *Al-Sahab Media Production Organization*, 18 May 2008.
Usama bin Laden, "Practical steps for the liberation of Palestine," *Al-Sahab Media Production Organization*, 14 March 2009.
Usama bin Ladin, "To Muslims in Pakistan," *Al-Jazirah Satellite Television*, 3 June 2009.
"No glory without jihad," *Al-Ghurbah Establishment* (Internet), 31 August 2009.
Osama bin Laden, "Address to the American people," *Al-Sahab Media Production Organization*, 14 September 2009.
Osama bin Laden, "The way to save the earth," *Al-Sahab Media Production Organization*, 29 January 2010.

PRIMARY SOURCES PERTAINING TO BIN LADEN

Abdullah Azzam, "I have never laid my eyes on a man like him," *Fi Dhilal Surat at-Tawbah*, p. 301, in English at http://forums.islamicawakening.com/f18/abdullah-azzam-usamah-bin-ladin-i-have-never-laid-my-eyes-man-like-him-1090/.
Khalid al-Batarfi, "Denying she is angry with him, saying she prays to God to guide him on the right path, mother of Usama bin Ladin says: 'I do not agree with my son,'" *Al-Madinah*, 8 December 2001, p. 1.
Khalid al-Batarfi, "Osama is very sweet, very kind, very considerate . . . ," *Mail on Sunday* (Internet version), 23 December 2001.
Khalid M. al-Batarfi, "Growing up with Osama: 2 youths took different paths," http://www.seatlletimes.nwsource.com, 6 January 2007.
Shaykh Abdul Aziz bin Baz, "The nullifiers of Islam," http://theclearsunnah.wordpress.com/2007/05/05/10-nullifiers-of-Islam/.
Peter L. Bergen, *The Osama bin Laden I Know*. New York: Free Press, 2006.
Carmen bin Laden, *Inside the Kingdom. My Life in Saudi Arabia*. New York: Grand Central Publishing, 2004.
Najwa bin Laden, Omar bin Laden, and Jean Sasson, *Growing Up bin Laden: Osama's Wife and Son Take Us inside Their Secret World*. New York: St. Martin's Press, 2009.
"Clerics in Afghanistan issue fatwa on necessity to move U.S. forces out of the Gulf; Saudi oppositionist Usamah bin Ladin supports it," *Al-Quds al-Arabi*, 14 May 1998, p. 4.
Issam Darraz, "Impressions of an Arab journalist in Afghanistan," in Abdullah Azzam, *The Lofty Mountain*, first edition, http://www.maktabah.net/store/images/35/Lofty%20mountain.pdf.
Jamil al-Dhiyabi, "Interview with Shaykh Musa al-Qarni, three parts," *Al-Hayah* (Internet version), 8 March, 9 March, and 10 March 2006.
Khlaid al-Hammadi, "Al-Qaeda from within, narrated by Abu Jandal, 11 parts," *Al-Quds al-Arabi*, 3 August 2004–29 March 2005.
Marianne Macdonald, "O Brother, where art thou?" *Evening Standard*, 26 May 2006.
"Al-Qaeda family: At home with Osama bin Laden," *CBC News Online*, 3 March 2004.

Muhammad Saddiq, "Bin Laden family statement," *Al-Sharq al-Awsat* (Internet version), 15 September 2001.
Saudi bin Laden Group Web site, http://www.sbg.com.sa/aboutus.html.
Abu Musab al-Suri, "A Drama of faith and jihad: The Mujahedin (Arabs-al-Qaida) and Ansar (Afghans-Taleban)," *Open Source Center Summary*, 16–17 October 2009.
Ahmad Muwaffaq Zaydan, *Usama bin Ladin without Mask: Interviews the Taliban Banned*. Beirut: World Book Publishing, 2003.

SECONDARY SOURCES: BOOKS

Khalil Khalil Asad. *Warrior from Mecca. The Complete Story of Osama bin Ladin*. London: Al-Ilam li al-Nashr, 2000.
Abdel Bari Atwan. *The Secret History of al Qaeda*. Berkeley: University of California Press, 2006.
Peter L. Bergen. *Holy War, Inc.: Inside the Secret World of Osama bin Laden*. New York: Free Press, 2001.
Gary Bernsten. *Jawbreaker. The Attack on Bin Laden and Al Qaeda: A Personal Account by the CIA's Key Field Commander*. New York: Three Rivers, 2006.
Jason Burke. *Al-Qaeda. Casting a Shadow of Terror*. London: I. B. Taurus, 2003.
Steve Coll. *The Bin Ladens. An Arabian Family in the American Century*. New York: Penguin, 2008.
———. *Ghost Wars. The Secret History of the CIA, Afghanistan, and bin Laden, From the Soviet Invasion to September 10, 2001*. New York: Penguin, 2005.
John L. Esposito and Dalia Mogahed. *Who Speaks for Islam? What a Billion Muslims Really Think*. New York: Gallup, 2007.
Richard A. Gabriel. *Muhammad. Islam's First Great General*. Norman: University of Oklahoma Press, 2007.
Fawaz A. Gerges. *The Far Enemy. Why Jihad Went Global*. New York: Cambridge University Press, 2005.
Rohan Gunaratna. *Inside al-Qaeda. Global Network of Terror*. New York: Columbia University Press, 2002.
Roy Gutman. *How We Missed the Story. Osama bin Laden, the Taliban, and the Hijacking of Afghanistan*. Washington, D.C.: United States Institute of Peace, 2008.
Randall B. Hamud, ed. *Osama bin Laden. America's Enemy in His Own Words*. San Diego: Nadeem Publishing, 2005.
Mary Habeck. *Knowing the Enemy. Jihadist Ideology and the War on Terror*. New Haven: Yale University Press, 2006.
Chris Hedges. *Empire of Illusion. The End of Literacy and the Triumph of Spectacle*. New York: Nation Books, 2009.
Geoffrey Hindley. *Saladin. Hero of Islam*. Barnsley, UK: Pen and Sword Books, 1976.
Mark Huband. *Brutal Truths, Fragile Myths. Power Politics and Western Adventurism in the Arab World*. Boulder: Westview, 2004.
Raymond Ibrahim, ed. and trans. *The al-Qaeda Reader*. New York: Broadway Books, 2007.
Efraim Karsh. *Islamic Imperialism. A History*. New Haven: Yale University Press, 2007.
John Kelsay. *Arguing the Just War in Islam*. Cambridge: Harvard University Press, 2007.
David Kilcullen. *The Accidental Guerrilla. Fighting Small Wars in the Midst of a Big One*. New York: Oxford University Press, 2009.
Bruce B. Lawrence, ed. *Messages to the World. The Statements of Osama bin Laden*. London: Verso, 2005.

Bernard Lewis. *What Went Wrong? Western Impact and Middle Eastern Response*. New York: Oxford University Press, 2002.

Brynjar Lia. *Architect of Global Jihad. The Life of al-Qaeda Strategist Abu Musab al-Suri*. New York: Columbia University Press, 2008.

Martin Lings. *Muhammad. His Life Based on the Earliest Sources*. Rochester, Vt.: Inner Traditions International, 1983.

David Loyn. *In Afghanistan. Two Hundred Years of British, Russian and American Occupation*. New York: Palgrave Macmillan, 2009.

Amin Maalouf. *The Crusades through Arab Eyes*. New York: Schocken Books, 1984.

Omar Nasiri. *Inside the Jihad. My Life with al-Qaeda: A Spy's Story*. New York: Basic Books, 2006.

Rudolph Peters. *Jihad in Classical and Modern Islam*. Princeton, N.J.: Markus Wiener, 1996.

Elizabeth Brown Pryor. *Reading the Man. A Portrait of Robert E. Lee through His Private Letters*. New York: Viking, 2007.

Jonathan Randall. *Osama. The Making of a Terrorist*. New York: Alfred A. Knopf, 2004.

Simon Reeve. *The New Jackals. Ramzi Yousef, Osama bin Laden, and the Future of Terrorism*. Boston: Northeastern University Press, 1999.

Bruce Riedel. *The Search for al-Qaeda. Its Leadership, Ideology, and Future*. Washington, D.C.: Brookings Institution, 2008.

James Reston, Jr. *Warriors of God. Richard the Lionheart and Saladin in the Third Crusade*. New York: Anchor Books, 2002.

Louise Richardson. *What Terrorists Want. Understanding the Enemy, Containing the Threat*. New York: Random House, 2006.

Marc Sageman. *Understanding Terror Networks*. Philadelphia: University of Pennsylvania Press, 2004.

Michael Scheuer. *Through Our Enemies' Eyes. Osama bin Laden, Radical Islam, and the Future of America*. Revised edition. Dulles, Va.: Potomac Books, 2006.

Philip Smucker. *Al Qaeda's Great Escape. The Military and the Media on Terror's Trail*. Washington, D.C.: Brassey's, 2004.

Camille Tawil. *Brothers in Arms: The Story of Al-Qaida and the Arab Jihadists*. London: Saqi Books, 2010.

Yaroslav Trofimov. *The Siege of Mecca. The Forgotten Uprising in Islam's Holiest Shrine and the Birth of al-Qaeda*. New York: Doubleday, 2007.

Michael Vlahos. *Fighting Identity. Sacred War and World Change*. Westport, Conn: Praeger Security International, 2009.

Bob Woodward. *Bush at War*. New York: Simon and Schuster, 2002.

Lawrence Wright. *The Looming Tower. Al-Qaeda and the Road to 9/11*. New York: Alfred A. Knopf, 2006.

Muhammad Yusaf and Mark Adkin. *The Bear Trap. Afghanistan's Untold Story*. Lahore: Jang Publishers, 1992.

Abdul Salam Zaeef. *My Life with the Taliban*. New York: Columbia University Press, 2010.

SECONDARY SOURCES: ARTICLES, ESSAYS, ADDRESSES, LETTERS, ETC.

"A call to Salafi groups in Gaza to join forces and confront Hamas," *MEMRI Special Dispatch Series*, No. 1946, 3 June 2008, http://www.memri.org.

Akbar S. Ahmed, "Ibn Khaldun and anthropology: The failure of methodology in the post 9/11 world," *Contemporary Sociology*, Vol. 34, No. 6 (November 2005), pp. 591–596.

Taysir Alwani, "Bin Ladin weds Yemeni girl in simple ceremony in the presence of his supporters," *Al-Quds al-Arabi* (Internet version), 1 August 2000.

"The Arab Afghans, parts 1–3," *Al-Sharq al-Awsat* (Internet), 29 June, 1 July, and 9 July 2005.

Tim Arango, "Top Qaeda leaders in Iraq reported killed in raid," http://www.nytimes.com, 19 April 2010.

Atiyah to Abu Musab al-Zarqawi, http://ctc.usma.edu, 11 December 2005.

Abdel Bari Atwan, "Guns and fried eggs in a mountain cave," *Sunday Times* (Internet version), 16 September 2001.

Shaykh Salman al-Awdah, "Letter to Usama bin Ladin," *IslamToday* (Internet), 17 September 2007.

———, "Revisions and Objections," *Ukaz* (Internet version), 22 August 2009.

Samir Awwad, "Umar, son of bin Ladin, says during an important interview 'The Americans are not serious about finding my father,'" *Al-Rayah* (Internet version), 20 August 2008.

Shaykh Abdullah Azzam, "Defense of the Muslim lands," http://www.religioscope.com/info/doc/jihad/jihadfile.htm#defence.

———, "Join the caravan," http://www.islamistwatch.org.texts/azzam/caravan/reference.html.

Abu-Umar al-Baghdadi, "Religion is sincere advice," http://www.muslim.net, 14 February 2008.

———, "Stop them do not kill them," *Al-Fajr Media Center* (Internet), 23 March 2010.

Peter L. Bergen, "The battle for Tora Bora," *New Republic* (Internet version), 22 December 2009.

Peter L. Bergen and Paul Cruickshank, "The unraveling," *New Republic* (Internet version), 11 June 2008.

Peter Beaumont, "Arabs under siege as Israel tightens grip on Holy City," http://www.guardian.co.uk, 27 July 2008.

Stephen Biddle, "Afghanistan and the future of warfare. Implications for army and defense policy," Carlisle, Pa.: Strategic Studies Institute, U.S. Army War College, 2002.

"Bin Ladin building new bases in Kandahar area," *Sunday Telegraph* (Internet version), 4 October 1998.

"Bin Ladin loved Sudan, adored its people, adjusted to their customs. His life in Sudan was simple," *Al-Quds al-Arabi* (Internet version), 26 November 2001.

"Bin Laden not top Islamist thinker: Study," *Reuters*, 16 November 2006.

"Biography of Usamah bin Laden," *Islamic Observation Center* (Internet), 22 April 2000.

David Blair, "Man who harboured bin Laden is lodestar for terrorists," http://www.telegraph.co.uk, 30 January 2006.

Tim Butcher, "My life in al-Qaeda, by bin Laden's bodyguard," http://www.telegraph.co.uk, 26 March 2008.

Steve Coll, "Osama in America. The final answer," *New Yorker* (Internet version), 30 June 2009.

———, "Osama's trust fund," *New Yorker* (Internet version), 2 October 2008.

———, "Young Osama," *New Yorker* (Internet version), 12 December 2005.

Martin Chulov, "Al-Qaeda bombs hit three Baghdad embassies," http://www.guardian.co.uk, 5 April 2010.

Alan Culinson, "Inside al-Qaeda's hard drive," *Atlantic Monthly*, September 2004, pp. 55–70.

Turki al-Dakhil, "Interview with Saudi cleric Salman al-Awdah," *Al-Arabiyah Television*, 28 August 2009.

R. Hrair Dekmejian, "The rise of political Islam in Saudi Arabia," *Middle East Journal*, Vol. 48, No. 4 (Autumn 1994), pp. 627–643.

Christopher Dickey, "Portrait of a family," *Newsweek*, 5 April 2004.

"Documentary on life with bin Laden," http://www.chinadaily.com, 7 March 2004.

Andrew Duffy, "Radicalized in Ottawa," *Ottawa Citizen* (Internet version), 11 May 2008.

W. G. Dunlop, "First edition of Al-Qaeda magazine published," Agence-France Presse, 12 July 2010.

Michael Collins Dunn, "Usama bin Laden. The nature of the challenge," *Middle East Policy*, Vol. 6, No. 2 (October 1998), pp. 23–28.

"11 September and some doubts," *Open Source Center*, 5 May 2010.

David Ensor et al., "Bin Laden family believes Osama is alive," *CNN Daybreak*, 19 March 2002.

Khaled Abou El Fadl, "Islam and the theology of power," *Middle East Report*, No. 221, (Winter 2001), pp. 28–33.

Khaled Abou El Fadl, "The Crusader," *Boston Review* (Internet version), Vol. 31, No. 2 (March/April 2006).

Shaykh Nasir bin Hamd al-Fahd, "A treatise on the legal status of using weapons of mass destruction against infidels" (Internet), May 2003.

Leah Farrall, "Hotline to jihad," *Australian* (Internet version), 7 December 2009.

Martin Fletcher, "The impenetrable jungle of Osama bin Laden's family tree," http://www.timesonline.co.uk, 23 December 2009.

Michael Freund, "The growing al-Qaeda threat to Israel," *Jerusalem Post* (Internet version), 21 October 2008.

Mamoun Fundy, "Safar al-Hawali. Saudi Islamist or Saudi nationalist," *Islam and Christian-Muslim Relations*, Vol. 9, No. 1, (March, 1998), pp. 5–21.

Kim Gamel, "Al-Qaeda in Iraq claims deadly central bank attack," Associated Press, 18 June 2010.

Abu Abd al-Rahman al-Ghazzawi, "An announcement and statement to the Islamic nation," *Media Division of Fatah al-Islam*, 13 February 2008.

Evan R. Goldstein, "How just is Islam's just war tradition?" *Chronicle of Higher Education* (Internet version), Vol. 54, No. 32 (11 April 2008).

Lenn Evan Goodman, "Ibn Khaldun and Thucydides," *Journal of the American Oriental Society*, Vol. 92, No. 2 (April-June 1972), pp. 250–270.

J. J. Green, "Al-Qaeda considered a 'joke' to jihadists," http://www.wtop.com, 29 April 2010.

Rosalind W. Gwynne, "Usama bin Ladin, the Qur'an, and jihad," *Religion*, Vol. 36 (2006), pp. 61–90.

Thomas Hagghammer, "Abdullah Azzam, imam of the jihad." In Gilles Kepel and Jean-Pierre Milelli, eds., *Al-Qaeda in Its Own Words*, Cambridge: Belknap Press of Harvard University Press, 2008, pp. 81–101.

Amos Harel, "Al-Qaeda in Israel. Fertile ground for terrorism," http://www.haaretz.com, 20 July 2008.

John Harlow, "Pray silence for bin Laden the wedding poet," http://www.timesonline.co.uk, 21 September 2008.

Mehdi Hasan, "The NS Interview. Omar bin Laden," http://www.newstatesman.com, 19 November 2009.

"Have Taleban changed their stand about Osama," *Jang*, 17 February 1999, p.4.
"Shakyh Safar al-Hawali," *Atlas of Islamist Ideology*, http://ctc.usma.edu/atlas/Atlas-ReserachCompensium.pdf.
Safar ibn Abdur Rahman al-Hawali, "An open letter to President Bush," http://www.sunnahonline.com, 15 October 2001.
Bernard Haykel, "Osama bin Laden, a purveyor of poetic terrorism," http://www.thedailystar.com.lb, 19 July 2008.
Scott Helfstein, Nassir Adullah, and Muhammad al-Obaidi, "Deadly vanguards. A study of al-Qaida's violence against Muslims," http://www.ctc.usma.edu/Deadly%Vanguards_Complete_L.pdf (December 2009).
Christopher Henzel, "The origins of al-Qaeda's ideology. Implications for U.S. strategy," *Parameters*, Vol. 35 (Spring 2005), pp. 69–80.
Cherrie Heywood, "Israeli intelligence warns of new Israeli terror," *Middle East Times* (Internet version), 30 September 2008.
Andrew Hill, "The bin Laden tapes," *Journal for Cultural Research*, Vol. 10, No. 1 (January 2006), pp. 35–46.
Joachim Hoelzgen, "The rulers of Kandahar," *Der Spiegel*, 9 November 1998, pp. 216–220.
"Interview with Egyptian Islamist lawyer Muntasir al-Zayyat," *Al-Sharq al-Awsat*, 12 July 1999, p. 2.
"Interview with Sa'd al-Faqih," *PBS Frontline Online*, April 1999.
"Iraq in 'open war' with Qaeda after bombings," http://www.kuwaittimes.com, 8 April 2010.
"Islamic State of Iraq. A statement on the blessed Tikrit raid," *Al-Fajr Media Center* (Internet), 9 December 2009.
"Islamic State of Iraq. A statement on the fifth wave of the prison raid in Baghdad," *Al-Fajr Media Center* (Internet), 8 April 2010.
"Jaysh al-Islam threatens Hamas," *Al-Arabiyah Television*, 26 September 2008.
AsadAl-Jihad2, "The timing of the entrance of the al-Qaeda organization to Palestine," http://www.al-boraq.info, 28 January 2008.
Calvert Jones, "Al-Qaeda's innovative improvisers: Learning in a diffuse international network," *Cambridge Review of International Affairs*, Vol. 19, No. 4 (December 2006), pp. 555–569.
"Journal to publish bin Laden's poetry," *Australian Broadcasting Company News* (Internet), 23 September 2008.
Sebastian Junger, "The Lion in winter," *National Geographic Adventure*, March/April 2001.
Ibrahim A. Karawan, "Takfir," *The Oxford Encyclopedia of the Islamic World*, http://www.oxfordislamicstudies.com.
"Ibn Khaldun," *The Oxford Encyclopedia of the Islamic World*, http://www.oxfordislamic-studies.com.
Aimal Khan, "Arab radicals declare Usama a non-Muslim," *Frontier Post*, 10 March 1999, p.1.
———, "Osama said mediating between Hekmatyar, Sayyaf," *Frontier Post*, 29 December 1998, pp. 1, 12.
———, "Usama bin Ladin steps up public appearances in Kabul," *Frontier Post*, 7 September 1999, p. 12.
Behroz Khan, "Bin Ladin makes 'rare' public appearance in Kandahar," *The News*, 22 January 1999.
Liaquat Ali Khan, "Who is feeding the bin Laden legend," http://www.thedailystar.net, 28 December 2004.

Jamal Khashoggi, "Interview with Prince Turki al-Faisal, 6 parts," *Arab News* (Internet version), 4, 5, 6, 7, 8, and 9 November 2001.

Ibrahim Zayd al-Kilani, "Usamah bin Ladin, the eagle of Islam," *Al-Sabil*, 19 October 1999, p. 20.

Kiyohito Kokita and Yuji Moronaga, "Terrorist asks writer to compile a biography—Testimony of Pakistanis who have met with bin Ladin," *AERA*, 8 October 2001, pp. 18–20.

Sami Kulyab, "Interview with Shaykh Abd-al-Majid al-Zindani," *Al-Jazirah Satellite Television*, 23 February 2007.

"Letter from al-Zawahiri to al-Zarqawi, 11 October, 2005," released by the Office of the Director of National Intelligence on 9 July 2006, www.dni.gov.

"Laden makes first appearance in Kandahar," *The News*, 11 April 1998, p. 12.

Stéphane Lacroix, "Ayman al-Zawahiri: Veteran of the jihad." In Gilles Kepel and Jean-Pierre Milelli, eds., *Al-Qaeda in Its Own Words*, Cambridge: Belknap Press of Harvard University Press, 2008, pp. 147–170.

Bruce B. Lawrence, "In bin Laden's words," *Chronicle of Higher Education* (Internet version), 4 November 2005.

Guy Lawson, "Osama's prodigal son," http://www.rollingstone.com, 20 January 2010.

Bernard Lewis, "Freedom and justice in the modern Middle East," *Foreign Affairs* (Internet version), Vol. 84, No. 3 (May/June 2005).

———, "License to kill," *Foreign Affairs* (Internet version), Vol. 77, No. 6 (November/December 1998).

Abraham Lincoln, "State of the Union Message," 3 December 1861.

Mark Long, "Ribat, al-Qaida and the Challenge for U.S. Foreign Policy," *Middle East Journal*, Vol. 63, No. 1 (Winter 2009), pp. 31–47.

William Maclean, "Al-Qaeda ideologue in Syrian detention," http://www.reuters.com, 10 June 2009.

"Husayn bin Mahmud comments on Bin Ladin's message," *Sada al-Jihad* (Internet version), Issue 24, 12 April 2008.

Husayn bin Mahmud, "This is al-Qaeda (1)," *Islamic al-Fallujah Forums* (Internet), 6 August 2009.

Asaf Maliach, "Bin Ladin, Palestine, and al-Qaida's operational strategy," *Middle Eastern Studies*, Vol. 44, No. 3 (May 2008), pp. 353–375.

Abu Muadh al-Maqdisi, "To the lions of al-Qassam in the relentless den," *Bayt al-Maqdis Islamic Forums* (Internet), 22 February 2008.

Abu Muhammad al-Maqdisi, "Obama's speech versus Osama's speech," http://al-faloja.org/vb/, 12 June 2009.

Jane Mayer, "The house of bin Laden," *New Yorker* (Internet version), 12 September 2002.

Andrew McGregor, "'Jihad and the rifle alone.' Abdullah Azzam and the Islamist Revolution," *Journal of Conflict Studies* (Internet version), Vol. 23, No. 2 (Fall 2003).

Muhammad Shamsaddin Megalommoatis, "Avert the founding of the al-Qaeda state 'Kurdistan' in northern Iraq," http://www.americanchronicle.com, 24 February 2010.

"Middle East. New militant group emerges in Gaza," http://www.adnkronos.com, 2 September 2008.

Flagg Miller, "Al-Qaida as a 'pragmatic base.' Contributions of area studies to sociolinguistics," *Language and Communications* (Internet version), Vol. 28 (2008), pp. 386–408.

Assaf Moghhhadam, "Motives for martyrdom," *International Security*, Vol. 33, No. 3 (Winter 2008/2009), pp. 46–78.

Professor Mohyuddin, "Something with regard to Saudi Arabia, Syria, and Yemen," *Ausaf* (Internet version), 8 January 2010.

Malik Mufti, "Jihad as statecraft. Ibn Khaldun on the conduct of war and empire," *History of Political Thought*, Vol. 30, No. 3 (Autumn 2009), pp. 385–410.

Nidal al-Mughrabi, "Pro-al-Qaeda fighters train in Gaza strip," http://www.alertnet.org, 1 September 2008.

Abu Hamza al-Muhajir, "The paths of victory," *Al-Fuqran Establishment for Media Production*, 19 April 2008.

"Mullah Omar declines bin Laden's offer to leave Afghanistan," *Ausaf*, 19 December 2000, pp. 1, 7.

"Mullah Omar ready for dialogue with Hekmatyar," *Ausaf*, 21 March 2001, pp. 1, 7.

"Muslim duty is to put Bin Ladin's words 'into practice'—Yemeni Islamists," ABC.es, 11 October 2009.

"Naif calls al-Qaeda khawarij," *Arab News* (Internet version), 17 March 2010.

Sally Neighbor, "The granny who denies she is public enemy No. 1," *Australian* (Internet version), 29 January 2008.

Rod Norlund, "Bin Laden's former bodyguard speaks," http://www.msnbc.msn.com, 26 August 2007.

Cherif Ouazai, "The bin Laden mystery. An investigation into the man who has defied America," *Jeune Afrique*, 7 September 1998.

"Part one of a series of reports on bin Ladin's life in Sudan," *Al-Quds al-Arabi* (Internet version), 24 November 2001.

Daniel Pipes, "Jihad through history," *New York Sun*, 31 May 2005, http://www.danielpipes.org/2662/jihad-through-history.

Giovanni Porzio, "Bin-Ladin: I will tell you about the super-terrorist seen from up close," *Panorama* (Internet version), 11 February 2010, pp. 86–92.

John Prendergast and Don Cheadle, "Lose this friendship with bin Laden crony in Sudan," *Houston Chronicle* (Internet version), 20 February 2006.

"Al-Qaeda affiliated group in Gaza," *Al-Arabiyah Television*, 3 September 2008.

"Al-Qaeda in Iraq confirms death of two top commanders," *Agence-France Presse*, 18 April 2010.

"Al-Qaeda in Iraq shifting its tactics," http://www.CNN.com. 16 December 2009.

Ibrahim Qannan, "Exclusive. New Salafist Gaza faction numbers 11,000," http://www.maannews.net, 23 April 2010.

Raid Qusti, "Bin Laden an intelligence agent," http://www.arabnews.com, 21 September 2006.

Abdallah al-Rashid, "Will option of containment succeed? Al-Qaida is dragging [the Saudi] government into a war of legitimacy," *Shu'un Sa'udiyah* (Internet version), 4 July 2004.

Madawi al-Rashid, "Islam today: From the jurisprudence scholars to the men of the cave," *Al-Quds al-Arabi* (Internet version), 6 February 2006.

"Renewed fear of al-Qaeda return to Anbar," http://www.nigash.org, 17 February 2010.

"Response by Shaykh Abu Muhammad al-Maqdisi," http://www.alboraq.info, 3 April 2009.

Urayb al-Rintawi, "Gaza's Salafis and takfiris," *Al-Dustur* (Internet version), 12 September 2008.

Sharon Rofe-Ofir, "Shaykh Salah: Israeli leaders [are] 'murderers and criminals," *Ynetnews*, 29 November 2008.

Bill Roggio, "Al-Qaeda in Iraq is 'broken,' cut off from leaders in Pakistan, says top U.S. general," http://www.longwarjournal.org, 5 June 2010.

Malise Ruthven, "The eleventh of September and the Sudanese mahdiya in the context of Ibn Khaldun's theory of Islamic history," *International Affairs*, Vol. 78, No. 2 (April 2002), pp. 339–351.

Ubaidah al-Saif, "Qassam brigades in Gaza issue urgent appeal to leaders of al-Qaeda," http://www.jiahdunspun.com, 26 June 2008.

Muhammad Salah, "Ali al-Rashidi: The Egyptian policeman who paved the way for 'Afghan Arabs' in Africa and prepared them to take revenge against the Americans," *Al-Hayah*, 30 September 1998, pp. 1, 6.

Rick Salutin, "Why Osama is hooked on classics," http://www.theglobeandmail.com, 8 August 2008.

Marc Santora, "Attacks threaten fragile security gains in cradle of Iraq insurgency," http://www.ocala.com, 17 November 2009.

Cathy Scott-Clark and Adrian Levy, "Rebel cult in blood feud with 'infidel' bin Laden," *Sunday Times* (Internet version), 18 July 1999.

Muhammad al-Shafi'i, "Al-Qaeda fundamentalist. Bin Laden believed the media exaggerations about him . . . ," *Al Sharq al-Awsat*, 12 July 2002, p. 4.

———, "Al-Qaeda ideologue recounts details of conflict between hawks and doves in organization on weapons of mass destruction," *Al-Sharq al-Awsat*, 12 September 2002, p. 7.

———, "Arab Afghan says Usama bin Ladin's force strength overblown," *Al-Sharq al-Awsat* (Internet version), 6 October 2001.

———, "Interview with Isam Darraz," *Al-Sharq al-Awsat*, 17 January 2002, p. 3.

———, "'Arab Afghans' theorist writes in book found by U.S. forces after Taleban's fall, Part 1," *Al-Sharq al-Awsat* (Internet version), 24 October 2006.

———, "Chatter on the world's rooftop," *Al-Sharq al-Awsat* (Internet version), 29 October 2006.

———, "The story of Abu Walid al-Masri," *Al-Sharq al-Awsat* (Internet version), 11 February 2007.

Michael Slackman, "Bin Laden's mother tried to stop him, Syrian kin say," *Chicago Tribune*, 13 November 2001, p. 5.

"Statement by the Ministry of Shariah Commissions in the Islamic State of Iraq," *Al-Fajr Media Center* (Internet), 25 April 2010.

"String of bombs in Iraq follow leadership losses for insurgency," http://www.dallasnews.com, 23 April 20.

"The al-Tahadi Network exclusively interviews one of the commanders of the Ma'sadat al-Mujahein, Shaykh Abu-Ubaydah al-Ansari, may God protect him," *Al-Fallujah Islamic Forums* (Internet), 14 February 2010.

Rauf Tahir, "Persecutions instead of comforts," *Fact Magazine*, 1–31 October 2007.

"Taleban confirms its intention to try bin Ladin. Pakistan prevented him for attending an Islamic conference," *Al-Quds al-Arabi*, 28 October 1998, p. 1.

"Taleban forces foil attempt to assassinate bin Ladin, uncover hireling network in Kandahar and Peshawar," *Al-Quds al-Arabi* (Internet version), 29 July 1999.

Shada Umar, "The Event," *Lebanese Broadcasting Company Satellite Television*, 12 September 2004.

"U.S. aid for Ahmed Shah Massoud against Usamah," *Jang*, 29 December 1998, p. 10.

Muhammad al-Uwayn, "Ideology of Takfir," *Kingdom of Saudi Arabia TV 1*, 10 August 2004.

Michael Vlahos, "Examining the war of ideas," *Washington Times* (Internet version), 19–22 July 2004.

———, "The Muslim Renovatio and U.S. strategy," http://www.2techcentralstation.com, 27 April 2004.
———, "Terror's mask. Insurgency within Islam," published by Johns Hopkins University/Applied Physics Laboratory; Laurel, Maryland, May 2002.
Joas Wagemakers, "A purist Jihadi-Salafi. The ideology of Abu Muhammad al-Maqdisi," *British Journal of Middle Eastern Studies* (Internet version), Vol. 36, No. 2 (August 2009).
Mary Anne Weaver, "The real bin Laden," *New Yorker* (Internet version), 24 January 2000.
"Welcome in Yemen, bin Ladin, but!" *al-Mahrusah* (Internet), 6 December 2002.
"The West at war: Bin Laden's son: Dad has become invisible: Always on his guard," *Sunday Mirror* (Internet version), 14 October 2001.
Quintan Wiktorowicz, "Anatomy of the Salafi movement," *Studies in Conflict and Terrorism* (Internet version), Vol. 29, No. 3 (May 2006).
———, "Framing jihad. Intra-movement framing contests and al-Qaeda's struggle for sacred authority," *International Review of Social History*, Vol. 49 (2004), pp. 159–177.
Quintan Wiktorowicz and Karl Kaltenthaler, "The rationality of radical Islam," *Political Science Quarterly*, Vol. 121, No. 2 (2006), pp. 295–319.
Quintan Wiktorowicz and John Kaltner, "Killing in the name of Islam: Al-Qaeda's justification for September 11," *Middle East Policy*, Vol. 10, No. 2 (September 2003), pp. 76–92.
Isambard Wilkinson, "Profile: Osama bin Laden's family," http://www.telegraph.co.uk, 23 July 2009.
Lawrence Wright, "The rebellion within," *New Yorker* (Internet version), 2 June 2008.
Rahimullah Yusufzai, "In the way of Allah," *Pakistan* (Internet version), 15 June 1998.
———, "Myth and man," *Newsline*, 1 September, 1998.
———, "Osama bin Laden: Al-Qaeda," in Harenda Baweja, ed., *Most wanted: Profiles of terror*. New Delhi: Lotus Collection, Roli Books, 2002, pp. 18–37.
———, "Taleban foil attempt on bin Ladin's life by Saudis," *The News*, 26 December 1998.
———, "Taleban let bin Laden break his silence," *The News* (Internet version), 6 January 1999.
———, "Face to face with Usama," *Guardian* (Internet version), 26 September 2001.
Ahmad Muwaffaq Zaydan, "Bin Ladin is in 'Tora Bora' south of Jalalabad," *Al-Hayah*, 17 February 1999, p. 16.
———, "Interview with Mustafa Abu al-Yazid, supervisor general of al-Qaeda in Afghanistan," *Al-Jazirah Satellite Television*, 8 June 2009.
———, "Taleban execute young Saudi for performing hostile activities against bin Ladin," *Al-Hayah*, 5 October 1998, p. 1.
Ayman al-Zawahiri, "Five years after the invasion of Iraq and decades of injustice by tyrants," *Al-Sahab Media Production Organization*, 18 April 2008.
———, "Open Interview, 2," *Al-Sahab Media Production Organization*, 22 April 2008.
———, "The Zionist-Crusader aggression on Gaza and Lebanon," *Al-Sahab Media Production Organization*, July 28, 2006.

INDEX

Note: Members of the Saudi royal family are gathered in the S entries under the "al-Saud" treatment of their names.

Note: The article "al-" is ignored in alphabetization. Thus, "al-Qaeda" appears under the Qs.